THE
INCORRUPTIBLE
SEED

A HISTORY AND DEFENSE OF THE HOLY BIBLE

UPDATED AND EXPANDED
14th ANNIVERSARY EDITION

THE INCORRUPTIBLE SEED

A HISTORY AND DEFENSE OF THE HOLY BIBLE

UPDATED AND EXPANDED
14th ANNIVERSARY EDITION

DANIEL BAER

ARI'EL PRESS

DEDICATED
TO
MY FATHERS IN THE FAITH

C. Fred Young
Pastor
Gospel Assembly Church, Akron, Ohio
(November 1980 – May 1984)
Who first gave me an unquenchable thirst for the Word of God

Richard K. Moore
Pastor
Gospel Assembly Church, Akron, Ohio
(June 1990 – Present)
*Whose fatherly guidance and burning faith
have kept the flame alive in my heart*

Charles H. Beougher
My Grandfather
*Who raised me as his own son
and showed me the truest example of spiritual manhood
I have ever known*

SPECIAL THANKS TO
Diana Marsan
for her labor in editing and final preparation

TABLE OF CONTENTS

TITLES OF THE WORD OF GOD

The Words of the Covenant *Exodus 34:28*
The Book of the Law *II Chronicles 34:15*
The Commandment of His lips *Job 23:12*
The Words of His mouth *Job 23:12*
The Law of the Lord *Psalms 1:2*
The Testimony of the Lord *Psalms 19:7*
The Statutes of the Lord *Psalms 19:7*
The Counsel of the Lord *Psalms 33:11*
The Book *Psalms 40:7, Revelation 22:19*
God's "Testimonies, Precepts, Statutes, Judgments, Law,
Commandments and Word" *Psalms 119*
The Law of Thy mouth *Psalms 119:72*
The Ordinances of the Lord *Psalms 119:91*
The Word of Thy Righteousness *Psalms 119:123*
The Book of the Lord *Isaiah 34:16*
The Scripture of Truth *Daniel 10:21*
The Word of God *Mark 7:13, Romans 10:17, Hebrews 4:12*
The Word of Christ *Colossians 3:16*
The Gospel of Christ *Romans 1:16*
The Word of Truth *II Timothy 2:15*
The Word of Life *Philippians 2:16*
The Lively Oracles *Acts 7:38*
The Oracles of God *Romans 3:2, Hebrews 5:12, I Peter 4:11*
The Scripture *Mark 15:28, John 7:38, II Timothy 3:16-17*
The Scriptures *Luke 24:27, John 5:39, Acts 17:11*
The Holy Scriptures *Romans 1:2, II Timothy 3:15*
The Law of Moses, the Prophets and the Psalms *Luke 24:25*
The Law and the Prophets *Matthew 5:17, Acts 13:15*
The Promises *Romans 9:4-5, 15:8*
The Sword of the Spirit *Ephesians 6:17*
The Engrafted Word *James 1:21*
The Perfect Law of Liberty *James 1:25*

So shall my word be that goeth forth out of my mouth:
it shall not return unto me void,
but it shall accomplish that which I please,
and it shall prosper in the thing whereto I sent it.
Isaiah 55:11

THE LIVING WORD OF GOD

1

Any study of the origins and transmission of the scriptures must begin with a clear understanding of the purpose and nature of the Bible. The evidence for scriptural infallibility (the state of being without mistake or error of any kind) can be demonstrated in a threefold manner: first, the testimony of the Bible itself; second, the extra biblical witnesses to the inerrancy of scripture (secular literature, history, and archaeology); finally, the life and breath that exudes from the scripture, as demonstrated by its effects on mankind and on society.

THE BIBLE IN THIS PRESENT AGE

It is especially important in our present age to have an understanding of the role the Bible has played and the effect it has had on the lives of men throughout history. We live in a time when all knowledge is questioned from a skeptical perspective. Those areas of knowledge that are based on faith and emotion are the most severely criticized by our neo-scientific generation. Many of the leaders of the world today have no use for the Bible or for the disciplines that it requires. The Bible and the way of life that it espouses have become devalued in our modern society. They have been mocked and ridiculed by the leading minds of our time. The intellectuals of our age tell us that there is no pure truth; they demand that truth is determined by the individual's own perspective. The Bible cuts completely cross-grain to this type of reasoning, as it clearly declares itself to not only be absolute truth, but to be the only truth.

As our present age grows darker and draws closer to its anticipated end, it is critical that we have the knowledge to be able to defend our faith. The secular reasoning that decries the Bible is based on old prejudices and incomplete arguments. Not one page of the Holy Scriptures has ever been demonstrated to be inaccurate. Whenever doubt or criticism has arisen through man's speculation, time has borne out witness to the Bible through both scientific and archaeological discoveries. Any supposed contradictions or discrepancies are easily cleared away with a proper understanding of the Bible's literary style, knowledge of the transmission of the text from the original writers to our modern-day translations, and, most importantly, the revelation of the Spirit of God. Paul, in his first letter to the church at Corinth (I Corinthians 2:6-16), makes it abundantly clear that the truth of God's message cannot be correctly comprehended by the mind of man without the indwelling of the Spirit to give illumination and clarity to the understanding.

WHY WE MUST HAVE ABSOLUTE TRUST IN THE BIBLE

The Holy Bible is the root and anchor of our faith. In it is recorded communication to man from the one true and eternal God. Without this precious collection of writings we would know nothing of God, the creation of the world, and the bloodline and history of God's chosen people. We would know nothing of the law of God, without which we could not obey him. We would know nothing of the promises of God, without which we would have no hope. The plan of God, descriptive of His actions toward man and the responsibility of man to God, is encapsulated in its pages.

If we do not have the scriptures to show us God, then all religious and philosophical understanding is open to individual interpretation. Every man could create his own god(s) and shape them according to his whims. Without this book the foundations of our faith and hope would crumble. Without this revelation, there would be no knowledge of the terrible price that was paid for our sin through the blood of the sacrifice shed to make us clean. What inestimable loss would it be not to know that one name…**Jesus**.

The impact of our faith and reliance on the Bible is critical and far reaching. As Christians, people of the Book, we must be able to have an absolute trust in the word of God as given through his anointed messengers and holy prophets. If we are taught to develop seeds of doubt and a critical spirit toward the Bible, then our foundation is washed away. The firm footing of our faith must be upon the bedrock of scriptural truth.

Let us consider what great injury can be brought upon the faith of God's people by taking away their faith in the inspiration of the Word. What if the textual critics decide that certain references to Jesus as the Way were not meant to be part of the original writings? What if modern theologians and scholars, who would pervert the truth in order to advance their own agendas and beliefs, decided that certain scriptures could not have been a part of the original writings? Why? Because those beliefs do not agree with the god they have created for themselves. Since the "god" they believe in could not have made such statements, then they must not have been in the original manuscripts.

This is precisely the path taken by some modern scholars. They twist and wrench the Book of God to match their own carnal beliefs about the Creator. Consider John 14:6…*I am the way, the truth, and the life: no man cometh unto the Father, but by me.* If this scripture and others like it could be stripped away, then the door would be opened to blind ecuminicism. Any and all religions and belief systems would be just as effectual a route of spiritual sustenance for man. This would remove all walls between religions such as Islam, Buddhism, or Hinduism. Man could take any path he chose and he would end up at the same goal in the end. This is precisely what the Bible is so firmly set against. There is only ONE way to God and salvation. There is only ONE righteous standard and absolute measure by which truth may be known. There is only ONE book that contains the oracles of God. There is only ONE eternal absolute that cannot fluctuate, by which all men will be judged.

We either believe that the word of God is exactly what it says it is, the only true and unfailing message from God to man, or we do not. If we are of the latter opinion, whether we desire to serve God or not, we are nothing more than atheists parading in the robes of religionists. The word of God, in its original transmission, must be entirely infallible or entirely false; its testimony to itself leaves no room for any other option. It is certain that discrepancies can be found within the individual translations and copies as these were the works of men's hands. But the source of these copies still lives on in near perfect translation in our hands. Recent finds such as the Dead Sea scrolls demonstrate that the scripture we hold in our hands today is a near perfect copy of the ancient writings.

The intellectual reasoning of men and their carnal philosophy and the socio-cultural forces of our age cannot and must not define what is and is not scripture. It is for the children of God, as kings and priests of His kingdom, to seek to know the message of God from His perspective and with His purpose and not by the corrupted interpretations of carnal man. The heart and mind of man cannot perceive the truth of God without the indwelling and quickening life of the Spirit. The Spirit of God must bring us into all knowledge: God defining and interpreting His word through us (and in spite of us). The interpretation and understanding does not come from within us, as we know no scripture is given by private interpretation, but is from without and through us by the flowing current of the Spirit.

Through a proper understanding of its inspiration and anointing, structure and design, transmission and translation, we can come to understand that this book is a supernatural construct, a living and divine oracle, the fire of the Almighty shining forth through vessels of clay. For such were the authors of this wondrous book, mere men constructed of earth, but filled with His quickening Spirit!

It is of paramount importance that we have a proper respect for its sacred message. We must understand the priceless value of this book that so often is taken for granted.

HOW WE KNOW THAT THE BIBLE IS THE WORD OF GOD

Consider the absolute uniqueness of the Bible:

Among all the "sacred" texts of the religions of the world, it is the only book to contain verifiable prophetic truth. Hundreds of biblical prophecies have been fulfilled with undeniable accuracy, while many more prophecies are coming to their fruition in this very age.[1] Prophecy is God's own stamp of authenticity on this Book of books. It is like a watermark on the scriptures, a signature to validate that they are the genuine creation of the Eternal Author. There is but one true God and His absolute uniqueness is demonstrated in that He alone knows the end from the beginning:

Isaiah 46:9-10 *Remember the former things of old: for I am God, and there is none else; I am God, and there is none like me, Declaring the end from the beginning, and from ancient times the things that are not yet done, saying, My counsel shall stand, and I will do all my pleasure:*

The Lord claims that prophetic foreknowledge is the evidence of deity and the sign by which it can be known that he is the only true God:

---

[1]Numerous excellent resources are available for further study on fulfilled and future prophecy. *Encyclopedia of Biblical Prophecy* (J. Barton Payne, 1973, Baker Books) and *Major Bible Prophecies* (John F. Walvoord, 1991, Zondervan Publishing House) are good starting points for study in this area.

Isaiah 41:21-23 *Produce your cause, saith the Lord; bring forth your strong reasons, saith the King of Jacob. Let them bring them forth, and show us what shall happen: let them show the former things, what they may be, that we may consider them, and know the latter end of them; or declare us things for to come. Show the things that are to come hereafter, that we may know that ye are gods…*
Isaiah 44:7-8 *And who, as I, shall call, and shall declare it, and set it in order for me, since I appointed the ancient people? and the things that are coming, and shall come, let them show unto them. Fear ye not, neither be afraid: have I not told thee from that time, and have declared it? ye are even my witnesses. Is there a God beside me? yea, there is no God; I know not any.*

Jesus uses this same method in foretelling the betrayal of Judas, by this prophetic truth demonstrating that he is the Christ.
John 13:18-19…*He that eateth bread with me hath lifted up his heel against me. Now I tell you before it come, that, when it is come to pass, ye may believe that I am he.*

Chuck Missler, Bible researcher and head of Koinonia House, describes it this way: *Since God has the technology to create us in the first place, He certainly has the technology to get a message to us. But how does He authenticate his message? How does He assure us that the message is really from Him and not a fraud or a contrivance? …One way to authenticate the message is to demonstrate that its source is from outside our time domain. God declares, "I alone know the end from the beginning." His message includes history written in advance. This is called "prophecy."…we now discover it [the Bible] is an integrated message from outside our time domain. It repeatedly authenticates this uniqueness by describing history before it happens.*[2]

---

[2] Chuck Missler, *Cosmic Codes*, p. 46, Koinonia House 1999.

As an historical book, the Bible is the most complete and accurate record known to man, covering the time period from the beginning of creation to the end of the world. The peoples, places, and events chronicled in its pages have been found to be unerringly precise. Skeptics have often maligned the scriptural record of history, arguing that many of the people and places were fabricated by the writers or purely mythological. This has been disproved time and time again by the discoveries of archaeology and its sister sciences.[3] Dr. William F. Albright, a world-class archaeologist, wrote that every archaeological discovery establishes more firmly that the Bible is historically accurate. Dr. Nelson Glueck, considered to have been one of the greatest authorities on Israeli archaeology, stated that *No archaeological discovery has ever controverted a Biblical reference. Scores of archaeological findings have been made which confirm in clear outline or in exact detail historical statements in the Bible. And, by the same token, proper evaluation of Biblical descriptions has often led to amazing discoveries.*[4]

Archaeology has often made finds that appeared to contradict the biblical historical record, but as more discoveries and advances have been made the apparent variances are worked out to create a fuller picture. These testimonies have often become the best evidences for biblical accuracy. Often the finds that appear to disprove the scriptural record become the strongest witnesses to its truth. The deeper we dig into the world of the past, the more evident it is that the Bible was a book of unerring historical accuracy.

---

[3] One of the best resources for further study on Biblical archaeological discoveries is the *Biblical Archaeology Review* magazine published by the Biblical Archaeology Society. There are also many excellent books available for further study in this area.

[4] Nelson Glueck, *Rivers in the Desert*, p. 31, Farrar, Strauss and Cudahy, 1959.

It has been the most widely circulated and read book in the history of the world and has been translated into more than 2200 languages.[5] Billions of copies of the Bible have been printed and distributed. The United Bible Society, which is the largest distributor of Bibles, distributed 24,965,609 Bibles and 12,583,933 copies of the New Testament in 2004 alone.[6] The Bible has been and still is the best-selling book of all time; no other book, whether religious, philosophical, or fictional, has ever come close to its distribution.

The character and actions of the historical figures and nations recorded in the Bible are dealt with directly and honestly. Individual character defects and mistakes are openly admitted by the authors as they record the history of the Biblical characters. If this was a book written for the propagation of man's beliefs, it would not be found so full of the mistakes and shortcomings of its heroes. Lewis Chafer, founder of the Dallas Theological Seminary, is famous for saying, *"The Bible is not such a book a man would write if he could, or could write if he would."* What truth is in those simple words. No man attempting to create a belief system or a mythological framework would be so forthright in his descriptions.

The Bible is primarily written by Israelites, yet is the nation of Israel demonstrated to be great and good? By no means! Israel is most often described in the Bible as a backslidden and unfaithful wife. The Scriptures testify clearly of man's sin and failures, and they declare the way that man can be forgiven and made clean in God's sight. This is no book written by man about God; it is God's own handwriting revealing Himself and His relationship with man, from its breaking to its remaking. Arthur W. Pink summarizes this thought perfectly: *In the repeated mention we have in the Old Testament of Israel's sins, we*

---

[5] The United Bible Societies have translated the Bible into more than 2,200 languages, accounting for approximately 90% of the earth's population.

[6] United Bible Society, Scripture Distribution Report, 2004.

discover, in light as clear as day, the absolute honesty and candor of those who recorded Israel's history. No attempt whatsoever is made to conceal their folly, their unbelief, and their wickedness; instead, the corrupt condition of their hearts is made fully manifest, and this, by writers who belonged to, and were born of the same nation. In the whole realm of literature there is no parallel.[7]

Josephus, the 1st century Jewish historian, is a perfect example of the tendency of man to aggrandize the life and activities of historical figures of his race or nation. In order to build a case for the excellence and superiority of the Jewish race, Josephus at times exaggerates the ability or avoids addressing the sin of those whose lives he is recording. He adds and subtracts to the biblical record as needed to justify his case. The Dictionary of New Testament Background states that Josephus *adds, subtracts and modifies, usually in minor respects but sometimes in major shifts as well. One such case is that of Jehoash, who in the Bible (II Kings 13:11) is said to have done evil in the sight of the Lord. Yet in Josephus he is described as a good man (Ant. 9.8.6). Again, Josephus goes so far as to transform Jehoiachin, who in the Bible is said to have done evil in the sight of the Lord (II Kings 24:9, II Chronicles 36:9), into a king who is described as kind and just (Ant. 10.7.1).*[8]

This is the case throughout recorded history. Those who write the histories of men and nations do so according to their own conscious or subconscious biases and preferences. This is also true of the Bible. God, who knows the end from the beginning, is the author of history itself and the inspirer of the historical writers of the Bible. The bias and prejudice of man is not a factor in its choice of selections.

---

[7] Arthur W. Pink, *The Divine Inspiration of the Bible*, Books for the Ages, 1997.
[8] *The Dictionary of New Testament Background*, Josephus: Interpretive Methods and Tendencies, p. 591, IVP, 2000.

The Bible influenced the development of the positive accomplishments of Western civilization and culture at every level. The Bible was a primary influence on the development of Western civilization and culture, especially that of the United States. From its governmental and legal systems to its educational and social structures, the United States was shaped according to a Biblical blueprint and has been blessed accordingly. Built primarily upon Christian principles of governance, it has demonstrated itself to be one of the greatest systems of government the world has ever known. As long as that nation has kept itself yielded to the word of God and obedient to His statutes, it has had prosperity and blessing. Any variance from these foundational principles has brought about underlying structural weakness.

The highest musical and artistic expression of the Western world reveals an underlying influence of the Scripture. It is a simple act to trace the decline of our Western society in all areas of civilization by its turning away from these original foundations.

The Bible, though written by more than three dozen different authors from various backgrounds and educational levels, has an incredible harmony and complex integration throughout its individual books. The deeper an understanding that you gain of the scriptures, the more their tight integration is revealed. There is no contradiction or disagreement between the varying accounts when a proper method of interpretation is used. The apparent contradictions in the Scripture are the guideposts that direct the spiritual man to the deeper meaning and layers within the text. When properly harmonized through the aid of the Spirit, those things that at first glance appear to oppose each other, when illuminated by the life of the Spirit, develop into a more complete and complex thought. With the light of the Holy Spirit illuminating the reader, the dense network of thought and design can be discerned. Consider the words of Paul to the church at Corinth:

I Corinthians 2:6-16 *Howbeit we speak wisdom among them that are perfect: yet not the wisdom of this world, nor of the princes[9] of this world, that come to naught: But* **we speak the wisdom of God in a mystery, even the hidden wisdom**, *which God ordained before the world unto our glory: Which none of the princes of this world knew: for had they known it, they would not have crucified the Lord of glory. But as it is written, Eye hath not seen, nor ear heard, neither have entered into the heart of man, the things which God hath prepared for them that love him.* **But God hath revealed them unto us by his Spirit: for the Spirit searcheth all things, yea, the deep things of God.** *For what man knoweth the things of man save the spirit of man which is in him? even so* **the things of God knoweth no man, but the Spirit of God.** *Now we have received, not the spirit of the world, but the spirit which is of God; that we might know the things that are freely given to us of God. Which things also we speak, not in the words which man's wisdom teacheth, but which the Holy Ghost teacheth; comparing[10] spiritual things with spiritual.* **But the natural man receiveth not the things of the Spirit of God: for they are foolishness unto him: neither can he know them, because they are spiritually discerned.** *But he that is spiritual judgeth all things, yet he himself is judged of no man. For who hath known the mind of the Lord, that he may instruct him? But we have the mind of Christ.*

---

[9] This word translated "princes" is the Greek *archon*, meaning rulers or leaders. These are the great minds and influences of the age, both intellectual and philosophical, who through their own carnal knowledge cannot discern the spiritual things of God.

[10] This word translated "comparing" is the Greek **sunkrino**, which means to join together, compare, interpret, or judge one thing in comparison with another. This corresponds exactly with the revelation of God's complex harmony by the Spirit. These things that are hard to understand are manifested through the Spirit by being joined together and combined in comparison and relation to each other.

For those who have made a serious study of the Bible and have yielded their hearts and minds over to its Author, this is one of the most powerful evidences for its divine design. Conversely, it is impossible for the skeptic who will not open his heart to the Spirit of truth to ever have the capability to truly comprehend the Oracles of God.

The Bible was and is thousands of years ahead of its time in its knowledge of God's creation. The scientific statements contained in its verses were antithetical to the beliefs of their time and only in the last few centuries are some of these statements being demonstrated to be true. The Bible is not necessarily written in order to reveal scientific understanding of the universe. Its primary purpose is to reveal the Creator of the universe and His will for His creation. It can be seen though, that in statements inspired by the Spirit of God or spoken by His voice, truths have been manifested that were unknown in their time, and there is knowledge in the Book that is still far ahead of the advances of modern science.

INTERNAL AND EXTERNAL TESTIMONIES TO THE UNIQUENESS OF THE SCRIPTURES

2

THE TESTIMONY OF THE SCRIPTURES

The writers of scripture did not need to defend the veracity of the word that proceeded from God. The Bible presupposes the reality of God and of His truth. It is demonstrated by its life and power to be the dynamic communication of a Holy God whose ways are beyond human imagination.

The terrible truths of His word stand across a vast chasm of separation from the literary and philosophical works of man. None of man's compositions match the dignity and simplicity of the scripture. Nothing else from the hand of man, whether religious or intellectual, has been able to so starkly separate and demonstrate the contrast of God and man, truth and falsehood. The heart and mind of mankind is revealed through its testimony, darkness revealed, and light made manifest. Throughout its pages it bears perfect witness to its own perfect truths.

II Samuel 7:28
And now, O Lord God, thou art that God, and thy words be true...

II Samuel 22:31/Psalms 18:30
As for God, his way is perfect: the word of the Lord is tried...

II Kings 10:10
*Know now that there shall fall unto the earth
nothing of the word of the Lord,*

Psalm 12:6
*The words of the Lord are pure words:
as silver tried in a furnace of earth, purified seven times*

Psalm 19:7-9
*The law of the Lord is perfect, converting the soul:
the testimony of the Lord is sure, making wise the simple.
The statutes of the Lord are right, rejoicing the heart:
the commandment of the Lord is pure, enlightening the eyes.
The fear of the Lord is clean, enduring forever:
the judgments of the Lord are true and righteous altogether.*

Psalm 33:4
For the word of the Lord is right; and all his works are done in truth.

Psalm 33:11
*The counsel of the Lord standeth forever,
the thoughts of his heart to all generations.*

Psalm 93:5
*Thy testimonies are very sure: holiness becometh thine house,
O Lord, for ever.*

Psalms 119:86[11]
All thy commandments are faithful...

Psalm 119:89-90
For ever, O Lord, thy word is settled in heaven.
Thy faithfulness is unto all generations:

Psalm 119:128
Therefore I esteem all thy precepts concerning all things to be right;
and I hate every false way.

Psalms 119:137-144
Righteous art thou, O Lord, and upright are thy judgments.
Thy testimonies that thou hast commanded are righteous and very
faithful. My zeal hath consumed me, because mine enemies have
forgotten thy words. Thy word is very pure: therefore thy servant
loveth it.
I am small and despised: yet do I not forget thy precepts.
Thy righteousness is an everlasting righteousness, and thy law is the
truth. Trouble and anguish have taken hold on me: yet thy
commandments are my delights. The righteousness of thy testimonies
is everlasting:
give me understanding and I shall live.

Psalm 119:151-152
Thou art near, O Lord; and all thy commandments are truth.
Concerning thy testimonies, I have known of old that thou hast
founded them for ever.

---

[11]The 119th Psalm is full of wonderful testimonies of the quickening power of the word of God. Of the 176 verses in this Psalm, all refer to God's word in some way, and all but a handful have a title of the word of God contained in them.

Psalm 119:160
Thy word is true from the beginning:
and every one of thy righteous judgments endureth for ever.

Proverbs 30:5-6
Every word of God is pure: he is a shield unto them
that put their trust in him. Add not unto his words,
lest he reprove thee, and thou be found a liar.

Isaiah 30:8
Now go, write it before them in a table, and note it in a book,
that it may be for the time to come forever and ever:

Isaiah 34:16
Seek ye out the book of the Lord, and read: no one of these shall fail,
none shall want her mate: for my mouth it hath commanded,
and his spirit it hath gathered them

Isaiah 40:8
The grass withereth, the flower fadeth:
but the word of our God shall stand for ever.

Isaiah 45:23
I have sworn by myself, the word is gone out of my mouth
in righteousness, and shall not return,

Isaiah 46:9-10
Remember the former things of old: for I am God, and there is none
else; I am God, and there is none like me, Declaring the end from the
beginning, and from ancient times the things that are not yet done,
saying, My counsel shall stand, and I will do all my pleasure:

Isaiah 55:11
So shall my word be that goeth forth out of my mouth:
it shall not return unto me void,[12] but it shall accomplish that which I
please, and it shall prosper in the thing whereto I sent it.

Isaiah 59:21
As for me, this is my covenant with them, saith the Lord;
My spirit that is upon thee, and my words which I have put in thy
mouth, shall not depart out of thy mouth, nor out of the mouth of thy
seed, nor out of the mouth of thy seed's seed, saith the Lord,
from henceforth and for ever.

Habakkuk 2:3
For the vision is yet for an appointed time, but at the end it shall
speak, and not lie:[13] though it tarry, wait for it; because it will surely
come, it will not tarry.[14]

Matthew 5:18
For verily I say unto you, Till heaven and earth pass, one jot or one
tittle shall in no wise pass from the law, till all be fulfilled.

Mark 13:31
Heaven and earth shall pass away,
but my words shall not pass away.

---

[12] The Hebrew **reyqam**, meaning "empty", "without effect" or in "vain".

[13] This is the Hebrew word **kazab**, the primary meaning of which is "to lie", but it can also mean "to fail" or "to disappoint".

[14] The first word translated tarry in this verse is **mahahh**, which means "to hesitate", "to wait," or "to delay". The second tarry is **achar**, generally meaning to cause to be delayed or kept back. The idea that seems to be represented here is that the vision may seem to be held back or delayed, but it will be accomplished at exactly the time God has appointed and His time clock will not be affected.

Luke 16:17
And it is easier for heaven and earth to pass,
than one tittle of the law to fail.

John 10:35
...the scripture cannot be broken;

John 17:17
Sanctify them through thy truth: thy word is truth.

Acts 5:38-39
...for if this counsel or this work be of men, it will come to naught:
But if it be of God, ye cannot overthrow it;

II Timothy 3:16-17
All scripture is given by inspiration of God, and is profitable for
doctrine, for reproof, for correction, for instruction in righteousness:
That the man of God may be perfect, throughly furnished unto all
good works.

I Peter 1:23-25
Being born again, not of corruptible seed, but of incorruptible,
by the word of God, which liveth and abideth forever.
For all flesh is as grass, and all the glory of man as the flower of
grass. The grass withereth, and the flower thereof falleth away:
But the word of the Lord endureth forever.
And this is the word which by the gospel is preached unto you.

Revelation 21:5
And he that sat upon the throne said, Behold, I make all things new.
And he said unto me, Write: for these words are true and faithful.

Thus, we can see that the Bible itself has a great deal to say about the testimony of the scripture contained within its covers. The Bible states its claim as the direct inspiration of God thousands of times throughout its pages. The scriptures are interspersed with prefaces such as "Thus saith the Lord" and "The word of the Lord came unto me, saying."

The Bible makes the clear assumption from beginning to end that it is the express communication of God to man. Dr. Henry Morris states, *In the Old Testament, the writers with great frequency claim to be recording the very words of the Lord…Those who have attempted to count these and other similar statements in the Old Testament have come up with the following approximate figures:*

    Pentateuch: 680 claims of inspiration
    Prophetical books: 1,307 claims of inspiration
    Historical books: 418 claims of inspiration
    Poetical books: 195 claims of inspiration
    Entire Old Testament: 2,600 claims of inspiration[15]

In the Old Testament alone we have at least 2,600 claims made by the scripture as to its origin!

We can see that the scriptures testify to their own absolute veracity, but what of the authors? To understand the faithfulness of the word of God, it is important to establish that the individual writers did not put down the thoughts of their own minds. Paul and Peter both testify to the source of the inspiration of scripture:

II Timothy 3:16 *All scripture is given by inspiration of God,*
II Peter 1:20-21 *Knowing this first, that no prophecy of the Scripture is of any private interpretation. For the prophecy came not in old time by the will of man: but holy men of God spake as they were moved by the Holy Ghost.*

---

[15] *Many Infallible Proofs*, Creation Life Publisher, Inc., 1974.

If we then establish that God is the originator and source author of all scripture, what testimony do we have to His faithfulness and truth regarding His word? Throughout His book the Lord affirms His unwavering commitment to His word:

Joshua 21:45 *There failed not aught of any good thing which the Lord hath spoken unto the house of Israel; all came to pass.*

Joshua 23:14...*Ye know in your hearts and in all your souls, that not one thing hath failed of all the good things which the Lord your God spake concerning you; all are come to pass unto you, and not one thing hath failed thereof.*

II Peter 3:9 *The Lord is not slack concerning his promise, as some men count slackness;*

Jesus's life and words testify to the validity and critical importance that he placed on the scriptures. His first great series of temptations demonstrates the precedence of scripture for establishing truth. Directly after his baptism he was taken up by the Spirit into the wilderness. After a forty-day fast he was tempted by the devil. Satan repeatedly attacked Jesus' faith and commitment to his calling. Throughout this tirade, the only replies Jesus made were quotes directly from the scripture. The tempter told Jesus that if he was truly the Son of God, let him turn the stones that lie at his feet to bread. Jesus, quoting from Deuteronomy 8:3, replied: ...*It is written, Man shall not live by bread alone, but by every word that proceedeth out of the mouth of God.* This is not only a purely scriptural defense; Jesus quoted a scripture that specifically demonstrated the dynamic importance of the word of God itself.

The tempter then took Jesus atop the pinnacle of the temple and told him if he was truly the Son of God, he should prove this by leaping from that high place, since the angels would then be obligated to keep him from harm. Jesus again quoted from Deuteronomy 6:16: ...*it is written again, Thou shalt not tempt the Lord thy God.*

Finally, the devil took Jesus up upon a high mountain and showed him the kingdoms of the world, offering them to him if he would worship him. Jesus final response was once again from the book of Deuteronomy, quoting Deuteronomy 6:13 and 10:20: ...*Get thee hence, Satan: for it is written, Thou shalt worship the Lord thy God, and him only shalt thou serve.* This final scriptural barrage drove Satan back and he left Jesus.

Just as Jesus before us, we must recognize the fact that it is God's word that is the answer to all of our needs. It is the Bible that is the sword of attack and defense that we carry into spiritual battle. This Book is the undergirding support upon which all truth is established.

EXTERNAL SECULAR TESTIMONIES TO THE SCRIPTURES

My tongue shall speak of thy word:
for all thy commandments are righteousness.
Psalm 119:172

There have been a great number of men and women of secular influence and standing who have testified to the great and abiding power of the Bible. Some of the most gifted minds and powerful personalities have recognized the eternal truth of God's word to man.

The story has been told that an African prince came as an ambassador to the court of Queen Victoria. During his audience with the Queen he asked her if she could tell him the secret of England's greatness. The Queen showed him none of the great treasures of her Empire but upon giving him a copy of the Bible, said, "Tell the prince that this is the secret of England's greatness."

It was said that just before his death Sir Walter Scott asked his son-in-law to read to him. "From what book shall I read?" said he. "And you ask?" Scott replied. "There is but one."

From the founders and statesmen of the United States to the great minds of science, philosophy, and the arts, testimonies have rung out in defense of this Holy Book, to which there is no equal. Here are some of those testimonies.

It is impossible to rightly govern the world without God and the Bible.
GEORGE WASHINGTON (1st U.S. President)

The Bible is the best book in the world. It contains more than all the libraries I have seen.

Suppose a nation in some distant region should take the Bible for their only law book, and every member should regulate his conduct by the precepts there exhibited! Every member would be obligated in conscience, to temperance, frugality, and industry; to justice, kindness, and charity towards his fellow men; and to piety, love, and reverence toward Almighty God...What a Utopia, what a paradise would this region be.
JOHN ADAMS (2nd U.S. President)

I have always said that a studious perusal of the sacred volume will make better citizens, better fathers, and better husbands.
THOMAS JEFFERSON (3rd U.S. President)

The first and almost the only book deserving of universal attention is the Bible.

So great is my veneration of the Bible, that the earlier my children begin to read it the more confident will be my hope that they will prove useful citizens of their country and respectable members of society.

I say to you, Search the Scriptures! The Bible is the book of all others, to be read at all ages, and in all conditions of human life; not to be read once or twice or thrice through, and then laid aside, but to be read in small portions of one or two chapters every day, and never to be intermitted, unless by some overruling necessity.
JOHN QUINCY ADAMS (6th U.S. President)

It is worth all other books which were ever printed.
PATRICK HENRY (American Patriot and Statesman)

The moral principles and precepts contained in the Scriptures ought to form the basis of all our civil constitutions and laws. All the miseries and evils which men suffer from –vice, crime, ambition, injustice, oppression, slavery, and war–proceed from their despising or neglecting the precepts found in the Bible.

The Bible is the chief moral cause of all that is good, and the best corrector of all that is evil in human society; the best book for regulating the temporal concerns of men, and the only book that can serve as an infallible guide to future felicity.
NOAH WEBSTER (American Lexicographer and Developer of Webster's Dictionary)

The Bible grows more beautiful as we grow in our understanding of it.
JOHANN WOLFGANG VON GOETHE (German Poet)

The New Testament is the very best book that ever was or ever will be known in the world.
CHARLES DICKENS (Author)

I have read the Bible through many times, and now make it a practice to read it through once every year…I pity the man who cannot find in it a rich supply of thought and of rules for conduct. It fits a man for life–it prepares him for death.

If we abide by the principle taught in the Bible, our country will go on prospering.
DANIEL WEBSTER (U.S. Statesman and Orator)

There came a time in my life when I doubted the divinity of the Scriptures, and I resolved as a lawyer and a judge I would try the book as I would try anything in the courtroom, taking evidence for and against. It was a long, serious, and profound study; and using the same principles of evidence in this religious matter as I always do in secular matters, I have come to the decision that the Bible is a supernatural book, that it has come from God, and that the only safety for the human race is to follow its teachings.
SALMON P. CHASE (U.S. Chief Justice)

The nearer I approach the end of my pilgrimage, the clearer is the evidence of the divine origin of the Bible
SAMUEL MORSE (Inventor of the telegraph)

It is impossible to mentally or socially enslave a Bible-reading people.
HORACE GREELEY (U.S. Journalist and Political Leader)

We account the Scriptures of God to be the most sublime philosophy.

I have a fundamental belief in the Bible as the Word of God, written by men who were inspired. I study the Bible daily.

I find more sure marks of authenticity in the Bible than in any profane history whatsoever.
ISAAC NEWTON (Scientist and Mathematician)

The most learned, acute, and diligent student cannot, in the longest life, obtain an entire knowledge of the Bible. The more deeply he works the mine, the richer and more abundant he finds the ore; new light continually beams from this source of heavenly knowledge, to direct the conduct, and illustrate the work of God and the ways of men; and he will at last leave the world confessing, that the more he studied the Scriptures, the fuller conviction he had of his own ignorance, and of their inestimable value.
SIR WALTER SCOTT (English Poet)

There are no songs comparable to the songs of Zion, no orations equal to those of the prophets, and no politics like those which the Scriptures teach.
JOHN MILTON (English Poet)

The gospel is not merely a book—it is a living power—a book surpassing all others. I never omit to read it, and every day with the same pleasure. The gospel possesses a secret virtue, a mysterious efficacy, warmth which penetrates and soothes the heart. One finds in meditating upon it that which one experiences in contemplating the heavens. The gospel is not a book; it is a living being, with an action, a power, which invades everything that opposes its extension.
NAPOLEON BONAPARTE (Emperor of France)

How petty are the books of the philosophers with all their pomp compared with the Gospels!
JEAN JACQUES ROUSSEAU (French Philosopher and Writer)

*I know the Bible is inspired because
it finds me at a greater depth of my being than any other book.*
SAMUEL TAYLOR COLERIDGE (English Poet)

That book, sir, is the rock on which our republic rests.
ANDREW JACKSON (7th U.S. President)

I believe the Bible is the best gift God has ever given to man. All the good from the Savior of the world is communicated to us through this book.
ABRAHAM LINCOLN (16th U.S. President)

In all my perplexities and distresses, the Bible has never failed to give me light and strength.

There are things in the old Book which I may not be able to explain, but I fully accept it as the infallible Word of God, and receive its teachings as inspired by the Holy Spirit.
ROBERT E. LEE (Confederate Army General)

Hold fast to the Bible as the sheet anchor of your liberties; write its precepts in your hearts, and practice them in your lives.
ULYSSES S. GRANT (18th U.S. President)

I have known ninety-five of the world's great men in my time, and of those eighty-seven were followers of the Bible.
W.E. GLADSTONE (British Prime Minister)

The more profoundly we study this wonderful Book, and the more closely we observe its divine precepts, the better citizens we will become and the higher will be our destiny as a nation.
WILLIAM MCKINLEY (25th U.S. President)

A thorough knowledge of the Bible is worth more than a college education.
THEODORE ROOSEVELT (26th U.S. President)

Give the Bible to the people, unadulterated, pure, unaltered, unexplained, uncheapened, and then see it work through the whole nature. It is very difficult indeed for a man or for a boy who knows the Scriptures ever to get away from it. It follows him like the memory of his mother. It haunts him like an old song. It reminds him like the word of an old and revered teacher. It forms a part of the warp and woof of his life.

I am sorry for men who do not read the Bible every day. I wonder why they deprive themselves of the strength and the pleasure.
WOODROW WILSON (28th U.S. President)

The foundations of our society and our government rest so much on the teachings of the Bible that it would be difficult to support them if faith in these teachings would cease to be practically universal in our country.
CALVIN COOLIDGE (30th U.S. President)

The whole inspiration of our civilization springs from the teachings of Christ and the lessons of the prophets. To read the Bible for these fundamentals is a necessity of American life.
HERBERT HOOVER (31st U.S. President)

We cannot read the history of our rise and development as a nation, without reckoning the place the Bible has occupied in shaping the advances of the Republic.

It is a fountain of strength and now, as always, an aid in attaining the highest aspirations of the human soul.
FRANKLIN D. ROOSEVELT (32nd U.S. President)

The Bible is endorsed by the ages. Our civilization is built upon its words. In no other book is there such a collection of inspired wisdom, reality, and hope.
DWIGHT D. EISENHOWER (34th U.S. President)

I never had any doubt about it being of divine origin...point out to me any similar collection of writings that has lasted for as many thousands of years and is still a Best-seller, world-wide. It had to be of divine origin.

Within the covers of the Bible are all the answers for all the problems men face. The Bible can touch hearts, order minds and refresh souls.
RONALD WILSON REAGAN (40th U.S. President)

HISTORICAL TESTIMONIES TO
BIBLICAL PERSONAGES AND EVENTS

The testimonies to the events and accuracy of the Biblical record are not only inclusive to those of the Christian faith. The historicity of its events, especially those recorded in the New Testament, has been attested to by secular scholars as well. The majority of these extra-Biblical testimonies were made by historians who lived and wrote concurrently with the personalities of the Bible.

Josephus, the 1st century Jewish historian, testified not only to the events surrounding the early Christian church, but to the historical reality of Jesus' life, death, and resurrection: *Now there was about this time Jesus, a wise man, if it be lawful to call him a man, for he was a doer of wonderful works, a teacher of such men as receive the truth with pleasure. He drew over to him both many of the Jews, and many of the Gentiles. He was [the] Christ. And when Pilate, at the suggestion of the principal men among us, had condemned him to the cross, those that loved him at the first did not forsake him; for he appeared to them alive again the third day; as the divine prophets had foretold these and ten thousand other wonderful things concerning him. And the tribe of Christians so named from him are not extinct at this day.*[16]

Josephus also mentioned both John the Baptist's ministry and the trial and martyrdom of James, the brother of Jesus: *Now some of the Jews thought that the destruction of Herod's army came from God, and that very justly, as a punishment of what he did against John, that was called the Baptist: for Herod slew him, who was a good man, and commanded the Jews to exercise virtue, both as to righteousness towards one another, and piety towards God, and so to come to baptism; for that the washing would be acceptable to him, if they made use of it, not in order to the putting away of some sins, but for the*

---

[16] Josephus, *Antiquities of the Jews*, XVIII, iii, 3.

purification of the body; supposing still that the soul was purified beforehand by righteousness.[17] *...he assembled the Sanhedrim of judges, and brought before them the brother of Jesus, who was called Christ, whose name was James, and some others; and when he had formed an accusation against them as breakers of the law, he delivered them to be stoned.*[18]

Julius Africanus quoted the 1st century Roman historian Thallus describing the events surrounding the crucifixion of Jesus: *On the whole world there pressed a most fearful darkness; and the rocks were rent by an earthquake,*[19] *and many places in Judea and other districts were thrown down.*[20]

Tacitus, another 1st century Roman historian, in detailing the persecution by Nero, testified to the existence of Jesus, even mentioning his trial by Pilate: *Nero...falsely charged with the guilt, and punished with the most exquisite tortures, the persons commonly called Christians, who were hated for their enormities. Christus, the founder of that name, was put to death as a criminal by Pontius Pilate, procurator of Judea in the reign of Tiberius.*[21]

The Roman historian Suetonius also mentioned Nero's persecution of the Christians: *Punishment [by Nero] was inflicted on the Christians, a class of men given to a new and mischievous superstition.*[22]

---

[17] Josephus, *Antiquities of the Jews*, XVIII, vi, 2.

[18] Josephus, *Antiquities of the Jews,* XX, xix.

[19] This was believed by Julius Africanus to be referring to the earthquake and darkening of the sun that occurred at the death of Jesus (Matthew 27:51, Luke 23:44-45). Thallus wrote his history about 52 A.D.

[20] Julius Africanus, Extant Writings, XVIII in *The Ante-Nicene Fathers* (Eerdmans, 1973).

[21] Tacitus, *Annals* xv, 44. The Oxford Translation, Revised, p. 423.

[22] Suetonius, *The Lives of the Caesars*, Nero xvi. Loeb Classical Library English translation by J. C. Rolfe, Vol. II, p. 111.

The 2nd century Roman historian Pliny described the activity and character attributed to the early Christians: *...they were in the habit of meeting on a certain fixed day before it was light, when they sang in alternate verses a hymn to Christ, as to a god, and bound themselves by a solemn oath, not to any wicked deeds, but never to commit any fraud, theft, or adultery, never to falsify their word, nor to deny a trust when they should be called on to deliver it up.*[23]

Lucian, writing in the 2nd century stated that the founder of the Christian faith had been crucified in Palestine: *...because he introduced this new cult into the world....Furthermore, their first lawgiver persuaded them that they are all brothers one of another after they have transgressed once for all by denying the Greek gods and by worshipping that crucified sophist himself and living under his laws.*[24]

It has been argued that the Talmud contains numerous derogatory references to Jesus Christ and the Christian faith. One of the clearest testimonies to Jesus's crucifixion is in *The Babylonian Talmud: On the eve of the Passover Yeshu*[25] *was hanged.*[26]

---

[23] Pliny, *Letters* X, xcvi. Loeb Classical Library. English translation by W. Melmoth, Vol. II, p. 103.

[24] Lucian, *The Passing of Peregrinus* 12, 13. Loeb Classical Library. English translation by A. M. Harmon, pp. 13, 15.

[25] Yeshu, or Yeshua, was the Hebrew name for Jesus. The word "hanged" may have been the term used for the crucifixion as it is thus used in Galatians 3:13.

[26] *The Babylonian Talmud*, vol. III, Sanhedrin 43a.

ARCHAEOLOGICAL TESTIMONY FOR THE BIBLE

Luke 19:40
*I tell you that, if these should hold their peace,
the stones would immediately cry out.*

Archaeology has been one of the most dynamic witnesses to the truth of the biblical record, and at the same time it has been the hammer used most often by critics and skeptics to strike at its historical accuracy. Though it has been used to try to break the rock, it has done no more than scatter the dust and revealed the word's truth yet more clearly. A number of archaeologists have testified to the undeniable accuracy of the Book.

Archaeology has confirmed countless passages which had been rejected by critics as unhistorical or contrary to known facts.[27]
Archaeologist Joseph Free

Luke's history is unsurpassed in respect of its trustworthiness.[28]

I began with a mind unfavorable to it...but more recently I found myself brought into contact with the Book of Acts as an authority for the topography, antiquities, and society of Asia Minor. It was gradually borne upon me that in various details the narrative showed marvelous truth.[29]

---

[27] Joseph Free, *Archaeology and Bible History* (Wheaton, IL: Scripture Press, 1969), p. 1.
[28] William Mitchell Ramsay, *Luke the Physician*, p. 177.
[29] William Mitchell Ramsay, *St. Paul the Traveler and the Roman Citizen*, p. 8.

Luke is a historian of the first rank; not merely are his statements of fact trustworthy; he is possessed of the true historic sense...this author should be placed along with the very greatest of historians.[30]
Archaeologist Sir William Ramsay

It...may be stated categorically that no archaeological discovery has ever controverted a biblical reference. Scores of archeological findings have been made which confirm in clear outline or exact detail historical statements in the Bible.[31]
Archaeologist Nelson Glueck

...archaeological work has unquestionably strengthened confidence in the reliability of the scriptural record. More than one archaeologist has found his respect for the Bible increased by the experience of excavation in Palestine.
Millar Burrows

In every instance where the findings of archaeology pertain to the Biblical record, the archaeological evidence confirms, sometimes in detailed fashion, the historical accuracy of Scripture. In those instances where the archaeological findings seem to be at variance with the Bible, the discrepancy lies with the archaeological evidence, i.e., improper interpretation, lack of evidence, etc.–not with the Bible.
Archaeologist Dr. Bryant C. Wood

There can be no doubt that archaeology has confirmed the substantial historicity of Old Testament traditions.
Archaeologist William F. Albright

---

[30] William Mitchell Ramsay, *The Bearing of Recent Discovery on the Trustworthiness of the New Testament*, p. 222.
[31] Nelson Glueck, *Rivers in the Desert* (New York: Farar, Straus and Cudahy, 1959), p. 136.

As has been testified to by numerous archaeologists, some of which are quoted above, the historical record of the Bible has never been maligned by archaeological discoveries. Discoveries have been made that have brought the Bible's statements into question, but time and further discovery have always unseated any question or contradiction that has arisen. The vast majority of archaeological discoveries have further validated the scripture. The key phrase in the study of the Bible, whether spiritual or archaeological is, "Dig a little deeper." The more that is unearthed the more evidence for the Bible mounts up, the more of God's truth is revealed.

In regard to archaeological or scientific understanding, we must take the Bible first and foremost as the foundation of truth. All human theories and speculations must adhere to its eternal witness. Time has always borne this out.

There are many key discoveries that have been unearthed in the field of Biblical archaeology, and many more are yet to be found. Many of the cities and locations described in the Bible have been found, among them Haran, Shechem, the store cities of Pithom and Raamses, Jericho, Dan, Megiddo, Ashkelon, Gezer, Shiloh, Ashdod, Beth Shemesh, the pool at Gibeon, Saul's fortress and capital city of Gibeah, Beth Shean, Beersheba, Samaria, Hazor, Carchemish, Babylon, Susa, and many others. Many of the cities and locations of the New Testament have also been located by archaeologists. Among these are Nazareth, Bethsaida, Cana, Capernaum, Jacob's Well near Sychar, the pool of Bethesda, Bethany, Tiberias, Caesarea Philippi, Herod's palace, Pilate's praetorium, Damascus, the Areopagus at Athens, Ephesus, Antioch, Philippi, Thessalonica, and others. Some of the most critical discoveries are worth examining.

ARCHAEOLOGICAL FINDS
THAT VALIDATE BIBLICAL ACCOUNTS

THE SUMERIAN KING LIST
(Evidence for the Flood of Genesis 7-8)

- List of the Sumerian kings on several clay tablets and prisms found in Mesopotamia
- Copies of this list date to 2100 B.C.
- The list is divided into two groups: kings ruling before a "flood that swept over the earth" and kings ruling after the flood
- The life spans and reigns of the group after the flood were much shorter than those before the flood, just as is the case in the biblical genealogies

THE GILGAMESH EPIC
(Evidence for the flood of Genesis 7-8)

- The story of the Babylonian king Gilgamesh on clay tablets found at Nineveh
- The Nineveh copies date to around the 7th century B.C.
- Tablet 11 contains a detailed account of the flood that is amazingly accurate
- The tablet states that the great flood was brought about by the god's wrath, there was one who built a ship, filled it with animals, and used birds to assure that the water had receded

THE SILVER SCRIPTURE AMULETS
(Evidence for the book of Numbers having been written long
before Ezra's time)

- Two silver amulets rolled up like miniature scrolls were found in tombs in Jerusalem
- These were dated to about 600 B.C. and contained the passage from Numbers 6:24-26: *The Lord bless thee and keep thee; The Lord make his face shine upon thee, and be gracious unto thee: The Lord lift up his countenance upon thee, and give thee peace.*
- These are the oldest examples of Scripture ever found

BOGHAZKOY, CAPITAL CITY OF THE HITTITE NATION
(Evidence for the existence of the Hittites)

- Modern critics accused the biblical authors of inventing the Hittites as no evidence of their existence had been found
- Boghazkoy, the capital of the Hittite nation, was discovered 90 miles east of Ankara in Turkey
- This find demonstrated that the Hittite people existed, once again validating the biblical record

THE MERNEPTAH STELE
(Evidence for the existence of Israel in the Promised Land)

- Many modern critics believed Israel was never a true nation in Canaan
- The Merneptah Stele records the victories of Pharaoh Merneptah over the people of Palestine and Libya
- It is believed to have been written about 1230 B.C. and contains the first historical mention of Israel outside of the Bible

THE SHISHAK RELIEF
(Evidence for the historicity of Pharaoh Shishak's invasion of Judah
recorded in I Kings 14 and II Chronicles 12)

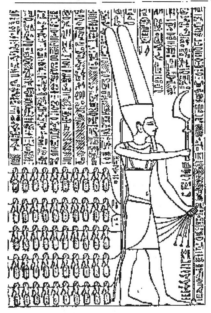

- Carvings found on the walls of the Karnak Temple of Amun
- The Shishak Relief shows the captives taken from Judah and was carved to commemorate the Pharaoh's victory over Rehoboam

THE TEL DAN INSCRIPTION
(Evidence for King David's monarchy)

- Modern critics believed that the biblical authors invented a mythical king named David and that there had never been such a historical figure
- Three pieces of black basalt stone were found during the excavation of the city of Dan
- One of the inscriptions was dated to within a few hundred years of David
- Part of the inscription, describing a king of Israel and a king of Judah reads in Aramaic, "the house of David"

THE HOUSE OF YAHWEH OSTRACON
(Evidence for the Temple of Solomon)

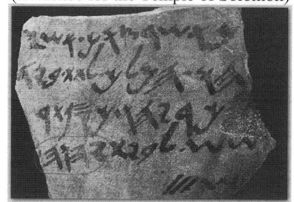

- A receipt written on a small piece of pottery dated between 835 and 796 B.C. about 130 years after the building of the Temple
- It records a donation of three shekels of silver to the Temple of Solomon, called the 'House of Yahweh'

SEALS OF THE KINGS OF ISRAEL AND JUDAH
(Evidence for the Bible's historical record of these kings)

- Numerous excavations have recovered carved semi-precious stones used as seals
- These are dated from about 900 to 600 B.C.
- Seals were found with the names of Uzziah, Hoshea, Hezekiah, and others
- The most well-known seal contains the phrase: "belonging to Shema, servant of Jeroboam"

THE MOABITE STONE
(Evidence for the historicity of Kings Omri, Ahab, and the Moabites)

- Many critics did not believe the Moabites existed
- This stone slab was found near Dibon and was dated to about 850 B.C.
- This stone records the humbling of Moab by Kings Omri and Ahab of Israel
- Some scholars have claimed it contains the phrase "the house of David"

THE BLACK OBELISK
(Evidence for the historicity of King Jehu)

- This black basalt obelisk was discovered in the palace at Nimrud and dated to about 841 B.C.
- Describes and depicts King Jehu bringing tribute to the Assyrian King Shalmaneser

KING UZZIAH'S BURIAL PLAQUE
(Evidence for the historicity of King Uzziah)

- This stone plaque was found on the Mount of Olives
- It contains the inscription "Here, the bones of Uzziah, King of Judah, were brought"

THE CYRUS CYLINDER
(Evidence of Cyrus' decree that the captives could return to

Jerusalem
- This is a clay cylinder found at Babylon and dated to about 539 B.C.
- Includes the decree of Cyrus to allow Babylonian captives to return to their homelands and rebuild their temples

THE DEAD SEA SCROLLS

- These include hundreds of pieces dated from 300 B.C. to 70 A.D.
- About 1/3ʳᵈ of the scrolls contained portions of books of the Old Testament, and nearly the entire book of Isaiah is intact
- This is one of the most incredible witnesses to the highly accurate transmission of the Scripture by the scribal traditions of the Masoretes and others
- *Of the 166 words in Isaiah 53, there are only 17 letters in question. Ten of these letters are simply a matter of spelling, which does not affect the sense. Four more letters are minor stylistic changes, such as conjunctions. The three remaining letters comprise the word LIGHT, which is added in verse 11 and which does not affect the meaning greatly. Furthermore, this word is supported by the LXX. Thus, in one chapter of 166 words, there is only one word (three letters) in question after a thousand years of transmission – and this word does not significantly change the meaning of the passage."*[32]

---

[32] Norman Geisler and William Nix, *A General Introduction to the Bible,* Chicago: Moody Press, p. 263.

THE PONTIUS PILATE INSCRIPTION
(Evidence for the historicity of Pontius Pilate)

- Inscription found in the ruins of Caesarea Maritima
- This inscription contains the name "Pontius Pilate"

THE POLITARCH INSCRIPTIONS
(Evidence for the historical accuracy of Luke)

- Many modern critics believed Luke was inaccurate in using this term for a political official as it had never been found
- Thirty-two inscriptions have been found containing the title "politarch"

THE NAZARETH DECREE
(Potential evidence for the resurrection of Christ)

- A decree made by the Roman Emperor Claudius, who ruled between 41 to 54 A.D.
- This unusual decree, discovered in Nazareth in 1878, addresses the removal of bodies from tombs, and decrees capital punishment for anyone doing so
- Given the fact that this appeared to address this issue in Israel soon after the time of the resurrection of Christ, this may have been made as a response to the message of Christ not being found in the tomb
- The decree states: "It is my decision [concerning] graves and tombs— whoever has made them for the religious observances of parents, or children, or household members – that these remain undisturbed forever. But if anyone legally charges that another person has destroyed, or has in any manner extracted those who have been buried, or has moved with wicked intent those who have been buried to other places, committing a crime against them, or has moved sepulchre-sealing stones, against

such a person...I wish that [violator] to suffer capital punishment under the title of tomb-breaker."

THE GALLIO INSCRIPTION
(Evidence for the historicity of the proconsul Gallio)

- A stone inscription found at Delphi in Greece and dated to about 53 A.D.
- This inscription mentions Gallio, Roman governor of Achaia

THE TESTIMONY OF SCIENTIFIC FOREKNOWLEDGE: SCIENTIFIC OBSERVATIONS IN THE BIBLE THAT PRECEDED MODERN DISCOVERY

Isaiah 48:6
Thou hast heard, see all this; and will not ye declare it?
I have shewed thee new things from this time, even hidden things,
and thou didst not know them.

MEDICAL EVIDENCES

One of the most powerful testimonies to the advanced understanding and divine inspiration of the Bible is the medically based observations made in the Mosaic Law. As has been observed, Moses was thoroughly schooled in the most advanced knowledge of his day by the most developed culture of that time. It is abundantly clear from a study of the Egyptian medical practices of Moses' day that they were seriously deficient in understanding of proper sanitation and cleanliness and that there was no comprehension of the nature of germs and bacteria and their effect on health.

Consider these "cutting-edge" medical treatments used in Egypt in the time of Moses' day, as related in the Ebers Papyrus and elsewhere:
- The treatment for healing an infected splinter wound includes applying a mixture containing the blood of worms and the feces of a donkey.[33]
- A painful tumor would be treated with fly dung mixed with sycamore juice.

---

[33] This treatment would be guaranteed to make the situation worse, as dung carries numerous diseases, including tetanus.

- The treatment for hair loss was to spread, on the man's scalp, a mixture of fats from a cat, snake, horse, and a crocodile as well as a donkey tooth crushed in honey.
- Curing a baby's excessive crying? One sure cure is a mixture of seeds and fly dung from the wall, strained and drunk for four days. The prescription promises "the crying will cease instantly" (no doubt when the child died).
- Some of the other common ingredients in ancient Egyptian prescriptions: snake skins, swine's teeth, rotten meat, goose grease, lizard's blood, donkey's hoofs, "stinking" fat, moisture from a pig's ear, and human and animal excrement (such as flies, donkeys, cats, gazelles, hippopotamuses and antelopes).

One of the most powerful promises God made to the nation of Israel after leaving Egypt was in regard to health:

Exodus 15:26...*If thou wilt diligently hearken to the voice of the Lord thy God, and wilt do that which is right in his sight, and wilt give ear to his commandments, and keep all his statutes, I will put none of these diseases upon thee, which I have brought upon the Egyptians: for I am the Lord that healeth thee.*

There are two currents of thought involved in this statement. Primarily and most critical is that the people obey the Lord and do that which is right in His sight. Secondarily, they must pay attention to His commandments and keep His statutes. In the first sense, the obedience to God is that of the heart. If the people of Israel were attentive to God's will and obedient to Him in their spiritual lives, they would be given divine protection from the diseases brought upon the world by the curse. In addition, if they obeyed the commandments and statutes of the law through its specific ordinances of purification and sanitation, they would be physically predisposed to a healthier condition.

Proper Sanitation Is Critical to Maintaining Health
Finally established in the 16th and 17th centuries,
about 3,000 years after the Bible

Many deadly diseases are directly caused by improper sanitary conditions. Up until the end of the 18th century in many modern cities of Europe and America, human excrement was dumped onto the streets. This attracted flies and other vermin that bred among the filth. This and the germs spread by the refuse caused cholera, typhoid, dysentery, and other diseases.

Moses gave clear instructions on proper sanitation:

> **Deuteronomy 23:12-13** *Thou shalt have a place also without the camp, whither thou shalt go abroad: And thou shalt have a paddle upon thy weapon; and it shall be, when thou shalt ease thyself abroad, thou shalt dig therewith, and shalt turn back and cover that which cometh from thee…*

Obedience to this command alone would have significantly reduced the mortality rate of the children of Israel in comparison to the nations surrounding them.

Quarantine and Purification Methods

The Levitical instructions regarding purification and cleanliness are revealing. Included in the dietary laws of Leviticus 11 are some interesting statements:

Leviticus 11:24-25 *...whosoever toucheth the carcasses of them [dead animals] shall be unclean until the even. And whosoever beareth aught of the carcasses of them shall wash his clothes, and be unclean until the even.*

Leviticus 11:31-33 *...whosoever doth touch them, when they be dead, shall be unclean until the even. And upon whatsoever any of them, when they are dead, doth fall, it shall be unclean; whether it be any vessel of wood, or raiment, or skin, or sack, whatsoever vessel it be, wherein any work is done, it must be put into water, and it shall be unclean until the even; so it shall be cleansed. And every earthen vessel, whereinto any of them falleth, whatsoever is in it shall be unclean; and ye shall break it.*

Leviticus 11:34 *Of all meat which may be eaten, that on which such water* [water used to cleanse unclean items] *cometh shall be unclean: and all drink that may be drunk in every such vessel shall be unclean.*

The Old Testament laws regarding purification and quarantine periods for disease and sickness are dealt with in great detail in Leviticus chapters 13, 14, and 15. These requirements were thousands of years ahead of the medicinal knowledge of their day.

There are a number of symbolic activities involved that are representative of spiritual principles and types, but the practical methodologies involved are those that we are examining for their scientific value. Consider the fact that the cleansing of the body by washing to remove germs and bacteria was unknown until the 16th century. The 15th chapter of Leviticus in particular has detailed insight into this procedure. Any person who had contact with one who was sick or diseased was required to wash himself in water.

Leviticus 15:11 *And whomsoever he toucheth that hath the issue, and hath not rinsed his hands in water, he shall wash his clothes, and bathe himself in water, and be unclean until the even.*

Not only were the Israelites required to cleanse themselves if they had contact with the sick, but the bed, clothing, and anything else that could carry the germs of disease or sickness were also to be treated as unclean. This element alone is demonstrative of a highly advanced understanding of disease-carrying germs.

One very revealing illustration of this is recorded by Dr. S.I. McMillen: *Let me give an example by citing what happened in Vienna in the 1840's...in one of the most famous teaching hospitals of that day, Allegemeine Krakenhause. In the maternity wards of this celebrated hospital, one out of every six women died, and this frightening mortality rate was similar in other hospitals around the world. The obstetricians ascribed the deaths to constipation, delayed lactation, fear, and poisonous air. The first order of each morning was the entrance of the physicians and medical students into the morgue to perform autopsies...afterward, without cleansing their hands, the doctors with their retinue of students marched into the maternity wards to make pelvic examinations on the living women. Of course, no rubber gloves were worn. In the early 1840's a young doctor named Ignaz Semmelweis was given charge over one of the obstetrical wards. He observed that it was particularly the women who were examined by the teachers and students who became sick and died. After watching this heartbreaking situation for three years, he established a rule that, in his ward, every physician and medical student who had participated in the autopsies of the dead must carefully wash his hands before examining the living medical patients. In April, 1847, before the new rule went into effect, fifty-seven women died; in June, only one out of every forty-two women died; in July, only one out of every eighty-four.*

The statistics strongly indicated that fatal infections had been carried from corpses to living patients.[34]

Dr. Roswell Park records his experiences with the lack of antiseptic methods: *When I began my work, in 1876, as a hospital interne, in one of the largest hospitals in this country, it happened that during my first winter's experience, with but one or two exceptions, every patient operated upon in that hospital, and that by men who were esteemed the peers of any one in their day, died of blood poisoning.*[35]

In the two years following this statement, Louis Pasteur and Sir Joseph Lister, both staunch Christians and believers in the Bible, developed the antiseptic methods that are used today to ensure cleanliness and to control the spread of bacteria.

The Mosaic Law required that the individuals who were the original vessels of the disease, after they had been cleansed of their sickness (the sickness had passed), were to wash. What is critical here is that the bearer of the sickness must wash in "running water." This is precisely what would have been necessary for any disease-bearing germs to be carried away from the body.

> **Leviticus 15:13** *And when he that hath an issue is cleansed of his issue; then shall he number himself seven days for his cleansing, and wash his clothes, and bathe his flesh in running water, and shall be clean.*

This verse, among many others, also demonstrates the secondary requirement for the sick, the period of quarantine. This of course would control the disease from spreading. This is but another advanced medical principle beyond the understanding of its time.

---

[34] S.I. McMillen, *None of These Diseases*, pp. 13-14, Spire Books, 1967.

[35] Cancer of Cervix and Non-Jews, *Journal of the American Medical Association*, p. 1069, July 23, 1949.

Blood Is an Essential Component
for the Body's Survival and Health
Properly comprehended by science in the 19th century

The Bible is decidedly clear on the importance of the blood to the operations and life of the body:

Genesis 9:4 *...flesh with the life thereof, which is the blood thereof, shall ye not eat.*

Leviticus 17:11, 14 *For the life of the flesh is in the blood:...For it is the life of all flesh; the blood of it is for the life thereof:...Ye shall eat the blood of no manner of flesh: for the life of all flesh is the blood thereof...*

Deuteronomy 12:23 *Only be sure that thou eat not the blood: for the blood is the life; and thou mayest not eat the life of the flesh.*

God puts a great degree of importance on blood in the Bible. It is mentioned approximately 375 times in the scriptures. Blood is the life of the flesh both naturally and spiritually. From a natural standpoint, blood is one of the most critical components of life. It is the fuel of the heart and circulatory system; it aids in fighting disease and provides strength and life to the body. From a spiritual standpoint, it is our covering, without which we would be dead in our trespasses and sins. The lifeblood that was poured out for us on Calvary enables us to be free from the bondage of sin.

Less than 200 years ago it was common practice to "bleed" the sick to aid in their recovery. Bleeding the sick, or phlebotomy, as it is properly called, is one of the oldest medical practices. It is believed to have originated in the ancient Egyptian and Grecian cultures.[36] This practice continued until the 19th century when the development of bacteriological and germ theory demonstrated the true source of disease.

---

[36] Red Gold, 2002, Educational Broadcasting Corporation.

The infamous story of the final illness of George Washington amply illustrates the dangers of bloodletting. Washington had been riding horseback on his farm during a cold, rainy December day. When he came into the house in the late afternoon he did not immediately change out of his wet clothing. The damp and the cold caused him to develop what was believed to be a severe case of pneumonia. He woke early in the morning barely able to breathe. After applying a number of home remedies, he asked for Rawlins, his farm overseer, who was experienced in veterinary medicine. Washington requested that Rawlins bleed him and a pint of the President's blood was taken. Four hours later, Washington's family doctor, Dr. Craik, arrived. He immediately bled him again. He then gave him vinegar and sage tea to gargle and, when no improvement was shown, bled him again. Two additional doctors were then summoned. When Dr. Brown and Dr. Dick arrived three hours later, Washington was much worse, his skin had turned blue, and he was having great difficulty breathing. The three doctors conferred and Drs. Brown and Craik felt that Washington should be bled again. Dr. Dick argued against this, saying that this would only diminish the President's strength. He was overruled and a quart of Washington's blood was taken. This caused him to become weaker, which led to his death that afternoon. The story of Washington's death, in which his treatment was strongly responsible, demonstrates the danger of misunderstanding the importance of blood to life and health.

We now know that blood is one of the most important elements in the human body. It carries water and oxygen to all the cells in the body. It maintains the body's temperature and aids in the removal of waste material from cells. It is certainly true that the life is in the blood.

The high value of the blood is attested to in the commandment of God that there is to be no blood eaten with the flesh:

Genesis 9:4 ...*flesh with the life thereof, which is the blood thereof, shall ye not eat.*
Leviticus 7:26-27 ...*Whatsoever soul it be that eateth any manner of blood, even that soul shall be cut off from his people.*
Leviticus 17:13-14 ...*he shall even pour out the blood thereof, and cover it with dust. For it is the life of all flesh; the blood of it is for the life thereof: therefore I said unto the children of Israel, Ye shall eat the blood of no manner of flesh: for the life of all flesh is the blood thereof: whosoever eateth it shall be cut off.*

The Act of Circumcision

God first commanded the act of circumcision to Abraham and his family. Circumcision was to be done on the eighth day after a child was born.

Genesis 17:12 *And he that is eight days old shall be circumcised among you, every man child in your generations, he that is born in the house, or bought with money of any stranger, which is not of thy seed.*

The eighth-day requirement, from a medical perspective, is amazing. During the first seven days of a baby's life its blood is saturated with antibodies from the mother. After this first week (seven days), these antibodies begin to decrease to a normal level. Vitamin K, which allows the blood to coagulate, is formed between days five and seven and is not usually at full strength until the eighth day. Prothrombin, another important element that aids in the clotting of the blood, reaches 110% of its normal level on the eighth day, dropping back to normal levels afterward. Any surgical procedure performed on the child before this time could result in serious hemorrhaging or infection. The elements to protect against this happening are at their peak on the eighth day!

SCIENTIFIC EVIDENCES

The Law of Conservation of Energy and Mass

The first law of thermodynamics essentially states that energy and mass within a closed system remain constant. Thus no new energy or mass is being created or destroyed. Anything that appears to be new is actually a redistribution of energy already in existence. From a scriptural standpoint, this can be demonstrated in that all secondary creation proceeds from a previously created thing. Humans, plants, and animals carry the seed within themselves to create new generations of life; this life is created by the seed within them, not from out of nothing. Only God can create ex nihilo, and it is by God's Spirit that all things continue to exist:

> **Nehemiah 9:6** *Thou, even thou, art Lord alone; thou hast made heaven, the heaven of heavens, with all their host, the earth, and all things that are therein, the seas, and all that is therein, and thou preservest them all; and the host of heaven worshippeth thee.*
>
> **Acts 17:28** *For in him we live, and move, and have our being; as certain also of your own poets have said, For we are also his offspring.*
>
> **Colossians 1:17** *And he is before all things, and by him all things consist.*[37]
>
> **II Peter 3:7** *But the heavens and the earth, which are now, by the same word are kept in store, reserved unto fire against the day of judgment and perdition of ungodly men.*

As God brought His creation into being in the first chapter of Genesis we are told that He saw everything that He had made, and, behold, it was very good. All divine creation was brought to an end at this point in time, and the law of conservation took effect.

---

[37] Literally meaning "are held together" or "sustained."

Genesis 1:12 *And the earth brought forth grass, and herb yielding seed after his kind, and the tree yielding fruit, whose seed was in itself, after his kind: and God saw that it was good.*

Ecclesiastes 1:9 *The thing which hath been, it is that which shall be; and that which is done is that which shall be done: and there is no new thing under the sun.*

Ecclesiastes 3:14-15 *I know that, whatsoever God doeth, it shall be forever: nothing can be put to it, nor any thing taken from it: and God doeth it, that men should fear before him. That which hath been is now; and that which is to be hath already been; and God requireth that which is past.*

The Law of Entropy

The law of entropy essentially states that disorder must increase. Thus, all systems are becoming less organized and are losing energy. We can see this demonstrated in all of the creation. Physically, man is in a constant state of degeneration. We are all slowly dying. This state is the same for all of created things. Anything that is built, whether structure or machine, is in a continual state of wearing down. Things do not become more ordered. They become less ordered. Over time, metal objects rust, cloth deteriorates, and rocks are worn away. Man, animals, and plants are "growing" continually toward their deaths.

The law of entropy was not originally intended to be a part of God's creation. Creation, in its original state, was intended to be a thing of perfect order and symmetry, good in all ways. When man stepped outside this order by choosing to disobey the will of God, the perfect creation was marred. God had warned man from the beginning that this would be the result of disobedience:

Genesis 2:17 *But of the tree of the knowledge of good and evil, thou shalt not eat*
of it: for in the day that thou eatest thereof thou shalt surely die.

Man chose to disobey his Creator and death and disorder was brought upon all of creation by his act:

Genesis 3:17-19 *And unto Adam he said, Because thou hast hearkened to the voice of thy wife, and hast eaten of the tree, of which I commanded thee, saying, Thou shalt not eat of it: cursed is the ground for thy sake; in sorrow shalt thou eat of it all the days of thy life; Thorns also and thistles shall it bring forth to thee; and thou shalt eat the herb of the field; In the sweat of thy face shalt thou eat bread, till thou return unto the ground; for out of it wast thou taken: for dust thou art, and unto dust shalt thou return.*

This state that was brought upon all the earth is referred to in the scripture as the "bondage of corruption."[38]

Romans 8:19-23 *For the earnest expectation of the creature waiteth for the manifestation of the sons of God. For the creature was made subject to vanity, not willingly, but by reason of him who hath subjected the same in hope, Because the creature itself also shall be delivered from the bondage of corruption into the glorious liberty of the children of God. For we know that the whole creation groaneth and travaileth in pain together until now. And not only they, but ourselves also, which have the firstfruits of the Spirit, even we ourselves groan within ourselves, waiting for the adoption, to wit, the redemption of our body.*

---

[38] In the spiritual sense, this is the bondage of the will to the carnal nature to sin.

The Shape of the Earth
Not proven until Magellan's voyage in 1521 A.D.

Throughout the history of the world most all civilizations believed that the earth was flat. The Chinese thought the earth was square, the Mesopotamians described it as a floating boat, and the Egyptians thought it was rectangular. During the 15th and 16th centuries, the major sea voyages of discovery disproved these theories. Isaiah 40:22, written in the 8th century B.C., demonstrates the Biblical understanding of the earth's shape: *It is he that sitteth upon the circle of the earth,...*

David's poetic statement in Psalm 103:12 takes on much more meaning when understood from the perspective of a spherical earth: *As far as the east is from the west, so far hath he removed our transgressions from us.* The east is an immeasurable distance from the west on a sphere like the earth, which has no edges, in contrast to a flat surface that could be measured from edge to edge.

The Earth Suspended in Nothing
Gravitational forces first began to be comprehended
in the 16th and 17th centuries A.D.

Job 26:7 *He...hangeth the earth upon nothing.*

Man's ancient beliefs ranged from the earth sitting on the back of a giant turtle to sitting upon a man's shoulders. The Bible clearly states that the earth is floating in the substance of space.

The Stars Are Innumerable
(Galileo's telescope revealed the beginning of this idea in 1608 A.D.)

Genesis 15:5 *...Look now toward heaven, and tell the stars, if thou be able to number them: and he said unto him, So shall thy seed be.*
Genesis 22:17 *That in blessing I will bless thee, and in multiplying I will multiply thy seed as the stars of heaven, and as the sand which is upon the sea shore.*
Jeremiah 33:22 *As the host of heaven cannot be numbered, neither the sand of the sea measured: so will I multiply the seed of David my servant,...*

Before the telescope was developed by Galileo, men believed that they could number the stars. Ptolemy claimed there were 1,056 stars, Kepler counted 1,006. After the invention of the telescope and modern astronomical science, it has been demonstrated that the stars cannot be counted. It has been calculated that there are 100 billon stars in the Milky Way galaxy alone, with many other billions of galaxies existing in the universe.

Both Day and Night Exist at the Same Time on the Earth
(At the same moment of time, it is night on one side of the planet while it is daytime on the other, a fact not known during Jesus' day)

Luke 17:34-36 *I tell you, in that night there shall be two men in one bed; the one shall be taken, and the other shall be left. Two women shall be grinding together; the one shall be taken, and the other left. Two men shall be in the field; the one shall be taken, and the other left.*[39]

---

[39] Jesus was stating that this event would occur during the night for some people who would be sleeping, while others would be involved in their daytime work at the same moment.

The Hydrologic Cycle

The hydrologic cycle of storage, evaporation, condensation, precipitation, and runoff would have been impossible for the ancient writers to discern. Yet we find that the Bible contains reference to this very thing:

Ecclesiastes 1:7 *All the rivers run into the sea; yet the sea is not full; unto the place from whence the rivers come, thither they return again.*

Evaporation

Water rises in gaseous form to the lower atmosphere and is bound up in the clouds.

Psalm 135:7 *He causeth the vapours to ascend from the ends of the earth; ...*

Jeremiah 10:13 *When he uttereth his voice, there is a multitude of waters in the heavens, and he causeth the vapours to ascend from the ends of the earth;....*

Condensation

The next stage in which the water vapor is bound up in the clouds.

Job 26:8 *He bindeth up the waters in his thick clouds; and the cloud is not rent under them.*

Job 37:11, 16 *Also by watering he wearieth[40] the thick cloud:...dost thou know the balancing of the clouds, the wondrous works of him which is perfect in knowledge?*

Proverbs 30:4...*who hath bound the waters in a garment?...*

Precipitation

The recycling of the water through rain, sleet, etc.

Job 36:27-28 *For he maketh small the drops of water: they pour down rain according to the vapour thereof: Which the clouds do drop and distil upon man abundantly.*

Psalm 147:8 *Who covereth the heaven with clouds, who prepareth rain for the earth, who maketh grass to grow upon the mountains.*

Proverbs 3:20 *By his knowledge the depths are broken up, and the clouds drop down the dew.*

Runoff and Erosion

Precipitation causes runoff and erosion as it drains back down to lower levels.

Job 14:19 *The waters wear the stones: thou washest away the things which grow out of the dust of the earth; and thou destroyest the hope of man.*

Job 28:10 *He cutteth out rivers among the rocks; and his eye seeth every precious thing.*

---

[40] The word "wearieth" here means "overburdened", referring poetically to the water's weight.

The Wind Travels in Circuits

Ecclesiastes 1:6-7 *The wind goeth toward the south, and turneth about unto the north; it whirleth about continually, and the wind returneth again according to his circuits.*

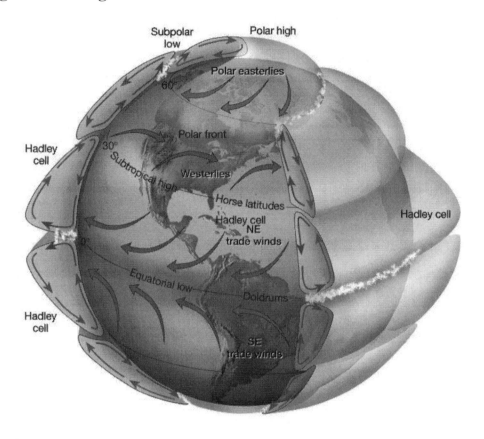

The Existence of Valleys in the Ocean

None of the ancient peoples had the technology to enable them to travel deep beneath the surface of the water or to measure its contours. Modern technology has enabled us to discover some of the incredible landscape that exists deep under the water. There are entire mountain ranges and valleys. God alone knew of the foundations of the world.

II Samuel 22:16 *And the channels[41] of the sea appeared, the foundations of the world were discovered, at the rebuking of the Lord, at the blast of the breath of his nostrils.*

The Existence of Ocean Currents (Paths in the Sea)
Discovered by Matthew Maury in 1854 A.D.

Maury, a naval captain, believed the Bible must be speaking truth when it claims the sea has paths. He was persistent in his research until he was able to verify the truth of the scriptural passage. It is now scientifically understood that the ocean has paths and currents.

Psalm 8:8 *The fowl of the air, and the fish of the sea, and whatsoever passeth through the paths of the seas.*

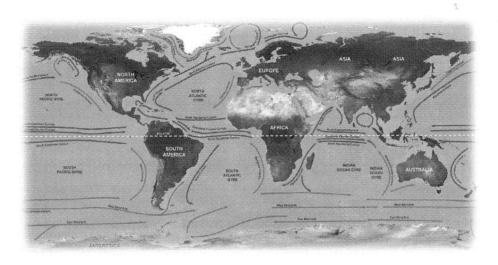

---

[41] "Channels" is the Hebrew word *aphiq*, meaning "channels" or "valleys".

Air Has Weight
Made known through the discovery of barometric pressure
by Torricelli in 1643 A.D.

All throughout known history man has believed that air was a weightless element. The Bible clearly understood this fact long before man had the capacity to measure the weight of air.

Job 28:25 *To make the weight for the winds; and he weigheth the waters by measure.*

THE TESTIMONY OF DIVINE PRESERVATION

Isaiah 40:8

The grass withereth, the flower fadeth:
but the word of our God shall stand for ever.

The book of God, like the people of God,
has, in every age, suffered persecution.
It has been tortured and ruptured,
pierced and ridiculed,
burned and buried,
but it has quenched the violence of fire,
escaped the edge of the sword,
stopped the mouths of lions,
and turned to flight the armies of the aliens.[42]

A thousand times over, the death knell of the Bible
has been sounded, the funeral procession formed,
the inscription cut on the tombstone, and committal read.
But somehow the corpse never stays put.
No other book has been so chopped, knived,
sifted, scrutinized, and vilified.
What book on philosophy or religion or psychology
or belles letters of classical or modern times
has been subjected to such mass attack as the Bible?
With such venom and skepticism?
With such thoroughness and erudition?
Upon every chapter, line and tenet?
The Bible is still loved by millions, read by millions,
and studied by millions.[43]

---

[42] *Handfuls on Purpose* IX, p. 90 (William B. Eerdmans Publishing Company).
[43] Bernard Ramm, *Protestant Christian Evidences*, pp. 232-233.

Last eve I passed beside a blacksmith's door
And heard the anvil ring the vesper chime;
When looking in, I saw upon the floor,
Old hammers worn with beating years of time.
"How many anvils have you had," said I,
"To wear and batter all these hammers so?"
"Just one," said he; then said with twinkling eye,
"The anvil wears the hammers out, you know."
And so, I thought, the anvil of God's word
For ages skeptics' blows have beat upon;
Yet, though noise of falling blows was heard,
The anvil is unharmed – the hammers gone![44]

Hammer away, ye unregenerate hands
Your hammer breaks, God's anvil stands
On a monument to the Huguenots in France

The Bible is a living vessel of communication given to us directly by the eternal Creator, the Ancient of Days who inhabits eternity. The Holy scriptures are infused with the life and breath of God, and as His living testimony to humankind they cannot be destroyed. These God-breathed oracles are a living organism, maintained by the pure breath of God that is eternal and can never die. The same indestructible energy that coursed through the body of Adam before his fall still lives and breathes out through the words of this holy book.

Throughout time God has both preserved His word through its transmission and translation and by protecting it from its adversaries. One of the most incredible evidences for the authenticity of the Bible is in its amazing resistance to the onslaughts of time and persecution. It has proven itself to be indestructible in the face of great hatred and oppression.

---

[44] John Clifford.

There are more ancient manuscripts of the scriptures in existence than all other ancient works of literature or history combined. There are literally thousands of manuscripts and fragments of scripture in existence, some of the Old Testament manuscripts dating back to before the time of Christ with New Testament manuscripts that have been dated to within 50 to 100 years of the original autographs.

These facts are incredible considering that the materials on which the scriptures were recorded did not have the capability to be resistant to time or weather. The nature of the basic materials available; whether papyrus, parchment, or vellum, was such that they did not have the capacity to last for an extended time. The chemical processes and protective coverings that we use to preserve paper-based books and documents today were not available at the time of the writing of the scriptures. These early manuscripts could be seriously damaged by exposure to weather or even light, and even when carefully taken care of and protected from exposure they would crumble away in time.

The ravages of weather and time have almost completely eradicated all evidence of many of the ancient works of literature, and the copies that are in existence were made many hundreds of years after the original autographs were written. The New Testament manuscripts have been numbered at over 24,000 pieces, some dating to within 25 years of the original writer. In comparison, the second most prevalent number of copies of an ancient work is Homer's Iliad. There are approximately 643 manuscript copies of the Iliad in existence, and the earliest was made 500 years after Homer's time. The Gallic Wars of Julius Caesar exist in 10 manuscript copies of which the earliest was made 1,000 years after the original autograph! The great majority of copies of ancient literature are of this kind, with only a handful of copies in existence, the oldest having been made anywhere from 700 to 1,400 years after the originals.

Time and weather were certainly not the only adversaries to the existence of the Bible. The greatest enemies of the scriptures were the nations and carnal men who attempted to destroy them. Satan raised many great and terrible foes against the Word of God in his attempt to take its life-giving words from God's people. From the very beginning there were those who in their pride and ignorance dashed themselves against the great Rock and were broken in pieces.

There were many also to whose generation the scriptures were lost, whether by those who did not have access to the scriptures or those who did not value God's word. During the ungodly reigns of many of the kings of Judah, there was no true worship of God or understanding of His word. The law of the Lord in its written form had been carelessly neglected and lost within the temple as it fell into a state of disuse and disrepair. We could assume that during this time, any worship of God was without the element of His word.

One of the first examples of an attempt to destroy the word of God is recorded in the book of Jeremiah. Jeremiah was commanded by the Lord to write His message on a scroll, that it would be a witness against the house of Israel and Judah.

> **Jeremiah 36:2** *Take thee a roll of a book and write therein all the words that I have spoken unto thee against Israel, and against Judah, and against all the nations, from the day I spake unto thee, from the days of Josiah, even unto this day.*

Jeremiah had begun prophesying in the 13th year of Josiah's reign, so it is apparent that this scroll was to include all the words of God spoken to Jeremiah from the beginning of his calling (about 20 years prior) to that time. God intended to have a written record of His declarations through Jeremiah, a piece of His testimony that would one day be passed down to us in the form of our modern Bibles.

Jeremiah commanded his scribe, Baruch, to take the scroll and read it before the people in the Lord's house. The word quickly spread until it had reached the ears of the princes of Judah. Baruch was brought before the princes to read the scroll of prophecy. After they had heard the scroll they were struck with fear. They knew the prophecy must be brought to the attention of the king. When they had told Jehoiakim, king of Judah, he sent immediately for the scroll:

Jeremiah 36:21-23 *So the king sent Jehudi to fetch the roll: and he took it from Elishama the scribe's chamber, And Jehudi read it in the ears of the king, and in the ears of all the princes which stood beside the king. Now the king sat in the winterhouse in the ninth month: and there was a fire on the hearth burning before him. And it came to pass, that when Jehudi had read three or four leaves, he cut it with the penknife, and cast it into the fire that was on the hearth, until all the roll was consumed in the fire that was on the hearth.*

Jehoiakim, in his arrogance and ignorance, did not even allow the entire message to be read before he had destroyed it. How those words must have cut to his heart, revealing his faltering lack of commitment to God and the failures of his nation. In his blind anger he utterly destroyed the word of God…or did he? The living word cannot be destroyed by fire or any other device of man. Once spoken into existence, His word cannot be made void. All that had been burned in the fire was the papyrus and ink through which it was communicated. The message itself lived on:

Jeremiah 36:27-28, 32 *Then the word of the Lord came to Jeremiah, after that the king had burned the roll, and the words which Baruch wrote at the mouth of Jeremiah, saying, Take thee again another roll, and write in it all the former words that were in the first roll, which Jehoiakim the king of Judah hath burned.…Then took Jeremiah another roll, and gave it to Baruch the scribe, the son of Neriah; who wrote therein from the mouth of Jeremiah all the words of the book which Jehoiakim king of Judah* *had burned in the fire: and there were added besides unto them many like words.*

Not only did the word of the Lord renew itself in its rewriting, but it grew in the flame of persecution!

The resistance to the word of God escalated as time marched forward. The Roman emperors severely persecuted the church and the word of God in the first few hundred years after the death of Christ. The church was finally officially sanctioned in the early 4th century when the Emperor Constantine claimed belief in Christ, but this did not end the opposition to God's truth. Pagan philosophies and mythology had already begun to infiltrate the church and had skewed the doctrinal perspectives of the church fathers. This instigated the long fall of the church into darkness. The doctrines and interpretations of God's word were perverted by the intellectual and philosophical wiles of the devil.

Soon after the Roman church began its persecution of any who stood against its non-biblical dogma. For 1,200 years Rome ruled over the Christian church with an iron hand, dispensing its version of truth to the common people. The scripture was forbidden to the common man and could not be translated into his tongue. Mother Rome brooked no resistance against its rule or the false doctrines it had developed. Many thousands gave their lives resisting the lies of Rome and attempting to bring the word of God to the common man. Later we will explore the relationship of the Roman church to the Bible.

H.L. Hastings recounts the story of a French king's attempted persecution of the church and the Bible: *Infidels for eighteen hundred years have been refuting and overthrowing this book, and yet [it] stands today as solid as a rock. Its circulation increases and it is more loved and cherished and read today than ever before. Infidels, with all their assaults, make about as much impression on this book as a man with a tack hammer would on the Pyramids of Egypt. When the French monarch proposed the persecution of the Christians in the dominion, an old statesman and warrior said to him, "Sire, the Church of God is an anvil that has worn out many hammers." So the hammers of infidels have been pecking away at this book for ages, but the hammers are worn out, and that anvil still endures. If this book had not been the book of God, men would have destroyed it long ago. Emperors and popes, kings and priests, princes and rulers have all tried their hand at it; they die and the book still lives.*[45]

Voltaire, the famed atheist philosopher, claimed that he would demonstrate how one Frenchman could destroy the Christian faith and the Bible within 50 years. He wrote and spoke all that he could against the faith of God throughout his life in a vain attempt to prove this foolish boast. Within 20 years of Voltaire's death the Geneva Bible Society purchased his house, and it was used as a headquarters for printing and distributing Bibles. Voltaire has long since gone to the dust, but the word of God lives on!

The great testimony to the divine preservation of the Bible is carried on the sound of many voices. Time has been unable to work its inevitable entropy upon the sacred word, unlike the things of man. When man's works have crumbled to dust the Bible has stood inviolate, anchored fast, kept alive by the breath of the living God.

Natures, both physical and spiritual, have not been able to destroy the word of God. Winds have torn at and beaten against the Rock, and it has never moved. Fire has burned its pages to ash, but the breath of the Almighty, written on eternal tables of stone, rose up from the ashes to greater life. Waters, both natural and doctrinal, have attempted to drown it. When the muddy waters receded, the word of God had not changed; it broke forth unstained and pure. The earth has swallowed it, burying it in the deep dark places, but its Fire could not be contained,

---

[45] John W. Lea, *The Greatest Book in the World*, pp. 17-18, Philadelphia, 1929.

could not die. With a great shout it rose up, like tongues of fire that could not be shut up in the dry bones of tradition and death.

The great powers of darkness have never been able to quench its light, for that light cannot die! Powers and principalities have brought all their might against it. The prince of this world has brought all his power to bear against it and has broken himself against its walls. The children of disobedience have torn at it through all the ages, but it still stands unscathed. This book is no book of man; it is the voice of the Ancient of Days echoing down the halls of eternity. This word cannot be moved, cannot be changed, it CANNOT die!

A.W. Pink wonderfully sums up the indestructible nature of the Bible: *Now suppose there was a man who had lived upon this earth for eighteen hundred years, that this man had oftentimes been thrown into the sea and yet could not be drowned; that he had frequently been cast before wild beasts who were unable to devour him; that he had many times been made to drink deadly poisons which never did him any harm; that he had often been bound in iron chains and locked in prison dungeons, yet he had always been able to throw off the chains and escape from his captivity; that he had repeatedly been hanged, till his enemies thought him dead, yet when his body was cut down he sprang to his feet and walked away as though nothing had happened; that hundreds of times he had been burned at the stake, till there seemed to be nothing left of him, yet as soon as the fires were out he leaped up from the ashes as well and as vigorous as ever—but we need not expand this idea any further; such a man would be super-human, a miracle of miracles. Yet this is exactly how we should regard the Bible! This is practically the way in which the Bible has been treated. It has been burned, drowned, chained, put in prison, and torn to pieces, yet never destroyed!*[46]

---

[46] A.W. Pink, *The Divine Inspiration of the Bible*, p. 67, Books for the Ages, 1997.

INFLUENCE OF THE BIBLE

3

THE INFLUENCE OF THE BIBLE ON
THE MORAL STANDARDS OF WESTERN CIVILIZATION[47]

The Bible has deeply influenced the moral fiber of Western civilization. Advances in cultural morality and ethical standards can be traced back to its principles and timeless truths. Mankind left to its own devices will create a socio-political system based on cruelty and the evolutionary caveat of the survival of the fittest, but the law of the Lord requires that man treat his fellowmen with love and respect.

This is in absolute contrast to the ancient founts of philosophical and cultural "wisdom." The empires that existed during the latter period of Israel's nationality and the birth and early days of the church were full of wickedness. The Greek and Roman empires have been often praised for their great culture and sophistication, but these empires were full of moral and philosophical disease. They had little sanctity for life or moral standards. One of the greatest sins of the ancient civilizations was their lack of value for human life. Infanticide, abortion, and violent entertainment were the norm. Until the influence of the Bible and the early Christians, there was no change in these barbaric practices.

---

[47] The Bible has had such an ingrained influence on the moral structures of Western civilization that it would take an entire book in itself to begin to deal with it effects. For the sake of brevity I will focus on only a handful of examples.

Infanticide and Abortion Outlawed

One of the cruelest acts of the Romans was the abandonment and murder of newly born babies. This act, called infanticide, was widespread in the Roman Empire during the early days of Christianity. Those who gave birth to an unwanted child would abandon it to the elements, drown it, or cut its throat. Plutarch recorded that the Carthagians regularly took the lives of their children, the mothers standing by without a tear or a moan.[48] Cicero and Seneca both testified to the fact that any child who was born weak or deformed was killed according to their laws. This terrible crime was a common occurrence not only among the Greeks and Romans but in many of the ancient societies around the world.

The early Christian church was in direct opposition to this barbaric practice. The Judaic and Christian standards were based on the sanctity of human life and the fact that man was created in the image of God. To the people of the Book, these murders were atrocities that could not continue. Those who did not have the fortitude to slay unwanted children often abandoned them. It was common practice among Greek and Roman society to abandon unwanted children. Throughout the years of the early church Christians opened their homes to these orphaned children, setting the stage for the later provisions made for orphans in modern society.

Abortion was also a widespread practice before the influence of Judeo-Christian ethics. This was another example of the low value for human life held by pagan societies. Plato, Aristotle, and other Greek thinkers were in complete support of abortion. Plato even argued that the state should have the ability to make a woman submit to an abortion to control population growth.[49] It was not until the Christian faith was

---

[48] Plutarch, *Moralia*, 2.171D.
[49] Plato, *The Republic*, 5.461.

legalized that the church had any power to influence these activities. The first Roman emperor to outlaw infanticide, child abandonment, and abortion was the emperor Valentinian in 374 A.D. This was due to the influence of the Christian bishops.

Gladiatorial Combat Outlawed

One of the most brutal and bloody pastimes of the Romans was the gladiatorial matches. Thousands died on the sand of the Coliseum, locked in deadly combat, mauled by wild animals, or tortured and abused. The early Christians were appalled by this devaluation of human life in which men were made to murder one another for the entertainment of the crowd.

A number of historians have demonstrated that the outlawing of these bloody spectacles was directly influenced by the Christians and the influence of biblical morality. Gladiatorial combat was finally outlawed for good by the Christian emperor Theodosius and his son Honorius in 404 A.D.

Care and Provision for the Sick and Needy

One of the most prominent characteristics of the Judeo-Christian culture is in its provision for and protection of the weak. Those who are less fortunate or who are unable to defend themselves must have someone to stand for them. Though it is in complete opposition to the humanistic law that the strong should survive, the Bible makes it abundantly clear that the strong must always be ready to protect and provide for the weak. Biblical morality introduced humane laws and helped to influence the downfall of dark pagan practices.

Isaiah 35:3 *Strengthen ye the weak hands, and confirm the feeble knees.*

Romans 15:1 *We then that are strong ought to bear the infirmities of the weak, and not to please ourselves.*

The teachings of Jesus stood in stark contrast to the barbarous paganism of the "great" civilizations of Greece and Rome. The principles of loving your neighbor, of caring for the poor, and providing for those who are in need were not even considered by the empires of the ancient world. The ruling principle was that of self above all else. With the explosive birth of Christianity in the first century, the seeds of change were sown.

The Christians believed it was their sacred duty to care for those in need. The first true hospitals were developed by Christians for the care of the sick and injured. The first charitable institutions and organizations were also the products of the biblical ethic of caring for your neighbor. Think of the many modern Christian charitable organizations that were created out of a desire to be obedient to the teachings of Jesus:

The YMCA (Young Men's Christian Association) founded about 1844
The YWCA (Young Women's Christian Association) founded in 1855
The Red Cross founded in 1864
The Salvation Army founded in 1865
The Charity Organizations Society (later the United Way) founded in 1887
and many others

THE INFLUENCE OF THE BIBLE ON EDUCATION

Proverbs 9:9
*Give instruction to a wise man, and he will be yet wiser:
teach a just man, and he will increase in learning.*

Language and Writing

The positive influence of Christianity on education began at its very roots. Many of the languages of the world today have been codified by Christian teachers and missionaries. There are many cultures throughout the world that would never have had a written language had it not been developed by these self-sacrificing men and women. This work still goes on today, as modern Christian missionaries work to develop written languages in the dark places of the world.

The men and women of these cultures would never have had the opportunity to be truly educated without the power of the written word and the communication that the writing of language allows. The development of writing for these cultures not only allowed them access to the Bible, but gave them a channel for expressing more complex ideas and principles. The Cyrillic alphabet is a perfect example of this. It is believed that it was developed in the 9th century by two missionary brothers, Cyril and Methodius. Rostislav, the founder of the Moravian Empire of the ninth century requested that Emperor Michael III of Byzantium send him missionaries to translate the liturgical services from Latin into Slavonic for the common people. The missionaries devised a new alphabet to aid in the translation. D. James Kennedy states, *During the days of the atheistic Soviet Union, most of their writing was done with an alphabet developed by a Christian to translate Christian writings!*[50]

---

[50] D. James Kennedy, *What if Jesus Had Never Been Born*, p. 42, Nelson, 1994.

The number of phrases and colloquialisms taken from the Scripture that have entered into common use since the time of the King James Bible translation is incredible. Consider some of the many words and phrases that have become a part of the English language via the conduit of the Bible:

Let there be light – Genesis 1:3

sweat of his brow – Genesis 3:19[51]

my brother's keeper – Genesis 4:9

the fat of the land – Genesis 45:18

the apple of his eye – Deuteronomy 32:10

arose as one man – Judges 20:8

a man after his own heart – I Samuel 13:14

how are the mighty fallen – II Samuel 1:25

from the sole of his foot to the crown of his head – II Samuel 14:25

still small voice – I Kings 19:12

gird up thy loins – II Kings 4:29

respect of persons – II Chronicles 19:7 and elsewhere

he stiffened his neck – II Chronicles 36:13

the shadow of death – Job 10:21

the skin of my teeth – Job 19:20

lovingkindness – Psalm 17:7 and elsewhere

the valley of the shadow of death – Psalm 23:4

tender mercies – Psalm 25:6 and elsewhere

lick the dust – Psalm 72:9, Isaiah 49:23, Micah 7:17

dark sayings – Psalm 78:2, Proverbs 1:6

at their wit's end – Psalm 107:27

a soft answer – Proverbs 15:1

a word in season – Proverbs 15:23, Isaiah 50:4

to eat, and to drink, and to be merry – Ecclesiastes 8:15

broken reed – Isaiah 36:6

as a drop of a bucket – Isaiah 40:15

---

[51] King James Version: "sweat of thy face."

weighed in the balance and found wanting – Daniel 5:27
the salt of the earth – Matthew 5:13
moth and rust corrupts – Matthew 6:19-20
signs of the times – Matthew 16:3
highways and hedges – Luke 14:23
a law unto themselves – Romans 2:14
the powers that be – Romans 13:1
a thorn in the flesh – II Corinthians 12:7
filthy lucre – I Timothy 3:3
root of all evil – I Timothy 6:10
fight the good fight – I Timothy 6:12
the pride of life – I John 2:16
clear as crystal – Revelation 21:11, 22:1

Educational Institutions

Education through organized institutions and schools was developed in America by the Pilgrims and Puritans who originally colonized this country. Between 1642 and 1647 the Puritans passed laws requiring that children be educated. In 1647 they passed the "Old Deluder Satan Act," which established schools by mandating towns to hire and pay teachers. This act included the following statement: *It being one chief project of that old deluder, Satan, to keep man from the knowledge of the Scriptures, as in former times, keeping them in an unknown tongue….It is therefore ordered by this Court, and authority thereof, that every township within this jurisdiction, after the Lord hath increased them to the number of fifty householders, shall then forthwith appoint one within their town to teach all such children as shall resort to him, to write and read…*[52]

It is clear from this statement that the most important aim of education to these early colonizers was that of the knowledge of the scriptures.

---

[52] Quoted in *What If Jesus Had Never Been Born* (see footnote 51).

These first schools were private and Christian in their beliefs and though they were the forerunners of our modern schools, they were nothing like the public secularized systems of our day. Modern-day universities and schools of higher learning can be traced back to their foundation in the middle ages. The three original models, dating back to around 1,200 A.D., were the schools at Oxford, Paris, and Bologna.[53] All three of these universities were Christian (Catholic) in structure and education. The curriculum of the schools at Oxford and Paris was primarily religious with a secondary focus on philosophy. The curriculum of Bologna was based on church studies and civil law. As other universities developed, their areas of study were always centered on biblical, theological, and canonical learning.

The formation of these schools of higher learning in the United States is even more revealing. Of the first 108 colleges and universities founded in America, 106 were founded on the study of the Bible and the Christian faith. Harvard, Princeton, and Yale are among the best-known and most prestigious colleges in the United States. It is interesting to see what their original foundations were based on. The rules and precepts governing Harvard University were set up in 1642 and included the following statements: *Let every Student be plainly instructed, and earnestly pressed to consider well, the maine end of his life and studies is, to know God and Jesus Christ which is eternall life, John 17:3 and therefore to lay Christ in the bottome, as the only foundation of all sound knowledge and Learning. And seeing the Lord only giveth wisdome, Let every one seriously set himselfe by prayer in secret to seeke it of him Prov. 2.3.*

> *Every one shall so exercise himself in reading the Scriptures twice a day, that he shall be ready to give such an account of his proficiency therein, both in theoretical observations of language and logic, and in practical and spiritual truths....*

---

[53] *The University and the City: From Medieval Origins to the Present*, Oxford University Press, 1988.

Princeton University was founded in 1746. It was attended by more of the founding fathers than any other. Its first president, Rev. Jonathan Dickinson stated, in regards to the education at Princeton: *...cursed be all learning that is contrary to the cross of Christ.* Princeton's official motto was, *Under God's Power She Flourishes,* and it is interesting to note that until 1902 every president of Princeton was a minister.

Yale College was founded in 1701 by 10 ministers with the following stated purpose: *To plant and under ye Divine blessing to propagate in this wilderness, the blessed reformed, Protestant religion, in ye purity of its order and worship.* Among the requirements for students of Yale was that they live a religious and prayer-filled life: *All scholars shall live religious, godly and blameless lives according to the rules of God's Word, diligently reading the Holy Scriptures, the fountain of light and truth; and constantly attend upon all the duties of religion, both in public and secret. Seeing God is the giver of all wisdom, every scholar, besides private or secret prayer, where all we are bound to ask wisdom shall be present morning and evening at public prayer in the hall at the accustomed hour.* Yale's primary educational goal, as outlined by its founders, was that *Every student shall consider the main end of his study to wit to know God in Jesus Christ and answerable to lead a Godly, sober life.*

Benjamin Rush, one of the Founding Fathers and a signer of the Declaration of Independence, was a strong proponent of the Bible's use in all phases of education. Rush was not only one of the most respected minds of his day, but was one of the top surgeons and the founder of the Pennsylvania Hospital. Rush wrote a treatise called *A Defence of the Use of the Bible in Schools.* In his preface to the work, he lists a number of reasons why the Bible should be the centerpiece of any education. Among these, are *That Christianity is the only true and perfect religion; and that in proportion as mankind adopt its principles, and obey its precepts, they will be wise and happy...That a better knowledge of this religion is to be acquired by reading the Bible than in any other way...That the Bible contains more knowledge necessary to man in his present state, than any other book in the world.*

Education for the Deaf and Blind

Charles Michel de l'Epee developed the first sign language for the deaf in 1775. Epee was a priest and it was his desire that the deaf be enabled to hear the gospel of Jesus. Thomas Gallaudet and Laurent Clerc took this development to the United States. Both men were Bible scholars who believed that the most important thing for their deaf students was the ability to learn the scriptures.

Louis Braille was a staunch Christian who had lost his sight early in life. In 1834 Braille developed the raised letters of the alphabet that bears his name. This invention gave literary "sight to the blind."

THE INFLUENCE OF THE BIBLE ON LITERATURE

Psalm 45:1
My heart is inditing a good matter:
I speak of the things which I have made touching the king:
my tongue is the pen of a ready writer.

Western literature has been saturated by the influence of biblical thought and terminology. It has been accurately stated that if the Bible were to be completely destroyed, it could be restored in all essential parts from the quotations contained in the books on the shelves of our public libraries. Many of the great Western literary giants have not only quoted from the Bible, but many of their themes, design, and illustrations are drawn from its narrative.

In a related manner, the King James Bible has had a tremendous affect on the literary style that followed it. Professor Gardiner, in one of his essays in the *Atlantic Monthly*, made the following statement: *in all study of English literature, if there be any one axiom which may be accepted without question, it is that the ultimate standard of English prose style is set by the King James version of the Bible.*[54]

William Shakespeare is one of the most preeminent Western literary writers. It has been stated that *No writer has assimilated the thoughts and reproduced the words of Holy Scripture more copiously than Shakespeare.* Dr. Furnivall says that *he is saturated with the Bible story,* and Capel Lloft stated that Shakespeare *had deeply imbibed the Scriptures.*

---

[54] *Atlantic Monthly*, May, 1900, p. 684.

The following are a small selection of the multitude of English literary writers whose narratives were stained with the indelible ink of the scripture:[55]

William Shakespeare
John Milton
John Bunyan
John Dryden
Joseph Addison
Alexander Pope
Lord Byron
Samuel Taylor Coleridge
Sir Walter Scott
William Wordsworth
Robert Browning
Elizabeth Barrett Browning
Thomas Carlyle
Charles Dickens
George Eliot
Lord Macaulay
John Ruskin
Robert Louis Stevenson
Alfred Tennyson
William Thackeray
Washington Irving
Henry Wadsworth Longfellow
John Greenleaf Whittier

---

[55] This is not to say that these were all men of Biblical character, but they were all men whose lives and writings were influenced by the scripture.

THE INFLUENCE OF THE BIBLE ON MUSIC

Ephesians 5:19
Speaking to yourselves in psalms and hymns and spiritual songs, singing and making melody in your heart to the Lord;

Great Musical Composers Who Believed in the Bible

Johann Sebastian Bach (1685–1750)
Bach, one of the greatest composers to ever live, was a committed Christian and a consistent Bible reader and student. He wrote many religious arrangements, both instrumental and vocal. It has been said that when he began a composition he would write the initials "J.J.," short for the Latin "Jesu Juva" or "Help me, Jesus," or "I.N.J.," short for the Latin "In Nomine Jesu" or "In the name of Jesus." At the end of the manuscript he would write the initials "S.D.G.," standing for "Soli Deo Gloria," Latin for "To God alone All Glory." Bach told his students that unless they committed their talents to Jesus Christ, they would never become great musicians.[56]

George Frideric Handel (1685–1759)
Handel, another of the great composers, was also a Bible-believing Christian. Among his many Christian compositions is the incomparable Messiah, which includes the Hallelujah Chorus.

---

[56] Alvin J. Schmidt, *Under the Influence*, p. 324, Zondervan, 2001.

Franz Joseph Haydn (1732–1809)

Haydn wrote many religious compositions, among these *The Seven Last Words of Christ, The Seasons,* and *The Creation.* He was quoted as saying in regard to the latter composition, *Never before was I so devout as when I composed The Creation. I knelt down each day to pray to God to give me strength for my work.*[57]

Wolfgang Amadeus Mozart (1756–1791)

Mozart wrote a number of religious compositions, the *Requiem* in particular is considered to be exceptionally spiritual.

Ludwig van Beethoven (1770–1827)

Beethoven also wrote religious compositions. Among these were *Christ on the Mount of Olives* and *Missa Solemnis.* He lived a difficult and lonely life and was once quoted as saying, *I have no friend. I know, however, that God is nearer to me than others; I go without fear to Him.*[58] He is recorded as having taken communion on his deathbed.[59]

Franz Peter Schubert (1797–1828)

Schubert's best-known religious compositions were *Ave Maria* and *Great Jehovah.* In his book on the spiritual lives of the great composers, Kavanaugh states *Through the tribulations of his tragic life, it was the combination of two elements in his nature-his faith in God and his God-given talent–that enabled him to create without applause or acclaim the many masterpieces we treasure today.*[60]

---

[57] Neil Butterworth, *Haydn: His Life and Times,* p. 122, Midas Books, 1977.
[58] Philip Kruseman, *Beethoven's Own Words,* p. 53, Henricksen, 1947.
[59] Paul Nettl, *The Book of Musical Documents,* p. 197, Philosophical Library, 1948.
[60] Patrick Kavanaugh, *Spiritual Lives of the Great Composers,* p. 71.

Felix Mendelssohn (1809–1847)

Mendelssohn was a Jew who was baptized by his parents into the Lutheran church. He was a committed Christian and a strong believer in the Bible. He wrote numerous religious hymns and compositions, among them *Elijah* and *St. Paul*. Charles Wesley wrote the words to *Hark the Herald Angels Sing*, but the music was written by Mendelssohn. It was said that when he set music to biblical text, he would make no changes or deviations from the exact scripture.[61]

Johannes Brahms (1833–1897)

Brahms, as Mendelssohn, was a Protestant Lutheran. Kavanaugh stated that he was a *diligent student of Martin Luther's German translation of the Bible, as well as Luther's book Table Talks.*[62] He was one of the greatest composers and a dedicated Christian.

Igor Stravinsky (1882–1971)

Stravinsky became a Christian at the age of 26. He once said that in order for one to compose religious music one had to be a believer in *the Person of the Lord, the Person of the Devil, and the Miracle of the Church.*[63] Among his religious compositions are *Pater Noster, Abraham and Isaac, The Flood,* and *The Tower of Babel.* Kavanaugh quotes him as saying once, *The more one separates himself from the canons of the Christian church, the further one distances himself from the truth.*[64]

---

[61] Patrick Kavanaugh, *Spiritual Lives of the Great Composers*, pp. 77-78.

[62] Patrick Kavanaugh, *Spiritual Lives of the Great Composers*, pp. 144.

[63] Stravinsky and Craft, *Conversations with Igor Stravinsky*, p. 125, University of California Press, 1960.

[64] Patrick Kavanaugh, *Spiritual Lives of the Great Composers*, p. 186.

THE INFLUENCE OF THE BIBLE ON SCIENCE

Proverbs 2:6
For the LORD giveth wisdom:
out of his mouth cometh knowledge and understanding.

Great Men Of Science Who Believed in the Bible
Including founders of many of the major scientific disciplines

Nicholas Copernicus (1473-1543) German/Polish astronomer. Copernicus was trained as a theologian in the Catholic Church, becoming a canon of the church. It is Copernicus who **introduced the revolutionary heliostatic theory** that the sun, rather than the earth was the gravitational center and that the earth revolved around the sun. This became known as **the Copernican Revolution** and changed the face of astronomy forever. Though Copernicus was a Catholic it is interesting to note that his masterwork on this subject was subsidized by a Protestant Lutheran prince, Duke Albrecht of Prussia, and that the printing was completed by two Lutherans, the theologian Andreas Osiander and the mathematician Georg Joachim Rheticus.

ASTRONOMY – Johann Kepler (1571-1630) German astronomer and mathematician. Founder of the field of **physical astronomy**. Kepler **developed the heliocentric system** from the heliostatic system introduced by Copernicus. Among his many discoveries, he was the first to note that the tides are caused by the moon. Kepler was also the first to uncover the error in our modern calendars. Our modern Gregorian calendar was developed by a monk named Dionysius Exiguus. Exiguus incorrectly calculated the date of the birth of Christ. Kepler's calculations determined that the actual date would have been between 4 and 5 B.C. Kepler stated in his writings, *Since we astronomers are the priests of the highest God in regard to the book of nature, it befits us to be thoughtful, not of the glory of our minds, but* *rather, above all else, of the glory of God,* and *...The chief aim of all investigation of the external world should be to discover the rational order and harmony which has been imposed on it by God.*

Blaise Pascal (1623-1662) French mathematician, physicist, and philosopher. Perhaps the greatest of the early mathematicians, Pascal helped lay the foundation for **hydrostatics, hydrodynamics, differential calculus, and the theory of probability**. Pascal's Wager is a classic Christian apologetic argument in which he asks, *How can you lose if you choose to be a Christian? If, when you die, there turns out to be no God and your faith was in vain, you have lost nothing–in fact, you've been happier in life than your non believing friends. If, however, there is a God and a heaven and hell, then you have gained heaven and your skeptical friends will have lost everything in hell!*

STATISTICS/MODERN ECONOMICS – William Petty (1623-1687) British mathematician and physician. One of the founders of **statistics and the modern study of economics**, Petty was a staunch defender of the Bible and Christianity, writing a number of articles on the evidence of God's design in nature.

MODERN CHEMISTRY – Robert Boyle (1627-1691) British chemist and physicist. Considered **the father of modern chemistry**. Boyle supported a number of Christian missions and Bible-translation projects.

NATURAL HISTORY (ENGLISH) – John Ray (1627-1705) British naturalist. Ray was **the father of English natural history**, deemed to be the premiere botanist and zoologist of his time. He was author of a book titled *The Wisdom of God Manifested in the Works of Creation*.

Sir. Isaac Newton (1642-1727) English mathematician and natural philosopher. He is believed by many to have been one of the greatest minds of all time. Newton created **calculus**, was the **discoverer of the laws of gravity and motion**, laid the foundation for the **understanding of the laws of thermodynamics**, among many other discoveries and inventions. He was a dedicated Christian and believer in the Bible and was a prolific author of Christian works. Consider these statements by Isaac Newton: *There is a being who made all things, who holds all things in his power, and is therefore to be feared,* and *...For it became him who created them* [the material elements of the universe] *to set them in order. And if He did so, its unphilosophical to seek for any other origin of the world, or to pretend that it might arise out of chaos by the mere law of nature.*

BIOLOGICAL TAXONOMY – Carolus Linnaeus (1707-1778) Swedish botanist. Linnaeus was the **father of biological taxonomy**, classifying animals and plants in an attempt to organize them by the original "kinds" of Genesis. He believed absolutely in the literal account of the creation in Genesis.

Joseph Priestly (1733-1804) English chemist and clergyman. Priestly **discovered oxygen, hydrochloric acid, nitrous oxide, and sulfur dioxide**. Throughout his life he argued for the teaching of Jesus Christ. He once wrote regarding Jesus, *The certainty of his resurrection was also evident from the conduct and miracles of the apostles....*

Wilhelm Friedrich Herschel (1738-1822) German-born astronomer and composer. Herschel made numerous astronomical finds, among them the discovery of the planet Uranus. Herschel stated that *the undevout astronomer must be mad!*

Alessandro Volta (1745-1827) Italian physicist. Volta was **discovered current electricity. The terms volt, voltage, etc., are coined from his name.** Volta was a committed Bible student, once making the statement, *I am not ashamed of the Gospel, may it produce good fruit!*

ATOMIC THEORY – John Dalton (1766-1844) British chemist and physicist. Dalton developed the **atomic theory upon which our modern physical science is founded**, being the first to publish the atomic weights of elements. He was also the discover of the condition of color blindness, the medical term of Daltonism, being named for him. He was a devout Christian and believer in the Bible.

COMPARATIVE ANATOMY – Georges Cuvier (1769-1832) French naturalist. Cuvier **founded the science of comparative anatomy**. He was deeply involved in **the development of modern paleontology**. Cuvier argued for creationism over evolution in many famous debates.

Andre Ampere (1775-1836) French physicist and mathematician. **A developer of the measurement of the strength of an electrical current, the unit, an ampere or amp, of which was named for him.** A Christian and Bible believer, he wrote, *One of the most striking evidences of the existence of God is the wonderful harmony by which the universe is preserved and living things are furnished in their organization with everything necessary to life.*

Georg Simon Ohm (1787-1854) German physicist. Ohm **formulated the equation known as Ohm's Law, which measures electrical resistance. The ohm, named for him, is the unit of this measurement.** Ohm was a dedicated Christian and in writing his first volume of *Molecular Physics*, he stated that he would write additional volumes, *if God gives me the length of days.*

Michael Faraday (1791-1867) English scientist. He was considered to be the greatest experimental scientist and physicist of his day. Faraday developed many **foundational scientific concepts involving electricity and magnetism** and laid the groundwork for **electromagnetic studies**. Among many other accomplishments, he was the **inventor of the electric generator**. He was a dedicated Christian and strong believer in the Bible, being a member of a fundamentalist Christian group known as the Glasists. This group firmly believed in the Bible and in Jesus as the Son of God.

COMPUTER SCIENCE – Charles Babbage (1792-1871) British mathematician and inventor. He **invented a number of mechanical computing machines that were pre-runners of our modern computers**. In his *Ninth Bridgewater Treatise* and *Passages from the Life of a Philosopher* he defended his belief in biblical miracles and reconciled them with science, in the latter book, writing that miracles were not *…the breach of established laws, but…indicate the existence of far higher laws.*

John Frederick Herschel (1792-1871) British astronomer. The son of Wilhelm Friedrich Herschel. Herschel was a contemporary and close friend of Charles Babbage. He is said to have **discovered over 500 stars** during his astronomical pursuits. In regard to his discoveries he stated *All human discoveries seem to be made only for the purpose of confirming more and more strongly the truths that come from on high and are contained in the Sacred Writings.* His father, William Herschel, was the astronomer who discovered Uranus. He said *The undevout astronomer must be mad.*

OCEANOGRAPHY – Matthew Maury (1806-1873) American naval officer and oceanographer. Maury was **the founder of oceanography**. His discoveries were based on his literal interpretation of Psalm 8:8: the *fish of the sea, and whatsoever passeth through the paths of the seas.* His belief in the accuracy of this scripture led him to chart out the winds and currents of the ocean, which enabled him to establish that the sea did indeed have paths.

James Simpson (1811-1870) British obstetrician. Simpson was the first British obstetrician to use ether in his practice. He also **introduced chloroform** into medical practice. When asked what his greatest discovery was, he stated, *It was not chloroform. It was to know I am a sinner and that I could be saved by the grace of God. A man has missed the whole meaning of life if he has not entered into an active, living relationship with God through Christ.*

George Gabriel Stokes (1819-1903) Irish physicist and mathematician. **He made many contributions to multiple fields of science, including mathematical physics, fluid dynamics, and optics**. In 1891 he published *Natural Theology,* and he was known for both speaking and writing of his belief in Jesus Christ and the resurrection.

GENETICS – Gregor Johann Mendel (1822-1884) Austrian monk. Mendel is considered by many to be **one of the originators of genetics and the study of heredity**. He was a contemporary of Charles Darwin, but believed strongly in the creationist view.

BACTERIOLOGY and MICROBIOLOGY– Louis Pasteur (1822-1895) French chemist and biologist. Pasteur is known as the **founder of microbiology and bacteriology**. A very dedicated Christian whose beliefs made him unpopular with the pro-Darwinian intelligentsia of his day.

ENTOMOLOGY – Jean-Henri Fabre (1823-1915) French physicist and entomologist. Considered **the father of modern entomology**. Fabre stated, *Without Him I understand nothing; without Him all is darkness...I regard Atheism as a mania. It is the malady of the age. You could take my skin from me more easily than my faith in God.*

Lord Kelvin (William Thompson) (1824-1907) British mathematician and physicist, and a **primary contributor to the definition of the laws of thermodynamics. He advanced numerous scientific fields and was considered one of the greatest physicists who ever lived**. Among his many accomplishments was the development of the Kelvin Scale, which measures absolute zero. Kelvin, a Bible-believing Christian, strongly opposed Darwinian evolution. He was quoted as saying, *With regard to the origin of life, science...positively affirms creative power* and, *If you think strongly enough, you will be forced by science to the belief in God.*

Georg Friedrich Bernard Riemann (1826-1866) German mathematician. Riemann was the **developer of non-Euclidian geometry**, which laid the groundwork for the theories of Einstein and in turn all modern theoretical physics. His biblical studies included evidences for Genesis based on mathematical principles.

Joseph Lister (1827-1912) British physician. Lister **discovered and developed the use of antiseptics for medical procedures**. This was a huge stride forward in the progress of medical science. Lister wrote, *I am a believer in the fundamental doctrines of Christianity.*

James Clerk Maxwell (1831-1879) British physicist. Maxwell **predicted the existence of electromagnetic waves and established the theory of gases**. His insights led to the greatest innovations of physics, including Einstein's theory of special relativity and quantum physics. He wrote that he was motivated to pursue his scientific studies by Genesis 1:28 in which God commands man to subdue the earth.

Lord Rayleigh (John Strutt) (1842-1919) British physicist. **Nobel Prize winner**, who, along with William Ramsay, **discovered the element argon**. He also **discovered the phenomenon now called Rayleigh scattering and predicted the existence of the surface waves now known as Rayleigh waves.**

ELECTRONICS – John Ambrose Fleming (1849-1945) British physicist and electrical engineer. **He made numerous contributions in the fields of electronics, photometry, wireless telegraphy, and electrical measurements**. Fleming **invented the two electrode radio rectifier**, which many consider to have been the beginning of electronics.

Max Born (1882-1970) German physicist. He was **one of the pioneers of quantum mechanics**. Born was **awarded the Nobel Prize in Physics** in 1953. He made the statement, *Those who say that the study of science makes man an atheist, must be rather silly people.*

Arthur Holly Compton (1892-1962) American physicist. Compton was **awarded the Nobel Prize in Physics** in 1927. He made numerous statements regarding his faith, including *For me, faith begins with the realization that a supreme intelligence brought the universe into being and created man. It is not difficult for me to have this faith, for an orderly, intelligent universe testifies to the greatest statement ever uttered; "In the beginning, God...."*

Wernher Von Braun (1912-1977) German-American engineer. Von Braun **developed the liquid fuel rocket and was considered the father of space science**. He wrote,...*the vast mysteries of the universe should only confirm our belief in the certainty of its Creator.*

THE INFLUENCE OF THE BIBLE ON
THE ESTABLISHMENT OF THE UNITED STATES[65]

Psalms 33:12
Blessed is the nation whose God is the LORD;
and the people whom he hath chosen for his own inheritance.

The modern discovery of the Americas is credited to Columbus around 1492. Some comments from his personal log, as recorded in Columbus's *Book of Prophecies*, are very illuminating. He stated that his purpose in seeking other worlds was *to bring the Gospel of Jesus Christ to the heathens... It was the Lord who put it into my mind...that it would be possible to sail from here to the Indies...I am the most unworthy sinner, but I have cried out to the Lord for grace and mercy, and they have covered me completely... No one should fear to undertake any task in the name of our Saviour, if it is just and if the intention is purely for His holy service.*

This is revealing as to the purpose and intent of Columbus. Without the Lord putting the thought in his mind of attempting the voyage, how long would it have been before this country would have been discovered? God directed Columbus' designs according to his timescale and plan for this world.

Consider the United States of America, a nation that would not exist as we know it today without the direct influence of the Bible and the Christian faith. The first settlers came to its shores specifically for religious reasons. Their driving desire was to establish a place of spiritual refuge and freedom of **Christian** worship. This can be very easily demonstrated through a study of the letters, documents, and

---

[65] Entire books have been written on this subject, and this is only intended as a brief overview.

charters written at the time, of which only a small cross section is recorded here for reference purposes.

The Charter for the Virginia Colony, established on April 10, 1606, makes a clear statement of its purpose: *To the glory of his divine Majesty, in propagating of the Christian religion to such people as yet live in ignorance of the true knowledge and worship of God....*

King James I of England certainly recognized the purpose underlying the colonization of America. In granting the charter of the Plymouth Council on November 3, 1620, he made this statement: *In the hope thereby to advance the enlargement of the Christian religion, to the glory of God Almighty....*

The Mayflower Compact of November 11, 1620, is another clear testimony to the intent of the settlers: *For the glory of God and advancement of ye Christian faith....*

The first Charter of Massachusetts, March 4, 1629, makes the following statement: *...whereby our people may be so religiously, peaceably, and civilly governed, as their good life and orderly conversation, may win and incite the natives of the country to the knowledge and obedience of the only true God and Savior of mankind, and the Christian faith....*

The Fundamental Orders of Connecticut in 1638, which was considered to be one of the first constitutions, even called the first American Constitution, demonstrates its purpose clearly: *...to maintain and preserve the liberty and purity of the gospel of our Lord Jesus Christ, which we now profess.*

When the governing body of New Hampshire was established on August 4, 1639, the reason for proper laws and government, and the example that was to be followed in their establishment was clearly set forth: *Considering with ourselves the holy will of God and our own necessity, that we should not live without wholesome laws and civil government among us, of which we are altogether destitute, do, in the name of Christ and in the sight of God, combine ourselves together to erect and set up among us such government as shall be, to our best discerning, agreeable to the will of God....*

The Charter of the New Haven Colony, established on April 3, 1644, is also absolutely clear on what foundation the law was to be founded: *That the judicial laws of God, as they were delivered by Moses...be a rule to all the courts in this jurisdiction.*

The Maryland Toleration Act, passed on April 21, 1649, provided for the legal protection of Christian believers. This stated specifically that **Christians** were not to be harassed: *Be it therefore...enacted...that no person or persons whatsoever within this province...professing to believe in Jesus Christ shall...henceforth be any ways troubled, molested (or disapproved of)...in respect of his or her religion nor in the free exercise thereof....*

The Great Law of Pennsylvania, April 25, 1689, is another example of the underlying understanding of the force and purpose behind the government of this country: *Whereas the glory of Almighty God and the good of mankind is the reason and the end of government...therefore government itself is a venerable ordinance of God....*

On July 12, 1775, the Continental Congress issued a proclamation that all citizens should fast and pray and confess their sin, beseeching God for his guidance in seceding from England and for his blessing upon their endeavors and their nation. The nation was to call upon God, and it was very clear which God was intended.

The Declaration of Independence, signed on July 4, 1776, was itself a testimony to the Christian and Bible-believing principles of the nation. The Declaration is full of spiritual insight. It was recorded that while the Declaration was being signed, Samuel Adams cried out, *We have this day restored the Sovereign to Whom all men ought to be obedient. He reigns in heaven, and from the rising to the setting of the sun, let his kingdom come!*

James Madison, who is considered the "architect" of the Constitution, made this statement: *We have staked the whole future of American civilization, not upon the power of government, far from it. We have staked the future...upon the capacity of each and all of us to govern ourselves, to sustain ourselves, according to the Ten Commandments of God.* For those who would like to believe that this nation was not founded specifically upon the Judeo-Christian God and His word, let us consider the fact that there is only one Book that contains the Ten Commandments revealed to Moses, and that book is the Bible.

Patrick Henry, who is famous for crying, *Give me liberty or give me death,* also said, *It cannot be emphasized too strongly or too often that this great nation was founded, not by religionists, but by Christians, not on religions, but on the Gospel of Jesus Christ!* This again demonstrates that the United States was built upon Christian and biblical foundations. It was the certain intent of its founders that this be the case.

The United States Constitution was finished on September 17, 1787. It has been testified that at least 50 of the 55 men who framed the Constitution were Bible-believing Christians.[66] Eleven of the first 13 states required faith in Jesus and the Bible as qualification for holding public office. This did not just mean that you had to be a religious

[66] M.E. Bradford, *A Worthy Company*, Plymouth Rock Foundation, 1982.

adherent to be a government official; it meant that you must be a Bible-believing Christian.

In George Washington's Inaugural Address on April 30, 1789, he made the following statement: *My fervent supplications to the Almighty Being who rules over the universe, Who presides in the council of nations, and Whose providential aid can supply every human defect, that His benediction may consecrate to the liberties and happiness of the people of the United States a government instituted by Himself for these essential purposes....*

John Adams, in a letter to Thomas Jefferson dated June 28, 1813, wrote: *The general principles on which the Fathers achieved independence, were...the general principles of Christianity.*

John Jay, the first Chief Justice of the Supreme Court, made it clear which type of governmental administrators should be chosen by the people: *Providence has given to our people the choice of their rulers. And it is the duty as well as the privilege and interest of a Christian nation to select and prefer Christians for their rulers.*

Daniel Webster, in an address in Plymouth, Massachusetts, on December 20, 1820, testified to the nation's biblical origin: *Let us not forget the religious character of our origin. Our fathers brought hither their high veneration for the Christian religion. They journeyed by its light, and labored in its hope.*

Alexis de Tocqueville, in *Democracy in America*, written in 1841, for the purpose of examining the structure of its government, wrote, *In the United States of America the sovereign authority is religious...there is no other country in the world in which the Christian religion retains a greater influence over the souls of men than in America.* It is said that he came to the United States to learn what quality enabled a small and insignificant group of people to defeat the mighty British Empire twice in 35 years. He looked for the greatness of America in her harbors and rivers, her fertile fields and boundless forests, mines and other natural resources. He studied America's schools, her Congress, and her matchless Constitution without comprehending America's power. Not, until he went into the churches of America and heard pulpits *aflame with righteousness* did he understand the secret of her genius and strength. De Tocqueville returned to France and wrote: *America is great because America is good, and if America ever ceases to be good, America will cease to be great.*

In the 1892 U.S. Supreme Court Case "Church of the Holy Trinity vs. United States 143 US 457, 36 L ed 226" the following statement was made by Supreme Court Justice Brewer: *Our laws and our institutions must necessarily be based upon and embody the teachings of the Redeemer of mankind. It is impossible that it should be otherwise; and in this sense and to this extent our civilization and our institutions are emphatically Christian...this is a religious people. This is historically true. From the discovery of this continent to the present hour, there is a single voice making this affirmation...we find everywhere a clear definition of the same truth...this is a Christian nation.*

President Woodrow Wilson, in a 1911 pre-presidential campaign speech, made this statement: *America was born a Christian nation. America was born to exemplify that devotion to the elements of righteousness, which are derived from the revelations of Holy Scriptures....Part of the destiny of Americans lies in their daily perusal of this great book of revelations. That if they would see America free and pure they will make their own spirits free and pure by this baptism of the Holy Spirit.*

President Dwight D. Eisenhower demonstrated his understanding of the biblical foundation in this statement: *It takes no brains to be an atheist. Any stupid person can deny the existence of a supernatural power because man's physical senses cannot detect it. But there cannot be ignored the influence of conscience, the respect we feel for the Moral Law, the mystery of first life...or the marvelous order in which the universe moves about us on this earth. All these evidence the handiwork of the beneficent Deity...That Deity is the God of the Bible and Jesus Christ, his son.*

Joint Resolution of the United States Congress in 1983, Public Law 97-280 (requesting the President proclaim 1983 as the Year of the Bible) included the following: *...the Bible, the Word of God, has made a unique contribution in shaping the United States as a distinctive and blessed nation and people...Deeply held religious convictions springing from the Holy Scriptures led to the early settlement of our nation...Biblical teachings inspired concepts of civil government that are contained in our Declaration of Independence and our Constitution of the United States.*

INSPIRATION OF THE SCRIPTURES

4

THE SOURCE OF INSPIRATION

II Timothy 3:16
All scripture is given by inspiration of God,....

It is often stated that the Bible is the inspired word of God, but what is truly meant by this statement? Is this saying that the Bible is man's description of the eternal God who cannot be known, that men wrote the Bible through their own spiritual understanding in an attempt to describe the unknowable in their own terms, that there are errors and mistakes in the scripture due to the source of transmission, that any book written by man can be disputed? OR, are we claiming that God Himself dictated the exact words of every line of scripture, that man had no more involvement in the process than the keys of a typewriter do as they print out the words of a book?

The first view, which many modern critical scholars are inclined to support, is hardly more than humanistic jargon. As we have demonstrated, the Bible is a supernatural structure, an indisputable witness to its own truth. Man could not have and would not have written such a book if he were attempting to carnally define God. The vision of man could not have reached the shuddering heights that the scripture ascends, nor could he have envisioned the fearful depths of eternal judgment. This book is a message transmitted from without our dimensions and span of time.

The second view, that man had no true involvement or understanding in the communication of the scripture, also fails to meet the character of the Holy Book. Man has always been a creature of free will, and it is that free will that makes him a proper conduit for God's message. God's plan would have no meaning had man no individual choice. In turn, God allows man to express His eternal truths through the vehicle of human language and cultural idioms. God speaks to man in his own tongue, though the source of the communication is the throne of heaven.

Man was designed as to be an interactive agent with his Maker. He was created as a perfect vessel of communication, an intricate and complex receptor for the transmission of God's Spirit and will. The intellect and emotions of man in their original Edenic state were attuned to the voice and presence of God. The sound of his voice created a resonating vibration that would have brought man into closer attunement with his Maker.

Just as a tuning fork, when struck, causes the key of a piano to vibrate in harmony, so man was created to maintain a relationship of harmonious attunement with God. The vibration and motion of molecular structures were, in their original state, in harmony with the Creator.

It is the Spirit of God that maintained this symbiotic and symphonic relationship. The separation from that Spirit, like the severing of an umbilical cord, cut off man from a perfect knowledge and understanding of his Creator. Man was not only alienated from the presence of God, but was cut off from the life-giving flow of spiritual nutrients. When man severed his connection with God, he turned to the desires of his own will and wickedness of his own imagination and understanding.

The scriptures clearly demonstrate that the source of all biblical inspiration is from the living God through His Spirit.

II Timothy 3:16 *All scripture is given by inspiration of God, and is profitable for doctrine, for reproof, for correction, for instruction in righteousness:*

II Peter 1:20-21 *Knowing this first, that no prophecy of the scripture is of any private interpretation. For the prophecy came not in old time by the will of man: but holy men of God spake as they were moved by the Holy Ghost.*[67]

God is both Spirit and light…

Isaiah 60:19-20 *The sun shall be no more thy light by day; neither for brightness shall the moon give light unto thee: but the Lord shall be unto thee an everlasting light, and thy God thy glory. Thy sun shall no more go down; neither shall thy moon withdraw itself: for the Lord shall be thine everlasting light, and thy God thy glory.*

I John 1:5 *…God is light, and in him is no darkness at all.*

It is by the light of revelation that truth is revealed. It is His light that illuminates our understanding, a light that is bourn on the tide of the Spirit. As we learn to be directed by the Spirit, God's light will illuminate our understanding.

As God is light, both in the sense of righteousness and purity, so the perfect revelation of His truth can only be made known in the clarity of His light and with the Spirit's interpretation. The more of the light of God that shines upon the mind of man, the more able he will be to properly interpret the word of God.

Psalm 18:28 *For thou wilt light my candle: the Lord my God will enlighten my darkness.*

Psalm 36:9 *For with thee is the fountain of life: in thy light we shall see light.*

---

[67] See II Samuel 23:2, Luke 1:70, etc.

Psalm 43:3 *O send out thy light and thy truth: let them lead me; let them bring me unto thy holy hill, and to thy tabernacles.*

God's word in and of itself is light, bringing spiritual enlightenment:
Psalm 19:8 *...the commandment of the Lord is pure, enlightening the eyes.*
Psalm 119:105 *Thy word is a lamp unto my feet, and a light unto my path.*
Psalm 119:130 *The entrance of thy words giveth light; it giveth understanding unto the simple.*
Proverbs 6:23 *For the commandment is a lamp; and the law is light; and reproofs of instruction are the way of life:*
Hosea 6:5 *Therefore have I hewed them by the prophets; I have slain them by the words of my mouth: and thy judgments are as the light that goeth forth.*

The first chapter of the book of John describes Jesus as the perfect manifestation of God's revelation of Himself. Jesus came to be the living Word of God, the perfect representative of his Father's light to the world.
John 1:1-2 *In the beginning was the Word, and the Word was with God, and the Word was God. The same was in the beginning with God.*

God's revelation is made known through vessels that bear His light. Man was designed to be a light bearer for the glory of God. In his resistance to God's will, he fell from this position of honor.

God brought His Son into human existence to bridge the gap that had been created by the fall, to restore man to the capacity to once again serve God as he was meant to do. Jesus was the perfect light bearer and image of the Father to man. He demonstrated the fullness of God's revelation and intention for man. It is through His Son that God created all things and made Himself manifest to man:

John 1:3 *All things were made by him; and without him was not any thing made that was made.*

Jesus is the arm of God (Isaiah 40:10, 52:10, 53:1, Jeremiah 32:17, etc.) created to do His express will in His name. He is the bearer of God's light, revealing God through his word and his life, the manifestation of God's word and His light.

> **Luke 2:32** *A light to lighten the Gentiles, and the glory of thy people Israel.*
>
> **John 1:4-9** *In him was life; and the life was the light of men. And the light shineth in darkness; and the darkness comprehended it not. ...That was the true Light, which lighteth every man that cometh into the world.*
>
> **John 5:35** *He was a burning and a shining light; and ye were willing for a season to rejoice in his light.*
>
> **John 8:12** *Then spake Jesus again unto them, saying, I am the light of the world: he that followeth me shall not walk in darkness, but shall have the light of life.*
>
> **John 9:5** *As long as I am in the world, I am the light of the world.*
>
> **II Corinthians 4:6** *For God, who commanded the light to shine out of darkness, hath shined in our hearts, to give the light of the knowledge of the glory of God in the face of Jesus Christ.*

The prophet Daniel was a perfect example of a man of God gifted with a measure of His truth revealed by His Spirit, through His light:

> **Daniel 2:20-22** *Daniel answered and said, Blessed be the name of God for ever and ever: for wisdom and might are his: And he changeth the times and the seasons: he removeth kings, and setteth up kings: he giveth wisdom to the wise, and knowledge to them that know understanding: He revealeth the deep and secret things: he knoweth what is in the darkness, and the light dwelleth with him.*
>
> **Daniel 5:11-14** *There is a man in thy kingdom, in whom is the spirit of the holy gods; and in the days of thy father light and understanding and wisdom, like the wisdom of the gods, was found*

in him;...Forasmuch as an excellent spirit, and knowledge, and understanding, interpreting of dreams, and shewing of hard sentences, and dissolving of doubts, were found in the same Daniel,...I have even heard of thee that the spirit of the gods is in thee, and that light and understanding and excellent wisdom is found in thee.

THE REFINING CHANNEL OF GOD'S WORD

The word proceeds from God in a pure stream; this liquid silver must then be processed and refined in the heart and mind of man both through the individual who is the channel of the message and through those who hear the words. If His word is not properly refined in the vessel of earth through which it passes, it will not come forth as a pure stream to the hearer.

Imagine a water pipe that through neglect and disuse has become full of rust and grime. No matter how pure and clean the water that goes in, that which comes out will be tainted and unclean. The pipe must be kept clean and unobstructed for the purity and constancy of the flow to be maintained.

We too must keep our bodies and minds pure from the filth of the world, so that God's Spirit and word can move in and through us with no obstruction. We must not communicate God's word to others if it has been tainted by its passage through us. This is why it is absolutely necessary to have the gift of the Holy Spirit active and alive in one's life in order to have a true understanding of God's word. The Spirit is that which makes the word alive and reveals its truth to our minds.

There are many different kinds of filters that we can place between God and ourselves. Most often we block out His voice with other voices: the television, radio, or social activities that keep us busy. We live our lives in the shadows of the gods we have created of our own desire. Imagine a great boulder in the desert, the bright sun low in the sky. One side of the rock is in bright light while the back side is in darkness and casts a shadow out behind it. It is in this darkness, in this long shadow of our own making, that we live out our lives, hiding from the light of God.

Just as the children of Israel could not look upon the face of Moses after he had been in the presence of God, so modern men cannot look directly upon the terrible light of His visage. Just as the children of Israel, modern man finds it easier to live with a veil over his eyes rather than looking upon the pure light of God and in turn having themselves revealed by that light. This is why we see God revealing His work in types and shadows, why we see Jesus speaking in parables. Jesus specifically took his disciples aside to interpret his words to them. It was only to his few chosen disciples that he revealed himself clearly:

> **Mark 4:11-12** *And he said unto them, Unto you it is given to know the mystery of the kingdom of God: but unto them that are without, all these things are done in parables: That seeing they may see, and not perceive; and hearing they may hear, and not understand; lest at any time they should be converted, and their sins should be forgiven them.*
>
> **Luke 8:10** *And he said, Unto you it is given to know the mysteries of the kingdom of God: but to others in parables; that seeing they might not see, and hearing they might not understand.*[68]

The mysteries and knowledge of God can be known only by His choosing and calling a man, and only through His Spirit. It is God's prerogative to whom He will reveal Himself and to what degree. As previously mentioned in the evidences given for biblical harmony, I Corinthians 2:6-16 clearly demonstrates that the things of God can be known only through the gift of his Spirit indwelling and illuminating the mind of man: *Howbeit we speak wisdom among them that are*

---

[68] See also Isaiah 6:9-10.

perfect: yet not the wisdom of this world, nor of the princes of this world, that come to nought: But we speak the wisdom of God in a mystery, even the hidden wisdom, which God ordained before the world unto our glory: Which none of the princes of this world knew: for had they known it, they would not have crucified the Lord of glory. But as it is written, Eye hath not seen, nor ear heard, neither have entered into the heart of man, the things which God hath prepared for them that love him. But God hath revealed them unto us by his Spirit: for the Spirit searcheth all things, yea, the deep things of God. For what man knoweth the things of a man, save the spirit of man which is in him? Even so the things of God knoweth no man, but the Spirit of God. Now we have received, not the spirit of the world, but the spirit which is of God; that we might know the things that are freely given to us of God. Which things also we speak, not in the words which man's wisdom teacheth, but which the Holy Ghost teacheth; comparing spiritual things with spiritual. But the natural man receiveth not the things of the Spirit of God: for they are foolishness unto him: neither can he know them, because they are spiritually discerned. But he that is spiritual judgeth all things, yet he himself is judged of no man. For who hath known the mind of the Lord, that he may instruct him? But we have the mind of Christ.

In order therefore for one to have the mind of Christ, which enables him to understand the things of God, one must have the Spirit's instruction. This is enabled only through the Spirit's life within man, and the Spirit is given only by baptism. This is not the same experience of repentance and water baptism, for John the Baptist was enabled to baptize unto repentance. The Spirit baptism is a secondary work, separate from the conversion experience and given by God through His Son alone. When we have experienced this baptism and have this Spirit dwelling within, we then can be taught the hidden wisdom and the deep things of God.

THE SEVEN GOLDEN CANDLESTICKS

The method by which God's word and will are made known to man is through the Spirit. From a spiritual and symbolic standpoint the illumination needed to know God shines forth from the 7 golden candlesticks, typified by the 7 branches of the lampstand in the Tabernacle of God. The flames burning atop the 7 branches of the lampstand represent the anointed illumination of the 7 spirits of God, through which His will and His truth can be perfectly known. These 7 spirits of God are the gifts of enlightenment through which man can come to fully know Him. Isaiah 11:1-2 reveals what these 7 spirits are: *And there shall come forth a rod out of the stem of Jesse, and a Branch shall grow out of his roots: And the spirit of the LORD shall rest upon him, the spirit of wisdom and understanding, the spirit of counsel and might, the spirit of knowledge and of the fear of the LORD;*

These 7 spirits of God are mentioned again in Revelation:
> **Revelation 4:5** *And out of the throne proceeded lightnings and thunderings and voices: and there were seven lamps of fire burning before the throne, which are the seven Spirits of God.*
> **Revelation 5:6** *And I beheld, and, lo, in the midst of the throne and of the four beasts, and in the midst of the elders, stood a Lamb as it had been slain, having seven horns and seven eyes, which are the seven Spirits of God sent forth into all the earth.*

These 7 Spirits are represented as horns and eyes, horns for the anointing that rests upon the bearer and eyes to typify the understanding and discernment imparted by the 7 spirits. The indwelling of these seven spiritual attributes gifts the bearer with an enhanced capacity to understand the will and revelation of God and brings man into resonance with His mind. The end result of this is a righteousness and equity reflecting God's original design for man.

Isaiah 11:3-5 *And shall make him of quick understanding in the fear of the LORD: and he shall not judge after the sight of his eyes, neither reprove after the hearing of his ears: But with righteousness shall he judge the poor, and reprove with equity for the meek of the earth: and he shall smite the earth with the rod of his mouth, and with the breath of his lips shall he slay the wicked. And righteousness shall be the girdle of his loins, and faithfulness the girdle of his reins.*

When the word of God has its full manifestation in and through the heart and mind of man, we will come into a complete understanding and unity with God:

Jeremiah 31:33[69] *But this shall be the covenant that I will make with the house of Israel; After those days, saith the LORD, I will put my law in their inward parts, and write it in their hearts; and will be their God, and they shall be my people.*

GOD'S WORD IS TRIED AND IT TRIES IN TURN

II Samuel 22:31 *As for God, his way is perfect; the word of the LORD is tried: he is a buckler to all them that trust in him.*

The word translated "perfect" in this verse is the Hebrew ***tamiym***, which carries the dual meaning of a thing being both complete and perfect, without spot or blemish. The way of God revealed through His word is perfect and true, complete and entire in itself. Notice that God clearly states that His word is not to be added to:

Deuteronomy 4:2 *Ye shall not add unto the word which I command you, neither shall ye diminish ought from it, that ye may keep the commandments of the Lord your God which I command you.*

Proverbs 30:6 *Add thou not unto his words, lest he reprove thee, and thou be found a liar.*

---

[69] See also Hebrews 8:10 and 10:16.

Revelation 22:18-19 *For I testify unto every man that heareth the words of the prophecy of this book, if any man shall add unto these things, God shall add unto him the plagues that are written in this book: And if any man shall take away from the words of the book of this prophecy, God shall take away his part out of the book of life, and out of the holy city, and from the things which are written in this book.*

"Tried" is the Hebrew word ***tsaraph***, meaning "to refine" or "to purify". This is usually used in the context of the process of refining or trying metal. God's word is not only tried in the sense that it is proven to be true, but it is put through a refining process in its revelation to the mind of man. This idea is further developed in Psalm 12:6: *The words of the Lord are pure words: as silver tried in a furnace of earth, purified seven times.*

The Hebrew word translated "pure" is ***tahor***, meaning "to be clean" or "to be pure". This can be from a physical, moral, or even ceremonial standpoint. Again the Lord demonstrates the absolute purity of His word.

God's words are tried (as silver) in a furnace of earth. There are several interesting metaphorical types involved in this statement. The earth here can be seen as the nations of the earth in which the seed of God's word takes conception and makes its judgments known. It also could be viewed as the earthy man himself, created of the dust of the earth, through whom God communicates His word.

The word of God has a dual activity in its relationship to man, it tries man and is tried through him. In Psalm 12:6 above, we see the word being tried through the vessel of man. Proverbs 17:3 is complementary to this in the sense of God trying man by His word: *The fining pot is for silver, and the furnace for gold: but the Lord trieth the hearts.*

Other scriptures that refer to God trying the hearts of men are I Chronicles 29:17, II Chronicles 32:31, Psalms 7:9, 17:3, 26:2, 139:23, Jeremiah 11:20, 12:3, 17:10, 20:12, and I Thessalonians 2:4.

In Genesis 2 God formed "man": **adam** out of the "dust": **aphar** of the "ground": **adamah**. The first man's name, Adam, is the root word from which the word ground comes and essentially means red or ruddy. In this context the word ground is representative of the rich red soil of the earth. This is the most fertile and nutrient-rich type of earth. In his pre-fallen state man was created to be a perfect receptacle for the life-giving Spirit of God. He was made in the image of God so as to be capable of communion with his Creator. It is this original state of receptivity and purity that we must attain in order to have a complete understanding of and capability to obey the word of God.

Isaiah 35:5-8[70] *Then the eyes of the blind shall be opened, and the ears of the deaf shall be unstopped. Then shall the lame man leap as an hart, and the tongue of the dumb sing: for in the wilderness shall waters break out, and streams in the desert. And the parched ground shall become a pool, and the thirsty land springs of water: in the habitation of dragons, where each lay, shall be grasses with reeds and rushes. And an highway shall be there, and a way, and it shall be called The way of holiness; the unclean shall not pass over it; but it shall be for those: the wayfaring men, though fools, shall not err therein.*

These scriptures speak of the outpouring of God's blessing and revelation through both His Spirit and His word, His Spirit upon man and His unadulterated word in its perfect revelation to man. There are those dead, without the Spirit and the understanding of His word, who shall be quickened and brought to life under its anointing.

---

[70] See also Isaiah 41:18, 43:19, and John 7:38-39.

To have a proper conception of the way in which God reveals Himself to man, it must be understood that revelation by God is accomplished based on a number of factors. There is a how and a when to the revelatory communication of God. The "how" corresponds to the methods He uses in relaying information to man. The "when" determines the time in which this information is supplied.

God moves in times and seasons according to His pre-ordained plan. This can be seen in the ages of time He has allotted for His creation and in the individual dispensations within these ages. Within each dispensation there is a ceiling on the level of revelatory understanding and vision that man can be given. God uses various methods of inspiration in each dispensation, but the level of spiritual maturity and perception of man and the dispensation itself determine how much revelation will be available.

METHODS OF INSPIRATION

God reveals Himself in times and seasons, in ways and means. He has multiple channels and instruments through which He is revealed, and He uses these in specific periods and dispensations of time.

From the beginning of creation God has made Himself known to man. He has communicated His presence and purpose to man through five specific vehicles of revelation:

1- Through the law of the inner man/the **CONSCIENCE** (the original image of God stamped on man's heart)
2- Through his **CREATIVE WORKS**
3- Through his **AUDIBLE VOICE**
4- Through his **EXTERNAL INSPIRATION** upon men by dreams, visions, or internal revelation
5- Through the **INTERNAL INSPIRATION** through the anointing of His Spirit within the mind of man

The Bible claims that all scripture is given by God either by *His voice* to men, *His inspiration* through men, or *His anointing* on men. He has also made Himself known through the silent voice of His creation and the inner voice of conscience. God spoke directly to Abraham, Moses, and others, both audibly and through dreams and visions. He inspired the words of David and Solomon, and His anointing on men such as Peter, Paul, and John gave them the insight into His character that was necessary to interpret His eternal truths.

The first two manifestations, the conscience and the creative works, bring an awareness of God. Through these two we can become aware of His will and His presence. We can become attuned to Him through the conscience and in awe of Him through His creation. The last three, the audible voice, inspiration, and anointing, bring a more personal understanding of God. These allow us to understand His specific requirements and desires for us.

It became necessary for God to speak directly and indirectly with man through the vehicles of speech, dreams, visions, and the power of the Spirit. Through the fall in the garden, man's perfect conscious awareness and unity with God were broken. As time went on, this rift between God and man grew wider. By the time of the flood, man had become so deviant that God was forced to begin afresh. From the time of Noah through Abraham, Isaac, Jacob, and eventually Moses, God spoke and directed man by speech and through inspiration and anointing.

This revelation of God through His word has been a progressive work. He has manifested Himself through the following vehicles:

THE CONSCIENCE

The first and most inherently complete revelation of God to man was through the inner conscience. This was part of the image of God placed in the heart of man at creation. It was to this image that God intended that man be conformed, the reflection of the Creator.

Man was brought into being with the capacity to fully know the will and ways of God, but his act of disobedience cut him off from this inner communication. God's will can be completely and perfectly revealed to us, but we must still choose to obey His ordinances. Often men long to know the will of God, but in their hearts they are not prepared to obey His voice. We must first learn obedience to His commands before He can properly direct our steps and guide us into His perfect will.

The establishment of the conscience began with the creation of man in the garden:

Genesis 1:26-27 *And God said, Let us make man in our image, after our likeness: and let them have dominion over the fish of the sea, and over the fowl of the air, and over the cattle, and over all the earth, and over every creeping thing that creepeth upon the earth. So God created man in his own image, in the image of God created he him; male and female created he them.*

The conscience of man was encoded in his mind as part of the image of God placed upon him. It was God's intention that man be in perfect harmony with Him and with all of the creation. It was this conscience and understanding that could allow man to have proper stewardship (dominion) over the creation. It was through this understanding of God that man could have lived in unity with and obedience to his Creator. It was this same conscience that the serpent had to slip past and debilitate in order to undermine man's relationship with God. It was then that the mind and desire of man, through his own ego and will, was allowed to overcome his inborn harmony with the will of God.

Genesis 3:7 *And the eyes of them both were opened, and they knew that they were naked; and they sewed fig leaves together, and made themselves aprons.*

Here was the first note of discord in the perfect harmony of God's earthly creation. Man separated his will and understanding from the mind of God. Man's ego supplanted the will of God for his life. This state of nakedness was not only physical, but even more importantly, it was spiritual. The covering of man by his relationship to God had been removed. The great war between the spiritual inner man and the carnal inner man began at this breaking point. In order that man can attempt to bring himself back into unity with his Maker, he must first attack the root cause of the separation. We are told throughout the scripture to keep the law of God in our hearts; by doing so we can come to know the will of God:

Deuteronomy 6:5-6 *And thou shalt love the Lord thy God with all thine heart, and with all thy soul, and with all thy might. And these words, which I command thee this day, shall be in thine heart:*

Psalm 37:31 *The law of his God is in his heart; none of his steps shall slide.*

Isaiah 51:7 *Hearken unto me, ye that know righteousness, the people in whose heart is my law; fear ye not the reproach of men, neither be ye afraid of their revilings.*

There are a multitude of scriptural passages discussing the writing of the law upon one's heart. This can be done from a natural standpoint by the physical and mental discipline of meditating on the word of God and committing it to memory. Spiritually though, the law is written on the fleshly tables of the heart when it begins to infiltrate the understanding and psyche of the mind and becomes an integrated part of the conscience.

The natural writing of the law on man's heart is relative to the covenant of Moses. The law was engraved on the hearts of the people by the iron pen of tradition, cut deep by repetition and habit, discipline, and obedience to the letter of the law. But this discipline was made strong in a covenant of death through fear. This was a covenant kept by the rule of action rather than thought.

In contrast, the spiritual writing of the law on man's heart is relative to the new covenant of Jesus Christ. This covenant of life is established by an act of sacrifice by love, and it is in this manner that it is kept. As Jesus did, we are to sacrifice our desires and the nature within us because of the love we have for him. The law of God was to once again become sibling to conscience, the law being known not through its commandments and restrictions, but through a spiritual relationship with its Author. This is the road to unity with God.

Jesus presented a perfect model of this in his relationship to God. As the last Adam, he demonstrated what man in unity with God is capable of, as the first Adam could have done had he not fallen. God has promised that we will once again be brought into the state of perfect unity with him:

Jeremiah 24:7 *And I will give them an heart to know me, that I am the Lord: and they shall be my people, and I will be their God: for they shall return unto me with their whole heart.*

Jeremiah 31:33 *But this shall be the covenant that I will make with the house of Israel; After those days, saith the Lord, I will put my law in their inward parts, and write it in their hearts; and will be their God, and they shall be my people.*[71]

Jeremiah 32:39-40 *And I will give them one heart, and one way, that they may fear me for ever, for the good of them, and of their children after them: And I will make an everlasting covenant with them, that I will not turn away from them, to do them good; but I will put fear in their hearts, that they shall not depart from me.*

---

[71] See also Hebrews 10:16.

Hebrews 8:10 *For this is the covenant that I will make with the house of Israel after those days, saith the Lord; I will put my laws into their mind, and write them on their hearts: and I will be to them a God, and they shall be to me a people.*

It is through the indwelling of the Spirit that we receive a new heart. The Spirit is the tool that God uses to heal the scarred consciences of men.

Ezekiel 11:19-20 *And I will give them one heart, and I will put a new spirit within you; and I will take the stony heart out of their flesh, and will give them an heart of flesh: That they may walk in my statutes, and keep my ordinances, and do them: and they shall be my people, and I will be their God.*

Ezekiel 36:26-27 *A new heart also will I give you, and a new spirit will I put within you: and I will take away the stony heart out of your flesh, and I will give you a heart of flesh. And I will put my spirit within you, and cause you to walk in my statutes, and ye shall keep my judgments, and do them.*

II Corinthians 3:3 *Forasmuch as ye are manifestly declared to be the epistle of Christ ministered by us, written not with ink, but with the Spirit of the living God; not in tables of stone, but in fleshly tables of the heart.*

This stony heart is that carnal spirit and state of mind that is a product of the natural man. It represents the place of separation in understanding and unity with God. It was the tables of stone that symbolized the Law of Moses, a law that could not save. It could only constrain sin and wall it off, separating man from God. It took the law of life, written in red blood on the cross of Calvary, to bring life and Spirit back into the soul of man.

GOD'S CREATIVE WORKS
The Testimony of the Creation

Romans 1:18-20 *For the wrath of God is revealed from heaven against all ungodliness and unrighteousness of men, who hold the truth in unrighteousness; Because that which may be known of God is manifest in them; for God hath shewed it unto them. For the invisible things of him from the creation of the world are clearly seen, being understood by the things that are made, even his eternal power and Godhead; so that they are without excuse.*

All of creation is a witness and evidence to the handiwork and presence of the Creator. The complexity and underlying harmony testify to a skilled craftsman. The creatures of the earth are aware of their Creator; it is man alone that has blinded himself to the Almighty.

> **Job 12:7-10** *But ask now the beasts, and they shall teach thee; and the fowls of the air, and they shall tell thee: Or speak to the earth, and it shall teach thee: and the fishes of the sea shall declare unto thee. Who knoweth not in all these that the hand of the Lord hath wrought this?...*
>
> **Psalm 19:1-4** *The heavens declare the glory of God; and the firmament sheweth his handywork. Day unto day uttereth speech, and night unto night sheweth knowledge. There is no speech nor language, where their voice is not heard. Their line is gone out through all the earth, and their words to the end of the world. In them hath he set a tabernacle for the sun,*
>
> **Luke 19:40** (metaphorically) *...I tell you that, if these should hold their peace, the stones would immediately cry out.*
>
> **Romans 1:18-20** *For the wrath of God is revealed from heaven against all ungodliness and unrighteousness of men, who hold the truth in unrighteousness; Because that which may be known of God is manifest in them; for God hath shewed it unto them. For the invisible things of him from the creation of the world are*

clearly seen, being understood by the things that are made, even his eternal power and Godhead; so that they are without excuse:

The creation of God and His works in the earth are made manifest to us for four reasons: that we may see, know, consider, and understand.
Isaiah 41:20 *That they may see, and know, and consider, and understand together, that the hand of the Lord hath done this, and the Holy One of Israel hath created it.*

To "see" is the Hebrew *ra'ah*, meaning to literally see in the sense of physical sight. To "know" is *yada*, meaning to know or perceive by experience of something. To "consider" is *sum*, meaning to assign something its proper place or determine something. To "understand" is *sakal*, meaning to understand a thing with wisdom or insight. This perfectly reveals the manner in which we learn the things of God through the majesty of His creation.

First we see those things that He has made, which then makes us aware of them through our mental perception. When we begin to properly perceive His works we then can begin to see the underlying structure and intelligent design of the Creator. This will develop in us an understanding and wisdom that give us evidence of the handiwork of God. This second manner of revelation is a perfect complement to the manifestation of God through the conscience. The structural design and evidence of God demonstrated through His works combined with the mind of God and Christ living in us by the conscience, if brought to a complete state of harmony with God, will bring us back full circle into the original relationship intended for us with God.

GOD'S AUDIBLE VOICE
The literal voice of God speaking
(directly or through an angelic messenger)

God's audible voice is usually heard through his angelic messengers, though at times there have been those who have spoken with Him directly. It would appear that Abraham spoke to the Lord Himself in the plains of Mamre.

Genesis 18:1-3 *And the Lord appeared unto him in the plains of Mamre: and he sat in the tent door in the heat of the day; And he lifted up his eyes and looked, and, lo, three men stood by him: and when he saw them, he ran to meet them from the tent door, and bowed himself toward the ground, And said, My Lord, if now I have found favor in thy sight, pass not away, I pray thee, from thy servant:*

The three men who appeared to Abraham were the Lord and two of His angels. Some have conjectured that all three were angels and that the Lord spoke through one or all of them. This does not fit the continued context of the story, however. The men went up to look over Sodom. It is at this point that the impending judgment of Sodom and Gomorrah is revealed to Abraham. After Abraham pleads with God for the righteous remnant in these cities, the Lord leaves.

Genesis 18:33 *And the LORD went his way, as soon as he had left communing with Abraham: and Abraham returned unto his place.*

We find in the very next verse (Genesis 19:1) that two angels arrived in Sodom that evening. These two must have been the angelic companions of the Lord previously mentioned.

The Lord spoke to Moses out of the burning bush. This was the voice of God speaking through an angelic manifestation:

Exodus 3:2-6 *And the angel of the LORD appeared unto him in a flame of fire out of the midst of a bush: and he looked, and, behold, the bush burned with fire, and the bush was not consumed. And Moses said, I will now turn aside, and see this great sight, why the* *bush is not burnt. And when the LORD saw that he turned aside to see, God called unto him out of the midst of the bush, and said, Moses, Moses. And he said, Here am I. And he said, Draw not nigh hither: put off thy shoes from off thy feet, for the place whereon thou standest is holy ground. Moreover he said, I am the God of thy father, the God of Abraham, the God of Isaac, and the God of Jacob. And Moses hid his face; for he was afraid to look upon God.* This event is spoken of by Stephen in Acts 7:30-31...*there appeared to him in the wilderness of mount Sina an angel of the Lord in a flame of fire in a bush. When Moses saw it, he wondered at the sight: and as he drew near to behold it, the voice of the Lord came unto him,*

It is evident by these passages that God spoke directly through the angel of the Lord. The angel appeared to Moses, but it was the voice of God Himself speaking through His messenger. ...*the angel of the Lord appeared unto him in a flame of fire out of the midst of a bush...God called unto him out of the midst of the bush...* Moses felt such fear at the presence of God manifested through the angel that he hid his face.

This is revealing in that Moses *was afraid to look upon God...*. He clearly understood that the angel that appeared to him in the bush was a direct manifestation of the divine presence. This angel was the image and mouthpiece of God Himself. This is not to say the angel **was** God.[72] The best interpretation of this passage is that the angel was the representative of God, an ambassador that spoke with the authority of his master. The angel of the Lord, or angel of His presence, is seen throughout the scripture as the manifest representative of God, the one who went before Israel in the wilderness.[73]

---

[72] Herein is made known the manifestation of the godhead, in that God makes Himself known through His messenger. This messenger is the perfect image of God in all respects, and the voice of God can be heard through him. Yet, this is not God Himself, but an image of the Almighty.

[73] See Exodus 14:19, 23:20, 32:34, 33:2, and Isaiah 63:9.

The Lord spoke audibly to Moses, Aaron, and Miriam during Israel's period in the wilderness.

Numbers 12:4-8 *And the LORD spake suddenly unto Moses, and unto Aaron, and unto Miriam, Come out ye three unto the tabernacle of the congregation. And they three came out. And the LORD came down in the pillar of the cloud, and stood in the door of the tabernacle, and called Aaron and Miriam: and they both came forth. And he said, Hear now my words: If there be a prophet among you, I the LORD will make myself known unto him in a vision, and will speak unto him in a dream. My servant Moses is not so, who is faithful in all mine house. With him will I speak mouth to mouth, even apparently, and not in dark speeches; and the similitude of the LORD shall he behold: wherefore then were ye not afraid to speak against my servant Moses?*

Moses was unique in his age in that God spoke with him *face to face.* This was clear and direct communication. Most prophecy must be interpreted or given clarification, but Moses conversed with God without the types and metaphors inherent in prophetic revelation.

Exodus 33:11 *And the Lord spake unto Moses face to face, as a man speaketh unto his friend....*

Deuteronomy 34:10 *And there arose not a prophet since in Israel like unto Moses, whom the Lord knew face to face,*

God spoke to the prophet Samuel as a young child.

I Samuel 3:3-4 *And ere the lamp of God went out in the temple of the LORD, where the ark of God was, and Samuel was laid down to sleep; That the LORD called Samuel: and he answered, Here am I.*

The Lord called out to Samuel three times in an audible voice. Samuel, thinking the voice was the priest Eli's, ran to him and asked if he had called him. Each time Eli sent him back to his bed, telling him he had not called him. After the third time Eli understood that the Lord was speaking to Samuel. He instructed him to return to his bed again, and if the Lord were to call him again he should reply, *Speak Lord, for thy servant heareth.* Again the Lord came and spoke to Samuel:

I Samuel 3:10-11 *And the LORD came, and stood, and called as at other times, Samuel, Samuel. Then Samuel answered, Speak; for thy servant heareth. And the LORD said to Samuel, Behold, I will do a thing in Israel, at which both the ears of every one that heareth it shall tingle.*

After the Lord spoke with Samuel and told him the fate of Eli's house, Samuel fell asleep.

I Samuel 3:15 *And Samuel lay until the morning, and opened the doors of the house of the Lord. And Samuel feared to show Eli the vision.*

Notice that the experience Samuel had with God was described as a vision. The term vision in the Bible is not always used in the way we think of it today. A biblical vision is a revelation of God in a very direct way, supernatural, but not in the same sense as a dream or a hallucination. It is clear that those who experienced a vision of the Lord were absolutely certain of what they had seen. The encounter was very real and lucid.

Throughout the scripture are found instances where God's voice is heard, whether directly or through a spiritual representative. Other examples are

Adam and Eve – Genesis 2:16-17, Genesis 3:8-24
Cain – Genesis 4:6-7, 9-16
Noah – Genesis 6:13-21, 7:1-4
Job – Job 38:1
Joshua – Joshua 5:13-15
Nebuchadnezzar – Daniel 4:31
Paul on the road to Damascus – Acts 9:3-7

INSPIRATION (EXTERNAL)
Through the intellectual vehicle of man
by dreams, visions, or revelation of knowledge

External inspiration is demonstrated most often in the revelatory experiences of the Old Testament prophets. This type of inspiration and understanding is external in the sense that the knowledge comes completely from an outside source. The Spirit's inspiration on the prophets gave them a temporary insight into the will of God for a specific purpose.

Let's begin by examining the individual types of inspiration dealt with in the Bible.

Dreams

Dreams come from several sources: through the carnal mind of man or through the spiritual consciousness, whether by God's communication or the devil's. The most common form of dream is the natural dream originated in the mind of man. As previously examined, we exist in a body that is designed to react to an outside stimulus; in its perfect state this would have been a harmonious reaction and interaction with God. With the fall of man, our bodies and minds became fertile ground for the stimulus of our own thoughts and the external stimulus of the adversary. Natural dreams, brought on by our own mind, are usually a product of our preoccupying thoughts. The busy whirlwind of our waking thoughts are often carried over into our subconscious sleep.

Ecclesiastes 5:3 *For a dream cometh through the multitude of business; and a fool's voice is known by multitude of words.*

Dreams can also come from spiritual sources outside the mind of man. Both God and the devil use dreams as a source of communication and inspiration. As in all his works, the deceiver uses this tool to attempt to thwart God's designs and to throw stumbling blocks before His people. The devil inspires men with false dreams in order to cause them to turn away from God:

Jeremiah 23:32 *Behold, I am against them that prophesy false dreams, saith the LORD, and do tell them, and cause my people to err by their lies, and by their lightness; yet I sent them not, nor commanded them: therefore they shall not profit this people at all, saith the LORD.*

Zechariah 10:2 *For the idols have spoken vanity, and the diviners have seen a lie, and have told false dreams; they comfort in vain: therefore they went their way as a flock, they were troubled, because there was no shepherd.*

Deuteronomy 13:1-3 *If there arise among you a prophet, or a dreamer of dreams, and giveth thee a sign or a wonder, And the sign or the wonder come to pass, whereof he spake unto thee, saying, Let us go after other gods, which thou hast not known, and let us serve them; Thou shalt not hearken unto the words of that prophet, or that dreamer of dreams: for the Lord your God proveth you, to know whether ye love the Lord your God with all your heart and with all your soul.*

God uses dreams as an indirect communication with man. It is often His purpose to hide His intention behind types and shadows. Given the nature of dreams, this does not allow man to be as certain of the source or validity of the message.

Job 33:14-17 *For God speaketh once, yea twice, yet man perceiveth it not. In a dream, in a vision of the night, when deep sleep falleth upon men, in slumberings upon the bed; Then he openeth the ears of men, and sealeth their instruction, That he may withdraw man from his purpose, and hide pride from man.*

God used dreams throughout the scripture to express His intent to man.

Jeremiah 23:28 *The prophet that hath a dream, let him tell a dream; and he that hath my word, let him speak my word faithfully. What is the chaff to the wheat? saith the LORD.*

Joel 2:28 *And it shall come to pass afterward, that I will pour out my spirit upon all flesh; and your sons and your daughters shall prophesy, your old men shall dream dreams, your young men shall see visions:*

Some of those in the Bible to whom God revealed his will through dreams follow:

Abimelech – Genesis 20:3
Jacob – Genesis 28:12-16, 31:10-13 and 46:2
Laban – Genesis 31:24
Joseph – Genesis 37:5-10
Pharaoh's butler and baker – Genesis 40
Pharaoh – Genesis 41:1-37
A Midianite – Judges 7:13-15
Solomon – I Kings 3:5-15
Eliphaz – Job 4:12-21
Nebuchadnezzar – Daniel 2:1-47, 4:1-27
Daniel – Daniel 2:19, chapter 7, etc.
Joseph – Matthew 1:20-24, 2:13, 19-21
The wise men – Matthew 2:12
Pilate's wife – Matthew 27:19
Paul – Acts 16:9-10 (or a vision)

Visions

Dreams and visions, from a biblical perspective, can be very different experiences. As seen in Samuel's early encounter with God, the vision he perceived was just as real as hearing the actual voice of the priest Eli. Generally, a vision could be considered a waking and conscious experience, whereas a dream occurs while the mind is in the semi-conscious realm of sleep. Though a dream can be called a vision,[74] a waking vision is a different experience than a sleeping dream.

One of the best examples of this type of experience is that recorded of Balaam:

Numbers 24:4 *He hath said, which heard the words of God, which saw the vision of the Almighty, falling into a trance, but having his eyes open:*

This, along with dreams, is one of the two primary ways in which God reveals Himself to His prophets:

Numbers 12:6 *And he said, Hear now my words: If there be a prophet among you, I the LORD will make myself known unto him in a vision, and will speak unto him in a dream.*

God often reveals Himself through a combination of the senses; in the case of Samuel God spoke audibly and manifested Himself to the boy in a vision.

I Samuel 3:15 *And Samuel lay until the morning, and opened the doors of the house of the LORD. And Samuel feared to shew Eli the vision.*

Daniel experienced many visions during his prophetic ministry; one of the most lucid was his vision of the Lord's messenger by the river Hiddekel:

---

[74] Genesis 46:2, Job 33:15, Isaiah 29:7, and Daniel 2:19, 7:2.

Daniel 10:7-8 *And I Daniel alone saw the vision: for the men that were with me saw not the vision; but a great quaking fell upon them, so that they fled to hide themselves. Therefore I was left alone, and saw this great vision, and there remained no strength in me: for my comeliness was turned in me into corruption, and I retained no strength.*

Peter was another example of one who received a vision in a trance-like state:

Acts 11:5 *I was in the city of Joppa praying: and in a trance I saw a vision, A certain vessel descend, as it had been a great sheet, let down from heaven by four corners; and it came even to me:*

Some to whom God revealed His will through waking visions follow:

Abraham – Genesis 15:1
Balaam – Numbers 22-24
The children of Israel – Exodus 24:9-17
Samuel – I Samuel 3:1-15
Elisha – II Kings 2:11-12
Elisha's servant – II Kings 6:17
Micaiah - I Kings 22:17-23
David – I Chronicles 21:15-21
Isaiah – Isaiah 6
Jeremiah – Jeremiah 1:11-13
Ezekiel – Ezekiel 1, 2:9, chapters 8-10, 37, 40-48, and throughout
Daniel – Daniel 7 (dream and visions), chapters 8-11 (dreams and visions), and throughout
Amos – Amos 7:1-9, chapters 8-9
Zechariah – Zechariah 1-6 and throughout
Zacharias – Luke 1:11-22
Jesus – Matthew 3:16-17, Mark 1:10, Luke 3:22, and John 1:32-34
John the Baptist – as above
Peter, James, and John – Matthew 17:1-9, Luke 9:28-36

Stephen – Acts 7:55-56
Paul – Acts 9:3-7, 16:9, 18:9-10, 22:17-21, and II Corinthians 12:1-4
Ananias – Acts 9:10-16
Cornelius – Acts 10:3-7
Peter – Acts 10:9-17
John – the Book of Revelation

ANOINTING (INTERNAL)
God speaking through man by His Spirit,
or by putting His words in his mouth

When God anoints a man to speak His word He can do so in multiple ways. The Spirit can come upon a man, opening up his insight and understanding to the message of God. God can also allow His precise words to be given to a man.

God put his precise words in the minds and mouths of select prophets. God Himself touched the lips of Jeremiah and placed His words in the prophet's mouth:

Jeremiah 1:9 *Then the Lord put forth his hand, and touched my mouth. And the Lord said unto me, Behold, I have put my words in thy mouth.*

The Lord did not say that He inspired Jeremiah's words or even that He had placed His words in Jeremiah's mind. Additionally this may have been true, but the specific phrase used here is that the Lord put His words in Jeremiah's mouth. These were the exact words God wished to be written down for the generations to come.

The anointing is spiritually complete and in its fullness when the mind of man is in complete unity with God. Jesus then, when he had come to full fruition in his calling, had his revelation of the Father through the anointing of his mind rather than external inspiration. He was in such perfect unity with the Father that his thoughts were the thoughts of God. This was brought to its full fruition when he yielded his mind and will entirely over to God in the garden of Gethsemane.

We see the breaking of this connection when the sin of the world fell upon him on the cross. For that short period of time he was cut off from the person and presence of God, and we can see the effect this had on him. It has been long debated by theologians how that Jesus could cry out to God, why hast thou forsaken me? At the moment that sin fell fully upon him, for the first time in his existence, a wall of separation came between Jesus and his Father.

In studying the effect of the Spirit's anointing, it is important to differentiate between the degree of the Spirit that is upon a man and the level of saturation with which he is permeated by the Spirit. The Spirit can come upon a person and can be on him for a time without him being filled with the Spirit in the New Testament sense. For the Spirit to dwell in a person it must saturate him completely; it must rest upon and within him long enough to take seed, effect change, and establish a permanent abode.

The Spirit upon a person brings about a transient change in the person's emotional state and may give temporary spiritual insight. When the Spirit saturates a person and the seed is brought to fruition and spiritual birth, a much deeper level of spiritual change and insight is afforded.

The Spirit is described first in scripture as being UPON a person, then IN a person, then finally FILLING a person. When a person has the Spirit come upon him, it can be a temporary occurrence in order to affect a specific purpose. The Spirit within a person gives him a deeper understanding of and harmony with God. When a person is full of the Spirit, he is afforded a living relationship that can develop and change him into the image of God, which can then open his mind to the spiritual truths of God. Those who were baptized with the Holy Spirit were given a channel of communication and harmony with God that had not existed in this form since the time of Adam.

Some of those who had the Spirit in or upon them
before the baptism of the Holy Spirit:

Joseph – Genesis 41:38
Bezaleel – Exodus 31:1-5
Moses / The Seventy Elders – Numbers 11:17, 25
Balaam – Numbers 24:2
Joshua – Numbers 27:18
Othniel – Judges 3:10
Gideon – Judges 6:34
Jephthah – Judges 11:29
Samson – Judges 13:25, 14:6, 19
Saul – I Samuel 10:6, 10
Azariah – II Chronicles 15:1
Zechariah – II Chronicles 24:20
Ezekiel – Ezekiel 11:5
Daniel – Daniel 4:8, 18, 5:11, 14
John the Baptist – Filled with the Spirit – Luke 1:15
Jesus – The Spirit was upon and within Christ – Isaiah 11:2, 42:1,
61:1, Matthew 1:18, 20 (of the Holy Ghost),
John 3:34 (but not by measure as had been done with those before
him)

THE WRITERS OF SCRIPTURE

5

II Peter 1:21
For the prophecy came not in old time by the will of man:
but holy men of God spake as they were moved by the Holy Ghost.

It is believed that there were approximately 40 different writers of the books of the Bible. What has been often noted is the amazing unity of this large group. The writers of the scriptures came from many different backgrounds and educational upbringings, and yet their message is perfect in unity and agreement.

The intention in the brief descriptions of each of the biblical writers is not so much to present a biographical sketch as to uncover their point of contact with God, to understand what qualities and abilities God provided each of these men with to enable them to record His message, and to demonstrate their individual callings as a vessel of His communication.

OLD TESTAMENT WRITERS

The Old Testament was written over the space of approximately 4,000 years and covered the time from the creation up until about 424 B.C.

THE HISTORICAL WRITERS

<u>Moses</u>

Nearly all biblical and Jewish tradition holds that Moses was the author and editor of the first five books of the Bible; **Genesis, Exodus, Leviticus, Numbers, and Deuteronomy**.

> **Deuteronomy 31:9, 24** *And Moses wrote this law, and delivered it unto the priests the sons of Levi, which bare the ark of the covenant of the Lord, and unto all the elders of Israel....And it came to pass, when Moses made an end of writing the words of this law in a book, until they were finished,*
>
> **Joshua 8:32** *And he* [Joshua] *wrote there upon the stones a copy of the law of Moses, which he* [Moses] *wrote in the presence of the children of Israel.*
>
> **John 1:45** Philip findeth Nathanael, and saith unto him, We have found him, of whom Moses in the law, and the prophets, did write, Jesus of Nazareth, the son of Joseph.

It is not known who the original author of Genesis was, though the narrative histories likely were passed down by Adam through his descendants by oral tradition before being eventually committed to writing. It is widely believed Moses was responsible for editing together these earliest scriptures and including them with the rest of the Law.

One viewpoint that has been proposed as to the original authorship of Genesis states that there were multiple original authors of the record. These authors would have passed down their testimonies by oral tradition or by etching them onto stone or clay tablets. Moses in turn would have gathered these collections into a single volume for their inclusion in the Law.

This theory assumes that each author completes his testimonial with the record of the generational descendants up to his point of reference. Thus the authors with each of their individual records as follows:

GENESIS 1:1 – 2:4	Adam as revealed to him by God
GENESIS 2:5 – 4:26	Adam
GENESIS 5:1 – 6:8	Noah
GENESIS 6:9 – 9:29	Noah / Shem
GENESIS 10:1 – 11:9	Shem
GENESIS 11:10 – 11:26	Terah / Abraham
GENESIS 11:27 – 25:18	Abraham / Isaac
GENESIS 25:19 – 37:1	Isaac / Jacob
GENESIS 37:2 – 50:21	Joseph
GENESIS 50:22-26	Moses

Though the generations of Ishmael and Esau are recorded, it is likely these would have been written by their brothers as the Scripture appears to have been recorded only by those in the chosen line of descent. The most likely separation points where each new writer began his record would be where the narrative indicates the death of the prior writer.

Moses then, as the editor, would have gained access to these records through those of the tribes of Israel who had preserved them during their sojourn in Egypt. It has been suggested by some that Moses gained this history through the libraries of Egypt, but this would seem highly unlikely as this tradition was very specifically oriented toward the Hebrews in particular and was completely opposite of the cosmological doctrines of the Egyptians.

Moses was brought up in the Egyptian court and given a royal education, as would befit a child of Pharaoh's daughter. The Talmudic tradition is that Moses was one of the greatest minds of his day and that he excelled in every area of learning. Josephus, the Jewish historian who lived not long after the time of Christ, describes Moses' early intellect in this way: *Now Moses's understanding became superior to his age, nay, far beyond that standard; and when he was taught, he discovered greater quickness of apprehension than was usual at his age....*[75]

Philo, the 1st century Jewish philosopher, sums up the Hebrew traditions regarding Moses upbringing: *Therefore the child being now thought worthy of a royal education and a royal attendance...exhibited a modest and dignified deportment in all his words and gestures, attending diligently to every lesson of every kind which could tend to the improvement of his mind. And immediately he had all kinds of masters, one after another, some coming of their own accord from the neighboring countries and different districts of Egypt, and some being procured from Greece...But in a short time he surpassed all their knowledge, anticipating all their lessons by the excellent natural endowments of his own genius; so that everything in his case appeared to be a recollecting* [a return to a knowledge already known in the original state of man] *rather than a learning, while he himself also, without any teacher, comprehended by his instinctive genius many difficult subjects; for great abilities cut for themselves many new roads to knowledge...Accordingly he speedily learnt arithmetic, and geometry, and the whole science of rhythm and harmony and metre, and the whole of music, by means of the use of musical instruments, and by lectures on the different arts, and by explanations of each topic....*

---

[75] *Antiquities of the Jews*, Flavius Josephus, Book 2, Chapter 9.6.

Moses was also thoroughly educated in the religion and philosophy of his day: ...*lessons on these subjects were given him by Egyptian philosophers, who also taught him the philosophy which is contained in the symbols, which they exhibit in those sacred characters of hieroglyphics, as they are called, and also that philosophy which is conversant about that respect which they pay to animals which they invest with the honours due to God. And all the other branches of encyclical education he learnt from the Greeks; and the philosophers from the adjacent countries taught him Assyrian literature[76] and the knowledge of the heavenly bodies so much studied by the Chaldaeans.*[77]

It is clear that the education of Moses was as thorough as the Egyptian culture could afford, and this was the most advanced culture of its day. He most likely received his education at the schools in Heliopolis, one of the major centers of learning in ancient Egypt. Luke testifies to the intensive education of Moses:

Acts 7:22 *And Moses was learned in all the wisdom of the Egyptians, and was mighty in words and deeds.*

Though he was trained in every possible branch of knowledge and philosophy available, it can be seen by a study of the five books attributed to him that this education did not influence his writing and interpretation of God's communication. Contrary to modern critics, the word of God revealed to Moses in the books of the law was not at all compatible with the religious and scientific understanding of the Egyptian schools.

---

[76] The Hebrew non-canonical book of Jubilees states that Moses was taught the Assyrian method of writing by his father Amram.

[77] *The Works of Philo*, On the Life of Moses, V. 20-23, Hendrickson Publishers, 1993.

The Egyptian religious beliefs were based on the worship of multiple gods[78] and the deification of animals. Their scientific and medicinal applications were primarily based on magical incantations and spiritism. The Egyptians believed that most illnesses were caused by adversarial demonic beings and the ghosts of the dead, and their magicians were believed to be as much responsible for the curing of disease as their physicians. The practical prescriptions for illness contained ingredients as diverse and unsanitary as the blood and droppings of various animals.

The intention of God was that His words given to Moses and entrusted to the Levitical priesthood would be copied and passed on for future generations:

Deuteronomy 17:1-15, 18-20 When thou art come unto the land which the Lord thy God giveth thee, and shalt possess it, and shall dwell therein, and shalt say, I will set a king over me, like as all the nations that are about me; Thou shalt in any wise set him king over thee, whom the Lord thy God shall choose: ...And it shall be, when he sitteth upon the throne of his kingdom, that he shall write him a copy of this law in a book out of that which is before the priests the Levites: And it shall be with him, and he shall read therein all the days of his life: that he may learn to fear the Lord his God, to keep all the words of this law and these statutes, to do them: That his heart be not lifted up above his brethren, and that he turn not aside from the commandment, to the right hand, or to the left: to the end that he may prolong his days in his kingdom, he, and his children, in the midst of Israel.

Deuteronomy 31:9-13 And Moses wrote this law, and delivered it unto the priests the sons of Levi, which bare the Ark of the Covenant of the Lord, and unto all the elders of Israel. And Moses

---

[78] It has been conjectured by some that Akhenaten (Amenhotep IV) was a monotheist based on his worship of the sun god Aten, but even if this were the case, it is abundantly clear that Aten was not the Hebrew God.

commanded them, saying, At the end of every seven years, in the solemnity of the year of release, in the feast of tabernacles, When all Israel is come to appear before the Lord thy God in the place which he shall choose, thou shalt read this law before all Israel in their hearing. Gather the people together, men, and women, and children, and thy stranger that is within thy gates, that they may hear, and that they may learn, and fear the Lord your God, and observe to do all the words of this law: And that their children, which have not known any thing, may hear, and learn to fear the Lord your God...

Moses made it very clear that this message from God was not to be tampered with. It must not be added to or taken from:

Deuteronomy 4:2 Ye shall not add unto the word which I command you, neither shall ye diminish aught from it, that ye may keep the commandments of the Lord   your   God   which   I command you.

The Talmudic tradition also credits Moses with the compiling of the book of **Job,** which is believed to be one of the oldest biblical books. This is uncertain though, and it is completely possible that Job himself wrote the book:

Job 19:23-24 *Oh that my words were now written! Oh that they were printed in a book! That they were graven with an iron pen and lead in the rock for ever!*

Moses is also author of **Psalm 90**, written after crossing the Red Sea.

Joshua

Joshua continued the scriptural transmission handed down from Moses:

> **Joshua 24:26-27** *And Joshua wrote these words in the book of the law of God, and took a great stone, and set it up there under an oak, that was by the sanctuary of the Lord. And Joshua said unto all the people, Behold, this stone shall be a witness unto us; for it hath heard all the words of the Lord which he spake unto us: it shall be therefore a witness unto you, lest ye deny your God.*

Jewish tradition holds that **Joshua** wrote the book of the Bible that bears his name, and this is most likely the case. The last five-verse epilogue of the book records the death of Joshua and thus must have been finished by one of his contemporaries.

Samuel

> **I Samuel 3:19** *And Samuel grew, and the Lord was with him, and did let none of his words fall to the ground.*

The Jewish Talmudic tradition ascribes authorship of the book of **Judges**, **Ruth,** and the books bearing his name to Samuel. The books of **I and II Samuel** could not have been written completely by Samuel though, as the events recorded extend past his death. Some believe that Nathan the prophet or perhaps Gad was the author of or completed I and II Samuel:

> **I Chronicles 29:29** *Now the acts of David the king, first and last, behold, they are written in the book of Samuel the seer, and in the book of Nathan the prophet, and in the book of Gad the seer,*

The book of Judges was probably written during the early stages of the kingdom period, during the time of Saul or David. Note that a number of chapters in Judges began with the statement that at the time of these events Israel had no king. Thus, the idea of Israel as a monarchy had been developed at the time of its compilation.

Judges 17:6 (see also 18:1, 19:1, and 21:25) *In those days there was no king in Israel, but every man did that which was right in his own eyes.*

It is interesting to note that this is also the final phrase of the book of Judges in Judges 21:25. As the story of Ruth gives the background of David's lineage through Boaz, it was probably written after Samuel's anointing of David as king of Israel.

Jeremiah

Jewish tradition states that Jeremiah was author of the books of **I and II Kings** as the historian of the southern kingdom of Judah. He is also author of the books of **Jeremiah** and **Lamentations**. See the section on prophetic writers for further commentary.

Ezra

The books of **I and II Chronicles** are usually assigned to **Ezra** along with the book that bears his name. The Jewish Talmud names Ezra as the author of these works as well as the co-author with Nehemiah of his book. Besides the testimony of the Jewish tradition there are a number of internal evidences that point to Ezra as the author. For example, the end of II Chronicles leads directly into the narrative of Ezra. The theme of the books of I and II Chronicles seem to be written from a priestly perspective as they are concerned with the temple worship and the Levitical priesthood. Ezra was known to be a priest and a skilled member of the scribal class, and as such was well qualified to write this type of history.

Ezra 7:6 *This Ezra went up from Babylon; and he was a ready scribe in the law of Moses, which the Lord God of Israel had given:*

and the king granted him all his request, according to the hand of the Lord his God upon him.

Ezra is believed to be responsible for the final compilation of the Old Testament books. In the Jewish order of the scriptures the final books are I and II Chronicles, which would make sense if Ezra were the compiler.

Nehemiah

Nehemiah, son of Hachaliah, was the author of the book bearing his name. Nehemiah was governor of Judah for 12 years during the rebuilding of Jerusalem's walls. This may have been written with the aid of Ezra, as Ezra was still alive at the time of the book of Nehemiah.

Mordecai

It is not certain who the author of **Esther** was. It could have been written by one of the Persian Jews in captivity, but there is a strong possibility that it was Mordecai himself as he was the author of the letters of warning sent to the Jewish exiles:

Esther 9:20, 29 *And Mordecai wrote these things, and sent letters unto all the Jews....Then Esther the queen, the daughter of Abihail, and Mordecai the Jew, wrote with all authority to confirm this second letter of Purim.*

Whoever the author may have been, it is likely he had access to the royal archives where the story was also recorded:

Esther 2:23, 6:1-2, and 10:2 ...it was written in the book of the chronicles before the king...he commanded to bring the book of records of the chronicles; and they were read before the king. And it was found written,...are they not written in the book of the chronicles of the kings of Media and Persia?

THE POETICAL WRITERS

David
"The sweet psalmist of Israel"

King David of Israel was the most prolific poetical writer in the Bible. Many of his psalms could also be classified as prophecy as they foretold future events involving the coming Messiah. David wrote at least 75 of the 150 **Psalms.** Seventy-three of these Psalms bear his name. Psalm 72 is a psalm for Solomon, which closes with the phrase: *The prayers of David the son of Jesse are ended,* making this clearly a Davidic psalm. Psalm 2 and Psalm 95 have no author named but the writers of the New Testament ascribe these to David:

Acts 4:25 (quoting Psalm 2:1) *Who by the mouth of thy servant David hast said, Why did the heathen rage, and the people imagine vain things?*

Hebrews 4:7 (quoting from Psalm 95:7-8) *Again, he limiteth a certain day, saying in David, Today, after so long a time; as it is said, Today if ye will hear his voice, harden not your hearts.*

We know that David was well qualified as an author of the Psalms. The Lord spoke to and through David. The Spirit of God rested upon him and anointed his mind with the spirit of both exhortation and prophecy:

I Samuel 16:13 *Then Samuel took the horn of oil, and anointed him in the midst of his brethren: and the Spirit of the LORD came upon David from that day forward. So Samuel rose up, and went to Ramah.*

II Samuel 23:1-2...*the man who was raised up on high, the anointed of the God of Jacob, and the sweet psalmist of Israel, said, The Spirit of the Lord spake by me, and his word was in my tongue.*

Psalm 89:19-20 *Then thou spakest in vision to thy holy one, and saidist, I have laid help upon one that is mighty; I have exalted one* *chosen out of the people. I have found David my servant; with my holy oil I have anointed him.*

Acts 1:16 *Men and brethren, this scripture must needs have been fulfilled, which the Holy Ghost by the mouth of David spake before concerning Judas, which was guide to them that took Jesus.*

Acts 2:29-30 *Men and brethren, let me freely speak unto you of the patriarch David, ...being a prophet, and knowing that God had sworn an oath to him....*

Acts 13:2 *...he raised up unto them David to be their king; to whom also he gave testimony, and said, I have found David the son of Jesse, a man after mine own heart, which shall fulfill all my will.*

God blessed him with an anointed skill to play and compose music:

I Samuel 16:18 *Then answered one of the servants, and said, Behold, I have seen a son of Jesse the Bethlehemite, that is cunning in playing, and a mighty valiant man, and a man of war, and prudent in matters, and a comely person, and the LORD is with him.*

The Sons of Korah

A number of the **Psalms**[79] were written for the sons of Korah. It has been debated whether these were written by the family of Korah, by David, or even by Asaph. The phrase translated "for the sons of Korah" can also be translated "of the sons of Korah." The sons of Korah are mentioned in I Chronicles 9:19 as workers in the Levitical priesthood: *And Shallum the son of Kore, the son of Ebiasaph, the son of Korah, and his brethren, of the house of his father, the Korahites, were over the work of the service, keepers of the gates of the tabernacle: and their fathers, being over the host of the Lord, were keepers of the entry.*

---

[79] It is interesting to note that other than the single Psalms written by Moses and Solomon, every Psalm not written by David was written by those of the Levitical lineage, with the possible exception of Ethan.

The sons of Korah were keepers of the entry to the tabernacle and thus the phrase in Psalm 84:10 is especially meaningful: *For a day in thy courts is better than a thousand. I had rather be a doorkeeper in the house of my God, than to dwell in the tents of wickedness.*

The Psalms written for or by the sons of Korah were Psalms 42, 44-49, 84, 85, 87, and 88 (written by Heman for the sons of Korah).

Asaph

Asaph was the writer of a number of the **Psalms**, 12 of which bear his name**.** These are Psalms 50 and 73-83. He is named along with David as one of the major psalm writers:

> **II Chronicles 29:30** *Moreover Hezekiah the king and the princes commanded the Levites to sing praise unto the LORD with the words of David, and of Asaph the seer. And they sang praises with gladness, and they bowed their heads and worshipped.*

He was one of the Levites chosen to go before the Ark of the Covenant on its return to Jerusalem from the house of Obed-edom.

> **I Chronicles 15:17, 19** *So the Levites appointed Heman the son of Joel; and of his brethren, Asaph the son of Berechiah....*

After its return to Jerusalem, Asaph was appointed chief over those who ministered before the Ark of the Lord:

> **I Chronicles 16:4-5** *And he appointed certain of the Levites to minister before the ark of the Lord, and to record and to thank and praise the Lord God of Israel: Asaph the chief, and next to him Zechariah, Jeiel, and Shemiramoth, and Jehiel, and Mattithiah, and Eliab, and Benaiah, and Obed-edom: and Jeiel with psalteries and with harps; but Asaph made a sound with cymbals;*

Asaph's appointment to these important positions demonstrates that he must have been a highly skilled singer and musician. He was also known as a seer. The Hebrew word *chozeh*, translated "seer", has the meaning of one who sees a vision or is a prophet. Thus, we see that Asaph, just as David, prophesied through the poetry and music of his psalms.

The musical gift of God bestowed upon Asaph clearly passed down to his descendants, as the children of Asaph are mentioned in their service to the tabernacle and the temple after it.[80]

Heman

Heman is the writer of **Psalm 88**. Some believe he was the grandson of Samuel the prophet.[81] Though Heman's father was corrupt and did not follow in the ways of Samuel,[82] it appears that Samuel's grandson was faithful to the Lord. Heman is mentioned as one of the singers, along with Asaph, that David set over the service of song in the house of the Lord:

> **I Chronicles 6:31-39** *And these are they whom David set over the service of song in the house of the Lord, after the ark had rest....Heman, a singer, the son of Joel,...And his brother[83] Asaph, who stood on his right hand, even Asaph the son of Berachiah,....*
>
> **I Chronicles 15:16-17** *And David spake to the chief of the Levites to appoint their brethren to be the singers with instruments of music, psalteries and harps and cymbals, sounding, by lifting up the voice with joy. So the Levites appointed Heman the son of Joel; and of his brethren, Asaph the son of Berechiah;....*

---

[80] See I Chronicles 25, II Chronicles 20:14, 35:15, Ezra 3:10, and Nehemiah 11:17, 22 and 12:35.

[81] See I Chronicles 6:33, where Samuel's name is spelled with the Hebrew spelling Shemuel.

[82] I Samuel 8:2-3.

[83] The term "brother" here is not used in the literal sense but is meant as one who is a fellow laborer or of the same kindred.

Like David and Asaph, Heman appears to have had a prophetic calling:

> **I Chronicles 25:5** *...Heman the king's seer in the words of God, to lift up the horn....*[84]

Just as with the family line of Asaph, Heman's progeny was blessed with their father's musical talent.

> **I Chronicles 25:5-6***...And God gave to Heman fourteen sons and three daughters. All these were under the hands of their father for song in the house of the Lord, with cymbals, psalteries, and harps, for the service of the house of God, according to the king's order to Asaph, Jeduthun, and Heman.*

Ethan

Ethan is named as the writer of **Psalm 89**. We know very little about Ethan other than that he may have been a descendant of the tribe of Judah. He must have been a man of great wisdom as he is compared, with Heman, as one whom Solomon had outshone in understanding.

> **I Kings 4:31** *For he* [Solomon] *was wiser than all men; than Ethan the Ezrahite, and Heman, and Chalcol, and Darda, the sons of Mahol: and his fame was in all nations round about.*

It is possible that this is the same Ethan referred to in the company of Asaph and Heman as a singer in the service of the house of the Lord.[85]

---

[84] This is not intended to mean horn as an instrument of music, but is a Hebrew idiom meaning to raise him up or bless him. This follows into the next statement about his children, which would appear to be the blessing referred to.
[85] See I Chronicles 6:44 and 15:17.

Solomon

Solomon wrote **Psalm 127** (Psalm 72 was written by David for Solomon) and is also the author of the majority, if not all, of the book of **Proverbs**, the books of **Ecclesiastes,** and **Song of Solomon**. The writings of Solomon are generally proverbial in nature. He wrote for the purpose of imparting wisdom, and he was certainly well qualified to do so. Not long after he became king of Israel, God appeared to Solomon:

> **I Kings 3:5-12** *In Gibeon the LORD appeared to Solomon in a dream by night: and God said, Ask what I shall give thee. And Solomon said, Thou hast shewed unto thy servant David my father great mercy, according as he walked before thee in truth, and in righteousness, and in uprightness of heart with thee; and thou hast kept for him this great kindness, that thou hast given him a son to sit on his throne, as it is this day. And now, O LORD my God, thou hast made thy servant king instead of David my father: and I am but a little child: I know not how to go out or come in. And thy servant is in the midst of thy people which thou hast chosen, a great people, that cannot be numbered nor counted for multitude. Give therefore thy servant an understanding heart to judge thy people, that I may discern between good and bad: for who is able to judge this thy so great a people? And the speech pleased the Lord, that Solomon had asked this thing. And God said unto him, Because thou hast asked this thing, and hast not asked for thyself long life; neither hast asked riches for thyself, nor hast asked the life of thine enemies; but hast asked for thyself understanding to discern judgment; Behold, I have done according to thy words: lo, I have given thee a wise and an understanding heart; so that there was none like thee before thee, neither after thee shall any arise like unto thee.*

Solomon demonstrated his first and greatest act of wisdom by the manner of request he made of God. God blessed him with wisdom and understanding beyond any man before or after him. Solomon's downfall was that he did not learn to apply wisdom in his own life and thus lived a life of sin and idolatry. Though his proverbs and writings are some of the wisest statements known to man, it is a sad fact that he did not practice what he preached.

Agur and Lemuel

Agur and Lemuel are named as the writers of **Proverbs 30** and **31** respectively. Rabbinic tradition says that these are pseudonyms used by Solomon and not separate writers.[86] Other than the words recorded in their writing, we have no other background on either writer.

---

[86] Louis Ginzberg, *The Legends of the Jews*, Volume 6, 1946, p. 277.

THE PROPHETICAL WRITERS

<u>Isaiah</u>

From the very beginning and throughout his prophecies, Isaiah states his authorship.

Isaiah 1:1 *The vision of Isaiah the son of Amoz, which he saw concerning Judah and Jerusalem in the days of Uzziah, Jotham, Ahaz, and Hezekiah, kings of Judah.*

Isaiah 2:1 *The word that Isaiah the son of Amoz saw concerning Judah and Jerusalem.*

Isaiah 13:1 *The burden[87] of Babylon, which Isaiah the son of Amoz did see.*

Isaiah 20:2 *At the same time spake the Lord by Isaiah the son of Amoz,....*

The first recorded call of Isaiah to the office of a prophet came during the year of the death of King Uzziah.

Isaiah 6:1-10 *In the year that king Uzziah died I saw also the Lord sitting upon a throne, high and lifted up, and his train filled the temple. Above it stood the seraphims: each one had six wings; with twain he covered his face, and with twain he covered his feet, and with twain he did fly. And one cried unto another, and said, Holy, holy, holy, is the LORD of hosts: the whole earth is full of his glory. And the posts of the door moved at the voice of him that cried, and the house was filled with smoke. Then said I, Woe is me! for I am undone; because I am a man of unclean lips, and I dwell in the midst of a people of unclean lips: for mine eyes have seen the King,*

---

[87] Isaiah often uses the term "burden" in describing the message of judgment or warning that he brings. The Hebrew word translated "burden", ***massa***, is beautifully demonstrative of Isaiah's view of the message. This word means burden in the sense of a load that must be carried. How Isaiah must have felt the great weight of the burden of his anointing.

the LORD of hosts. Then flew one of the seraphims unto me, having a live coal in his hand, which he had taken with the tongs from off the altar: And he laid it upon my mouth, and said, Lo, this hath touched thy lips; and thine iniquity is taken away, and thy sin purged. Also I heard the voice of the Lord, saying, Whom shall I send, and who will go for us? Then said I, Here am I; send me. And he said, Go, and tell this people, Hear ye indeed, but understand not; and see ye indeed, but perceive not. Make the heart of this people fat, and make their ears heavy, and shut their eyes; lest they see with their eyes, and hear with their ears, and understand with their heart, and convert, and be healed.

This was probably not the original call of Isaiah. First, Isaiah probably ministered during a period of Uzziah's reign before the year of his death in which he saw the vision of God in the temple. Second, the book of Isaiah is arranged relatively chronologically, so this event most likely happened during his later ministry. It is clear that the Lord wanted Isaiah to record the prophecy for future generations. He is told to take a roll (tablet) and write out the words of the prophecy God revealed to him.

Isaiah 8:1 *Moreover, the Lord said unto me, Take thee a great roll*[88] ["roll" here is the] *and write in it with a man's pen....*
Isaiah 30:8 *Now go, write it before them in a table,*[89] *and note it in a book,*[90] *that it may be for the time to come for ever and ever....*

Isaiah did not speak as one using his own words or thoughts; approximately thirty-five times throughout his prophecies he states

---

[88] "Roll" is the Hebrew word **gillayon**, meaning a "writing tablet".
[89] "Table" is the Hebrew word **luach**, meaning a "tablet". This is the same word used in Exodus and Deuteronomy to describe the two tables of the law given to Moses.
[90] "Book" is the Hebrew word **sepher**, usually translated "book" or "scroll", the exact meaning is "that which is written".

"Thus saith the Lord." It was clear that he was an instrument through which God revealed His will.

Isaiah was one of the greatest of the Old Testament prophets. There are more prophesies of the Messiah in his writings than any other prophet. Some Jewish traditions believe that he was the leader of the school of prophets (the sons of the prophets) in the tradition of Elijah and Elisha who directly preceded him; Elisha died about 808 B.C., 24 years before Isaiah's prophetic dispensation.

The most complete of the ancient manuscripts discovered at Qumran was the scroll of Isaiah, which has been placed on display in the Shrine of the Book in Jerusalem.

Jeremiah

Jeremiah is believed by Jewish tradition to have written **I and II Kings** as well as the prophecies recorded in the books of **Jeremiah** and **Lamentations**.

> **Jeremiah 1:1-2** *The words of Jeremiah the son of Hilkiah, of the priests that were in Anathoth in the land of Benjamin: To whom the word of the LORD came in the days of Josiah the son of Amon king of Judah, in the thirteenth year of his reign.*
>
> **Jeremiah 36:2** *Take thee a roll of a book, and write therein all the words that I have spoken unto thee against Israel, and against Judah, and against all the nations, from the day I spake unto thee, from the days of Josiah, even unto this day.*

The Lord put His own words in Jeremiah's mouth. The inspiration of the Spirit was on Jeremiah in his prophecy, but the precise words God wished to be spoken by His prophet would come forth through the anointing of the Spirit.

> **Jeremiah 20:9** *Then I said, I will not make mention of him, nor speak any more in his name. But his word was in mine heart as a*

burning fire shut up in my bones, and I was weary with forbearing, and I could not stay.

The Lord chose Jeremiah for a prophetic ministry at a young age. Most scholars believe he was in his late teens to early twenties when the Lord first spoke to him:

Jeremiah 1:4-10 *Then the word of the LORD came unto me, saying, Before I formed thee in the belly I knew thee; and before thou camest forth out of the womb I sanctified thee, and I ordained thee a prophet unto the nations. Then said I, Ah, Lord GOD! behold, I cannot speak: for I am a child. But the LORD said unto me, Say not, I am a child: for thou shalt go to all that I shall send thee, and whatsoever I command thee thou shalt speak. Be not afraid of their faces: for I am with thee to deliver thee, saith the LORD. Then the LORD put forth his hand, and touched my mouth. And the LORD said unto me, Behold, I have put my words in thy mouth. See, I have this day set thee over the nations and over the kingdoms, to root out, and to pull down, and to destroy, and to throw down, to build, and to plant.*

As can be seen in the above passage, the Lord put His words into the mouth of Jeremiah. As God called Jeremiah He promised him that if he would speak His word, he would have divine protection:

Jeremiah 1:17-19 *Thou therefore gird up thy loins, and arise, and speak unto them all that I command thee: be not dismayed at their faces, lest I confound thee before them. For, behold, I have made thee this day a defenced city, and an iron pillar, and brasen walls against the whole land, against the kings of Judah, against the princes thereof, against the priests thereof, and against the people of the land. And they shall fight against thee; but they shall not prevail against thee; for I am with thee, saith the LORD, to deliver thee.*

Ezekiel

Ezekiel was both a prophet and a priest of the Levitical line, in the same tradition as Jeremiah and Zechariah. It was in Babylon that Ezekiel received his prophetic call.

Ezekiel 1:1-3 *Now it came to pass in the thirtieth year, in the fourth month, in the fifth day of the month, as I was among the captives by the river of Chebar, that the heavens were opened, and I saw visions of God. In the fifth day of the month, which was the fifth year of king Jehoiachin's captivity, The word of the LORD came expressly unto Ezekiel the priest, the son of Buzi, in the land of the Chaldeans by the river Chebar; and the hand of the LORD was there upon him.*

Isaiah, Jeremiah, and Ezekiel, who wrote more than any other of the prophets, were all described as having the word of the Lord put in their mouths. In Ezekiel's case he was commanded to eat the words:

Ezekiel 2:8–3:4 *But thou, son of man, hear what I say unto thee; Be not thou rebellious like that rebellious house: open thy mouth, and eat that I give thee. And when I looked, behold, an hand was sent unto me; and, lo, a roll of a book was therein; And he spread it before me; and it was written within and without: and there was written therein lamentations, and mourning, and woe. Moreover he said unto me, Son of man, eat that thou findest; eat this roll, and go speak unto the house of Israel. So I opened my mouth, and he caused me to eat that roll. And he said unto me, Son of man, cause thy belly to eat, and fill thy bowels with this roll that I give thee. Then did I eat it; and it was in my mouth as honey for sweetness. And he said unto me, Son of man, go, get thee unto the house of Israel, and speak with my words unto them.*

Daniel

Daniel was the writer of the book bearing his name, written during his captivity in Babylon. He was a man of great intelligence and learning:

Daniel 1:3-4 *And the king spake unto Ashpenaz the master of his eunuchs, that he should bring certain of the children of Israel, and of the king's seed, and of the princes; Children in whom was no blemish, but well favoured, and skilful in all wisdom, and cunning in knowledge, and understanding science, and such as had an ability in them to stand in the king's palace, and whom they might teach the learning and the tongue of the Chaldeans.*

Daniel had the word of God revealed to him through a number of different manifestations. He had the word of God revealed to him directly by the angel Gabriel as well as in dreams and visions.

Daniel 8:1-2, 15-19 *In the third year of the reign of king Belshazzar a vision appeared unto me, even unto me Daniel, after that which appeared unto me at the first. And I saw in a vision;...And it came to pass, when I, even I Daniel, had seen the vision, and sought for the meaning, then, behold, there stood before me as the appearance of a man. And I heard a man's voice between the banks of Ulai, which called, and said, Gabriel, make this man to understand the vision. So he came near where I stood: and when he came, I was afraid, and fell upon my face: but he said unto me, Understand, O son of man: for at the time of the end shall be the vision. Now as he was speaking with me, I was in a deep sleep on my face toward the ground: but he touched me, and set me upright. And he said, Behold, I will make thee know what shall be in the last end of the indignation:....*

Daniel 9:20-23 *...whiles I was speaking in prayer, even the man Gabriel, whom I had seen in the vision at the beginning, being caused to fly swiftly, touched me about the time of the evening oblation. And he informed me, and talked with me, and said, O Daniel, I am now come forth to give thee skill and understanding.*

At the beginning of thy supplications the commandment came forth, and I am come to show thee; for thou art greatly beloved: therefore understand the matter, and consider the vision.

Daniel also had the word of God revealed to him through his interpretation of other's dreams. It is made clear through this gift of interpretation that Daniel had, as Joseph before him, a capacity to understand the communication of God through prophetic insight.

Daniel 1:17 *As for these four children, God gave them knowledge and skill in all learning and wisdom: and Daniel had understanding in all visions and dreams.*

Daniel 5:11-12 *There is a man in thy kingdom, in whom is the spirit of the holy gods; and in the days of thy father light and understanding and wisdom, like the wisdom of the gods, was found in him; whom the king Nebuchadnezzar thy father, the king, I say, thy father, made master of the magicians, astrologers, Chaldeans, and soothsayers; Forasmuch as an excellent spirit, and knowledge, and understanding, interpreting of dreams, and shewing of hard sentences, and dissolving of doubts, were found in the same Daniel, whom the king named Belteshazzar: now let Daniel be called, and he will shew the interpretation.*

Hosea

Hosea 1:1 *The word of the LORD that came unto Hosea, the son of Beeri, in the days of Uzziah, Jotham, Ahaz, and Hezekiah, kings of Judah, and in the days of Jeroboam the son of Joash, king of Israel.*

Hosea 3:1 *Then said the LORD unto me, Go yet, love a woman beloved of her friend, yet an adulteress, according to the love of the LORD toward the children of Israel, who look to other gods, and love flagons of wine.*

Little is known of Hosea, though some have theorized that he could have been a baker, based on the metaphor used in Hosea 7:4, though this is probably not the case. Hosea gave his father's name as Beeri, though we have no background on his family other than that he was commanded of the Lord to marry a harlot named Gomer, symbolically representing God's marriage to Israel. With this wife he had three children, Jezreel, Lo-ruhamah, and Lo-ammi.

Joel

Joel 1:1 *The word of the Lord that came to Joel the son of Pethuel.*

Nothing is known of Joel other than his father's name mentioned above. It is likely that he lived in or around Jerusalem based on his focus and references to the area.

Amos

Amos 1:1 *The words of Amos, who was among the herdmen of Tekoa, which he saw concerning Israel in the days of Uzziah king of Judah, and in the days of Jeroboam the son of Joash king of Israel, two years before the earthquake.*

It is theorized that Amos worked as both a shepherd and a dresser of trees when he was called by God.
> **Amos 1:1** *The words of Amos, who was among the herdmen of Tekoa....*
> **Amos 7:14-15** *Then answered Amos, and said to Amaziah, I was no prophet, neither was I a prophet's son; but I was an herdman, and a gatherer of sycomore fruit: And the Lord took me as I followed the flock, and the Lord said unto me, Go, prophesy unto my people Israel.*

Amos clearly believed that God was communicating directly with him, stating multiple times, *Thus saith the Lord* and *Thus hath the Lord God shown unto me.*

<u>Obadiah</u>

Obadiah 1:1 *The vision of Obadiah. Thus saith the Lord GOD concerning Edom; We have heard a rumour from the LORD, and an ambassador is sent among the heathen, Arise ye, and let us rise up against her in battle.*

Nothing is known of Obadiah other than his prophecies.

<u>Jonah</u>

Jonah 1:1 *Now the word of the Lord came unto Jonah the son of Ammitai, saying,*
Jonah 3:1 *And the word of the Lord came unto Jonah the second time, saying,*

Nothing is known of Jonah outside of Jewish legend. These legends claim that he was the son of the widow of Zarephath, and was the youth that Elisha sent to anoint Jehu as king over Israel. Though this is an interesting theory, most historians strongly disagree.

<u>Micah</u>

Micah 1:1 *The word of the Lord that came to Micah...which he saw....*

Nothing is known of Micah other than the fact that he was believed to have been brought up among the poorer class of country folk from the area of Moresheth, as this is where his prophesying primarily took place.

Nahum

Nahum 1:1 *The burden of Nineveh. The book of the vision of Nahum the Elkoshite.*

Nothing is known of Nahum outside of his prophecies. Though he is called an Elkoshite, the location of Elkosh has not yet been determined.

Habakkuk

Habakkuk 1:1 *The burden which Habakkuk the prophet did see.*

As other prophets before him, Habakkuk was instructed to record the revelation of God for future generations:
> **Habakkuk 2:2** *And the Lord answered me, and said, Write the vision, and make it plain upon tables, that he may run that readeth it.*

Little is known of Habakkuk though Jewish legend claims he was the son of the Shunammite woman in II Kings:
> **II Kings 4:16-17** *And he said, About this season, according to the time of life, thou shalt embrace a son. And she said, Nay, my lord, thou man of God, do not lie unto thine handmaid. And the woman conceived, and bare a son at that season that Elisha had said unto her, according to the time of life.*

Historians tend to disagree with this belief as Habakkuk was probably born long after this time. Other traditions state that Habakkuk was a Levitical priest. Though the story is likely to be fanciful, the apocryphal book of Bel and the Dragon describes Habakkuk being taken to Babylon by an angel to feed Daniel while he was in the lion's den.

Zephaniah

Zephaniah 1:1 *The word of the LORD which came unto Zephaniah the son of Cushi, the son of Gedaliah, the son of Amariah, the son of Hizkiah, in the days of Josiah the son of Amon, king of Judah.*

Nothing is known of Zephaniah outside of his prophecies.

Haggai

Haggai 1:1-3 *In the second year of Darius the king, in the sixth month, in the first day of the month, came the word of the LORD by Haggai the prophet unto Zerubbabel the son of Shealtiel, governor of Judah, and to Joshua the son of Josedech, the high priest, saying, Thus speaketh the LORD of hosts, saying, This people say, The time is not come, the time that the LORD'S house should be built. Then came the word of the LORD by Haggai the prophet, saying,*
Haggai 1:13 *Then spake Haggai the LORD'S messenger in the LORD'S message unto the people, saying, I am with you, saith the LORD.*

Nothing is known of Haggai outside of his prophecies.

Zechariah

Zechariah 1:1 *In the eighth month, in the second year of Darius, came the word of the LORD unto Zechariah, the son of Berechiah, the son of Iddo the prophet, saying,*

Zechariah, like Daniel before him, had the word of God revealed to him through angelic messengers.
Zechariah 1:7-9 *Upon the four and twentieth day of the eleventh month, which is the month Sebat, in the second year of Darius, came the word of the LORD unto Zechariah, the son of Berechiah,*

the son of Iddo the prophet, saying, I saw by night, and behold a man riding upon a red horse, and he stood among the myrtle trees that were in the bottom; and behind him were there red horses, speckled, and white. Then said I, O my lord, what are these? And the angel that talked with me said unto me, I will shew thee what these be.

Throughout the book of Zechariah, the prophet converses with angels who reveal the word and vision to him.

Zechariah was the grandson of Iddo,[91] the head of one of the priestly families that returned from Babylon. This infers that Zechariah was likely a priest himself. Zechariah would have been a contemporary of Haggai, beginning his prophetic ministry within a year of Haggai's final prophecy.

Malachi

Malachi 1:1 *The burden of the word of the Lord to Israel by Malachi.*

Nothing is known of Malachi outside of his prophecies. Some ancient Hebrew traditions believed that Malachi was actually an angel as the name Malachi can mean "my angel" or "my messenger" in Hebrew.

---

[91] Zechariah is called the son of Iddo in Ezra 5:1 and 6:14. This may have been due to his father passing away, which would have placed him in the succession of carrying on his grandfather's line and calling.

NEW TESTAMENT WRITERS

In contrast to the Old Testament, which was written by men of various backgrounds over the space of approximately 4,000 years, the New Testament writers were all either students of Jesus or of his disciples and wrote their testimonies within a space of about 70 years. Many generations came and went as the Old Testament was being compiled, whereas the New Testament took form within one generation.

The writers of the New Testament had a distinct advantage over the Old Testament writers. They were given a deeper insight and understanding of the scriptures both through their interaction with Jesus and through the gift of the Holy Spirit. It was given to them to understand the hidden things of the Bible, thus the phrase "the New is in the Old concealed and the Old is in the New revealed."

Jesus himself opened up and made known the scriptures to these men, both through his teaching and through the Holy Spirit.
   Matthew 11:25-27 *At that time Jesus answered and said, I thank thee, O Father, Lord of heaven and earth, because thou hast hid these things from the wise and prudent, and hast revealed them unto babes.[92] Even so, Father: for so it seemed good in thy sight. All things are delivered unto me of my Father: and no man knoweth the Son, but the Father; neither knoweth any man the Father, save the Son, and he to whomsoever the Son will reveal him.*

Before the gift of the Holy Spirit, the disciples had the living Word of God to open their eyes and ears to the truth. Within his parables and instruction were the truths that he revealed to his disciples.
   Matthew 13:10-17 (see also Mark 4:11 and Luke 8:10) *And the disciples came, and said unto him, Why speakest thou unto them in*

---

[92] These men were both babes in comparison of intellect with the wise of this world and babes through their new birth in the Spirit.

parables? He answered and said unto them, Because it is given unto you to know the mysteries of the kingdom of heaven, but to them it is not given. For whosoever hath, to him shall be given, and he shall have more abundance: but whosoever hath not, from him shall be taken away even that he hath. Therefore speak I to them in parables: because they seeing see not; and hearing they hear not, neither do they understand. And in them is fulfilled the prophecy of Esaias, which saith, By hearing ye shall hear, and shall not understand; and seeing ye shall see, and shall not perceive: For this people's heart is waxed gross, and their ears are dull of hearing, and their eyes they have closed; lest at any time they should see with their eyes, and hear with their ears, and should understand with their heart, and should be converted, and I should heal them. But blessed are your eyes, for they see: and your ears, for they hear. For verily I say unto you, That many prophets and righteous men have desired to see those things which ye see, and have not seen them; and to hear those things which ye hear, and have not heard them.

Matthew 13:34-35 *All these things spake Jesus unto the multitude in parables; and without a parable spake he not unto them: That it might be fulfilled which was spoken by the prophet, saying, I will open my mouth in parables; I will utter things which have been kept secret from the foundation of the world.*

<u>Matthew</u>

The book of **Matthew** was written by the apostle who bears its name, Matthew, who was also called Levi. Throughout the book he authored he refers to himself as Matthew, whereas Mark and Luke, in their gospels, refer to him as Levi.[93]

Matthew was a customs officer, otherwise known as a publican or tax collector. Individuals who held these positions were some of the most despised persons in society. They were considered traitors by many of their Jewish brethren for collecting taxes for the Roman government that was then occupying Palestine. This type of occupation would have required that he would have been skilled in the form of shorthand used in that day, which would have enabled him to write down much of the details of Jesus' messages. Some of the longest and most complete messages of Jesus are found in the book of Matthew, and it may be that Matthew was able to write many of these down verbatim.

The early church fathers testified strongly to Matthew's authorship.
- Origen (*Ecclesiastical History* VI 14.5) – *...the first gospel was written by Matthew, who was once a tax collector, but who was afterwards an apostle of Jesus Christ, and it was prepared for the converts from Judaism, and published in the Hebrew tongue.*
- Irenaeus (*Against Heresies* III 1.1) – *Matthew also published a book of the gospel among the Hebrews, in their own dialect, while Peter and Paul were preaching the gospel in Rome and founding the church.*
- Eusebius (*Ecclesiastical History* III 24.5) – *Matthew, who preached earlier to the Hebrews, committed his gospel to writing in his native tongue, and so compensated by his writing for the loss of his presence.*

---

[93] Mark 2:14 and Luke 5:27.

<u>Mark</u>

The book of **Mark** was written by John Mark, the cousin of Barnabas.

> **Colossians 4:10** *Aristarchus my fellowprisoner saluteth you, and Marcus, sister's son[94] to Barnabas, (touching whom ye received commandments: if he come unto you, receive him;)*

Mark was a companion of Paul and Barnabas on their missionary travels.

> **Acts 12:25** *And Barnabas and Saul returned from Jerusalem, when they had fulfilled their ministry, and took with them John, whose surname was Mark.*
>
> **Acts 13:5** (first missionary journey) *And when they were at Salamis, they preached the word of God in the synagogues of the Jews: and they had also John to their minister.*

Mark later departed from the company to return to Jerusalem.

> **Acts 13:13** *Now when Paul and his company loosed from Paphos, they came to Perga in Pamphylia: and John departing from them returned to Jerusalem.*

Mark's departure clearly angered Paul. When he and Barnabas were choosing their companions for their second missionary journey, Paul did not want Mark included due to the fact he felt he had deserted them on their first missionary journey.

> **Acts 15:36-40** *And some days after Paul said unto Barnabas, Let us go again and visit our brethren in every city where we have preached the word of the Lord, and see how they do. And Barnabas determined to take with them John, whose surname was Mark. But Paul thought not good to take him with them, who departed from them from Pamphylia, and went not with them to the work. And the contention was so sharp between them, that they departed asunder one from the other: and so Barnabas took Mark, and sailed unto*

---

[94] The term "sister's son" actually means "cousin" in the Greek.

Cyprus; and Paul chose Silas, and departed, being recommended by the brethren unto the grace of God.

It is clear Paul and Mark reconciled at some point as Paul speaks favorably of him in his letters to the church at Colossi, Timothy, and Philemon.

Colossians 4:10...*and Marcus, sister's son to Barnabas, (touching whom ye received commandments: if he come unto you, receive him;)*

II Timothy 4:11...*Take Mark, and bring him with thee: for he is profitable to me for the ministry.*

Philemon 24 *Marcus, Aristarchus, Demas, Lucas, my fellowlabourers.*

It was Mark's mother's home that Peter came to after he was delivered from prison by the angel.

Acts 12:12...*he came to the house of Mary the mother of John, whose surname was Mark; where many were gathered together praying.*

Mark was a disciple of Peter, and church tradition states he was the writer of the gospel bearing his name, as dictated to him by Peter. He may have been Peter's scribe, responsible for writing down the recollections of Peter's time with Jesus and transcribing them into the Greek.

I Peter 5:13 *The church that is at Babylon, elected together with you, saluteth you; and so doth Marcus my son.*

Many of the later church fathers testified to Mark's authorship:
- Eusebius, quoting Papias (*Ecclesiastical History* III, 39) – *And John the presbyter also said this, Mark being the interpreter of Peter, whatsoever he recorded he wrote with great accuracy, ...in the order in which it was spoken or done by our Lord, but as before said, he was in company with Peter, who gave him such instruction as was necessary, but not to give a history of our Lord's discourse:*

wherefore Mark has not erred in any thing, by writing some things as he has recorded them; for he was carefully attentive to one thing, not to pass by any thing he had heard, or to state any thing falsely in these accounts.

- Irenaeus stated that after the departure of Peter and Paul...*Mark, the disciple and interpreter of Peter, also transmitted to us in writing what had been preached by Peter.*
- Tertullian (*Against Marcion* IV, 5) – [the gospel] *which Mark published may be affirmed to be Peter's, whose interpreter Mark was.*

Luke

Luke was considered to be the author of both the books of **Luke** and **Acts**. Both the early church tradition and that of the church fathers were virtually unanimous in naming him as writer of both books. It is certain that the writers of Luke and Acts were the same individual. Both books were addressed to Theophilus and contain the same literary structure and language.

Luke is mentioned only three times in the New Testament, and all of these by Paul.

Colossians 4:14 *Luke, the beloved physician...*
II Timothy 4:11 *Only Luke is with me....*
Philemon 24 *...Lucas, my fellowlabourers.*

Luke most certainly must have been a physician, and due to this was probably a man of sharp intellect and education. Hobart, in *The Medical Language of Luke*, found 400 terms that Luke used in his writings that were terms used by the Greek medical writers of his time.

Luke would have been a companion of Paul and may have seen much of the activity recorded in Acts firsthand. The term "we" is used throughout the book, inferring his presence, and he is the only viable companion of Paul who could have witnessed all these events.

John

There are many evidences to demonstrate that the apostle **John** was the author of the gospel that bears his name. The tradition and testimony of the Early Church testifies to his authorship and both Papias and Irenaeus firmly believed that the elder of Ephesus was the writer of this gospel and that this elder was John the apostle.

The internal evidences for his authorship are exceptionally strong. Throughout this gospel the writer calls himself "the disciple whom Jesus loved." The author of John never mentions himself by name in his gospel, but he certainly was an eyewitness of the events recorded therein. The gospel ends with Jesus' discussion with Peter and John and John's statement:

> **John 21:24** *This is the disciple which testifieth of these things, and wrote these things: and we know that his testimony is true.*

The writer was, along with Andrew, a disciple of John the Baptist before coming into contact with Jesus.

> **John 1:35-40** *Again the next day after John* [the Baptist] *stood, and two of his disciples; And looking upon Jesus as he walked, he saith, Behold the Lamb of God! And the two disciples heard him speak, and they followed Jesus. Then Jesus turned, and saw them following, and saith unto them, What seek ye? They said unto him, Rabbi, (which is to say, being interpreted, Master,) where dwellest thou? He saith unto them, Come and see. They came and saw where he dwelt, and abode with him that day: for it was about the tenth hour. One of the two which heard John speak, and followed him, was Andrew, Simon Peter's brother.*

This second disciple could not have been Peter as Andrew later found Peter and brought him to meet Jesus

> **John 1:41** *He first findeth his own brother Simon, and saith unto him, We have found the Messias, which is, being interpreted, the Christ. And he brought him to Jesus....*

After this initial contact, Jesus called them as disciples after the imprisonment of John the Baptist. Notice the first four disciples called in Matthew's gospel:

Matthew 4:18-22 *And Jesus, walking by the sea of Galilee, saw two brethren, Simon called Peter, and Andrew his brother, casting a net into the sea: for they were fishers. And he saith unto them, Follow me, and I will make you fishers of men. And they straightway left their nets, and followed him. And going on from thence, he saw two other brethren, James the son of Zebedee, and John his brother, in a ship with Zebedee their father, mending their nets; and he called them. And they immediately left the ship and their father, and followed him.*

Of these first four disciples, the only two that could have been the unnamed disciple in John 1:35-40 would have been John or his brother James; the most likely of the two to have been the author of the gospel was John as James was martyred around 44 A.D. and the book of John was believed to have been written about 85 A.D. These two accounts demonstrate that Jesus had contact with at least two of these first four disciples before his calling of them on the shores of Galilee.

John and his brother James were called "sons of thunder" by Jesus, which may have been a reference to their fiery zeal for the work of God.

Mark 3:17 *And James, the son of Zebedee, and John the brother of James; and he surnamed them Boanerges, which is, The sons of thunder:*

John was one of the three disciples along with Peter and James, who were closest to Jesus and a part of his "inner circle." These three were the only disciples who were allowed to be present with Jesus at the healing of Jairus' daughter, his transfiguration, and his private prayer in the garden of Gethsemane.

Mark 5:37 (Luke 8:51) *...And he suffered no man to follow him,* [to the house of Jairus] *save Peter, and James, and John the brother of James.*

Matthew 17:1 (Mark 9:2, Luke 9:28) *And after six days Jesus taketh Peter, James, and John his brother, and bringeth them up into an high mountain apart, And was transfigured before them: and his face did shine as the sun, and his raiment was white as the light.*

Matthew 26:36-37 *Then cometh Jesus with them unto a place called Gethsemane, and saith unto the disciples, Sit ye here, while I go and pray yonder. And he took with him Peter and the two sons of Zebedee, and began to be sorrowful and very heavy.*

John was one of the leaders of the Early Church and was involved in some of the most significant activity. It was John and Peter who healed the lame man at the gate of the Temple:

Acts 3:1-10 *Now Peter and John went up together into the temple at the hour of prayer, being the ninth hour. And a certain man lame from his mother's womb was carried, whom they laid daily at the gate of the temple which is called Beautiful, to ask alms of them that entered into the temple; Who seeing Peter and John about to go into the temple asked an alms. And Peter, fastening his eyes upon him with John, said, Look on us. And he gave heed unto them, expecting to receive something of them. Then Peter said, Silver and gold have I none; but such as I have give I thee: In the name of Jesus Christ of Nazareth rise up and walk. And he took him by the right hand, and lifted him up: and immediately his feet and ankle bones received strength. And he leaping up stood, and walked, and entered with them into the temple, walking, and leaping, and praising God. And all the people saw him walking and praising God: And they knew that it was he which sat for alms at the Beautiful gate of the temple: and they were filled with wonder and amazement at that which had happened unto him.*

John was arrested and tried with Peter for healing the lame man and for preaching about Jesus:

Acts 4:1-22 *And as they spake unto the people, the priests, and the captain of the temple, and the Sadducees, came upon them, Being grieved that they taught the people, and preached through Jesus the resurrection from the dead. And they laid hands on them, and put them in hold unto the next day: for it was now eventide. Howbeit many of them which heard the word believed; and the number of the men was about five thousand. And it came to pass on the morrow, that their rulers, and elders, and scribes, And Annas the high priest, and Caiaphas, and John, and Alexander, and as many as were of the kindred of the high priest, were gathered together at Jerusalem. And when they had set them in the midst, they asked, By what power, or by what name, have ye done this? Then Peter, filled with the Holy Ghost, said unto them, Ye rulers of the people, and elders of Israel, If we this day be examined of the good deed done to the impotent man, by what means he is made whole; Be it known unto you all, and to all the people of Israel, that by the name of Jesus Christ of Nazareth, whom ye crucified, whom God raised from the dead, even by him doth this man stand here before you whole. This is the stone which was set at nought of you builders, which is become the head of the corner. Neither is there salvation in any other: for there is none other name under heaven given among men, whereby we must be saved. Now when they saw the boldness of Peter and John, and perceived that they were unlearned and ignorant men, they marvelled; and they took knowledge of them, that they had been with Jesus. And beholding the man which was healed standing with them, they could say nothing against it. But when they had commanded them to go aside out of the council, they conferred among themselves, Saying, What shall we do to these men? for that indeed a notable miracle hath been done by them is manifest to all them that dwell in Jerusalem; and we cannot deny it. But that it spread no further among the people, let us straitly threaten them, that they speak henceforth to no man in this* *name. And they called them, and commanded them not to speak at all nor teach in the name of Jesus. But Peter and John answered and said unto them, Whether it be right in the sight of God to hearken unto you more than unto God, judge ye. For we cannot but speak the things which we have seen and heard. So when they had further threatened them, they let them go, finding nothing how they might punish them, because of the people: for all men glorified God for that which was done. For the man was above forty years old, on whom this miracle of healing was shewed.*

John was sent with Peter to Samaria to aid in the Samaritans' reception of the Holy Spirit:

Acts 8:14-17 *Now when the apostles which were at Jerusalem heard that Samaria had received the word of God, they sent unto them Peter and John: Who, when they were come down, prayed for them, that they might receive the Holy Ghost: (For as yet he was fallen upon none of them: only they were baptized in the name of the Lord Jesus.) Then laid they their hands on them, and they received the Holy Ghost.*

John was mentioned by Paul, along with Peter and James, as pillars of the Church:

Galatians 2:9 *And when James, Cephas, and John, who seemed to be pillars, perceived the grace that was given unto me, they gave to me and Barnabas the right hands of fellowship; that we should go unto the heathen, and they unto the circumcision.*

John is also credited with the writing of the three epistles that bear his name, **I, II, and III John,** and the book of **Revelation**. There are a number of internal evidences that demonstrate John's authorship. One of the strongest validations is the vocabulary that is used exclusively in John's writing: terms such as *The Word, the Lamb of God,* the term *overcome* in relationship to sin, and others. II and III John both begin as letters from "the elder," which has been assumed to be the apostle

John. This term would have been fitting for John as at the time of the writing of these books, he would have been much older and almost certainly the only apostle remaining alive.

The book of Revelation is clearly stated as belonging to the writings of John. It contains much of the same terminology used in his other writings. The book is claimed to have been written by John, and as there was no other significant member of the Early Church named John, this most certainly would have meant the apostle.

Revelation 1:1,4,9 *The Revelation of Jesus Christ, which God gave unto him, to shew unto his servants things which must shortly come to pass; and he sent and signified it by his angel unto his servant John,...John to the seven churches which are in Asia:...I John, who am also your brother, and companion in tribulation, and in the kingdom and patience of Jesus Christ, was in the isle that is called Patmos, for the word of God, and for the testimony of Jesus Christ.*

Revelation 21:2 *And I John saw the holy city, new Jerusalem, coming down from God out of heaven, prepared as a bride adorned for her husband.*

Revelation 22:8 *And I John saw these things, and heard them. And when I had heard and seen, I fell down to worship before the feet of the angel which shewed me these things.*

Paul

The apostle Paul was the writer of more New Testament books than any other writer, being responsible for **Romans**, **I and II Corinthians**, **Galatians**, **Ephesians**, **Philippians**, **Colossians**, **I and II Thessalonians**, **I and II Timothy**, **Titus**, and **Philemon**. Tradition also considers him the author of the book of **Hebrews**.

There have been a number of different opinions regarding the authorship of Hebrews. Most traditions claim Paul as author, but some have theorized otherwise. This is usually based on the fact that the literary style of Hebrews seems to be different from Paul's other writings. Tertullian claimed that Barnabas was the writer. Martin Luther believed it was most likely Apollos. Other possible authors presented as candidates have been Silas, Aquila and Priscilla, and Clement of Rome.

Paul was the apostle to the Gentiles, and it is primarily to the Gentiles that he writes.

> **Romans 11:13** *For I speak to you Gentiles, inasmuch as I am the apostle of the Gentiles, I magnify mine office:*

Paul was called by Jesus to the office of an apostle after the resurrection. He had not been one of Jesus' disciples, nor was he a witness to the things Jesus' inner circle had experienced. Paul himself realized that he was one who had been brought into his leadership position in the Church much later than the other apostles and those who had received the baptism of the Spirit at the first.

> **I Corinthians 15:8-9** *And last of all he was seen of me also, as of one born out of due time. For I am the least of the apostles, that am not meet to be called an apostle, because I persecuted the church of God.*

Paul was probably from a well-to-do family. Paul was both a Jew and a Roman citizen, meaning that his father likely had purchased Roman citizenship. Paul did not purchase this citizenship himself as he states clearly that he was free born.

> **Acts 22:25-29** *And as they bound him with thongs, Paul said unto the centurion that stood by, Is it lawful for you to scourge a man that is a Roman, and uncondemned? When the centurion heard that, he went and told the chief captain, saying, Take heed what thou doest: for this man is a Roman. Then the chief captain came, and said unto him, Tell me, art thou a Roman? He said, Yea. And the chief captain answered, With a great sum obtained I this freedom. And Paul said, But I was free born. Then straightway they departed from him which should have examined him: and the chief captain also was afraid, after he knew that he was a Roman, and because he had bound him.*

One other factor that demonstrates the likelihood of Paul being from a wealthy family is his educational upbringing. He was brought up under the tutelage of Gamaliel I, considered to be one of the greatest rabbinical minds of the 1st century. Paul's exceptional intelligence and natural gift for the study of the scriptures may have also contributed to his becoming a student of Gamaliel.

> **Acts 22:3** *I am verily a man which am a Jew, born in Tarsus, a city in Cilicia, yet brought up in this city at the feet of Gamaliel, and taught according to the perfect manner of the law of the fathers, and was zealous toward God, as ye all are this day.*

Before his meeting with his Savior on the Damascus road, Paul was deeply committed to the Hebrew religion. He was so zealous for the faith of his fathers that he persecuted the Christians whom he felt were defiling it.

> **Acts 7:57-58, 8:1-3** *Then they cried out with a loud voice, and stopped their ears, and ran upon him with one accord, And cast him out of the city, and stoned him: and the witnesses laid down their*

clothes at a young man's feet, whose name was Saul....And Saul was consenting unto his death. And at that time there was a great persecution against the church which was at Jerusalem;...As for Saul, he made havock of the church, entering into every house, and haling men and women committed them to prison.

Acts 9:1-2 (see also verses 13 and 21) *And Saul, yet breathing out threatenings and slaughter against the disciples of the Lord, went unto the high priest, And desired of him letters to Damascus to the synagogues, that if he found any of this way, whether they were men or women, he might bring them bound to Jerusalem.*

Acts 22:4 *And I persecuted this way unto the death, binding and delivering into prisons both men and women.*

Acts 26:10-11 *Which thing I also did in Jerusalem: and many of the saints did I shut up in prison, having received authority from the chief priests; and when they were put to death, I gave my voice against them. And I punished them oft in every synagogue, and compelled them to blaspheme; and being exceedingly mad against them, I persecuted them even unto strange cities.*

I Corinthians 15:9 *For I am the least of the apostles, that am not meet to be called an apostle, because I persecuted the church of God.*

Galatians 1:13-14 *For ye have heard of my conversation in time past in the Jews' religion, how that beyond measure I persecuted the church of God, and wasted it: And profited in the Jews' religion above many my equals in mine own nation, being more exceedingly zealous of the traditions of my fathers.*

Philippians 3:5-6 *Circumcised the eighth day, of the stock of Israel, of the tribe of Benjamin, an Hebrew of the Hebrews; as touching the law, a Pharisee; Concerning zeal, persecuting the church; touching the righteousness which is in the law, blameless.*

I Timothy 1:12-13 *And I thank Christ Jesus our Lord, who hath enabled me, for that he counted me faithful, putting me into the ministry; Who was before a blasphemer, and a persecutor, and* *injurious: but I obtained mercy, because I did it ignorantly in unbelief.*

Paul was clearly a man of great zeal and passion for his belief; even to the extreme of persecuting those who he felt were causing it harm. God would take this intensity and desire and shape it to His will, making Paul one of the greatest evangelists the world has ever known, pleading for the very beliefs he had persecuted so fiercely.

There were a number of men who aided Paul in his work and who were co-writers and senders of the letters to the churches. Sosthenes, Timothy, and Silas all are mentioned with Paul in communications to the churches.

Silas

Silas was the co-sender with Paul and Timothy of I and II Thessalonians. He was a prominent member of the church in Jerusalem.

> **Acts 15:22** *Then pleased it the apostles and elders, with the whole church, to send chosen men of their own company to Antioch with Paul and Barnabas; namely, Judas surnamed Barsabas, and Silas, chief men among the brethren:*

Silas, like Paul, was likely a Roman citizen. Paul appears to claim citizenship for both himself and Silas in Acts 16:37. Silas accompanied Paul on his missionary journeys and was imprisoned with him at Philippi (Acts 16:12-40).

> **Acts 15:40-41** *And Paul chose Silas, and departed, being recommended by the brethren unto the grace of God. And he went through Syria and Cilicia, confirming the churches.*
> **II Corinthians 1:19** *For the Son of God, Jesus Christ, who was preached among you by us, even by me and Silvanus and Timotheus, was not yea and nay, but in him was yea.*

This is likely to be the same Silvanus that was mentioned by Peter as having aided him in the writing of his letter.

I Peter 5:12 *By Silvanus, a faithful brother unto you, as I suppose, I have written briefly, exhorting, and testifying that this is the true grace of God wherein ye stand.*

Sosthenes

Sosthenes is only known through his mention by Paul. He was the co-sender of the book of I Corinthians. It has been suggested that this is the same Sosthenes who was the successor to Crispus as chief ruler of the synagogue in Corinth. Thus, he would have been the one who led the persecution against Paul and who was later beaten by the Greeks. Though this is unlikely, if this were the case, it would be yet another example of one who persecuted the faith turning and becoming a Christian.

Timothy

Timothy was the co-sender with Paul of the epistles of II Corinthians, Philippians, Colossians, I and II Thessalonians, and Philemon. Timothy was half Jewish and half Greek and was a third-generation member of the Church on his mother's side.

Acts 16:1-3 *Then came he to Derbe and Lystra: and, behold, a certain disciple was there, named Timotheus, the son of a certain woman, which was a Jewess, and believed; but his father was a Greek: Which was well reported of by the brethren....*

II Timothy 1:5 *When I call to remembrance the unfeigned faith that is in thee, which dwelt first in thy grandmother Lois, and thy mother Eunice; and I am persuaded that in thee also.*

He was a traveling companion of Paul on his journeys and a student under Paul in the ministry. Paul sent Timothy out to minister to the churches.

I Corinthians 4:17 *For this cause have I sent unto you Timotheus, who is my beloved son, and faithful in the Lord, who shall bring you into remembrance of my ways which be in Christ, as I teach every where in every church.*

Philippians 2:19 *But I trust in the Lord Jesus to send Timotheus shortly unto you, that I also may be of good comfort, when I know your state.*

I Thessalonians 3:2 *And sent Timotheus, our brother, and minister of God, and our fellowlabourer in the gospel of Christ, to establish you, and to comfort you concerning your faith:*

James

James, the brother of John, and James, the brother of Jesus, have both been argued for as the writer of the book of **James**. There are numerous strong evidences for this having been James, the brother of Jesus. James, the son of Zebedee and brother of John, was one of the first martyrs of the Early Church, losing his life about 44 A.D., whereas the book of James was believed to have been written during the years following this event.

James would have been one of the brothers of Jesus spoken of in the gospels.

Matthew 13:55-56 (Mark 6:3) *Is not this the carpenter's son? is not his mother called Mary? and his brethren, James, and Joses, and Simon, and Judas? And his sisters, are they not all with us? Whence then hath this man all these things?*

Paul mentions James in his letter to the church at Galatia, naming him as the brother of Jesus.

Galatians 1:19 *But other of the apostles saw I none, save James the Lord's brother.*

It appears that Jesus's brothers did not believe on him at the beginning and possibly did not follow him until after his resurrection.

John 7:5 *For neither did his brethren believe in him.*

Though they did not at first believe, they were later numbered with the 120 in the upper room on the day of Pentecost.

Acts 1:14 *These all continued with one accord in prayer and supplication, with the women, and Mary the mother of Jesus, and with his brethren.*

James later became one of the pillars of the early church and was considered by many historians to have been the leader of the church at Jerusalem. It is revealing to note, that after Peter was released from prison by the angel of God, the first individuals that he specifically wanted the news carried to were James and the brethren.

Acts 12:16-17 *But Peter continued knocking: and when they had opened the door, and saw him, they were astonished. But he, beckoning unto them with the hand to hold their peace, declared unto them how the Lord had brought him out of the prison. And he said, Go shew these things unto James, and to the brethren.*

Peter also seemed to be concerned about how James would view his fellowshipping with the Gentiles, going as far as withdrawing himself from the Gentiles in fear of James' opinion.

Galatians 2:11-12 *But when Peter was come to Antioch, I withstood him to the face, because he was to be blamed. For before that certain came from James, he did eat with the Gentiles: but when they were come, he withdrew and separated himself, fearing them which were of the circumcision.*

During the disputation over the Gentiles at the council at Jerusalem in Acts 15, James appears to speak with authority, his statement clearly being the final decision ending the debate.

Acts 15:12-13, 19 *...after they had held their peace, James answered, saying, Men and brethren, hearken unto me:...*

Luke and Paul both testify to the position of apostolic authority and influence that James appeared to hold in the Church. The authority with which the book of James is written is consistent with the position and influence of Jesus' brother James, who clearly was one of the leaders of the Early Church.

Acts 21:17-18 *And when we were come to Jerusalem, the brethren received us gladly. And the day following Paul went in with us unto James; and all the elders were present.*

Galatians 1:18 *Then after three years I went up to Jerusalem to see Peter, and abode with him fifteen days. But other of the apostles saw I none, save James the Lord's brother*

Galatians 2:9 *And when James, Cephas [Peter], and John, who seemed to be pillars...*

<u>Peter</u>

Peter, the brother of Andrew, was the author of the epistles of **I and II Peter** and was the influence behind Mark's gospel. His brother Andrew was a disciple of John the Baptist, and Peter may have been also. It was his brother that first introduced him to Jesus. Jesus called Simon Peter by the name Cephas, the Aramaic transliteration of his Hebrew name, Peter.

> **John 1:40-42** *One of the two which heard John speak, and followed him, was Andrew, Simon Peter's brother. He first findeth his own brother Simon, and saith unto him, We have found the Messias, which is, being interpreted, the Christ. And he brought him to Jesus. And when Jesus beheld him, he said, Thou art Simon the son of Jona: thou shalt be called Cephas, which is by interpretation, A stone.*

Truly Peter was a rock, <u>one</u> of the "living" foundation stones (I Peter 2:5) upon which the Church was built:

> **Revelation 21:14** *And the wall of the city had twelve foundations, and in them the names of the twelve apostles of the Lamb.*

…but he was not <u>the</u> Rock; the bedrock upon which the foundation stones of the Church were sunk into was Jesus himself.

> **I Corinthians 3:11** *For other foundation can no man lay than that is laid, which is Jesus Christ.*

From the beginning Peter was a leader among the disciples. In every list of the disciples, and later the apostles, Peter's name is given first in order (Matthew 10:2, Mark 3:16, Luke 6:14-16, and Acts 1:13). He is mentioned in the gospels more than any other disciple. Along with James and John, he was a part of Jesus' closest inner circle. He was a spokesperson on a number of occasions, whether due to some deference on the part of the other disciples or by reason of his outspoken nature. He speaks more often than any of the disciples in the Gospels and is spoken to by Jesus more often than any other. He is often the specific disciple named as asking questions or making comments to Jesus.

On the day of Pentecost, it is Peter who becomes the spokesperson for the apostles:

> **Acts 2:14-40** *But Peter, standing up with the eleven, lifted up his voice, and said unto them...Now when they heard this, they were pricked in their heart, and said unto Peter and to the rest of the apostles, Men and brethren, what shall we do? Then Peter said unto them, Repent and be baptized every one of you in the name of Jesus Christ for the remission of sins, and ye shall receive the gift of the Holy Ghost. For the promise is unto you, and to your children, and to all that are afar off, even as many as the Lord our God shall call. And with many other words did he testify and exhort,....*

Peter was the apostle who passed judgment upon Ananias and Sapphira (Acts 5:1-11), demonstrating his authority and office.

He was a man of high passion and emotion. The gospels record several of his arguments with Jesus, and when the temple guards came to arrest Jesus, it was Peter who attacked them.

> **John 18:10** *Then Simon Peter having a sword drew it, and smote the high priest's servant, and cut off his right ear....*

Scholars have debated over whether Peter could have written both of the epistles that have been credited to him. It appears that the literary style in each is very different and one of the writers is more skillful in the Greek language. This is not a difficulty when we understand that Peter likely had Silas as his scribe in writing at least one of the letters, just as Mark had written down Peter's version of the gospel.

> **I Peter 5:12** *By Silvanus, a faithful brother unto you, as I suppose, I have written briefly, exhorting, and testifying that this is the true grace of God wherein ye stand.*

Jude

The writer of the book of Jude would most likely have been Jude, the brother of James and of Jesus, though this may have been Judas the apostle, the brother of James and the son of Alphaeus (not Judas Iscariot).

THE LANGUAGES OF THE BIBLE

6

It is important in any study of the literary and structural design of the Bible to have an understanding of the languages God used to communicate His word. Each of the languages used in the original transmission of the Bible has capabilities and qualities that allow for the perfect flow and dispensational revelation of His plan for man.

HEBREW

The Hebrew tongue is one of the most ancient languages in the world. Some have speculated that the Hebrew of the patriarchs and Israel may have been a direct descendant of the one universal language that existed before the fall of Babel.

Biblical Hebrew is made up of a 22-letter alphabet consisting of consonants only. There were no vowels or vowel pointings[95] in the original language. In addition, many times the text of the ancient languages was written without spaces between the words. To contrast this with our modern languages, imagine the difficulty involved in understanding John 3:16 in English:

> With spaces:
> *Fr Gd s lvd th wrld tht h gv hs nly bgttn Sn tht whsvr blvth n hm shld nt prsh bt hv vrlstng lf*
> Without spaces:
> *FrGdslvdthwrldththgvhsnlybgttnSnthtwhsvrblvthnhmshldntprs hbthvvrlstngf*

---

[95] Vowel pointings, or **nikud**, were later accents added to the Hebrew letters to show what vowel sounds were to be included in the reading of the text.

Hebrew is a concise language in which much fewer words are used to describe a thought than in the Greek, or in modern English. It compresses complex thoughts into short phrases and words, and though this makes it harder to translate into modern terms, it gives it a depth of power and beauty beyond that of other languages with various shades of meaning.

The language of Israel was not referred to as Hebrew in the Old Testament. It was called "the Jews' language" or "language of Canaan."

> **Nehemiah 13:24** *And their children spake half in the speech of Ashdod, and could not speak in the Jews' language, but according to the language of each people.*[96]
> **Isaiah 19:18** *In that day shall five cities in the land of Egypt speak the language of Canaan, and swear to the LORD of hosts; one shall be called, The city of destruction.*

"Hebrew" was what the language was referred to as in the New Testament.
> **Luke 23:38** *And a superscription also was written over him in letters of Greek, and Latin, and Hebrew, THIS IS THE KING OF THE JEWS.*
> **Acts 21:40** *...he spake unto them in the Hebrew tongue, saying,*

The idiomatic language of Hebrew is built upon visual expression and outward observation rather than inner reflection or philosophical thought. It is designed to be felt by the emotions and seen by the eyes of the mind, painting visual images to describe thoughts and ideas. It expresses itself pictorially in many ways throughout the Bible. Some of the many examples follow:

---

[96] This means the language of Judah.

in the sweat of thy face – Genesis 3:19
Abraham lifted up his eyes – Genesis 22:4
and he arose, and went – Genesis 24:10
lift up thine head – Genesis 40:13
unstable as water – Genesis 49:4
a land flowing with milk and honey – Exodus 3:8
sheep which have no shepherd – Numbers 27:17
whatsoever is right in his own eyes – Deuteronomy 12:8
the apple of his eye – Deuteronomy 32:10
a man after his own heart – I Samuel 13:14
how are the mighty fallen – II Samuel 1:25
from the sole of his foot to the crown of his head – II Samuel 14:25
stole the hearts – II Samuel 15:6
horn of my salvation – II Samuel 22:3
a still small voice – I Kings 19:12
gird up thy loins – II Kings 4:29
he stiffened his neck – II Chronicles 36:13
the shadow of death – Job 10:21
the skin of my teeth – Job 19:20
the land of the living – Job 28:13
incline thine ear – Psalm 17:6
my cup runneth over – Psalm 23:5
my tongue is the pen of a ready writer – Psalm 45:1
at their wit's end – Psalm 107:27
heap coals of fire upon his head – Proverbs 25:22
iron sharpeneth iron – Proverbs 27:17
as a drop of a bucket – Isaiah 40:15

The roots from which many of the words developed demonstrate Hebrew's picturesque nature.

- "To decide" originally meant "to cut," showing a picture of a thing being cut in two so that there is a separation and division.
- "To be right" meant "to be straight," in contrast to the root of "sin" which means "to be crooked" or "to miss the mark."
- "To be true" meant "to be firmly fixed," a beautiful picture of the anchored and faithful nature of being true.

The Hebrew Scriptures are richly seasoned with a multitude of similes, metaphors, and poetic structures. Some scholars have estimated that a third or more of the Hebrew Old Testament is written in poetic form. Only seven books in the Old Testament are said to be without distinct poetic structure: Leviticus, Ruth, Ezra, Nehemiah, Esther, Haggai, and Malachi. E.W. Bullinger spent years analyzing and cataloging the poetic structures contained in the Bible.[97] Many of these poetic structures take the form of parallelism. Parallelism is a poetic form containing parallel line or statements.

---

[97] See *The Companion Bible*, E.W. Bullinger.

POETIC STRUCTURE AND PARALLELISM IN THE BIBLE

SYNONYMOUS PARALLELISM
Repeating parallel lines expressing an analogous thought
in different words

Psalm 3:1
Lord, how are they increased that trouble me!
many are they that rise up against me.

Proverbs 19:29
Judgments are prepared for scorners,
and stripes for the back of fools.

Isaiah 1:3
...Israel doth not know, my people doth not consider.

Matthew 11:30
For my yoke is easy, and my burden is light.

ANTITHETIC/CONTRASTIVE PARALLELISM
Made up of contrasting parallel lines

Psalm 1:6
For the Lord knoweth the way of the righteous:
but the way of the ungodly shall perish.

Psalm 90:6
In the morning it flourisheth, and groweth up;
in the evening it is cut down, and withereth.

Proverbs 10:1 (and throughout the chapter)
...A wise son maketh a glad father:
but a foolish son is the heaviness of his mother.

Proverbs 27:6
Faithful are the wounds of a friend;
but the kisses of an enemy are deceitful.

SYNTHETIC/COMPLETIVE PARALLELISM
A statement or series of statements reaching a logical conclusion

Psalm 1:1-3
Blessed is the man that walketh not in the counsel of the ungodly,
nor standeth in the way of sinners,
nor sitteth in the seat of the scornful.
But his delight is in the law of the Lord;
and in his law doth he meditate day and night.
And he shall be like a tree planted by the rivers of water,
that bringeth forth his fruit in his season;
his leaf also shall not wither;
and whatsoever he doeth shall prosper.

Psalm 46:1
God is our refuge and strength,
a very present help in trouble.

CHIASTIC STRUCTURE
A series of statements arranged in a reflective, mirror-like pattern

Amos 5:4-6
For thus saith the Lord unto the house of Israel,
Seek ye me, and ye shall live: (A)
But seek not Bethel,   (B)
nor enter into Gilgal,   (C)
and pass not to Beer-sheba:
for Gilgal shall surely go into captivity,   (C)
and Bethel shall come to nought.   (B)
Seek the Lord, and ye shall live;.... (A)

ACROSTIC STRUCTURE
A form in which lines or phrases begin with
consecutive letters of the alphabet

The 22-letter Hebrew alphabet is displayed in acrostic structure in nine of the Psalms. The most dynamic example of this is in the 119th Psalm, where every eighth verse begins with the next consecutive letter of the alphabet. Other examples are Psalms 9, 10, 25, 34 (with minor exceptions), 37 (every second verse), 111, 112, and 145.[98]

---

[98] Psalm 145 is missing the Hebrew letter *nun* in the King James Version, though it does occur in the Septuagint.

ARAMAIC

Aramaic was a sister language to Hebrew, using much of the same terminology. Aramaic, though, was a fuller and more precise language, with a larger and more exact vocabulary. During the later Old Testament times, Aramaic became the common language of the Near East, operating as a trade language for the peoples of that part of the world. In the Old Testament, Aramaic is also referred to as Syriac or Chaldean, which would have primarily been the eastern Aramaic dialect.

There are eight passages in the Bible where Aramaic is used, five in the Old Testament and three in the New.

Old Testament Passages in Aramaic

Genesis 31:45-47 *And Jacob took a stone, and set it up for a pillar. And Jacob said unto his brethren, Gather stones; and they took stones, and made an heap: and they did eat there upon the heap. And Laban called it* **Jegarsahadutha**: *but Jacob called it Galeed.*

Laban's term for the "witness heap" was the Aramaic word *Jegarsahadutha*, whereas Jacob used the Hebrew word *Galeed*.

Jeremiah 10:11 *Thus shall ye say unto them, The gods that have not made the heavens and the earth, even they shall perish from the earth, and from under these heavens.*

The entire verse is in the Aramaic. This is the only verse in the book of Jeremiah so written. A number of theories have been put forward as to why Jeremiah would have written this verse in Aramaic. Modern critical scholars tend to believe that this verse was added by a later scribe; this would have been exceptionally careless on his part not to transcribe it into Hebrew. Others feel that this may have been a common phrase during the time his book was written, so he quoted it from its original language. It is also very possible that God's intention was for the statement to be made in the Aramaic directly to those who used that tongue.

Daniel 2:4–7:28 *Then spake the Chaldeans to the king in Syriack,....Hitherto is the end of the matter. As for me Daniel, my cogitations much troubled me, and my countenance changed in me: but I kept the matter in my heart.*

From the beginning of the Chaldeans speaking to the king to the finalization of prophecy regarding the Gentile kingdoms, this entire section of Daniel is written in the eastern dialect of the Aramaic. This may be due to the nature of the prophecy and its Gentile overtones.

Ezra 4:8–6:18 *Rehum the chancellor and Shimshai the scribe wrote a letter against Jerusalem to Artaxerxes the king in this sort: ...And they set the priests in their divisions, and the Levites in their courses, for the service of God, which is at Jerusalem; as it is written in the book of Moses.*

This section records the letters written by the adversaries of Israel to Darius and his reply. It is most likely that this is an exact quote of the correspondence that had taken place and thus is quoted directly from the source language. This section is introduced by the statement in the preceding verse (4:7): *...the writing of the letter was written in the Syrian tongue, and interpreted in the Syrian tongue.*

Ezra 7:12-26 *Artaxerxes, king of kings, unto Ezra the priest,.....And whosoever will not do the law of thy God, and the law of the king, let judgment be executed speedily upon him, whether it be unto death, or to banishment, or to confiscation of goods, or to imprisonment.*

Just as with the prior example, this series of verses is preceded by an introductory statement: *Now this is the copy of the letter that the king Artaxerxes gave unto Ezra the priest,....*This is another example of a letter being quoted from its original language by the Biblical writer.

ARAMAIC WORDS USED IN THE NEW TESTAMENT

WORD(S)	PASSAGE(S)
Abba	Mark 14:36. Romans 8:15. Galatians 4:6.
Aceldama (Akeldama)	Acts 1:19.
Aeneas (Ainias)	Acts 9:33,34.
Alphaeus (Alphaios)	Matthew 10:3. Mark 2:14; 3:18. Luke 6:15. Acts 1:13.
Annas	Luke 3:2. John 18:13, 24. Acts 4:6.
Barabbas	Matthew 27:16, 17, 20, 21, 26. Mark 15:7, 11, 15. Luke 23:18. John 18:40.
Bar-Jesus (Bar-iesous)	Acts 13:6.
Bar-Jona (Bar-iona)	Matthew 16:17.
Barnabas	Acts 4:36, etc. 1 Corinthians 9:6. Galatians 2:1, 9, 13. Colossians 4:10.
Barsabas	Acts 1:23; 15:22.
Bartholomew (Bartholomaios)	Matthew 10:3. Mark 3:18. Luke 6:14. Acts 1:13.
Bartimaeus (Bartimaios)	Mark 10:46.
Beelzebub (Beel-zeboul)	Matthew 10:25; 12:24, 27. Mark 3:22. Luke 11:15, 18, 19.
Bethesda	John 5:2.
Bethphage	Matthew 21:1. Mark 11:1. Luke 19:29.
Bethsaida	Matthew 11:21. Mark 6:45; 8:22. Luke 9:10; 10:13. John 1:44; 12:21.
Boanerges	Mark 3:17.
Cephas (Kephas)	John 1:42. 1 Corinthians 1:12; 3:22; 9:5; 15:5. Galatians 2:9.
Cleopas (Kleopas)	Luke 24:18.
Eli/Eloi	Matthew 27:46. Mark 15:34.
Ephphatha	Mark 7:34.
Gethsemane	Matthew 26:36. Mark 14:32.
Golgotha	Matthew 27:33. Mark 15:22. John 19:17.

Hosanna	Matthew 21:9, 9, 15. Mark 11:9, 10. John 12:13.
Jona (Ioannes)	John 1:42; 21:15, 16, 17.
Klopas	John 19:25.
Lama	Matthew 27:46. Mark 15:34.
Mammon (Mammonas)	Matthew 6:24. Luke 16:9, 11, 13.
Maranatha	1 Corinthians 16:22.
Martha	Luke 10:38, 40, 41. John 11:1, etc.
Matthew (Matthaios)	Matthew 9:9; 10:3. Mark 3:18. Luke 6:15. Acts 1:13.
Nazareth (-et)	Matthew 2:23; 4:13, 21:11. Mark 1:9. Luke 1:26; 2:4, 39, 51; 4:16. John 1:45, 46. Acts 10:38.
Passover (Pascha)	Matthew 26:2, 17, 18, 19. Mark 14:1, 12, 12, 14, 16. Luke 2:41; 22:1, 7 8, 11, 13, 15. John 2:13, 23; 6:4; 11:55, 55; 12:1; 13:1; 18:28, 39; 19:14. Acts 12:4. 1 Corinthians 5:7. Hebrews 11:28.
Rabboni, Rabbouni	Mark 10:51. John 20:16.
Raka	Matthew 5:22.
Sabachthani	Matthew 27:46. Mark 15:34.
Sabbath (Sabbata)	Matthew 12:1, 5, 10, 11, 12, etc.
Tabitha	Acts 9:36, 40.
Talitha cumi	Mark 5:41.
Thaddaeus (Thaddaios)	Matthew 10:3. Mark 3:18.
Thomas	Matthew 10:3. Mark 3:18. Luke 6:15. John 11:16; 14:5; 20:24, 26, 27, 28, 29; 21:2. Acts 1:13.
Zacchaeus (Zakchaios)	Luke 19:2, 5, 8.
Zebedee (Zebedaios)	Matthew 4:21; 10:2; 20:20; 26:37; 27:56. Mark 1:19, 20; 3:17; 10:35. Luke 5:10. John 21:2.

GREEK

ΑΒΓΔΕΖΗΘ
ΙΚΛΜΝΞΟΠ
ΡΣΤΥΦΧΨΩ
αβγδεζηθικλμ
νξοπρστυφχψ

The Greek language, in which the New Testament is written, is a much more complex and flexible language than the Semitic languages of Hebrew and Aramaic. The structure of Greek allows for very detailed shades of meaning. It has a rich depth of expression that is not contained in the sparse ancient tongues. This complexity of design makes Greek a much more philosophical and reflective language than Hebrew.

Hebrew was a language of emotion and feeling, whereas Greek stressed intellectual thought. These contrasts actually cause these languages to complement each other well in their development of Biblical revelation. The Greek takes the direct expressions of the Hebrew and further develops them with finer precision. In relation to the rock of Scripture, Hebrew represents the stonecutter who mines out and gives the stone its basic shape; Greek, the sculptor who carves the intricate details into the raw stone.

Greek is very precise in its tenses and grammatical constructs. This makes it perfect for the complicated theological discussions of Paul and the other apostles. With its grammatical exactness, what is being addressed in a statement can easily be determined specifically.

Scholars believe that the Greek alphabet had its origins in the same original root alphabet from which Hebrew and Phoenician came. The first two letters in the Hebrew alphabet are called **aleph** and **bet**. In the Greek they are **alpha** and **beta**, from which we get the English word *alphabet.*

Just as with Hebrew, Greek was originally written from right to left. During its later development it was written in alternation with the first line written right to left, the second left to right, and so on. It finally became written from left to write like English.

In New Testament times, Greek was written in all capital letters, called uncials. There was no division between the words and no punctuation. Modern readers would probably find this very difficult. The phrase *For God so loved the world* would have been written FORGODSOLOVEDTHEWORLD. In later stages the minuscule script began to be used. The minuscule or cursive writing would have been closer to our modern writing with both capital and lowercase letters used.

Just as Aramaic had become the trade language of the East during the captivity of the Jews, so Greek became the common language of the Eastern nations after the military conquests of Alexander the Great. Alexander spread Greek language and culture throughout the East and especially in the nations bordering the Mediterranean Sea.

During the time of the Roman Empire the Greek language was the common trade tongue used in the nations under Rome's control, which would have included Israel. This common Greek language, used to write the books of the New Testament, was referred to as **koine** (or common) Greek.

Latin, the Roman tongue, would have been used primarily for military and political communication, with Greek being the predominant language of the day. Even though Aramaic was still commonly used by the Jews in Palestine, Greek would have been the language the New Testament was written in, especially as its letters and writings were disbursed throughout the other Roman colonies.

The Greek language went through a number of developmental stages. The Greek of the New Testament is not the classical Greek that the philosophers Socrates and Aristotle would have used. As has previously been stated, this was a common usage form of Greek, unlike the classical Greek used by the ancient philosophers and Greek intelligentsia.

Modern scholars have often used the classical forms and definitions to explain the Greek meanings of the biblical text, but this should not be done. The biblical Greek is a unique language of its own and should be dealt with as such. E.C. Hoskins wrote, *The New Testament documents were, no doubt, written in a language intelligible to the generality of Greek-speaking people; yet to suppose that they emerged from the background of Greek thought and experience would be to misunderstand them completely. There is a strange and awkward element in the language which not only affects the meanings of words, not only disturbs the grammar and syntax, but lurks everywhere in a maze of literary allusions which no ordinary Greek man or woman could conceivably have understood or even detected. The truth is that behind these writings there lies an intractable Hebraic, Aramaic, Palestinian material. It is this foreign matter that complicates New Testament Greek. ...The tension between the Jewish heritage and the Greek world vitally affects the language of the New Testament.*[99]

---

[99] E.C. Hoskins, *The Riddle of the New Testament*, 1931, pp. 19-20.

A number of other scholars have attested to the unique nature of the Greek used in the New Testament. The phraseology and flavor of the Greek used in the Bible is unlike any other Greek manuscript. It is imbued with a distinctly Hebrew tone that creates a form completely its own. Martin Luther stated, *One cannot fully understand the New Testament books without a knowledge of the Hebrew language. For the New Testament, although it is written in Greek, is full of Hebraisms and betrays the Hebrew style of writing.*[100]

Greek then, in its New Testament usage, has a linguistic form that is completely its own. It appears to have been specially suited in this way to transmit the interpretive understanding of the Old Testament more expressively and completely in a linguistic sense, just as the types and shadows of the Old Testament became revealed by the illumination of the Holy Spirit through the dispensation of the New Covenant.

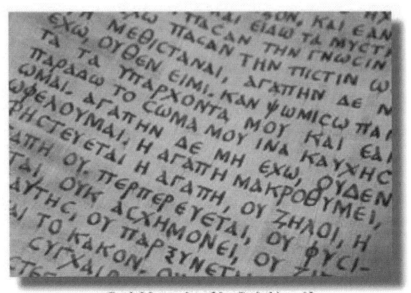

Greek Manuscript of 1st Corinthians 13

---

[100] Martin Luther, *Table Talks*, 1.525.

WRITING TOOLS AND MATERIALS

7

Throughout history the scriptures have been written and copied on a variety of different materials. For thousands of years, writing and copying was done completely by hand on materials that did not have the capacity to withstand the conditions of nature and time. Only in the modern age have chemical additives and protective substances been developed to aid in the preservation of documents.

It is believed that the most ancient records were chiseled into stone and etched into clay tablets. The Mesopotamian nations of Sumeria and Babylon used clay and stone to make a permanent record of laws and events. Hammurabi, king of Babylon from about 1792 to 1750 B.C., made a record of his legal judgments on a stone stele, called the **Code of Hammurabi**. This ancient judicial record was found by archaeologists near Susa in 1902. It has been considered one of the best witnesses to the writings of these early cultures.

Other finds, such as the **Rosetta Stone** and the **Moabite Stone**, have added to this evidence.

It is generally believed that writing of this kind was in existence by 3500 B.C. or earlier. Hammer and chisel were the instruments of choice in carving words into stone, whereas a metal stylus was used to make etchings in tablets of clay.

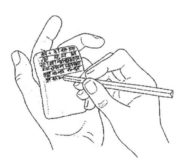

In Exodus 31-34 God gives the Ten Commandments to Moses engraved on tablets of hewn stone.

Exodus 31:18 ...*two tables of testimony, tables of stone, written with the finger of God.*

Deuteronomy 9:10 *And the LORD delivered unto me two tables of stone written with the finger of God; and on them was written according to all the words, which the LORD spake with you in the mount out of the midst of the fire in the day of the assembly.*

A number of passages testify to this type of penmanship:

Deuteronomy 27:4-8 (completed in Joshua 8:32) *Therefore it shall be when ye be gone over Jordan, that ye shall set up these stones, which I command you this day, in mount Ebal, and thou shalt plaister them with plaister....And thou shalt write upon the stones all the words of this law very plainly.*

II Corinthians 3:7 *But if the ministration of death* [the law of Moses], *written and engraven in stones, was glorious, so that the children of Israel could not stedfastly behold the face of Moses for the glory of his countenance; which glory was to be done away:*

Job 19:23-24 *Oh that my words were now written! oh that they were printed*[101] *in a book! That they were graven with an iron pen and lead in the rock for ever!*

Isaiah 30:8 *Now go, write it before them in a table, and note it in a book, that it may be for the time to come forever and ever:*

Habakkuk 2:2 *And the Lord answered me, and said, Write the vision, and make it plain upon tables, that he may run that readeth it.*

The first forerunner of our modern writing material would have been **papyrus**, the root of our English word "paper." Papyrus was developed in Egypt and around the area of the Mediterranean Sea. Papyrus is actually a reed plant of the sedge family. It is a large plant, sometimes growing up to 10 feet tall. The stem and root of a papyrus plant are nearly as thick as a human arm and it is from this stem that its paper was made.

---

[101] "Printed" is the Hebrew word *chaqaq*, the actual meaning of which is "to engrave" or "to inscribe".

In order to make papyrus sheets for writing, the pith of the stem was cut into strips, usually about 12 to 15 inches long. These were than laid in layers running lengthwise and crosswise to one another. This mat was then moistened with water and beaten out flat with mallets. The natural moisture and sugars in the plant helped to bond the layers together. The finishing process was accomplished by rubbing the sheet smooth with bone, ivory, or smooth shells and trimming off the rough edges. Normally the side of paper with the horizontal layer showing was used first as it would have been the smoothest. This side was later called the "recto." The backside of the vertical layer was called the "verso." The edges of the sheets were overlapped and glued or sewn together to create long rolls, which were then wound around dowels for keeping, creating the scrolls of biblical times.[102]

Papyrus was believed to have been in use in Egypt as early as 2000 to 3000 B.C.[103] The Greeks were known to have used papyrus by the 5th century B.C. The oldest known Hebrew papyrus document was found near Qumran at Wadi Murabba'at and is dated from the 7th to 8th century B.C. Papyrus documents are exceptionally rare as the material is easily damaged by light or moisture and crumbles away over time. Ancient papyrus documents are usually found in dry climates such as Egypt and Arabia.

---

[102] See Pliny's *Naturalis Historia*, section 13, for detailed descriptions of the making and uses of papyrus during the 1st century.
[103] *International Standard Bible Encyclopedia*, article on "Papyrus" and *Anchor Bible Dictionary*, article on "Writing and Writing Materials."

The bulrushes mentioned in the making of the boat that carried the baby Moses were probably papyrus plants. It is interesting to consider that this same material that carried the future lawgiver was the vessel used to contain the law of Moses in its written form.

Other writing materials that were used contemporary with papyrus were made from the skins of animals. Both leather and parchment appear to have been used almost as early as papyrus. These materials were more durable and easier to write on, but were also much more expensive.

Leather was usually made from the skins of sheep or goats. The skin was shaved and scraped clean and dried out to prepare it for writing. The Talmud recorded that all copies of the law used in public worship were to be written on the skins of clean animals.[104] Thus the copies of the scriptures used in the temple and the synagogues would have been written on leather or parchment. The manuscript discoveries at Qumran validate this fact as many of the scrolls found were written on leather, particularly the Isaiah scroll displayed in the Shrine of the Book in Jerusalem.

Parchment and **vellum** were the highest qualities of leather writing material. These were taken from the skins of younger animals in the same way as regular leather. The skin was cleaned and scraped on both sides, then rubbed smooth with powdered pumice. They would then be bleached white by being soaked in lime water. Bruce Metzger describes the difference between parchment and vellum: *The younger the animal, the finer was the quality of skin. Vellum was the finest*

---

[104] Sir. Frederic George Kenyon, *Our Bible and the Ancient Manuscripts*, p. 37.

quality of extra-thin parchment, sometimes obtained from animals not yet born.[105]

In their original form, the manuscripts that make up our modern Bibles would probably be unrecognizable to us. Our modern books were derived from codices, which were groups of individual books and letters that were bound together. These first originated as sheets and scrolls, which were later glued or sewn together to create a book known as a codex.

---

[105] Bruce Metzger, *Manuscripts of the Greek Bible*, p. 14, Oxford University Press, 1981.

SCRIBAL TRADITIONS

8

The scribal families were the copyists and keepers of the scriptures from the very beginning of the organized writing of the Scripture. These very likely originated with and worked hand in hand with their brothers in the Levitical priesthood.

It is believed that the scribes formed themselves into guilds, usually by family. This was especially the case in the time period following the destruction of Jerusalem and up into the time of the Masoretic scribes from 500 to 1000 A.D. The scribes had already begun to be separated by family in the time of their sojourn in Israel:

I Chronicles 2:55 *And the families of the scribes which dwelt at Jabez; the Tirathites, the Shimeathites, and Suchathites. These are the Kenites that came of Hemath, the father of the house of Rechab.*

The scribes had a number of responsibilities in the Old Testament times. They were the keepers of the law, copying and maintaining the books of scripture:

II Chronicles 34:13-16 *Also they were over the bearers of burdens, and were overseers of all that wrought the work in any manner of service: and of the Levites there were scribes, and officers, and porters. And when they brought out the money that was brought into the house of the LORD, Hilkiah the priest found a book of the law of the LORD given by Moses. And Hilkiah answered and said to Shaphan the scribe, I have found the book of the law in the house of the LORD. And Hilkiah delivered the book to Shaphan. And Shaphan carried the book to the king, and brought the king word back again, saying, All that was committed to thy servants, they do it.*

Though Hilkiah the priest found the book of the law, he gave the book to Shaphan the scribe to bring to the king's attention. It is clear from this passage that the scribal office held a great deal of authority in regard to the safeguarding of the law.

Baruch, Jeremiah's scribe, copied down Jeremiah's words as given by God:

Jeremiah 36:4-6 *Then Jeremiah called Baruch the son of Neriah: and Baruch wrote from the mouth of Jeremiah all the words of the LORD, which he had spoken unto him, upon a roll of a book. And Jeremiah commanded Baruch, saying, I am shut up; I cannot go into the house of the LORD: Therefore go thou, and read in the roll, which thou hast written from my mouth, the words of the LORD in the ears of the people in the LORD'S house upon the fasting day:*

and also thou shalt read them in the ears of all Judah that come out of their cities.

The scribes also held roles as administrators and accountants for the kings of Israel:

Under Solomon
I Kings 4:1-3 *So king Solomon was king over all Israel. And these were the princes which he had; Azariah the son of Zadok the priest, Elihoreph and Ahiah, the sons of Shisha, scribes; Jehoshaphat the son of Ahilud, the recorder.*

Under Uzziah
II Chronicles 26:11 *Moreover Uzziah had an host of fighting men, that went out to war by bands, according to the number of their account by the hand of Jeiel the scribe and Maaseiah the ruler, under the hand of Hananiah, one of the king's captains.*

Under Jehoash
II Kings 12:10-11 *And it was so, when they saw that there was much money in the chest, that the king's scribe and the high priest came up, and they put up in bags, and told the money that was found in the house of the LORD. And they gave the money, being told, into the hands of them that did the work, that had the oversight of the house of the LORD: and they laid it out to the carpenters and builders, that wrought upon the house of the LORD,*

Under Hezekiah
II Kings 18:18 *And when they had called to the king, there came out to them Eliakim the son of Hilkiah, which was over the household, and Shebna the scribe, and Joah the son of Asaph the recorder.*

Ezra was both a priest and a scribe, uniting both Levitical traditions.

Ezra 7:6 *This Ezra went up from Babylon; and he was a ready scribe in the law of Moses, which the LORD God of Israel had given: and the king granted him all his request, according to the hand of the LORD his God upon him.*

Ezra 7:11-12 *Now this is the copy of the letter that the king Artaxerxes gave unto Ezra the priest, the scribe, even a scribe of the words of the commandments of the LORD, and of his statutes to Israel. Artaxerxes, king of kings, unto Ezra the priest, a scribe of the law of the God of heaven, perfect peace, and at such a time.*

In Ezra we begin to see the culmination of the scribal tradition. From Ezra's time forward the scribes appear to speak with even more authority. They are considered not only the keepers of the word of God, but also the teachers and interpreters. Consider the example of Ezra recorded in Nehemiah 8:

Nehemiah 8:1-8 *And all the people gathered themselves together as one man into the street that was before the water gate; and they spake unto Ezra the scribe to bring the book of the law of Moses, which the LORD had commanded to Israel. And Ezra the priest brought the law before the congregation both of men and women, and all that could hear with understanding, upon the first day of the seventh month. And he read therein before the street that was before the water gate from the morning until midday, before the men and the women, and those that could understand; and the ears of all the people were attentive unto the book of the law. And Ezra the scribe stood upon a pulpit of wood, which they had made for the purpose; and beside him stood Mattithiah, and Shema, and Anaiah, and Urijah, and Hilkiah, and Maaseiah, on his right hand; and on his left hand, Pedaiah, and Mishael, and Malchiah, and Hashum, and Hashbadana, Zechariah, and Meshullam. And Ezra opened the book in the sight of all the people; (for he was above all the people;) and when he opened it, all the people stood up: And Ezra blessed the LORD, the great God. And all the people* *answered, Amen, Amen, with lifting up their hands: and they bowed their heads, and worshipped the LORD with their faces to the ground. Also Jeshua, and Bani, and Sherebiah, Jamin, Akkub, Shabbethai, Hodijah, Maaseiah, Kelita, Azariah, Jozabad, Hanan, Pelaiah, and the Levites, caused the people to understand the law: and the people stood in their place. So they read in the book in the law of God distinctly, and gave the sense, and caused them to understand the reading.*

There are three specific things that Ezra and his assistants accomplished in their reading of the law to the people:
1) They read the law of God distinctly
2) They gave the sense
3) They caused them to understand

Here we see the scribal office as that of a teacher and instructor in the law. The law was read distinctly: clearly Ezra and his assistants were skilled in the law and its interpretation to the people. They gave the sense: they were able to clarify and reveal the meaning of the law. They caused them to understand: they were able to bring the life of the word of God directly into the hearts of the people, to give them an understanding of the word of God in a way that could bring illumination.

By the time of Jesus, the scribes had become an elite group who were an integral part of the instructive arm of the synagogue and temple worship. They were usually found in the company of other religious leaders, evidenced in such phrases as "the chief priests and scribes," and "the scribes and the Pharisees." They were experts on the interpretation and explanation of the law. Jesus used them as a simile in his parable of the householder:

Matthew 13:52 *Then he said unto them, Therefore every scribe which is instructed unto the kingdom of heaven is like unto a man* *that is an householder, which bringeth forth out of his treasure things new and old.*

The disciples inferred that the scribes were considered the interpreters of the law in their question to Jesus regarding Elijah:

Matthew 17:10 *And his disciples asked him, saying, Why then say the scribes that Elias must first come?*

Jesus also referred to this interpretative capacity of the scribes in regard to the lineage of the Messiah:

Mark 12:35 *And Jesus answered and said, while he taught in the temple, How say the scribes that Christ is the son of David?*

Jesus referred to their position of authority in regard to the law, though they themselves were not obedient to the law:

Matthew 23:1-3 *Then spake Jesus to the multitude, and to his disciples, Saying, The scribes and the Pharisees sit in Moses' seat: All therefore whatsoever they bid you observe, that observe and do; but do not ye after their works: for they say, and do not.*

Jesus himself had the full and complete understanding of the scriptures, and his authority went well beyond the spiritually skin-deep authority of the scribes:

Mark 1:22 *And they were astonished at his doctrine: for he taught them as one that had authority, and not as the scribes.*

The scribes that supported the Pharisee sect spoke with authority before the Sanhedrin at the trial of Paul:

Acts 23:9 *And there arose a great cry: and the scribes that were of the Pharisees' part arose, and strove, saying, We find no evil in this man: but if a spirit or an angel hath spoken to him, let us not fight against God.*

The Jewish rabbis and teachers of the law were descendants of this scribal tradition. Gamaliel, the early instructor of the apostle Paul, may have been a member of this class.

The scribal tradition began to take form in an organized way during the time of the Babylonian captivity. The Jewish religious leaders felt the need to establish a means to make certain that the law would continue uncorrupted.

The first of these organized scribes would have been the **Sopherim**, the title of which comes from the Hebrew root **saphar**, meaning "scribe" or "numbered". The **Sopherim** operated from about 500 B.C. to 100 A.D. This was the scribal tradition ascribed to Ezra and the other scribes returning from the Babylonian captivity. There were also those who remained in Babylon and other lands of the Dispersia who were responsible for the keeping and interpreting of the law and prophets. The Babylonian Talmud states, *The early* [scholars] *were called soferim because they used to count all the letters in the Torah.* This requirement of numbering the letters and divisions of the scripture for the sake of accuracy continued on through the later scribal copyists.

The **Tannaim** were the next historical group of scribes. The term **tannaim** comes from the Hebrew, meaning "to hand down orally", "to study", or "to teach". The **Tannaim** worked from about 20 to 200 A.D. and were responsible for the development of the Mishnah and the Gemara. The Mishnah is a set of Jewish oral traditions that expounded on the Old Testament law; the Gemara was a later commentary on the Mishnah.

The **Amoraim** were the next scribes to come on the scene, working from about 200 to 500 A.D. **Amoraim** means "expositors", and this is precisely the work that they did. The **Amoraim** began the development of the Talmud. The Talmud was a further commentary and exposition on the Old Testament law, the Mishnah, and the Gemara. They operated in two general centers of activity, Babylon and Palestine, thus the Babylonian and Palestinian Talmuds. It was during the time of the *Amoraim* that verse divisions began to be made in the Hebrew Bible.

The last of the ancient scribal traditions was that of the **Masoretes.** The **Masoretes** were scribes from about 500 to 1000 A.D. There were two locations in which the **Masoretes** carried out their work: in the East in Babylon and in the West in Palestine, and later at Tiberias on the Sea of Galilee.

By the end of the 10th century there were two major **Masoretic** family lines involved in the copying of the scripture: the Ben Asher and Ben Naphtali families. The Ben Asher eventually became the predominant text and underlies the later Hebrew and English translations of the Old Testament. Of all the scribes, they were the ones responsible for introducing the most number of changes to the biblical text. At the same time they may have had the most reverence toward the structure of the scriptures. The changes that were introduced by the Masoretes were not in the translational sense; changes were introduced to enable the writings to be better understood, codified, and validated.
Vowel pointings were one of the most important additions that the Masoretes added to the text. The Hebrew words did not contain vowels; the words were inferred by the context. The Masoretic scribes introduced points and accents to the letters, which clarified the words and gave them modern vowel forms. This significantly added to the understanding and clarity of the text for future translators and copyists. Many other minor corrections were added to the text by the Masoretes during this period.

One of the most distinctive characteristics of the Masoretes was their great respect for and veneration of the manuscripts themselves. They were said to have counted nearly every part of the text; the number of letters, verses, and divisions were closely counted and codified to ensure perfect accuracy in copying. An example of this is found in the final Masorah[106] at the end of the Torah:

Total verses in the Torah
5, 845
All the Sedarim[107] of the Torah
167
Total number of words in the Torah
97, 856
Total number of letters in the Torah
400,945

---

[106] **Masoretic** notation on the text.
[107] Hebrew divisional sections.

HEBREW AND MASORETIC RULES
FOR COPYING THE SCRIPTURES

In preparing the official copies of the scripture for use in the synagogues, known as the Synagogue Rolls, the scribes had very detailed and specific rules.

- Must be written on the skins of clean animals.
- Must be prepared for synagogue use by a Jew only.
- Must be fastened together with strings taken from clean animals.
- Each skin must contain an exact number of columns, which must be equal throughout the entire manuscript.
- The length of each column must be between 48 and 60 lines.
- The breadth of each column must consist of 30 letters.
- The whole copy must be first lined; if three words were written without a line, it was considered worthless.
- The ink must be black only and prepared according to a special recipe that was used only for the copying of scripture.
- The original used to make the copy must be authentic, it must not be deviated from by the copyist, and the scribe must say each word aloud as he wrote it.
- No word or letter could ever be written from memory; the scribe must always look first at the original before writing his copy.
- A space of a hair or thread must intervene between each consonant.
- A space of the breadth of nine consonants must come between each section.
- No word must ever touch another.
- A space of three lines must come between every book.
- The fifth book of Moses (Deuteronomy) must end exactly with a line.
- Before copying, the scribe must wash his whole body.
- While copying, the scribe must sit in full Jewish dress.

- The scribe must write the name of God with a pen newly dipped into the ink.
- Each time the scribe came across the Hebrew word for God, he had to wipe his pen clean. And when he came across the name of God, Jehovah (*YHWH*), he had to wash his whole body before he could write it.
- Should a king address the scribe while writing that name, he must take no notice.
- If a sheet of parchment had one mistake on it, the sheet was condemned. If there were three mistakes found on any page, the whole manuscript was condemned. Each scroll had to be checked within 30 days of its writing, or it was considered unholy.
- Every word and every letter was counted. If a letter or word was omitted, the manuscript was condemned.

In his book, *Story of Our English Bible*, W. Scott wrote, ...*It is well known that among the Jews it was the profession of the Masorites, or doctors of tradition, to transcribe the scriptures. We know to what extent these indefatigable scholars carried their respect for the letter; and when we read the rules under which their labours were carried on, we understand the use that the providence of God (who had "confided his oracles to the Jews") made of their superstition. They reckoned the number of verses, words, and letters in each book. They tell us, for instance, that the letter A occurs forty-two thousand three hundred and seventy-seven times in the Bible; the letter B thirty-eight thousand two hundred and eighteen times; and so on to the end. They were scrupulous of changing the position even of a letter, though evidently misplaced, but limited themselves to noting in the margin, supposing some mystery was involved. They tell us which is the middle letter of the Pentateuch, as well as of each of the books of which it is composed. They never allowed themselves to correct their manuscript; and if any mistake escaped them, they rejected the papyrus or the skin which they had blemished, and recommenced upon a fresh one; for they were equally interdicted from even correcting one of their own errors, and from retaining for their sacred volume a single parchment or skin in which an error had been made....*

The incredible accuracy of these scribes has been attested to by the discovery of ancient manuscripts, which have been found to be virtually identical with copies made by scribes over a thousand years later. The care that was taken by the copyists of the Hebrew scriptures is demonstrated by the very small number of deviations in comparable manuscripts.

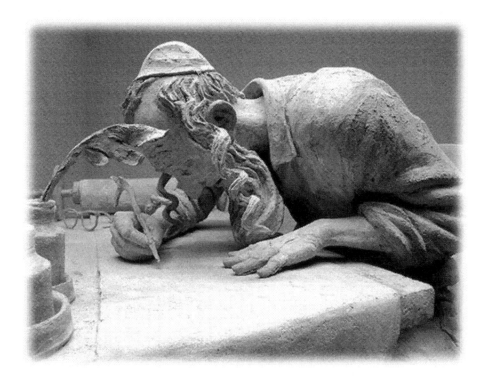

Kennicott's edition of the Hebrew Bible deals with consonantal variants in over 600 different manuscripts. Dr. Robert Dick Wilson stated that there are about 284,000,000 letters in the manuscripts considered by Kennicott and that among these manuscripts there are about 900,000 variants, approximately 750,000 of which are the insignificant variation of w and y. Among these, there is only about one variant for 316 letters and, apart from the w and y variation, only about one variant for 1,580 letters. The variants for the most part are supported by only one or by only a few of the manuscripts.[108] Dr. Wilson has elsewhere said that there are hardly any variant readings in these manuscripts with the support of more than one out of the 200 to 400 manuscripts in which each book is found, except in the full and defective writing of the vowels, a matter which has no bearing on either the pronunciation or the meaning of the text.[109]

R. Laird Harris stated, *We can now be sure that copyists worked with great care and accuracy on the Old Testament, even back to 225 B.C....indeed, it would be rash skepticism that would now deny that we have our Old Testament in a form very close to that used by Ezra when he taught the word of the Lord to those who had returned from the Babylonian captivity.*[110]

When discussing the significance of the Dead Sea Scrolls in demonstrating the exceptional accuracy of the Masoretic scribes, F.F. Bruce stated, *The new evidence confirms what we had already good reason to believe that the Jewish scribes of the early Christian centuries copied and recopied the text of the Hebrew Bible with the utmost fidelity.*[111]

[108] Robert Dick Wilson, "The Textual Criticism of the Old Testament", *The Princeton Theological Review,* XXVII (1929) pp. 40f.
[109] *A Scientific Investigation of the Old Testament*, 1959, Moody Press, pp. 61f.
[110] R. Laird Harris, *Can I Trust My Bible?*, 1963, Moody Press, p. 124.
[111] F.F. Bruce, *Second Thoughts on the Dead Sea Scrolls*, 1956, pp. 61-62.

ORDER AND STRUCTURE OF THE BIBLICAL BOOKS

9

The structure of the Bible has undergone a number of progressive stages throughout its history. In its earliest stages of formation, the scriptures were made up of both the written word and oral tradition. The earliest books of the Bible would have been Genesis and Job, and they were probably passed down until eventually they were officially canonized during the time of Moses.

There are 66 books in our modern Bibles. This series of books is divided into the Old and New Testaments. The 39 books of the Old Testament were the oracles of God revealed to the Hebrew people before the time of Christ. The 27 books of the New Testament were added by the Early Church to create the complete biblical record we have today.

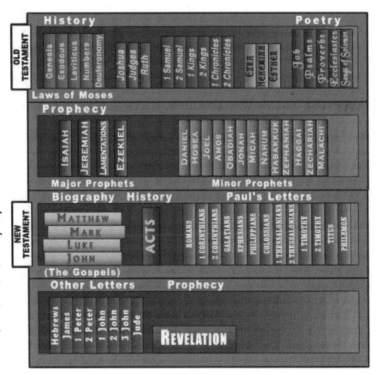

THE OLD TESTAMENT/THE HEBREW BIBLE

Thirty-nine books comprise the writings of the Old Testament. The Hebrew people originally divided these into three groups made up of the law, called the Torah in Hebrew; the Prophets, called Neviim; and the Writings, called Khetuvim. In the first few centuries after Jesus, the Jews called these writings the *Mikra,* which means *that which is read.* This was replaced by the term *Tanakh* around the 5th or 6th century.[112] The acronym *Tanakh,* formed by combining the letters of Torah, Neviim, and Khetuvim, is used by the Jews to encompass the entire series of books.

In the earliest traditions regarding the Hebrew scriptures there were between 22 and 24 books. This is due to the fact that some of the original books were later separated into two parts. Examples of this would be the books of Samuel, Kings, and Chronicles, which were originally made up of one book each. Ezra and Nehemiah were another example as well as the 12 Minor Prophets, which at one time were a single book.

The original Hebrew division of the biblical books may have been as follows:

Genesis, Exodus, Leviticus, Numbers, Deuteronomy, Joshua, Judges, Ruth, Samuel, Kings, Chronicles, Ezra/Nehemiah, Esther, Job, Psalms, Proverbs, Ecclesiastes, Song of Solomon, Isaiah, Jeremiah, Lamentations, Ezekiel, Daniel, and the Twelve Minor Prophets

The Jewish historian Josephus believed that Judges and Ruth were also originally combined, as well as Jeremiah and Lamentations, which would bring the number of books down to 22. This would perfectly correspond to the 22 letters of the Hebrew alphabet.

---

[112] Daniel J. Silver, *The Story of Scripture*, Basic Books Inc., 1990.

The original order of the Hebrew Bible was somewhat different than our present order. The three divisions of the Hebrew Bible were broken up into six sets of writings.

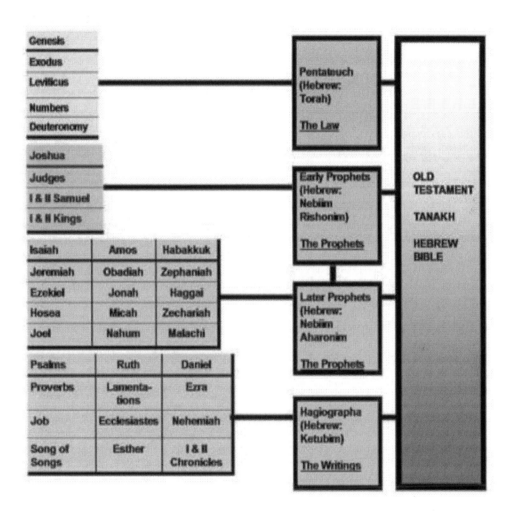

The law was considered to be one book of five parts rather than five individual books. The five divisions of the law may have stemmed from the limitations of scroll size. Due to the volume of the law, it would have had to have been divided into separate sections of manageable size. The Hebrew name for the five books of the law is the Torah.

The Christian term for these five books is the Pentateuch, which is the Greek phrase meaning "five books." This title was believed to have originated with Origen, though he may have borrowed this term from the Jews of Alexandria.[113]

The terms "Former" and "Latter" prophets can be somewhat misleading. The Former Prophets were written more from an historical perspective, whereas the Latter Prophets were much more prophetic in their communication. The terms "former" and "latter" do not necessarily infer that the former were written before, as some of the latter prophets were written during the time of the former prophets.

The Writings are divided into three sections. The Poetical books of Job, Psalms, and Proverbs are the capstone of all the poetic writings and have been called "the books of truth" by the Jews.[114]

The Five Rolls, or Megilloth, were books that were to be read in public (usually in the synagogue) to commemorate specific events or seasons. Song of Songs (Song of Solomon) was read at the feast of Passover in the early spring as it was believed to represent a type of the love of God for the nation of Israel. Ruth was read at the feast of Pentecost during the early summer wheat harvest. Lamentations was read on the ninth of Ab to commemorate the fall of Solomon's temple on that day in 586 B.C. Ecclesiastes was read during the Feast of Tabernacles in the early fall. Ecclesiastes deals with the futile vanity of life, and the Jews related this to the wilderness experience recalled in the Feast of Tabernacles. Esther was read during the Feast of Purim in the early spring in remembrance of the deliverance of the Jews from Haman.

---

[113] Origen, *Commentarii in evangelium Joannis* 5.6.1.5, 13.26.154.2, Selecta in Genesim 12.140.31, et. al.
[114] Harrison, *Introduction to the Old Testament*, p. 965.

The final Historical books in the Hebrew Bible were Daniel, Ezra, and Chronicles. Though Daniel would seem to belong with the prophetic books, the Jews placed it with the historical writings, possibly due to the fact that it contains a running narrative of part of the history of the captivity and the significant characters involved.

Jesus spoke of three distinct divisions of the Bible in his time. At times he would use the term "the Law and the Prophets," and at other times "the Law of Moses, the Prophets, and the Psalms." This second statement would clearly encompass the Hebrew divisions. The Psalms spoken of in this way are representative of the poetical books as a whole.

> **Luke 24:44-45** *And he said unto them, These are the words which I spake unto you, while I was yet with you, that all things must be fulfilled, which were written in the law of Moses, and in the prophets, and in the psalms, concerning me. Then he opened he their understanding, that they might understand the scriptures,*

This then defines the scriptures of Jesus's day (the Old Testament) as the Law, the Prophets, and the Psalms. The shorter title of the Law and the Prophets was also used by Jesus and the writers of scripture when referring to the Old Testament.[115]

The book of Chronicles was the final book of the Hebrew Bible. Jesus himself verified that the Hebrew scriptures were in this historical order in his day:

> **Luke 11:51** *From the blood of Abel unto the blood of Zacharias, which perished between the altar and the temple: verily I say unto you, It shall be required of this generation.*

This denotes the beginning of the Hebrew scriptures with Genesis and the death of righteous Abel:

---

[115] Matthew 7:12, 22:40, Luke 16:16, John 1:45, Acts 13:15, Romans 3:21, etc.

Genesis 4:8 *And Cain talked with Abel his brother: and it came to pass, when they were in the field, that Cain rose up against Abel his brother, and slew him.*

…and the last historical book of the scriptures where the death of Zechariah the priest is recorded:

II Chronicles 24:21 *And they conspired against him, and stoned him with stones at the commandment of the king in the court of the house of the Lord.*

The original Hebrew scriptures were not divided into chapters and verses. The first known sectional divisions made to the scriptures are believed to have been begun shortly before the Babylonian captivity, which occurred around 586 B.C. Scholars call this first division the **Palestinian sections**. This involved the five books of the Torah only. These were divided into 154 sections called Sedarim (Seder in the singular). These were arranged to allow for a three-year reading schedule. During the Babylonian captivity, probably from about 586 to 536 B.C., the Torah was divided into 54 more comprehensive sections called Parashiyyoth (Parasha in the singular). These divisions were known as the **Babylonian sections**. These 54 sections were later divided further into 669 sections. The Parashiyyoth sections were arranged along a one-year reading schedule. Around 165 B.C. the Prophetic books were divided into the **Maccabean sections**. These were 54 sections called Haphtarahs. This division was a continuation of the Sedarim division that had been made to the Torah.

The sectional division of our modern Old Testament is believed to have originated with the translators of the Septuagint sometime between 150 and 300 years before Christ. The Septuagint was the first known translation of the Hebrew scriptures into Greek. This was necessitated by the fact that the Greek language had become the predominant spoken language of the Western and Middle Eastern parts of the world. Many Jews living outside of Palestine spoke the Greek language and were no longer fluent in their native tongue.

The translators of the Septuagint organized the individual books according to their concept of the subject matter rather than by the scribal traditions. Our modern Old Testament is separated topically into three parts: the Historical Books, the Poetic Books, and the Prophetic Books.

The Historical Books (17)
Genesis, Exodus, Leviticus, Numbers, Deuteronomy, Joshua, Judges, Ruth, I and II Samuel, I and II Kings, I and II Chronicles, Ezra, Nehemiah, Esther

The Poetic Books (5)
Job, Psalms, Proverbs, Ecclesiastes, Song of Solomon

The Prophetic Books (17)
Isaiah, Jeremiah, Lamentations, Ezekiel, Daniel, Hosea, Joel, Amos, Obadiah, Jonah, Micah, Nahum, Habakkuk, Zephaniah, Haggai, Zechariah, Malachi

---

Stephen Langton, Archbishop of Canterbury, divided the Bible into chapters around 1227 A.D.[116] In 1382 A.D. the Wycliffe Bible used Langton's chapter divisions. The Wycliffe Bible was so influential upon the translations that followed it that all subsequent English translations used this same division of chapters. R. Nathan divided the Old Testament into verses in 1448 A.D. The New Testament was divided into verses by Robert Stephanus in 1551 A.D. The first Bible to contain complete chapter and verse divisions was the Geneva Bible in 1560 A.D.

---

[116] Norman Geisler and William Nix, *A General Introduction to the Bible*, p. 340, Moody Press, 1968, 1986.

THE NEW TESTAMENT

Twenty-six books comprise the body of New Testament writings. These are arranged according to three topical divisions: the Historical writings, the Epistles, or Letters to the churches, and the Prophetic writings.

There are generally considered to be two classes of Epistles: the Pauline Epistles (those written by the apostle Paul, usually to an individual or specific church) and the General or Church Epistles (written by a variety of authors and usually intended for the churches in general rather than specifically).

The Historical Books (5)
Matthew, Mark, Luke, John, Acts

The Epistles (21)
Pauline
Romans, I and II Corinthians, Galatians, Ephesians, Philippians, Colossians, I and II Thessalonians, I and II Timothy, Titus, Philemon
General
Hebrews, James, I and II Peter, I, II, and III John, Jude

The Prophetic Books (1)
Revelation

CANONIZATION OF THE BIBLICAL BOOKS

10

CANONIZATION OF THE OLD TESTAMENT

The term "canon" is used in regard to the Bible to signify the books that were accepted as divinely inspired by God. They were the officially sanctioned writings. The idea of canonization is often misunderstood. It is not the leaders or the laity that have the authority to decide what is and is not included in the sacred scriptures. That decision is God's alone. We can determine what has been accepted by man as God's inspired word, but we must understand how to determine why the individual books are either God's word or man's.

One of the most important evidences for canonicity in the Old Testament was the writer himself. In order for a book to be considered canonical, it must have been written by one who was a true and proven mouthpiece of God. So our first question in regard to canonicity must be, Was the writer a true prophet, a man of God whose words were demonstrated to have prophetic insight and anointing?

This is the most important verification of whether the writing is inspired of God. Throughout the scriptures we find that the men who wrote the words of God were those who had either a prophetic calling or a prophetic gift operating. The Jews believed that only a prophet could communicate the inspired word in this way.

Josephus, the 1st century Jewish historian wrote, *It therefore naturally, or rather necessarily, follows (seeing that with us it is not open to everybody to write the records, and that there is no discrepancy in what is written; seeing that on the contrary, the prophets alone had this privilege, obtaining their knowledge of the most remote and ancient history through the inspiration which they owed to God, and committing to writing a clear account of the events of their own time just as they occurred)—it follows, I say, that we do not possess myriads of inconsistent books, conflicting with each other. Our books, those which are justly accredited, are but two and twenty, and contain the record of all time...From Artaxerxes to our own time the complete history has been written, but has not been deemed worthy of equal credit with the earlier records, because of the failure of the exact succession of the prophets. We have given practical proof of our reverence for our own Scriptures. For, although such long ages have now passed, no one has ventured either to add, or to remove, or to alter a syllable; and it is instinct with every Jew, from the day of his birth, to regard them as the decrees of God, to abide by them, and, if need be, cheerfully to die for them.*[117]

The Jewish rabbinical tradition generally believed that the inspiration of the scripture ceased with the death of the last of the prophets, that the Holy Spirit no longer anointed men to write the divine words after the time of Malachi, about 425 B.C. The Tosefta Sotah contains the statement: *With the death of Haggai, Zechariah and Malachi the latter prophets, the Holy Spirit ceased out of Israel...*[118]

---

[117] *Contra Apion* 1.7-42.
[118] *Tosefta Sotah* 13.2.

According to some rabbis, the Spirit of prophecy had left Israel either at the time of the destruction of Solomon's temple or during the period between its destruction and the building of the second temple by the Jews returning from the Babylonian captivity.[119]

In some sense all the writers of the Old Testament could be considered prophets. The prophetic office is made known through the two operations of foretelling and forthtelling. All of the writers of the Old Testament were dispensaries of one or both of these gifts. Prophecy, as defined by our modern understanding, is the gift of foretelling, usually in the sense of foretelling future events. This was certainly a major part of the prophetic call in the Old and New Testaments. The Bible is full of future prophetic insights. Some of these events have come to pass and some are yet to be. This is the clearest evidence of an individual having heard the word of God, for God alone knows the end from the beginning. It is testimony to His power and foresight that He alone can know the end of all things.

> **Isaiah 44:7-8** *And who, as I, shall call, and shall declare it, and set it in order for me, since I appointed the ancient people? and the things that are coming, and shall come, let them show unto them. Fear ye not, neither be afraid: have not I told thee from that time, and have declared it? ye are even my witnesses. Is there a God beside me? yea, there is no God; I know not any.*
>
> **Isaiah 46:9-10** *Remember the former things of old: for I am God, and there is none else; I am God, and there is none like me, Declaring the end from the beginning, and from ancient times the things that are not yet done, saying, My counsel shall stand, and I will do all my pleasure:*

---

[119] *Babylonian Baba Bathra* 12a, 12b, etc.

In contrast to foretelling, forthtelling is communication of the present will and message of God. This is often done directly through the vessel of communication. Many of the commands and laws of God were given in this way. Forthtelling often was followed by an immediate demonstration of God's power, backing up the bearer of the message. Moses was a perfect example of this type of prophetic messenger. A number of the great men of the Bible were gifted in both of these prophetic functions; perhaps the greatest example would have been Jesus himself. Jesus not only foretold events that were to come in a future sense, but he spoke the present message of God with authority and with signs and power that validated his message.

There are three definite marks of a true prophet of God:

1. His prophecy must ALWAYS be in accord with the law of God:
Deuteronomy 13:1-5 *If there arise among you a prophet, or a dreamer of dreams, and giveth thee a sign or a wonder, And the sign or the wonder come to pass, whereof he spake unto thee, saying, Let us go after other gods, which thou hast not known, and let us serve them; Thou shalt not hearken unto the words of that prophet, or that dreamer of dreams: for the LORD your God proveth you, to know whether ye love the LORD your God with all your heart and with all your soul. Ye shall walk after the LORD your God, and fear him, and keep his commandments, and obey his voice, and ye shall serve him, and cleave unto him. And that prophet, or that dreamer of dreams, shall be put to death; because he hath spoken to turn you away from the LORD your God, which brought you out of the land of Egypt, and redeemed you out of the house of bondage, to thrust thee out of the way which the LORD thy God commanded thee to walk in. So shalt thou put the evil away from the midst of thee.*

2. His prophecy must ALWAYS come to pass:

Deuteronomy 18:21-22 *And if thou say in thine heart, How shall we know the word which the LORD hath not spoken? When a prophet speaketh in the name of the LORD, if the thing follow not, nor come to pass, that is the thing which the LORD hath not spoken, but the prophet hath spoken it presumptuously: thou shalt not be afraid of him.*

3. His prophecy is often validated by a sign. Moses asked the Lord for this type of witness in order that it would be known that he was the messenger of God:

Exodus 4:1-9 *And Moses answered and said, But, behold, they will not believe me, nor hearken unto my voice: for they will say, The LORD hath not appeared unto thee. And the LORD said unto him, What is that in thine hand? And he said, A rod. And he said, Cast it on the ground. And he cast it on the ground, and it became a serpent; and Moses fled from before it. And the LORD said unto Moses, Put forth thine hand, and take it by the tail. And he put forth his hand, and caught it, and it became a rod in his hand: That they may believe that the LORD God of their fathers, the God of Abraham, the God of Isaac, and the God of Jacob, hath appeared unto thee. And the LORD said furthermore unto him, Put now thine hand into thy bosom. And he put his hand into his bosom: and when he took it out, behold, his hand was leprous as snow. And he said, Put thine hand into thy bosom again. And he put his hand into his bosom again; and plucked it out of his bosom, and, behold, it was turned again as his other flesh. And it shall come to pass, if they will not believe thee, neither hearken to the voice of the first sign, that they will believe the voice of the latter sign. And it shall come to pass, if they will not believe also these two signs, neither hearken unto thy voice, that thou shalt take of the water of the river, and pour it upon the dry land: and the water which thou takest out of the river shall become blood upon the dry land.*

This was the type of witness given to Hezekiah by Isaiah the prophet to validate the truth of God's promise:

II Kings 20:8-11 *And Hezekiah said unto Isaiah, What shall be the sign that the LORD will heal me, and that I shall go up into the house of the LORD the third day? And Isaiah said, This sign shalt thou have of the LORD, that the LORD will do the thing that he hath spoken: shall the shadow go forward ten degrees, or go back ten degrees? And Hezekiah answered, It is a light thing for the shadow to go down ten degrees: nay, but let the shadow return backward ten degrees. And Isaiah the prophet cried unto the LORD: and he brought the shadow ten degrees backward, by which it had gone down in the dial of Ahaz.*

Elijah and Elisha were some of the most dynamic examples of this in the Old Testament. Their ministries were full of miraculous events that demonstrated their calling and authority. These men had powerful witnesses of God backing up their words: an answer of fire from heaven, the sick healed, and the dead raised to life.

The second thing we must establish in determining whether a book is canonical is to make certain that the writings themselves adhered to and were in harmony with God's prior revelation. Was the book in complete contradiction to that which had previously been revealed? Then it certainly could not be considered canonical. This is not to say that apparent contradictions should rule out a message as being from God. It is often found in the scripture that those things that appear to demonstrate contradiction are revealed through deeper study and the anointing of the Spirit to be themselves evidence of an even more intricate harmony.

A third factor that must be considered in a book's canonicity is whether it has dynamic life within its words. God's word is alive and active. The dynamic, quickening power of His word changes all that it comes into contact with. Its life saturates into anything it touches. The true word has this life in and of itself; it vibrates in tune with the thundering voice of the Almighty.

The last two considerations for canonicity are made up of the testimony of reliable witnesses and in a book's acceptance by the Jews. These are the two least important sources, and yet they are the most quoted by modern apologists. The quotations of the ancient sources can be good benchmarks of what books were considered canonical by the people of God, but they are no more than the opinions of men. This is also true in the sense of the Jewish scholars. It is certain, though, that the Jews were those to whom God committed His word, in its primary expression and in its preservation. Paul testified to this legacy in his letter to the Romans:

> **Romans 3:1** *What advantage then hath the Jew? or what profit is there of circumcision? Much every way: chiefly, because that unto them were committed the oracles of God.*

Through the painstakingly detailed copying of the Jewish scribes, the Old Testament text was passed down to us. Due to the great reverence that they held for the word of God, we can be certain that the testimony of the Jewish patriarchs has been properly maintained.

The final compilation of the books of the Torah (Genesis through Deuteronomy) took place under the hand of Moses. The books were given to the Levitical priesthood to preserve.

> **Deuteronomy 31:24-26** *And it came to pass, when Moses had made an end of writing the words of this law in a book, until they were finished, That Moses commanded the Levites, which bare the ark of the covenant of the Lord, saying, Take this book of the law, and put it in the side of the ark of the covenant of the Lord your God, that it may be there for a witness against thee.*

God Himself sealed the canon of the Torah with the statement He made to Moses: only that which He had commanded and revealed could be considered scripture:

Deuteronomy 4:2 *Ye shall not add unto the word which I command you, neither shall ye diminish aught from it, that ye may keep the commandments of the Lord your God which I command you.*

After the death of Moses, Joshua completed the last section of Deuteronomy and thus finished the editing and compilation of the books of the law. He continued to write the divine words and experiences as scripture, adding what the Lord divinely inspired him to record and including it with the books of the law.

Joshua 24:26-27 *And Joshua wrote these words in the book of the law of God, and took a great stone, and set it up there under an oak, that was by the sanctuary of the Lord. And Joshua said unto all the people, Behold, this stone shall be a witness unto us; for it hath heard all the words of the Lord which he spake unto us: it shall be therefore a witness unto you, lest ye deny your God.*

There were probably five major periods of compilation and canonization during the development of the Old Testament, corresponding to the dispensation of each particular group of writers.

THE FIVE PERIODS OF OLD TESTAMENT CANONIZATION

WRITER'S DISPENSATION	TIME PERIOD	BOOKS SANCTIONED
Moses and Joshua	1462–1372 B.C.	Genesis, Exodus, Leviticus, Numbers, Deuteronomy, Joshua, Job
Samuel, David, and Solomon	1073–945 B.C.	Judges, Ruth, I and II Samuel, the majority of Psalms, Proverbs, Ecclesiastes, Song of Solomon
Hezekiah and Isaiah	740–697 B.C.	Sections of Psalms, Proverbs, Ecclesiastes, and Song of Solomon, Isaiah and very likely Hosea, Joel, Amos, Obadiah, Jonah, and Micah
Josiah and Jeremiah	647–522 B.C.	I and II Kings, Jeremiah, Lamentations, and possibly some of the prophets (Ezekiel, Daniel, Nahum, Habakkuk, Zephaniah)
Ezra	About 450–400 B.C.	I and II Chronicles, Ezra, Nehemiah, Esther, Haggai, Zechariah, Malachi, and possibly some of the minor prophets (Ezekiel, Daniel, Nahum, Habakkuk, Zephaniah)

The first period would have taken place under the dispensation of Moses and Joshua as previously described. This probably occurred from about 1462 to 1372 B.C. and would have been made up of the editing of the ancient records of the patriarchal fathers and the revelation of the law through Moses and Joshua.

During the activity of Samuel, David, and Solomon, another period of addition and canonization would have taken place. Samuel probably wrote from about 1073 B.C. until his death around 1025 B.C. According to Talmudic tradition he is believed to have been responsible for recording the history of the 300-year period between the death of Joshua and the time of Saul and David. David wrote his Psalms before his death about 985 B.C. Solomon's poetic and proverbial contributions were completed by the time of his death about 945 B.C. The writings of Samuel and the Psalms and quotations of David and Solomon would likely have been made a part of the Biblical canon during the establishment of the Temple structure and order of worship. This was a time period of great contribution in the areas of poetry and wisdom literature by inspired men of God.

The next period in which canonization would have taken place would have been during the time of Hezekiah and Isaiah. Isaiah began his prophesying about 740 B.C. and Hezekiah became co-regent of Judah about 727 B.C. It is likely that a great deal of organization and structuring of the scripture was being completed during Hezekiah's reign, which lasted until his death about 697 B.C. A great reform took place during Hezekiah's rule that included the restoration of the Temple:

II Chronicles 29:1-11 *Hezekiah began to reign when he was five and twenty years old, and he reigned nine and twenty years in Jerusalem. And his mother's name was Abijah, the daughter of Zechariah. And he did that which was right in the sight of the LORD, according to all that David his father had done. He in the first year of his reign, in the first month, opened the doors of the* *house of the LORD, and repaired them. And he brought in the priests and the Levites, and gathered them together into the east street, And said unto them, Hear me, ye Levites, sanctify now yourselves, and sanctify the house of the LORD God of your fathers, and carry forth the filthiness out of the holy place. For our fathers have trespassed, and done that which was evil in the eyes of the LORD our God, and have forsaken him, and have turned away their faces from the habitation of the LORD, and turned their backs. Also they have shut up the doors of the porch, and put out the lamps, and have not burned incense nor offered burnt offerings in the holy place unto the God of Israel. Wherefore the wrath of the LORD was upon Judah and Jerusalem, and he hath delivered them to trouble, to astonishment, and to hissing, as ye see with your eyes. For, lo, our fathers have fallen by the sword, and our sons and our daughters and our wives are in captivity for this. Now it is in mine heart to make a covenant with the LORD God of Israel, that his fierce wrath may turn away from us. My sons, be not now negligent: for the LORD hath chosen you to stand before him, to serve him, and that ye should minister unto him, and burn incense.*

After the temple had been cleansed and purified, Hezekiah restored the sacrificial system and the musical service:

II Chronicles 29:20-36 *Then Hezekiah the king rose early, and gathered the rulers of the city, and went up to the house of the LORD. And they brought seven bullocks, and seven rams, and seven lambs, and seven he goats, for a sin offering for the kingdom, and for the sanctuary, and for Judah. And he commanded the priests the sons of Aaron to offer them on the altar of the LORD....And the priests killed them, and they made reconciliation with their blood upon the altar, to make an atonement for all Israel: for the king commanded that the burnt offering and the sin offering should be made for all Israel. And he set the Levites in the house of the LORD with cymbals, with psalteries, and with harps, according to the commandment of David, and of Gad the king's seer, and Nathan* *the prophet: for so was the commandment of the LORD by his prophets. And the Levites stood with the instruments of David, and the priests with the trumpets. And Hezekiah commanded to offer the burnt offering upon the altar. And when the burnt offering began, the song of the LORD began also with the trumpets, and with the instruments ordained by David king of Israel. And all the congregation worshipped, and the singers sang, and the trumpeters sounded: and all this continued until the burnt offering was finished. And when they had made an end of offering, the king and all that were present with him bowed themselves, and worshipped. Moreover Hezekiah the king and the princes commanded the Levites to sing praise unto the LORD with the words of David, and of Asaph the seer. And they sang praises with gladness, and they bowed their heads and worshipped....So the service of the house of the LORD was set in order. And Hezekiah rejoiced, and all the people, that God had prepared the people: for the thing was done suddenly.*

Hezekiah also restored the order of the priests, as well as the tithes and offerings:

II Chronicles 31:2-6 *And Hezekiah appointed the courses of the priests and the Levites after their courses, every man according to his service, the priests and Levites for burnt offerings and for peace offerings, to minister, and to give thanks, and to praise in the gates of the tents of the LORD....Moreover he commanded the people that dwelt in Jerusalem to give the portion of the priests and the Levites, that they might be encouraged in the law of the LORD. And as soon as the commandment came abroad, the children of Israel brought in abundance the firstfruits of corn, wine, and oil, and honey, and of all the increase of the field; and the tithe of all things brought they in abundantly. And concerning the children of Israel and Judah, that dwelt in the cities of Judah, they also brought in the tithe of oxen and sheep, and the tithe of holy things which were consecrated unto the LORD their God, and laid them by heaps.*

During this time of restoration Hezekiah was compiling and sanctioning portions of the scriptures. His scribes, mentioned in the book of Proverbs, were probably responsible for the compilation of sections of the books of Psalms and Proverbs.

Proverbs 25:1 *These are also proverbs of Solomon, which the men of Hezekiah king of Judah copied out.*

The Talmud states that parts of Proverbs, Ecclesiastes, Song of Solomon, the book of Isaiah, and some of the Minor Prophets were compiled by the scribes of Hezekiah.[120] It is possible that some of the Psalms may have been a part of this work also.

In the Hebrew manuscripts, the letters H Z K (in Hebrew) are placed at the end of every book of the Old Testament except the five books of the Megilloth (Ruth, Song of Solomon, Ecclesiastes, Lamentations, and Esther). It is believed by a number of scholars that this may have been a designation representing Hezekiah, as his name in Hebrew is spelled with these same three consonants. Books that were written after the time of Hezekiah also have this same three-letter seal, but this may be a testimony to Hezekiah's earlier work of restoring the word of God. Bullinger stated that an addition was added to the initials at the end of the books written after Hezekiah's time that read, "be bound, we will bind," which may represent the idea of the accepted canon being bound shut.

The meaning of the name Hezekiah in Hebrew can be translated "God has strengthened." The Hebrew roots that make up the name are ***yah*** which is the shortened form of ***Yahweh***, and ***chazaq***, which can mean "to strengthen", "to bind", or "to fasten". Thus, the name of Hezekiah carries the meaning of God binding or fastening a thing. God has not only strengthened His word, but He has bound and sealed it.

---

[120] *Baba Bathra* 15a.

Isaiah, who was the major prophet to the southern kingdom of Judah during this time, would certainly have had a part in the restoration and development of the scriptures during Hezekiah's reign. Isaiah was considered one of the greatest of the prophets, and his dynamic ministry would have added a crucial element to the restoration process.

The next period of canonization probably took place during the time of Josiah and Jeremiah. Little more than 50 years had passed and already the house of the Lord was in a state of disrepair. Josiah, king of Judah, commanded that the house of the Lord be repaired. During the building work the book of the law was discovered:

II Kings 22:3-8 *And it came to pass in the eighteenth year of king Josiah, that the king sent Shaphan the son of Azaliah, the son of Meshullam, the scribe, to the house of the LORD, saying, Go up to Hilkiah the high priest, that he may sum the silver which is brought into the house of the LORD, which the keepers of the door have gathered of the people: And let them deliver it into the hand of the doers of the work, that have the oversight of the house of the LORD: and let them give it to the doers of the work which is in the house of the LORD, to repair the breaches of the house, Unto carpenters, and builders, and masons, and to buy timber and hewn stone to repair the house. Howbeit there was no reckoning made with them of the money that was delivered into their hand, because they dealt faithfully. And Hilkiah the high priest said unto Shaphan the scribe, I have found the book of the law in the house of the LORD. And Hilkiah gave the book to Shaphan, and he read it.*

It is clear by the reaction of Hilkiah, Shaphan, and Josiah that the scriptures had been lost or misplaced. Josiah immediately recognized the importance of the discovery:

II Kings 22:9-13 *And Shaphan the scribe came to the king, and brought the king word again, and said, Thy servants have gathered the money that was found in the house, and have delivered it into the hand of them that do the work, that have the oversight of the* *house of the LORD. And Shaphan the scribe showed the king, saying, Hilkiah the priest hath delivered me a book. And Shaphan read it before the king. And it came to pass, when the king had heard the words of the book of the law, that he rent his clothes. And the king commanded Hilkiah the priest, and Ahikam the son of Shaphan, and Achbor the son of Michaiah, and Shaphan the scribe, and Asahiah a servant of the king's, saying, Go ye, inquire of the LORD for me, and for the people, and for all Judah, concerning the words of this book that is found: for great is the wrath of the LORD that is kindled against us, because our fathers have not hearkened unto the words of this book, to do according unto all that which is written concerning us.*

This discovery helped to inspire the great reformation under Josiah. Josiah was one of the few kings of Judah who was faithful and obedient to the will of God. He was the only king of Judah who completely eradicated the pagan worship in the land. It had been prophesied over a hundred years before his time that he would accomplish this work:

I Kings 13:1-2 *And, behold, there came a man of God out of Judah by the word of the LORD unto Bethel: and Jeroboam stood by the altar to burn incense. And he cried against the altar in the word of the LORD, and said, O altar, altar, thus saith the LORD; Behold, a child shall be born unto the house of David, Josiah by name; and upon thee shall he offer the priests of the high places that burn incense upon thee, and men's bones shall be burnt upon thee.*

This cleansing of the land took place just as it had been prophesied. The reading of the scriptures that had been found inspired Josiah to cast down all the pagan places of worship and renew the worship of God in the land.

II Kings 23:1-25 *And the king sent, and they gathered unto him all the elders of Judah and of Jerusalem. And the king went up into the house of the LORD, and all the men of Judah and all the inhabitants of Jerusalem with him, and the priests, and the prophets, and all* *the people, both small and great: and he read in their ears all the words of the book of the covenant which was found in the house of the LORD. And the king stood by a pillar, and made a covenant before the LORD, to walk after the LORD, and to keep his commandments and his testimonies and his statutes with all their heart and all their soul, to perform the words of this covenant that were written in this book. And all the people stood to the covenant. And the king commanded Hilkiah the high priest, and the priests of the second order, and the keepers of the door, to bring forth out of the temple of the LORD all the vessels that were made for Baal, and for the grove, and for all the host of heaven: and he burned them without Jerusalem in the fields of Kidron, and carried the ashes of them unto Bethel. And he put down the idolatrous priests....And he brought out the grove from the house of the LORD, without Jerusalem, unto the brook Kidron, and burned it at the brook Kidron, and stamped it small to powder, and cast the powder thereof upon the graves of the children of the people. And he brake down the houses of the sodomites, that were by the house of the LORD,.....And he brought all the priests out of the cities of Judah, and defiled the high places where the priests had burned incense, from Geba to Beersheba, and brake down the high places of the gates....And he defiled Topheth, which is in the valley of the children of Hinnom, that no man might make his son or his daughter to pass through the fire to Molech. And he took away the horses that the kings of Judah had given to the sun,...and burned the chariots of the sun with fire. And the altars that were on the top of the upper chamber of Ahaz,...and the altars which Manasseh had made...did the king beat down, and brake them down from thence, and cast the dust of them into the brook Kidron. And the high places that were before Jerusalem, which were on the right hand of the mount of corruption, which Solomon the king of Israel had builded for Ashtoreth the abomination of the Zidonians, and for Chemosh the abomination of the Moabites, and for Milcom the abomination of the children of Ammon, did the king defile. And he brake in pieces the images, and cut down the groves, and filled their places with the bones of men. Moreover the altar that was at Bethel, and the high place which Jeroboam the son of Nebat, who made Israel to sin, had made, both that altar and the high place he brake down, and burned the high place, and stamped it small to powder, and burned the grove. And as Josiah turned himself, he spied the sepulchres that were there in the mount, and sent, and took the bones out of the sepulchres, and burned them upon the altar, and polluted it, according to the word of the LORD which the man of God proclaimed, who proclaimed these words. Then he said, What title is that that I see? And the men of the city told him, It is the sepulchre of the man of God, which came from Judah, and proclaimed these things that thou hast done against the altar of Bethel. And he said, Let him alone; let no man move his bones. So they let his bones alone, with the bones of the prophet that came out of Samaria. And all the houses also of the high places that were in the cities of Samaria,....Josiah took away, and did to them according to all the acts that he had done in Bethel. And he slew all the priests of the high places that were there upon the altars, and burned men's bones upon them, and returned to Jerusalem. And the king commanded all the people, saying, Keep the passover unto the LORD your God, as it is written in the book of this covenant. Surely there was not holden such a passover from the days of the judges that judged Israel, nor in all the days of the kings of Israel, nor of the kings of Judah; But in the eighteenth year of king Josiah, wherein this passover was holden to the LORD in Jerusalem. Moreover the workers with familiar spirits, and the wizards, and the images, and the idols, and all the abominations that were spied in the land of Judah and in Jerusalem, did Josiah put away, that he might perform the words of the law which were written in the book that Hilkiah the priest found in the house of the LORD. And like unto him was there no king before him, that turned to the LORD with all his heart, and with all his soul, and with all his might, according to all the law of Moses; neither after him arose there any like him.*

Josiah began his reformation in the 12th year of his reign,[121] and Jeremiah began prophesying in the 13th year of Josiah's reign. The prophecies of Jeremiah were probably an integral part of the process of restoration. He would have written the books of Jeremiah and Lamentations during and after this time and is believed to have written I and II Kings.

The tradition that Jeremiah carried on the work of the canonization is especially credible in the light of his ministry and activities. He would have been the most likely candidate to preserve and make additions to the body of Scripture. Some traditions hold that Jeremiah removed the Ark of the Covenant from the Temple and hid it before the fall of Jerusalem to the Babylonians. This is based upon the statement made in the non-canonical book of II Maccabees (2:4-8): *It was also in the writing that the prophet, having received an oracle, ordered that the tent and the ark should follow with him, and that he went out to the mountain where Moses had gone up and had seen the inheritance of God. And Jeremiah came and found a cave, and he brought there the tent and the ark and the altar of incense, and he sealed up the entrance.* The books of Maccabees were not considered part of the Scripture and were probably written more than 500 years after the time of Jeremiah, but the tradition could have been based on true events in which Jeremiah may have preserved the holy things along with the writings that had been committed to him.

The final period of canonization under which the Old Testament was completed and sealed took place during the time of Ezra. This period began after the return of the dispersed Jews under Ezra, about 70 years after the time of Jeremiah. The activity of Ezra is usually dated about

---

[121] II Chronicles 34:3.

450–400 B.C. Jewish tradition states that Ezra was responsible for the final editing and compilation of the entire Old Testament canon. Many Jewish scholars, including David Kimchi (1160–1232 A.D.) and Elias Levita (1465–1549 A.D.) maintained that the final collection of the Old Testament canon was completed by Ezra and the members of the Great Synagogue in the 5th century.

Josephus, writing in the 1st century, stated: *We have but 22 books, containing the history of all time, books that are believed to be divine. Of these, 5 belong to Moses, containing his laws and the traditions of the origin of mankind down to the time of his death. From the death of Moses to the reign of Artaxerxes the prophets who succeeded Moses wrote the history of the events that occurred in their own time, in 13 books. The remaining 4 books comprise hymns to God and precepts for the conduct of human life. From the days of Artaxerxes to our own times every event has indeed been recorded; but these recent records have not been deemed worthy of equal credit with those which preceded them, on account of the failure of the exact succession of prophets. There is practical proof of the spirit in which we treat our Scriptures... although so great an interval of time has now passed, not a soul has ventured to add or to remove or to alter a syllable; and it is the instinct of every Jew, from the day of his birth, to consider these Scriptures as the teaching of God, and to abide by them, and, if need be, cheerfully to lay down his life in their behalf.*

Ezra certainly had the technical qualifications necessary to enable him to have finished the work of compilation and canonization. He was both a priest and a scribe, uniting the two lines of Levitical priest and scribal scholar. Ezra was known for his great skill as a scribe:

Ezra 7:6, 11-12 *This Ezra went up from Babylon; and he was a ready scribe in the law of Moses,...Ezra the priest, the scribe, even a scribe of the words of the commandments of the Lord, and of his statutes to Israel. Artaxerxes, king of kings, unto Ezra the priest, a scribe of the law of the God of heaven,....*

Nehemiah 8:1-8 *And all the people gathered themselves together as one man into the street that was before the water gate; and they spake unto Ezra the scribe to bring the book of the law of Moses, which the LORD had commanded to Israel. And Ezra the priest brought the law before the congregation both of men and women, and all that could hear with understanding, upon the first day of the seventh month. And he read therein before the street that was before the water gate from the morning until midday, before the men and the women, and those that could understand; and the ears of all the people were attentive unto the book of the law. And Ezra the scribe stood upon a pulpit of wood, which they had made for the purpose;...And Ezra opened the book in the sight of all the people; (for he was above all the people;) and when he opened it, all the people stood up: And Ezra blessed the LORD, the great God. And all the people answered, Amen, Amen, with lifting up their hands: and they bowed their heads, and worshipped the LORD with their faces to the ground. Also Jeshua, and Bani, and Sherebiah, Jamin, Akkub, Shabbethai, Hodijah, Maaseiah, Kelita, Azariah, Jozabad, Hanan, Pelaiah, and the Levites, caused the people to understand the law: and the people stood in their place. So they read in the book in the law of God distinctly, and gave the sense, and caused them to understand the reading.*

Ezra's work would have included the final compilation of the biblical books of the Old Testament. He finished the inspired historical record of Israel and bound together the remaining prophetic writings. He may also have updated the names of locales and cities in the older writings so that they could be more easily located by the reader. This would explain modernized names of locations being found in books that had been written long before being known by their later names.

It is believed that Ezra copied the scriptures in the square script. This would have distinctively set these copies apart from the older writings, which had been done in the ancient Paleo-Hebraic script. This would have demonstrated a marked separation between other cultural translations and the "official" compilation done under Ezra. It is certain that the scriptures passed down through this line of scribes and used during the time of Jesus were written in the square script. The jot and tittle referred to by Jesus in Matthew 5:18 and elsewhere are components of the square script. The jot or **yod** (**iota** in Greek) was the smallest Hebrew letter in the square script, whereas the tittle is the small pen stroke used to distinguish similar letters from one another. With the exception of five books, all of the books in our modern Old Testament were unanimously and absolutely agreed upon as the inspired word of God. Though the majority of the rabbinical scribes agreed upon the remaining five books, later rabbinical scholars argued over the canonicity of Esther, Proverbs, Ecclesiastes, Song of Solomon, and Ezekiel. Over time nearly all the scribal schools agreed upon the inclusion of these books in the sacred canon.

Esther was questioned primarily due to the fact that the name of God is not mentioned anywhere throughout. Some of the rabbis believed a book without the name of God could not be inspired of God. Once the structure and typological design of Esther are understood, it becomes clear that it is an integral part of the established canon.

The debate over the book of Proverbs centered on the fact that a number of rabbinical scholars felt that some of the statements were contradictory. Proverbs 26:4-5 is a perfect example of this apparent contradiction: *Answer not a fool according to his folly, lest thou also be like unto him. Answer a fool according to his folly, lest he be wise in his own conceit.*

The key to this type of supposed contradiction is in understanding the poetic and linguistic expression of the biblical Hebrew. This type of contradictive contrast is found throughout the scriptures.

Ecclesiastes was criticized due to its skeptical nature. Again, this is nothing more than a lack of understanding of the full intention of the book. The contrast being made in Ecclesiastes is between a life without purpose and a life with purpose. A life that is lived without God as its central purpose is void of meaning. The skepticism with which carnal existence is viewed is contrasted against the summary of the book:

Ecclesiastes 12:13 *Let us hear the conclusion of the whole matter: Fear God, and keep his commandments: for this is the whole duty of man.*

Song of Solomon was questioned due to its apparent sensual nature. The key to understanding the context of the Song of Solomon lies in recognizing the fact that a woman is often symbolic of a body of people or church in the Bible. Israel was called God's wife, and the purified and perfected Church is referred to as the Bride of Christ. Interpreting the book metaphorically opens up an entire range of meaning beneath the surface language.

The rabbinical scholars who disputed the canonicity of the book of Ezekiel did so because they felt that its teachings were contradictory with the revelation in the law of Moses. The dimensions described for the Temple were very different than any of the temples that had existed up to that time. These difficulties in understanding arise when the text is not applied and interpreted correctly. The Temple measurements in Ezekiel were clearly not meant to describe any of the earthly constructs the children of Israel had known. This was a spiritual type of the Temple of God.

One strong extra-biblical testimony to the canon of scripture is the 1st century Jewish historian Josephus. As quoted previously, Josephus believed in the absolute inspiration of the Bible. He defended the complete Old Testament Hebrew canon as we know it today. Josephus accompanied Titus, the Roman general who laid siege to and destroyed Jerusalem and the Temple. It is said that Titus allowed Josephus to remove the sacred scrolls from the Temple before it fell. This would have given Josephus access to the most perfectly preserved copies of the Old Testament scriptures in his day. He actually held the writings in his hands and certainly knew what was included as official scripture. The order and structure of these books were different from our modern design, but they were the same books held as canonical today. He named 22 books as completing the Hebrew canon, and these correspond exactly to the writings of the Masoretic Text used today. As previously discussed under the structure of the Bible, this was a lower number due to the combining of multiple books.

One of the greatest testimonies to the official acceptance and seal upon the Old Testament books for a Christian is in the many quotations from them found in the New Testament. Jesus quoted from all three of the Hebrew divisions of the Old Testament. The apostles quoted hundreds of times from the Old Testament books. Eighteen of the 22 books of the traditional Hebrew canon are quoted by the New Testament writers. The only books not directly quoted are Judges, Chronicles, Esther, and the Song of Solomon.

A number of scholars have attempted to collate the number of quotations from the Old Testament made in the New. The numbers vary widely due to the individual translations and specificity of the quotes. Counts have ranged from about 300 to thousands. The 1989 Jewish New Testament lists 695 direct quotations from the Old Testament.

CANONIZATION OF THE NEW TESTAMENT

The qualification for canonicity of the New Testament books is largely the same as that of the Old Testament. The validity of the writings was based on a number of factors. To begin with, the New Testament books were circulated widely among the Early Church during the lifetimes of the apostles who wrote them. Forged or false writings would have been quickly discovered during this period, and doctrinal deviances would have been put down by those who had been eyewitnesses to the life of Jesus. The acceptance of a book or letter by the Early Church would have been a statement of canonicity in and of itself.

One of the most important determinations of canonicity was whether the book had been authored by an apostle. All of the books of the New Testament were either written by the hand of an apostle or dictated by an apostle to a clerical or ministerial assistant.

The apostolic office was a parallel to the authority and anointing held by the prophets of the Old Testament. The twofold prophetic operation of forthtelling and foretelling was active in the apostles. They were bound to the same rule of prophetic utterance that was given in the Old Testament. First, he must ALWAYS be in accord with the revealed word of God, any prophetic foretelling must ALWAYS come to pass, and the word is often backed up by the Spirit through signs and wonders. Examples of this are found throughout the New Testament historical record:

> **Mark 16:17, 20** *And these signs shall follow them that believe;...And they went forth, and preached everywhere, the Lord working with them, and confirming the word with signs following. Amen*
>
> **Acts 2:22** *Ye men of Israel, hear these words; Jesus of Nazareth, a Man approved of God among you by miracles and wonders and signs, which God did by Him in the midst of you, as ye yourselves also know:*

Acts 4:29-33 *And now, Lord, behold their threatenings: and grant unto thy servants, that with all boldness they may speak thy word, By stretching forth thine hand to heal; and that signs and wonders may be done by the name of thy holy child Jesus. And when they had prayed, the place was shaken where they were assembled together; and they were filled with the Holy Ghost, and they spake the word of God with boldness....And with great power gave the apostles witness of the resurrection of the Lord Jesus: and great grace was upon them all.*

Acts 14:3 *Long time therefore abode they speaking boldly in the Lord, which gave testimony unto the word of his grace, and granted signs and wonders to be done by their hands.*

Romans 15:18-19 *For I will not dare to speak of any of those things which Christ hath not wrought by me, to make the Gentiles obedient, by word and deed, Through mighty signs and wonders, by the power of the Spirit of God; so that from Jerusalem, and round about Illyricum, I have fully preached the gospel of Christ.*

I Corinthians 2:3-5 *And I was with you in weakness, and in fear, and in much trembling. And my speech and my preaching was not with enticing words of man's wisdom, but in demonstration of the Spirit and of power: That your faith should not stand in the wisdom of men, but in the power of God.*

II Corinthians 12:12 *Truly the signs of an apostle were wrought among you in all patience, in signs, and wonders, and mighty deeds.*

Hebrews 2:3-4 *How shall we escape, if we neglect so great salvation, which at the first began to be spoken by the Lord, and was confirmed unto us by them that heard Him; God also bearing them witness, both with signs and wonders, and with divers miracles, and gifts of the Holy Ghost, according to his own will?*

We can see that the apostles were given the revelation of the word of God backed up by demonstration of power. It is not the signs and wonders that define whether a thing is of God though. The authority and validation of the word must be established by more than just the dynamic. Jesus warned his apostles that miraculous events could be demonstrated by false prophets as well:

Matthew 24:24 *For there shall arise false Christs, and false prophets, and shall shew great signs and wonders; insomuch that, if it were possible, they shall deceive the very elect.*

The apostles themselves quoted the New Testament writings of other apostles as Holy scripture. They placed the same emphasis and authority on one another's writings as they did on the books of the Old Testament. They also demonstrated the acceptance of individual books and letters by these quotations.

Jude quotes Peter's writings as part of the established canon:

Jude 17-18 (quoting from II Peter 3:3) *But, beloved, remember ye the words which were spoken before of the apostles of our Lord Jesus Christ; How that they told you there should be mockers in the last time, who should walk after their own ungodly lusts.*

Paul quotes Luke's writing as part of the scripture, going so far as to combine the words of Moses and Jesus together:

I Timothy 5:18 (quoting from Deuteronomy 25:4 and Luke 10:7) *For the scripture saith, Thou shalt not muzzle the ox that treadeth out the corn. And the labourer is worthy of his reward.*

Peter speaks of Paul's epistles, equating them with the scripture:

II Peter 3:15-16 *...even as our beloved brother Paul also according to the wisdom given unto him hath written unto you; As also in all his epistles, speaking in them of these things; in which are some things hard to be understood, which they that are unlearned and unstable wrest, as they do also the other scriptures, unto their own destruction.*

The New Testament canon was well established by the end of the 1st century. A number of scholars have attempted to demonstrate that the authorized writings of the New Testament were not officially accepted as scripture until the church councils of the 4th and 5th centuries, but this could not have been the case. This argument is usually based upon the idea that the earliest list given of the New Testament writings was about 170 A.D. by Origen and others. The first list usually cited as containing the 27 books of our New Testament was made by Athanasius of Alexandria in a letter in 367 A.D.

This belief that the acceptance of the individual books developed over a longer period of time is not viable in light of the testimony of the scriptures and the historical events surrounding the development of the Early Church. The writings of the apostles had made their way throughout the Early Church and were accepted as inspired scripture before 100 A.D. and the death of John, last of the 12. This canon had been established through use. The scriptures had already begun to take life and grow in the lives of the saints of the Early Church. The development and growth of the Christian faith depended upon knowledge of the events surrounding the life of Jesus and his apostles (the Gospels and Acts) and the understanding of Christian doctrine and teaching revealed in the writings of the apostles.

Just as had been the case with the Old Testament, there were those who questioned the canonicity of certain books. The epistle to the Hebrews was brought into question due to the anonymity of its author. Most traditional sources attribute it to Paul, though it may have been written by one of the other leaders of the Early Church.

James was strongly debated by Martin Luther in particular. The teachings of James and his statements regarding faith and works did not harmonize with Luther's beliefs on salvation through faith alone. Luther vehemently argued against the inclusion of James in the canon for this reason. As was the case with previous disputations, this type of argument is usually based on an improper interpretation and harmonizing of doctrinal truth.

The II epistle of Peter was also censured by some scholars. The debate centered on the difference in the linguistic style used in I and II Peter. This is not a difficulty, especially when understanding the writing process Peter would have used. It is very likely that he did not directly write both of the epistles with his own hand. I Peter 5:12 hints at this: *By Silvanus, a faithful brother unto you, as I suppose, I have written briefly,....*
Silvanus was Silas, the companion of Paul and Peter, and was probably the scribe Peter dictated this epistle to. This would have given the individual epistles a differing literary style as they would have been written down by different men.

The books of II and III John do not state the name of the author and due to this they also became an issue of contention. Both epistles are sent from "the elder." John certainly could have used such a title as his writings were completed closer to the end of his life, and he was the oldest living apostle at the time. The literary style contained in these letters is perfectly synonymous with that of his other writings and contains much of the same verbiage. In fact, they are so similar in style and flavor that assuming a different authorship is intellectually ridiculous.

The book of Jude was questioned as canonical due to a reference in it to an apocryphal work. Jude 14-15 refers to a verse that is believed to have originated in the non-canonical book of Enoch. To begin with, this does not prove that Jude was giving this book status as scripture because he quoted from it. The quote may have originated in a much older record and could have been repeated in the book of Enoch. In addition, reference to an extra-biblical work by a biblical author certainly cannot be used as an argument for non-canonicity. Joshua and Samuel both referred to the book of Jasher in Joshua 10:13 and II

Samuel 1:18. Paul alluded to a statement made by the Greek philosopher Epimenides in Titus 1:12 and mentioned a statement made by the Greek poet Aratus in Acts 17:28.

The canonicity of the book of Revelation was more hotly debated than any other. Most of the difficulty centered on theological disputation. This usually centered on the millennial reign and other prophetic issues that could not be understood or accepted by certain scholars. As is always the case with prophetic revelation, there will be those who cannot accept its message. Revelation was supported and accepted by some of the very earliest church fathers and is certainly part of the established canon.

PRE-NEW TESTAMENT PERIOD TRANSLATIONS

11

THE SAMARITAN PENTATEUCH

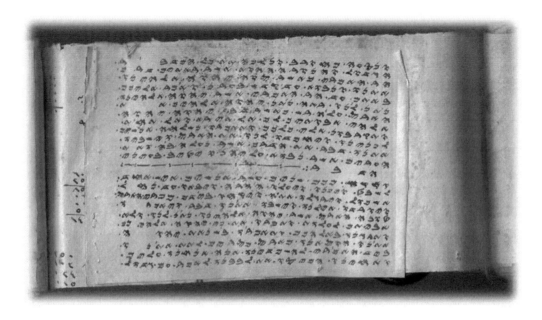

To understand the origin of the Samaritan Pentateuch, we must travel back to the original source of the Samaritan tradition. The Samaritans as a people were descendants of the northern tribes of Israel, primarily Ephraim and Manasseh. The name Samaritan comes from the city of Samaria, the political capital of the northern tribes, located within the ancestral boundaries of the tribe of Manasseh. The center of worship of the northern tribes was at Shechem and Mt. Gerizim.

The spiritual division of the northern and southern tribes can be traced back to the location of the sanctuary of God during the time of Joshua. The northern tribes believed that Joshua had erected a sanctuary to God on Mt. Gerizim in the north. This, they argued, was intended to be the center for Israel's worship and the location of the house of God. They claimed that Eli had disobeyed God's will in building the sanctuary at Shiloh. The later Samaritan priests would claim that this was the origin of the spiritual separation between the north and the south, and that the southern tribes had gone out of the will of God.

There are a number of problems with this argument. To begin with, the first mention in the Bible of the sanctuary at Shiloh states that it was set up there by the children of Israel.

Joshua 18:1 *And the whole congregation of the children of Israel assembled together at Shiloh, and set up the tabernacle of the congregation there....*

Later, during the time of the judges, the tribe of Dan (one of the northern tribes) attempted to set up their own order of priests in a system of image worship. Micah, who may have been an Ephraimite, had made a graven image and had hired a Levitical priest to lead in his household worship. Men of the tribe of Dan stole the image and appropriated the renegade priest to serve them. The priest, Jonathon, and his sons continued to serve in this capacity until the time of the Assyrian captivity.

Judges 18:30-31 *And the children of Dan set up the graven image: and Jonathan, the son of Gershom, the son of Manasseh, he and his sons were priests to the tribe of Dan until the day of the captivity of the land. And they set them up Micah's graven image, which he made, all the time that the house of God was in Shiloh.*

This desire of the northern tribes to have their own place of worship continued in the later actions of Jeroboam who set up places of worship at Bethel and Dan so that the northern tribes would not have to go to

Jerusalem to worship. He installed graven images in these shrines and created his own priests, who were not of the Levitical line to minister there.

I Kings 12:26-31 *And Jeroboam said in his heart, Now shall the kingdom return to the house of David: If this people go up to do sacrifice in the house of the LORD at Jerusalem, then shall the heart of this people turn again unto their lord, even unto Rehoboam king of Judah, and they shall kill me, and go again to Rehoboam king of Judah. Whereupon the king took counsel, and made two calves of gold, and said unto them, It is too much for you to go up to Jerusalem: behold thy gods, O Israel, which brought thee up out of the land of Egypt. And he set the one in Bethel, and the other put he in Dan. And this thing became a sin: for the people went to worship before the one, even unto Dan. And he made an house of high places, and made priests of the lowest of the people, which were not of the sons of Levi.*

The political division between north and south also originated during the time of Jeroboam. Jeroboam, an Ephraimite, had risen to power under Solomon. Ahijah the prophet had told him that the Lord would take the 10 northern tribes from Solomon and give him rulership over them due to Solomon's pagan practices. When Solomon became aware of this he sought his life, and Jeroboam was forced to flee to Egypt.

Rehoboam, son of Solomon, became king over the nation of Israel upon his father's death. Rehoboam came to Shechem in the north to be accepted as king by the northern tribes:

I Kings 12:1 *And Rehoboam went to Shechem: for all Israel were come to Shechem to make him king.*

Jeroboam and the representatives of the northern tribes told Rehoboam that they would serve him if he would ease their burden of labor. Rehoboam took counsel for three days with his advisors on how to answer this request. The elder men who had served with his father counseled him to deal graciously with the northern tribes, whereas the younger men who were his contemporaries advised him to deal harshly with them. Rehoboam took the advice of the younger men and responded roughly:

I Kings 12:14 *...My father made your yoke heavy, and I will add to your yoke: my father also chastised you with whips, but I will chastise you with scorpions.*

This insensitive reply of Rehoboam caused the northern tribes to respond with the decision that divided Israel and Judah from that point forward:

I Kings 12:16 *So when all Israel saw that the king hearkened not unto them, the people answered the king, saying, What portion have we in David? neither have we inheritance in the son of Jesse: to your tents, O Israel: now see to thine own house, David. So Israel departed unto their tents.*

It is probable that this final decision of the northern tribes had been developing long before this event. The spiritual and cultural differences that had crept in laid the foundation that eventually led to their final schism.

The next development that affected the northern tribes was the Assyrian invasion. Shalmaneser, king of Assyria, besieged Samaria for three years. Following his death in 722 B.C. his brother Sargon took the city, and approximately 28,000 Israelites were led away into captivity. After a continued deportation of the Israelites, Sargon brought men of foreign nations into the land to live.

II Kings 17:24 *And the king of Assyria brought men from Babylon, and from Cuthah, and from Ava, and from Hamath, and from Sepharvaim, and placed them in the cities of Samaria instead of the children of Israel: and they possessed Samaria, and dwelt in the cities thereof.*

These foreign settlers intermarried with the remnant of Israelites who were left in the land and combined a mixture of pagan beliefs with the worship of the Hebrew God. Thus began the Samaritan race that existed in the land at the time of Jesus. The Jews mark this period as the beginning of the Samaritan people, whom they viewed as a mongrel race.

The northern tribes were never completely removed from the land. Within a few years of the Assyrian deportation, Hezekiah, king of Judah, invited the northern tribes to attend the Passover at Jerusalem. The invitation was specifically sent to the remnant that remained. Some members of the tribes of Asher, Manasseh, and Zebulun accepted the invitation:

> **II Chronicles 30:6, 10-11** *So the posts went with the letters from the king and his princes throughout all Israel and Judah, and according to the commandment of the king, saying, Ye children of Israel, turn again unto the LORD God of Abraham, Isaac, and Israel, and he will return to the remnant of you, that are escaped out of the hand of the kings of Assyria....So the posts passed from city to city through the country of Ephraim and Manasseh even unto Zebulun: but they laughed them to scorn, and mocked them. Nevertheless divers of Asher and Manasseh and of Zebulun humbled themselves, and came to Jerusalem.*

During the reign of Josiah, king of Judah, the restoration of the Temple was begun. This occurred about 623 B.C., about 100 years after the fall of Samaria. The tribes of Ephraim and Manasseh are mentioned among the contributors to the restoration of the temple:

> **II Chronicles 34:9** *And when they came to Hilkiah the high priest, they delivered the money that was brought into the house of God, which the Levites that kept the doors had gathered of the hand of Manasseh and Ephraim, and of all the remnant of Israel, and of all Judah and Benjamin; and they returned to Jerusalem.*

The Samaritans had a desire to join in the rebuilding of the temple under Zerubbabel about 520 B.C., but were refused. The foreign settlement of the north was believed to have begun around 669 B.C., and by this time nearly four generational dispensations had passed.

Ezra 4:1-3 *Now when the adversaries of Judah and Benjamin heard that the children of the captivity builded the temple unto the LORD God of Israel; Then they came to Zerubbabel, and to the chief of the fathers, and said unto them, Let us build with you: for we seek your God, as ye do; and we do sacrifice unto him since the days of Esarhaddon king of Assur, which brought us up hither. But Zerubbabel, and Jeshua, and the rest of the chief of the fathers of Israel, said unto them, Ye have nothing to do with us to build an house unto our God; but we ourselves together will build unto the LORD God of Israel, as king Cyrus the king of Persia hath commanded us.*

The adversaries mentioned here would have been the Samaritan people who had remained in the land, led by the governor of Samaria, Sanballat, and the governor of Ammon, Tobiah. Nehemiah testifies to the surreptitious work of these and others in the area to undermine the work:

Nehemiah 2:9-10 *Then I came to the governors beyond the river, and gave them the king's letters. Now the king had sent captains of the army and horsemen with me. When Sanballat the Horonite, and Tobiah the servant, the Ammonite, heard of it, it grieved them exceedingly that there was come a man to seek the welfare of the children of Israel.*

Nehemiah 6:1-2 *Now it came to pass, when Sanballat, and Tobiah, and Geshem the Arabian, and the rest of our enemies, heard that I had builded the wall, and that there was no breach left therein; (though at that time I had not set up the doors upon the gates;) That Sanballat and Geshem sent unto me, saying, Come, let us meet together in some one of the villages in the plain of Ono. But they thought to do me mischief.*

Sanballat, the Samaritan leader, played a major role in the translation of the Samaritan Pentateuch. It is Sanballat who is credited by Josephus as being responsible for the building of the rival temple on Mt. Gerizim. This would clearly explain why he would be in opposition to the building going on at Jerusalem. Sanballat married his daughter to the grandson of the Jewish high priest Eliashib.[122]

> **Nehemiah 13:28** *And one of the sons of Joiada, the son of Eliashib the high priest, was son-in-law to Sanballat the Horonite: therefore I chased him from me.*

This marriage gave Sanballat a son-in-law who was of the Levitical priesthood. Sanballat could then install his own Levitical priest in the temple on Mt. Gerizim. This establishment of a rival place of worship would have cemented the schism between Jew and Samaritan. The last Halaka of Masseket Kutim, a Talmudic tractate, describes the Jewish attitude toward the Samaritans: *When shall we take them back? When they renounce Mount Gerizim and confess Jerusalem.*

It is believed that a copy of the Torah was brought to Mt. Gerizim during this time by Sanballat's son-in-law. This would have included only the five books of Moses. The Samaritans believed that only the books of Moses were canonical. The translation made from this copy of the Torah is what is believed to have become the Samaritan Pentateuch. The Samaritan Pentateuch was copied in the older Paleo-Hebraic script that had been used before the Babylonian captivity. This may have been one of the factors involved in the scribes of Ezra's day using the square script, as this would show a contrast between the accepted Jewish scripture and the renegade Samaritan Pentateuch.

There are a number of differences between this version and the Hebrew Torah in the spelling of names and places. The Samaritan Pentateuch

---

[122] Josephus stated that his name was Manasseh, and that his brother Jaddua later became high priest in Jerusalem.

also makes changes in the text in order to support the Samaritan religious beliefs. For example, the Masoretic Hebrew text states in Deuteronomy 27:4, *Therefore it shall be when ye be gone over Jordan, that ye shall set up these stones, which I command you this day, in mount Ebal,…*, whereas the Samaritan Pentateuch changes Ebal to Gerizim.

The oldest manuscripts of the Samaritan Pentateuch in existence today date from the 11th and 12th centuries A.D.

THE ARAMAIC TARGUMS

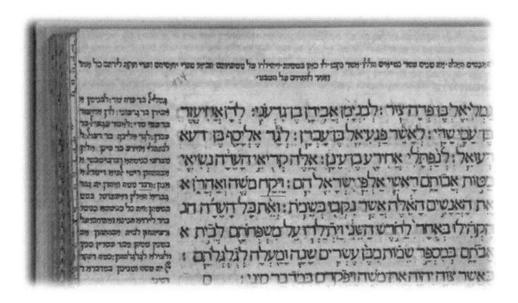

The Aramaic Targums are believed to have originated around the time of the return from the Babylonian captivity. Targum is the Aramaic word for translation, but these were not so much translations as paraphrases.

The Hebrew language had ceased from being the language of common use among the Jews in captivity in Babylon. The exiles had taken the language of Aramaic as their primary tongue. Aramaic was the common trade language of the Middle East during this period, and thus as the Jews became acclimated to the Babylonian culture, the Hebrew fell out of use except for its preservation by the scribes and priestly class.

The Aramaic paraphrases came into being to address these issues. As the common people understood Aramaic far better than Hebrew, the scribes felt the necessity to transliterate the Hebrew scriptures into the Aramaic tongue. This was probably begun during the period of Ezra. As previously addressed, it is interesting to note that during the reading of the scriptures to the people recorded in Nehemiah 8:7-8, Ezra and his scribal assistants…*caused the people to understand the law…they read in the book in the law of God distinctly, and gave the sense, and caused them to understand the reading.* This could have been done in two different ways. To begin with, the book of law would have been written in Hebrew and thus the scribes may have paraphrased and explained what they were reading for their listeners. This also may have involved commentary on the meaning of what was being read.

This would have led directly into the development of the Aramaic Targums. It is believed that the first Targums were oral only, and this would correspond well with the work of Ezra and the scribes of his day. In the later synagogues, the law was first read in Hebrew one statement at a time. It was then translated or paraphrased into Aramaic so that it could be discussed by the common people.

Some written Targums were discovered among the manuscripts of the Dead Sea scrolls, so we know that they could have been in existence before the time of Christ. It is likely that most were committed to writing in the 1st and 2nd centuries A.D.

THE SEPTUAGINT

Just as the Hebrew language had gone out of common use among the Babylonian exiles, Jews who had migrated to other areas of the world had often lost touch with their original tongue. Jews living in the Hellenistic centers of learning such as Alexandria, Egypt, eventually replaced their native Hebrew with Greek.

The Septuagint is a Greek translation of the Hebrew scriptures that was believed to have been translated sometime between 300 and 200 B.C. The story of the Septuagint is rife with legend. Most of the tale is taken from a letter said to be written by Aristeas, a member of the Alexandrian court of Ptolemy II from 285 to 246 B.C. According to the story, the translation was proposed by Demetrius, Ptolemy's librarian,[123] in order that the Hebrew scriptures could be added to the famed library at Alexandria. This library, one of the wonders of the ancient world, was later completely destroyed by the Muslims.

The story relates that Ptolemy sent a letter to Eleazar, the Jewish high priest at Jerusalem, requesting that he send six scribes from each of the 12 tribes of Israel to Alexandria in order that they might make the translation. This would have given the committee a total number of 72

---

[123] This part of the story would also appear to be false as Demetrius was exiled by Ptolemy upon his accession to the throne.

members, which is why the translation was called the Septuagint, Latin for "the seventy." The letters LXX, the Roman numerals for 70, are often used when referring to the Septuagint.

This gathering of scribes would almost certainly not have been possible, as it is believed that the majority of the tribes had been widely scattered by this time. Another problem with this story arises when we consider the fact that the high priest in Jerusalem would have had little influence on those of the northern tribes that remained, as they did not recognize his authority.

It was said that the 72 translators arrived with a copy of the law written in letters of gold on rolls of skins. The scribes were sequestered on the island of Pharos during the translation process. At the end of 72 days they completed the translation. It was claimed that even though each scribe had worked alone, the language of the final translation was in perfect harmony! It was said that Ptolemy, and in turn the Jews of Alexandria, was thrilled with this translation.

Philo, the Alexandrian scholar, and the historian Josephus, both 1st century Jews, wrote of the Septuagint translation and verified certain parts of Aristeas' account. Philo, in regard to the location of the translation, states, *Even to this very day, there is every year a solemn assembly held and a festival celebrated in the island of Pharos, to which not only the Jews but a great number of persons of other nations sail across, reverencing the place in which the first light of interpretation shone forth, and thanking God for that ancient piece of beneficence which was always young and fresh.*[124]

Aristobulus, a Jew living at the beginning of the 2nd century B.C., was the earliest writer to mention the Septuagint. In his comments, he only mentions the translation of the law during the time of Ptolemy

---

[124] Philo, *On the Life of Moses*, ll, Vll, (41).

Philadelphus. Josephus supports this: *...the Hebrews inform us, that only the five books of Moses were translated by them, and given to King Ptolemy.*

Modern scholars discount the legend of the Septuagint's unique creation, but many feel that this translation was done at Alexandria during this time frame. The first translation was believed to have been of the Torah, the remainder of the Septuagint being translated at a later date. A number of scholars believe that those who made the later additions were much less skilled than the translators of the Torah. The Septuagint is usually considered to be an inferior translation compared to the Masoretic texts.

THE BIBLE AND THE CHURCH OF ROME

12

Revelation 17:1-6

And there came one of the seven angels which had the seven vials, and talked with me, saying unto me, Come hither; I will shew unto thee the judgment of the great whore that sitteth upon many waters: With whom the kings of the earth have committed fornication, and the inhabitants of the earth have been made drunk with the wine of her fornication. So he carried me away in the spirit into the wilderness: and I saw a woman sit upon a scarlet coloured beast, full of names of blasphemy, having seven heads and ten horns. And the woman was arrayed in purple and scarlet colour, and decked with gold and precious stones and pearls, having a golden cup in her hand full of abominations and filthiness of her fornication: And upon her forehead was a name written, MYSTERY, BABYLON THE GREAT, THE MOTHER OF HARLOTS AND ABOMINATIONS OF THE EARTH. And I saw the woman drunken with the blood of the saints, and with the blood of the martyrs of Jesus: and when I saw her, I wondered with great admiration.

After the persecution of Christians was brought to an end by Constantine, the church became much more structured and political in its organization. The hierarchy of the church began to take on the form and substance of imperial Rome. The bishops of the church, rather than being ministers and shepherds of the flock, became lords over God's heritage. The favor bestowed upon the church allowed the once poor church to become prosperous in material wealth and indoctrinated into the political machinations of the imperial government.

As time went on, the largest metropolitan areas became the centers of influence and authority. These areas generally fell into line with the four prefectures into which Constantine had divided the empire. The bishops of Rome, Constantinople, Antioch, and Alexandria became the spiritual and political leaders of the larger areas under which their metropolitan governments held sway. These were the centers of activity and influence and were afforded a great deal of authority. The bishops of these centers gained more political influence as time passed. These men were not the best equipped in the knowledge of the Bible nor imbued by the spirit of Christ. They were men who knew how to wield power and to exact their influence in the same manner as the imperial politicians who preceded them. Positions in the church were bought and sold, and violent infighting erupted between doctrinal and political opponents.

As the Roman church gained ascendancy over Christendom, it was critical that "the doctrines of the church" be maintained against heresy. Any individual or group that stood against the beliefs of the mother church was quickly beaten into submission or murdered for its resistance. From the 4th to the 16th centuries Rome held the word of God bound in chains of darkness and tradition.

The Roman church controlled the teaching and transmission of the Bible with an iron fist. Anyone who attempted to translate or distribute the scripture in a language understandable to the common man was severely persecuted. Catholic Rome believed that it alone held the keys to the kingdom of heaven. This was a distinct parallel to the condition that caused Jesus to rebuke the scribes and Pharisees in his statement in Matthew 23:13, *But woe unto you, scribes and Pharisees, hypocrites! for ye shut up the kingdom of heaven against men: for ye neither go in yourselves, neither suffer ye them that are entering to go in.* The ecclesiastical power of the fallen church did not abide in the doctrines or truth of Christ, and it forbid any of the laity to have access to the Book to seek out the truth for themselves.

This resistance to the word of God continued throughout the history of the Catholic Church. With each successive church council, the truth of the Bible became more and more eclipsed by the doctrines and commandments of men, buried under ages of philosophy and deceit. As time passed the Roman Church became the final word in doctrinal matters. The Bible became little more than a record that was secondary in authority to the church, and that could be defined and interpreted by its leaders alone.

This descent into darkness began as early as the time of Constantine. Pope Damasus was the first to officially claim that he was the successor of Peter, opening the door to an authority that his bishopric was never given by scripture, or validated by history. Pope Leo the Great continued this ideology in arguing for papal supremacy during his rule in 383. Augustine, perhaps the greatest influence on the Catholic system of religion, wrote in the 5th century: *Rome has spoken; the case is closed.*[125]

Upon the death of Emperor Theodosius in 395 A.D., the Roman Empire once again split into Easter and Western divisions. During this time Leo the Great, Pope from 440–461 A.D., fought for the development of papal supremacy. He was supported in this by Emperor Valentinian III, who passed an edict in 445 A.D. stating that the clergy of both the Eastern and Western empires were to obey the bishop of Rome: *Inasmuch then as the primacy of the Apostolic See is assured by the merit of St. Peter, prince of the episcopate, by the rank of the City of Rome, and also by the authority of a sacred Synod, let not presumption endeavour to attempt anything contrary to that See.*

---

[125] Augustine, Sermon 131:10.

For then at length will the peace of the churches be everywhere maintained, if the whole body acknowledges its ruler...we decree by this perpetual edict that it shall not be lawful for the bishops of Gaul or of the other provinces, contrary to the ancient custom, to do aught without the authority of the venerable Pope of the Eternal City; and whatsoever the authority of the Apostolic See has enacted, or may hereafter enact, shall be the law for all.[126]

The Western Roman Empire finally collapsed completely in 476 A.D. under the onslaught of the barbarian tribes. During the ensuing chaos in the West, the Western church took up the reins of power and stepped directly into the void left by the empty imperial seat. In the East at Constantinople (Byzantium) the Byzantine Church was supreme. For hundreds of years the Eastern and Western churches would go through cycles of unity and division as each tried to position itself as the center of spiritual authority.

Where was the word of God during all of this turmoil? In the Western (Roman) Church the Latin and Vulgate translations held preeminence. Modern scholars would later refer to these manuscripts as Western or Alexandrian in source and textual family. In the Eastern (Byzantine) Church the Greek scriptures continued to be copied and passed down as they had been from the beginning. These Byzantine manuscripts would later be known as the Majority or Byzantine textual family. The manuscripts underlying these copies were those of Palestinian and Syrian origin, many originating around one of the first centers of the early church at Antioch.

The first major schism between the Eastern and Western Churches occurred from 484–519 A.D. when Pope Felix III excommunicated Acacius, Patriarch of Constantinople. Between 533 and 534 A.D., in a codex of the Emperor Justinian, the Pope is referred to as *the Head of*

---

[126] Edict in Support of Papal Authority, Valentinian III, July 8, 445 A.D.

all Churches. Though this was not an official title or position in the eyes of the Eastern church, it added to the mounting tensions between East and West.

Gregory the Great, Pope from 590 to 604 A.D., continued the declaration of papal supremacy, using terms such as *the head of all the churches, the head of the faith,* and *the holder of the place of Peter, the prince of the Apostles.* The more power that the Roman bishop acquired, the more intolerant the Roman church became to any disobedience or heresy.

From 633 to 642 A.D. Jerusalem, Antioch, and Alexandria fell to Muslim invaders. As these centers of church activity were swallowed into the Islamic states, authority in church matters became centered completely in the capitals of Rome and Constantinople. This continued to accelerate the division and contention between the East and West.

During the 8th and 9th centuries the Roman church presented a number of documents claiming its position and superiority. All of these were later demonstrated to be forgeries, but by that time they had already accomplished their purpose. The first writings to appear were the supposed letters of Clement, bishop of Rome in the 1st century. These letters established Peter as the leader of the apostles and the first bishop of the church at Rome.

Soon after the Pseudo-Isidorian decrees and the Pseudo-Constantian donation appeared. These stated that the Pope was above all authority as the head of the priesthood and that he should be considered the head of the universe! The Constantian donation was a letter purported to be from the Emperor Constantine giving his Imperial office as a gift to the Pope. This letter also ceded all the regions of Italy surrounding Rome to the Pope as the property of the church.

In 800 A.D. another schism erupted between East and West. Pope Leo III crowned Charlemagne as Emperor and effectually established the Holy Roman Empire. Leo separated from the Eastern church and claimed sole supremacy over all of the Western church.

During the latter 9th century the leaders of the Eastern church become embroiled in the Photian Schism. Ignatius and Photius vied for the Patriarchal seat of the Byzantine church. The 4th Council of Constantinople was called in 869 A.D. in which Photius was excommunicated and Ignatius returned to his position as Patriarch. This caused a great division in the church and eventually led to the Great Schism of 1054 A.D. Ten years later, in 879 A.D., the Pope of Rome and Patriarch of Constantinople excommunicated each other.

Rome and Constantinople struggled back and forth until finally in 1054 A.D. the battle came to a head. Both Rome and Constantinople felt they were the successors to the Imperial authority of the old Roman Empire. Rome considered itself the original seat of the Empire, whereas Constantinople claimed that the capital of the Empire had been moved from Rome to Byzantium. The Roman Pope had gained great power in the West while Byzantium had declined. Michael Curalarius, Patriarch of Constantinople, made charges against the Pope to one of the Western bishops. Pope Leo IX, enraged at this, excommunicated Curalarius, who in turn excommunicated Leo. This was considered the final schism between East and West.

With this last separation, the scriptural transmission became profoundly effected. The Eastern clerics continued to copy the scriptures in the Greek language as they had always done. In the West the Greek language finally went completely out of use and Latin became the language of the Western church. Knowledge of the Greek and of the Byzantine manuscripts passed from the West.
In the West, the political infighting and doctrinal disputes continued for the next few hundred years. Many of the false doctrines of the

Roman Church were developed during these Dark Ages. Celibacy for priests, transubstantiation, and the foundations for papal infallibility were hammered out in this long dark night of the Church.

Gregory VII, Pope from 1073 to 1085 A.D., demonstrated the Catholic attitude toward the Bible at the time: *For it is clear to those who reflect often upon it, that not without reason has it pleased Almighty God that holy scripture should be a secret in certain places lest, if it were plainly apparent to all men, perchance it would be little esteemed and be subject to disrespect; or it might be falsely understood by those of mediocre learning, and lead to error....*[127] Gregory wrote a Dictatus of declarations regarding the papal authority, including the statements that no one on earth can judge the Pope, the Roman church has never erred and can never err, and the Pope has the authority to depose bishops, kings, and emperors.

The 11th century ended with the beginning of the Crusades in 1095–1096 A.D. The Crusades were holy wars called up by the Pope of Rome. There were four general reasons behind the calling up of the various Crusades, very likely in the following order of importance:

- To enrich and expand the Roman church and the Western Lords
- To crush any "heretical" groups that believed or acted contrary to the established order and doctrine of the church
- To draw the feudal lords away from their constant infighting, which might damage the order established by the church
- To reclaim the Holy Land

Usually the last reason was the one given for the Crusade, though in reality this was of the least importance to the Pope. The second reason had become more necessary to the Roman Church as time passed. Small resistance groups that had always existed in opposition to the Catholic doctrine had begun to become larger and more influential.

---

[127] Cited in *Rome and the Bible*, David W. Cloud, 1996.

These dissenters must be crushed quickly and mercilessly. An example must be set for any who would stand against the authority of the mother church.

There had always been scattered groups that would not bow to the Roman pontiff, but they were often so small that they went unnoticed by the powers above them. When the Christian faith had first spread into Europe, there had been no established church. The Roman church eventually consolidated the lands and peoples of Europe under its covering and established its doctrines as orthodox. These doctrines were in conflict with the biblical beliefs of these early converts, and many continued to pass down the teachings their fathers had given them. Those who were brought to the attention of the church were usually condemned and often severely persecuted.

The ideologies behind these pockets of resistance could be traced back to the time of the first church councils when the church doctrines had begun to be shaped by the philosophical and political winds of change stirring in the empire. As the purity and spirit of the Early Church fell away, there remained a tiny nucleus of Bible-believing Christians who held tightly to their beliefs. These grassroots movements were usually the domain of the common folk. The intellectual and ecclesiastical elite were bound up in and blinded by the doctrinal system of their day.

The two most widespread groups during the 12th and 13th centuries were the Albigenses and the Waldenses. Some historians have speculated that these were in a direct line of spiritual descent from the early church period. Whether that is truly the case has not yet been proven, but it is certain that they believed themselves to be heirs of a spiritual line reaching back to the apostolic order of the early church.

Pius Melia lists 11 major "heretical" views the Waldenses held, all of which became the cry of the later Reformation:

- *The Church of God has failed*
- *The Holy Scriptures alone are sufficient to guide men to Salvation*
- *Catholic priests…have no authority; and the Pope of Rome is the chief of all heresiarchs*
- *Everyone has the right to preach publicly the word of God*
- *Purgatory is a dream, an invention of the sixth century*
- *The indulgences of the Church are an invention of covetous Priests*
- *The invocation of Saints cannot be admitted*[128]

The Waldenses (or Waldensians) were heavily involved in the teaching and distribution of the Bible. The Waldenses believed that the truth was to be found within the pages of the Bible, not within the cloistered walls of Rome and its man-made traditions. One manual on the Catholic inquisition wrote that Peter Waldo, the Waldensian leader from whom their name was taken, *arranged for the gospels and some other books of the Bible to be translated in the common speech…which he read very often, though without understanding their import. Infatuated with himself, he usurped the prerogatives of the Apostles by presuming to preach the Gospel in the streets, where he made many disciples….*[129]

In the mid-13th century the Catholic inquisitor Reinerius angrily described the Waldensian love for the Bible: *They can repeat by heart, in the vulgar tongue, the whole text of the New Testament and great part of the Old: and by adhering to the text alone, they reject decretals and decrees with the sayings and expositions of the Saints.*[130] In the

---

[128] Pius Melia, D.D., *The Origin, Persecutions, and Doctrines of the Waldenses,* pp. 101-129.
[129] Bernard Gui, *Manuel de l'Inquisiteur* as cited in *The Waldensians* by Giorgio Tourn, pp. 3-4.
[130] George Stanley Faber, *History of the Ancient Vallenses and Albigenses,* p. 596.

eyes of the Catholic church this was one of the greatest crimes of the Waldenses. They dared to place the words of the scripture above the traditions of the church. By 1215 A.D. they had been excommunicated and the persecutions began in earnest.

In the 4th Lateran Council in 1215 A.D. secular authorities were enjoined to aid the church in the extermination of heretics (including any who would translate or preach the Bible in the common tongue): *Secular authorities...shall be admonished and induced and if necessary compelled by ecclesiastical censure...for the defense of the faith they ought publicly to take an oath that they will strive in good faith and to the best of their ability to exterminate...all heretics pointed out by the Church....*[131]

Pope Innocent III stepped onto the stage of history in the midst of this spiritual war. He has been considered by many historians to have been the most powerful Pope ever to rule the church of Rome. He had a vicious hatred for any who dared to stand against Catholic Rome, and particularly those who attempted to bring the Bible to the common people: *they shall be seized for trial and penalties, who engage in the translation of the sacred volumes, or who hold secret conventicles, or who assume the office of preaching without the authority of their superiors....*[132] Schaff, in his *History of the Christian Church*, quotes Innocent as stating *...that as by the old law, the beast touching the holy mount was to be stoned to death, so simple and uneducated men were not to touch the Bible or to preach its doctrines....*[133] It was Innocent III who established the first official Inquisition.

---

[131] *The Disciplinary Decrees of the Ecumenical Council*, translated by H. J. Schroeder (St. Louis: B. Herder Book Co. , 1937), pp. 242-243.
[132] J.P. Callender, *Illustrations of Popery*, 1838, p. 387.
[133] Philip Schaff, *History of the Christian Church*, VI, p. 723.

The Inquisition went hand in hand with the Crusades. Whereas the Crusades were the civil arm of the church distributing "justice" and reclaiming territory, the Inquisition was the direct vengeance of the Church upon those deemed heretics. It was a system of mock trials, torture, and murder against any who were labeled heretics by the church. Ruckman, in his *History of the New Testament Church*, describes the purpose and spread of this murderous machine: *The Inquisition was purely and uniquely a Catholic institution; it was founded for the express purpose of exterminating every human being in Europe who differed from Roman Catholic beliefs and practices. It spread out from France, Milan, Geneva, Aragon, and Sardinia to Poland (14th century) and then to Bohemia and Rome (1543). It was not abolished in Spain until 1820.*[134]

The Inquisition of Pope Innocent III inspired the Crusade against the Albigenses in 1209 A.D. Innocent released a statement commanding all of Christendom to rise up against the heretics and destroy them. The King of France, who had many Albigensian subjects, bluntly refused this order. Innocent replied by offering an indulgence to any who would give him 40 days of service in the war against the heretics.

A huge mob of knights, clergy, and peasants attacked the predominantly Albigensian city of Bezier. This "spiritual" army included 20,000 cavalry troops. On the march to Bezier, the mob looted the countryside and killed any who stood in its way.

Many of the people of Bezier had locked themselves in the churches of St. Jude and St. Mary Magdalene. St. Mary Magdalene alone was crowded with over 7,000 women, children, and elderly. The invaders, while singing *Come ye Holy Spirit,* broke down the doors and massacred everyone inside. The entire city was sacked and over 60,000 people were killed. When someone complained that Catholics were

---

[134] Dr. Peter S. Ruckman, *History of the New Testament Church.*

being murdered along with the heretics, the papal legates told them to go on killing and not to be concerned, as "the Lord knows his own."

The Waldenses also fell under intense persecution. Armitage records, *Many of them were frozen to death, others were cast from high precipices and dashed to pieces. Some were driven into caverns, and by filling the mouths of their caves with fagots were suffocated. Others were hanged in cold blood, ripped open and disemboweled, pierced with prongs, drowned, racked limb from limb till death relieved them; were stabbed, worried by dogs, burned, or crucified with their heads downward. Foxe relates one case in which four hundred mothers who had taken refuge in the cave of Castelluzzo...were smothered with their infants in their arms....*[135]

The Inquisition continued to grind forward on its bloody path, directed by the popes and supported by Europe's most powerful rulers. Frederick II, ruler of the Holy Roman Empire, was in complete support of the Inquisition and aided in the persecution by creating further laws against heretics. In 1224 A.D. he condemned them to be either burned alive or to have their tongues torn out, at the judges' discretion.
Pope Gregory IX carried the Inquisition from Spain and France into all of Europe. In 1229 A.D. at the Council of Toulouse he declared, *It is the duty of every Catholic to persecute heretics.* This council also forbade translations in the common tongue or the use of the Bible to any but the priests: *We forbid the permission of the books of the Old and New Testament to laymen...expressly forbidding their having the other parts of the Bible translated into the vulgar tongue.*[136]

---

[135] Thomas Armitage, *A History of the Baptists*, I, pp. 311-312.
[136] Council Tolosanum, Pope Gregory IX, Anno. chr. 1229. Canons 2 and 14.

The Synod of Tarragona in 1234 A.D. ordered that all vernacular versions of the Bible be brought to the bishop to be burned.[137] Every layman daring to possess a Bible was in peril of the rack, the dungeon, and the stake.[138] Don Jayme of Aragon during the same year made an edict that *prohibited the use of any part of the Old or New Testament in the vernacular tongue, and commanded all, whether laity or clergy, who possessed such books, to deliver them to their ordinaries to be burnt, on the pain of being held suspected of heresy.*[139]

Innocent IV, in 1252 A.D., issued his Bull *Ad Extirpanda,* giving the inquisitors the authority to torture and commit whatever acts necessary to rid the church of heretics. He decreed that any disobedience, even in thought, was punishable.

Pope Clement V, near the beginning of the 14th century, rebuked King Edward II of England for forbidding torture in England: *We hear that you forbid torture as contrary to the laws of your land. But no state law can override canon law, our law. Therefore I command you at once to submit those men to torture.*[140]

Pope Clement XI in his Unigenitus (Dogmatic Constitution) issued in 1713 stated that the following statements[141] (believed by the Reformers) were to be condemned as false:

- *It is useful and necessary at all times, in all places, and for every kind of person, to study and to know the spirit, the piety, and the mysteries of Sacred Scripture*
- *The reading of Sacred Scripture is for all*

---

[137] P. Marion Simms, *The Bible from the Beginning*, p. 162.

[138] Blackburn, *Church History*, p. 309.

[139] Thomas M'Crie, *History of the Reformation in Spain*, pp. 190-191.

[140] Will and Ariel Durant, *The Story of Civilization*, V.

[141] Unigenitus Dei Filius, issued by Pope Clement XI on September 8, 1713.

- *The sacred obscurity of the Word of God is no reason for the laity to dispense themselves from reading it*
- *The Lord's Day ought to be sanctified by Christians with readings of pious works and above all of the Holy Scriptures. It is harmful for a Christian to wish to withdraw from this reading*
- *To snatch away from the hands of Christians the New Testament, or to hold it closed against them by taking away from them the means of understanding it, is to close for them the mouth of Christ*
- *To forbid Christians to read Sacred Scripture, especially the Gospels, is to forbid the use of light to the sons of light, and to cause them to suffer a kind of excommunication.*

The Roman Catholic torture and murder of Bible-believing reformers would continue on for hundreds of years. The hatred, misuse, and devaluation of the Bible by the Roman church continues still. Consider this small selection of testimonies:

- Pope Pius VII (1800–1823 A.D.) stated, *It is evidence from experience, that the holy Scriptures, when circulated in the vulgar tongue, have, through the temerity of men, produced more harm than benefit.*
- Pope Leo XII (in his Ubi Primum of 1824 A.D.) stated:, *...to allow holy Bibles in the ordinary language, wholesale and without distinction, would on account of human rashness cause more harm than good.*
- Pope Gregory XVI (1831–1846 A.D.) said that he was *against the publication, distribution, reading, and possession of books of the holy Scriptures translated into the vulgar tongue.*
- Pope Pius IX (1846–1878 A.D.) stated, *You, in your wisdom, perfectly understand, venerable brothers, with what vigilance and solicitude you ought to labour, that the faithful may fly with horror from this poisonous reading* [the translations of the Bible into the common tongue]; *and that they may remember that no man, supported by his own prudence, can arrogate to himself the right,*

and have the presumption, to interpret the Scriptures otherwise than as our holy mother the Church interprets them, to whom alone our Lord has confided the guardianship of the faith, judgment upon the true sense and interpretation of the divine books.[142]

- Pope Leo XIII (in his encyclical Providentissimus Deus of 1893) stated, *Wherefore it must be recognized that the sacred writings are wrapt in a certain religious obscurity, and that no one can enter into their interior without a guide...that in reading and making use of His Word, they must follow the Church as their guide and their teacher.*

  What of the church at Berea, considered more noble than others because the Bereans searched the scriptures daily to see whether Paul's teachings were correct?

- Leo also stated in his Apostolic Constitution Officiorum ac Munerum of 1897, *All versions of the Holy Bible, in any vernacular language, made by non-Catholics are prohibited.*

- Alexander Robertson recounts the following amazing story of events occurring at Vatican I: *A curious thing happened at the so called Ecumenical Council, held in the Vatican in 1869-70, at which the infallibility of the Pope was decreed. Dollinger and Dupanloup, in supporting their arguments against the insensate proposal, wished to refer to some passages of Scripture; but NO ONE HAD A BIBLE IN THE WHOLE COUNCIL, nor could one be procured for them within the bounds of the Church, so one had to be borrowed from the Protestant chaplain of the Prussian Embassy!*[143]

  Robertson also relates, *Students are not taught the Bible in the Papal seminaries. They have many text-books...but no Bible. Count Campello, ex-Canon of St. Peter's, was trained in the Academy of Noble Ecclesiastics, the highest training college in Rome, and yet during all his years of study HE NEVER EVEN SAW A BIBLE.*

---

[142] J.A. Wylie, *The Papacy*, 1888, p. 188.
[143] Alexander Robertson, *The Roman Catholic Church in Italy*, p. 216.

- The Universal Catholic Catechism states, *The task of interpreting the Word of God authentically has been entrusted solely to the Magisterium of the Church, that is, to the Pope and to the bishops in communion with him.*

- Johnan Faber (Catholic defender of the papacy): *If we must choose between the Holy Scriptures of God, and the old errors of the church, we should reject the former.*[144]

- Joseph Faa di Bruno in Catholic Belief: *Like two sacred rivers flowing from paradaise, the Bible and divine tradition contain the word of God, the precious gems of revealed truths. Though these two divine streams are in themselves, on account of their divine origin, of equal sacredness, and are both full of revealed truths, still of the two, tradition is to us more clear and safe.*[145]

- When Rome was made the capital of Italy in 1870, a papal law was passed that required that any copies of the Bible found in the possession of visitors were to be confiscated.[146]

- From Modern Bible Translations Unmasked: *In 1954, the Supreme Council of the Knights of Columbus, a fiercely Roman Catholic organization, made the bold claim that the Bible does not believe itself to be inspired or to be the complete Word of God; and that there is only one place in the world where you can be sure to prove the Bible is true and that is through the Catholic Church.*[147]

- From Modern Bible Translations Unmasked: *We do not profess faith in the Bible, but in Jesus Christ and His church, and its teachings.*[148]

---

[144] Merle d'Aubigne, *History of the Reformation*, Book 11, chapter 5, paragraph 9.

[145] Joseph Faa di Bruno, *Catholic Belief*, p. 45.

[146] Phillip Schaff, *History of the Christian Church*, VI, p. 727.

[147] Dr. Russell R. Standish, *Modern Bible Translations Unmasked*, p. 38.

[148] *Catholic Answers to "Bible Christians,"* cited in *Modern Bible Translations Unmasked*, Dr. Russell R. Standish, p. 37.

The dark centuries of oppression and persecution would take their toll. The murderous Inquisition would finally strike the spark that would burst forth into flame. Soon after the turn of the 14th century, John Wycliffe would rise up to translate the Bible into the English language. Within 100 years of his death, William Tyndale would translate the Bible into English from the original tongues and the church would be changed forever.

ENGLISH TRANSLATIONS AND PERSECUTION

13

JOHN WYCLIFFE

John Wycliffe was born in 1329 A.D. in Yorkshire, England. He was one of the first English churchmen to translate the entire Bible into the common tongue.

With the infighting and schisms taking place in the Roman church in the 14th century, the nation of England was able to become much more independent of the church and gradually more power was assumed by the king in ecclesiastical affairs. This opened the door for the first flickering light of Reformation to begin to shine.

Wycliffe had grown to despise the Catholic system, which he believed to be full of corruption. He was strongly opposed to many of the doctrines of Rome, and he wrote and spoke out against them at every opportunity. His courageous and dogged resistance to the established church earned him the later title "The Morning Star of the Reformation." Schaff wrote that *Wyclif brought Scripture and common sense to bear. His pen was as keen as a Damascus blade. Irony and invective, of which he was the master, he did not hesitate to use.*[149] Wycliffe was said to have been the first Englishman to call the Pope the anti-Christ.[150] He called the Catholic monks robbers, malicious foxes, ravishing wolves, gluttons, devils, and apes and said that their monasteries were little more than dens of thieves, nests of serpents, and houses of living devils.[151]

Wycliffe taught and lectured at Oxford University and other schools while continuing to serve in the church. He was a gifted scholar, and his lectures were always crowded with students. Many of these students would later become followers of his anti-Catholic beliefs.

Wycliffe's criticism of the church made him many powerful enemies. Though he had also developed a number of strong allies, the Roman church eventually influenced the officials at Oxford to remove Wycliffe from his position there. After his removal from Oxford, Wycliffe began a full-scale attack upon the church. He believed that all men should be able to read the Bible in their own tongue, stating, *It helpeth Christian men to study the Gospel in that tongue in which they know best Christ's sentence.*[152] It was for this belief above all others, and for his translation of the Bible into English, that he was branded a heretic by Rome. In 1377 Pope Gregory XI ordered that Wycliffe be seized and imprisoned for his heresy, but the Pope's orders were never carried out by the authorities in England.

[149] Philip Schaff, *History of the Christian Church*, Vol. 6, Eerdmans, 1910, p. 319.
[150] Ibid., p. 316.
[151] Will and Ariel Durant, *The Story of Civilization*, Vol. 6, Simon and Schuster, 1957, p. 34.
[152] W.A. Craigie, The English Versions, in *The Bible in Its Ancient and English Versions*, Oxford, 1940, p. 138.

Thomas Arundel, Archbishop of Canterbury, made a telling statement about the reason for hatred of Wycliffe: *This pestilential and most wretched John Wycliffe of damnable memory, a child of the old devil, and himself a child or pupil of Anti-Christ...crowned his wickedness by translating the Scriptures into the mother tongue.*[153]

Two other statements made by Catholic writers, recorded in *Annals of the English Bible,* are very revealing: *This Master John Wycliffe hath translated the Gospel out of Latin into English, which Christ had intrusted with the clergy and doctors of the Church, that they might minister it to the laity and weaker sort, according to the state of the times and the wants of men. So that by this means the Gospel is made vulgar, and laid more open to the laity, and even to women who can read, than it used to be to the most learned of the clergy and those of the best understanding!*[154] This statement demonstrates a lack of biblical knowledge. Again we must testify to Paul's praise of the church at Berea:

> **Acts 17:11** *These were more noble than those in Thessalonica, in that they received the word with all readiness of mind, and searched the scriptures daily, whether those things were so.*

The second witness is even more revealing: *The prelates ought not to suffer that every one at his pleasure should read the Scripture, translated even into Latin; because, as is plain from experience, this has been many ways the occasion of falling into heresies and errors. It is not, therefore, politic that any one, wheresoever and whensoever he will, should give himself to the frequent study of the Scriptures.*[155] This statement is even more blasphemous than the prior. David's writings in the Psalms alone testify to the great importance in which he held the frequent study and meditation in the word of God. The

---

[153] David Fountain, *John Wycliffe: The Dawn of the Reformation*, p. 45.
[154] Christopher Anderson, *Annals of the English Bible*, I, p. 4.
[155] Ibid.

119th Psalm itself is also a testimony to the need for the word of God to become a part of a person's everyday existence. It is this indwelling of the word that gives strength and life, light and understanding.

Due to the fact that Wycliffe was unskilled in the Hebrew and Greek tongues, he made his translation directly from the Latin manuscripts, primarily the Vulgate. Though this was certainly not a pure line of transmission, it broke the ground for future translations and opened the door for the Bible to be given to the people in their own language.

Wycliffe's first version of the New Testament was published in English in 1380 A.d. with the Old Testament completed in 1382 A.D. Later editions were done by his followers. John Purvey's edition of Wycliffe's translation in 1388 A.D. was the primary English Bible used up to the time of William Tyndale. This Bible was propagated and distributed after the death of Wycliffe by his followers, who had been labeled the Lollards, a derisive term for babblers.

A number of the phrases used by Wycliffe in his translation were carried directly over into the expressions of the King James Bible. Some examples of these follow:

strait is the gate, and narrow is the way – Matthew 7:14
whited sepulchers – Matthew 23:27
born again – John 3:3,7; I Peter 1:23
worship the Father in spirit and in truth – John 4:23
the Spirit of adoption – Romans 8:15
a living sacrifice – Romans 12:1
the revelation of the mystery – Romans 16:25
the deep things of God – I Corinthians 2:10
the cup of blessing which we bless – I Corinthians 10:16
what communion hath light with darkness – II Corinthians 6:14
upbraideth not – James 1:5

One of the most notable persons influenced by Wycliffe was the early reformer John Hus. Hus stood in strong opposition to the corruptions of the Catholic church. He was requested to attend the Council of Constance (1415–1418 A.D.) to explain his beliefs and was guaranteed protection from trial or punishment. During the council he was betrayed and condemned to death, being burned to death on his birthday. It was during this same council that Wycliffe's bones were ordered to be dug up, burned, and cast into the river that ran alongside his church.

THE LOLLARDS AND THE EARLY ENGLISH BIBLE

The Lollards were the disciples of John Wycliffe who carried on his work over the next few generations. These Wycliffites were given the derogatory name of Lollards, meaning "babblers." These men and women laid down the spiritual seed that would spring up into the later Reformation. Though their predecessor had died peacefully, the Lollards would be subject to intense persecution for their distributing and teaching of the Bible.

The Lollards held the belief that any man who was called of God to preach or teach was authorized by heaven to do so. The civil and religious powers of the day demanded that any person operating in this capacity must be ordained and approved by the established church. The Lollards were set strongly against this system. Their convictions and determination to resist the authority of the church and its corrupt prelates created many powerful enemies. But it also drew many proselytes to their ranks. It was said at one time that of any two people walking down the streets of England, one was a supporter of Wycliffe's teachings.

Long before the 95 theses of Martin Luther were nailed to the Wittenberg Castle door, the Lollards were nailing anti-Catholic and Wycliffite teachings to the cathedral doors of England. They were dedicated to resisting the Catholic order and in bringing spiritual understanding and light to the common man through the word of God. One of their primary works was spreading the word of God through the distribution of the Scriptures, tracts, and teaching of the Bible.

The circulation of the Bible by the Lollards was met with both great joy and terrible anger. The common people were overjoyed to have the opportunity to be able to read the scriptures in a language they could comprehend and to experience the word of God without an intermediary to interpret it to them.

During these early days of distribution, the copying of Bibles was a painstaking, time-consuming process. Before the invention of the printing press, every copy had to be done by hand. It took a professional copyist from 10 months to a year of full-time work to finish one Bible. The time and effort involved in the process allowed for only a limited number of complete copies, and these were highly valued by any who had access to them.

According to McClure, the cost of an entire hand-copied Bible was four marks and forty pence, the equivalent of a clergyman's entire salary for a year.[156] John Foxe relates the great value placed upon the scriptures by the common people of that time: *So scanty was the supply of Bibles at this time, that but few of those who craved its teaching could hope to possess the sacred volume...If only a single copy was owned in a neighborhood, these hard working laborers and artisans would be found together, after a weary day of toil, reading in turn, and listening to the words of life; and so sweet was the refreshment to their spirits, that sometimes the morning light surprised them with its call to a new day of labor, before they thought of sleep.*[157]

In contrast to the joy and reverence the common people had for the English Bible, the church of Rome had a crushing hatred for these common translations. The rulers of the church held tightly to the belief that they alone were capable of understanding and interpreting the Bible and that no other "unclean" hands should intrude upon their private interpretations. The church believed that it alone had power to define doctrine and it took the circulation of these "heretical" translations as a direct attack against its authority. From the end of the 14th century through the 15th century numerous proclamations and decrees were made by the civil and ecclesiastical authorities forbidding the use and possession of Wycliffe's translation and writings.

In 1399 A.D. the bishop of York crowned Henry VI King of England and charged him *to consolidate the throne, conciliate the clergy and sacrifice the Lollards.* Henry replied, *I will be the protector of the Church.*

---

[156] Alexander McClure, *Translators Revived*, Maranatha Bible Society, 1858, p. 15.
[157] John Foxe, *Christian Martyrs of the World*, Barbour and Co., 1985, p. 346.

The preaching and distribution of God's word by the Lollards eventually brought about decrees of church and state created to smother their activity. In 1401 A.D. the Act for Burning Heretics was passed by the English Parliament. Within eight days of the passage of the bill, the burnings began at Smithfield. The political resolutions surrounding this included the following statements: *...no one within...the realm or any other dominions subject to his royal Majesty shall presume to preach openly or secretly without first seeking and obtaining the license of the local diocesan...henceforth no one either openly or secretly shall preach, hold, teach or instruct, or produce or write any book, contrary to the Catholic faith or the determination of the holy Church, nor shall any of the* [Lollard] *sect hold conventicles anywhere or in any way keep or maintain schools for its wicked doctrines and opinions...And if any person...is convicted by sentence...of the said wicked preachings, doctrines, opinions, schools and heretical and erroneous instruction, or any of them, and if he refuses duly to abjure the same...then the sheriff of the county....the mayor and sheriffs or sheriff, or the mayor and bailiffs of the city, town or borough...shall, after such sentences are proclaimed, receive those persons...and shall cause them to be burned before the people in a prominent place, in order that such punishment may strike fear into the minds of others, to the end that no wicked doctrines and heretical and erroneous opinions, nor their authors and favorers, be sustained...or in any way tolerated.*[158]

Thomas Arundel, Archbishop of Canterbury, made this statement in 1408 A.D.: *We therefore decree and ordain that no man shall, hereafter, by his own authority, translate any text of the Scripture into English or any other tongue....*[159]

---

[158] William L. Sachse, editor, *English History in the Making*, Volume 1, Xerox College Publishing, 1967, p. 137.
[159] The Constitutions of Thomas Arundel, 1408 A.D.

In 1414 A.D. another law was passed commanding the persecution of those who read the Scriptures in English: *...a law was passed, declaring that all who read the Scriptures in the mother tongue should "forfeit land, cattle, life, and goods, from their heirs forever."*[160]

The Lollards were not only charged with possessing and distributing the scriptures, but were castigated and persecuted for their ability to memorize and repeat Bible verses by heart!

Many of the Lollards gave their lives for their beliefs, being burned at the stake at Smithfield and elsewhere. Often they were tied to the stake with their Bible translations and writings tied around their necks. The first martyr burned at Smithfield was William Satre. The crime that necessitated his death was that he was heard to say, *I adore not the cross upon which Christ died as much as the Christ who died upon the cross.* Foxe, in *Christian Martyrs of the World*, recounts a number of these martyrs' deaths as quoted in *Final Authority*: *One Christopher Shoemaker, who was burned alive at Newbury, was accused of having gone to the house of John Say, and "read to him, out of a book, the words which Christ spake to his disciples..." In 1519 seven martyrs were burned in one fire at Coventry, " for having taught their children and servants the Lord's prayer and the ten commandments in English..." Jenkin Butler accused his own brother of reading to him a certain book of Scripture, and persuading him to hearken unto the same. John Barret, goldsmith, of London, was arrested for having recited to his wife and maid servant the Epistle of St. James, without a book...Thomas Phillip and Lawrence Taylor were arrested for reading the Epistle to the Romans and the first chapter of St. Luke in English.*[161]

---

[160] John Eadie, *History of the English Bible*, I, p. 89

[161] William P. Grady, *Final Authority*, Grady Publications, Inc., 1993-2001, pp. 127-128.

Many of the Lollards were held at what later became known as the Lollards Tower. This tower was attached to the Archbishop of Canterbury's residence at Lambeth Palace. As poignantly captured in the documentary film *The Indestructible Book*, there is a small, cramped room at the top of the tower where the prisoners were held. Along its walls are rusty iron rings where they were manacled. Here they awaited the torture and death that was in store for them. Etchings made by the prisoners cover the walls. One of the most compelling of these was made by an individual who had undergone terrible tortures and death for his beliefs. The words etched into the wooden wall read in Latin *Jesus amor mias*: "Jesus is my friend".

One of the greatest supporters of the Lollards was Sir John Oldcastle, known by the title Lord Cobham. Lord Cobham would go so far as to stand by the Lollard preachers armed and in armor in order that they might speak without being assaulted. He also heavily distributed copies of Wycliffe's Bible among the people.

Due to the fact that Cobham was a favorite of King Henry IV, he was not brought to trial until 1413 A.D., after Henry's death. At his trial he declared, *I am willing to believe all that God desires, but that the Pope should have the authority to teach that which is contrary to the Scripture, that I can never believe.* Cobham later escaped from his cell in the Tower of London, a feat considered near to impossible. Cobham was finally recaptured and executed in 1417 A.D. at St. Giles Field. He was chained to a rotisserie and roasted alive over a slow fire. David Cloud describes the scene in Rome and the Bible: *As this barbarous execution proceeded, the hateful priests and monks reviled and cursed the poor man and did their best to prevent the people from praying for him. It was to no avail. The people loved the godly knight and they wept and prayed with him and for him. The last words which were heard, before his voice was drowned by the roaring flames, was "Praise God!"*[162]

The voices and pens of the Lollards were never stilled by the intense persecution they faced. Their activity went on from the end of the 14th century until after the time of William Tyndale in the mid-16th century. Their incredible example of courage and conviction inflamed the hearts of those who followed them.

---

[162] David W. Cloud, *Rome and the Bible*, 1996.

ERASMUS AND THE TEXTUS RECEPTUS

The suppression of the Bible and the persecution of its early translators sowed the seeds that would become the Reformation movement. The blood of the martyrs watered the cracked, ancient soil of tradition, sowing the seed that would allow the two witnesses of the Old and New Testament to return to life. The events of the 15th and 16th centuries signaled this time of new beginnings, and it was a time of great heroes of the faith and villainous opponents of the truth.

God began to lay the groundwork for the renewal of the ancient scriptures. It was time to uncover the truth that had been buried under the avalanche of centuries of tradition and false doctrine.

The original languages in which the Bible had been written had become almost unknown in the West. Hebrew and Greek were not considered necessary for an understanding of the Bible as the Roman Catholic Church believed that the most inspired version ever written was the Latin Vulgate completed by Jerome.

Just before the breaking forth of Reformation there was a revival in the study of the ancient Biblical languages. This came about in great part due to the fall of Constantinople to Muslim (Turkish) invaders in 1453 A.D. With the Muslim occupation of Constantinople, many scholars and clerics of the Eastern Church were forced to flee to the West, bringing their knowledge of the Greek scriptures and their precious ancient manuscripts. These Greek manuscripts had been faithfully copied from the original Greek texts of the New Testament during the division of the Eastern and Western churches. Many of these exiled

Greek scholars found teaching positions in the universities of Europe. With this influx of Greek culture and language, the foundations were laid for a return to the New Testament in its original form.

The second major event that opened up the doors to translation and distribution of the Bible was the invention of the printing press by Johann Gutenberg in 1450 A.D. The printing press enabled copies of the Bible and other written works to be made much more quickly and economically than had been previously possible. This invention allowed the new translations and versions to spread even faster. It became nearly impossible for the enemies of the Bible to stop their circulation.

During this same period of time, the Old Testament Hebrew began to rise from its Masoretic obscurity. The entire Old Testament was printed in Hebrew at Socino, Italy, in 1488 A.D. Jacob ben Chayyim's fully annotated edition of the Hebrew Bible was published in 1525 A.D. This edition became the Hebrew Bible upon which all other translations were based.

There were three contemporaries during this time who had a great deal of influence on the transmission of the Bible into the common tongues: Desiderius Erasmus, Martin Luther, and William Tyndale. What is not commonly known is that the work of these three men was closely interrelated. These men communicated and influenced one another with their ideas and actions.

Desiderius Erasmus was born in Rotterdam in 1467 A.D. His father and mother both died of the plague when he was only 11 years old, and he was taken in at an Augustinian monastery. In 1492 A.D. he took vows as an Augustinian monk.

Erasmus was exceptionally intelligent. He excelled at nearly all of his intellectual studies and was considered one of the greatest minds of his day. His amazing intellect and keen wit allowed him to develop friendships with many of the most influential scholars and most powerful personalities of his day. He was a friend of Popes and kings, princes and prelates.

During his peak, Erasmus was offered positions by nearly all of the great powers of Europe. The King of England and the Emperor of Germany both offered him any position in their kingdoms at whatever price he would name. These and other nations courted his citizenship. Even the Pope offered him a cardinalship, which Erasmus declined.

Erasmus wrote a number of treatises on the corruption and moral and political issues of the church of his day. Books such as *The Manual of the Christian Soldier* and *In Praise of Folly* stirred the hearts of those who had longed for a reformation in the church. His intention was not to divide the church as much as to cause it to be reformed from within. Though he felt that the church was full of error and corruption, he did not approve of the schism created by the later Reformation.

Erasmus may not have intended to create the renewal that followed, but he was certainly a major influence on its coming about. Erasmus was said to have communicated with Luther and was supportive of his ideas. Erasmus mailed copies of Luther's 95 theses to his friends. This relationship changed when Luther permanently broke away from the Catholic Church. Erasmus disapproved of Luther's schism. The statement has been made that Erasmus laid the egg and Luther hatched it. Great changes were created through the power of his written words and especially through the New Testament translation he would make from the Greek.

Erasmus considered the work of translation of great importance. He strongly believed that the common man should have access to the word of God. In his first edition he stated, *I vehemently dissent from those who would not have private persons read the Holy Scriptures nor have them translated into the vulgar tongues, as though either Christ taught such difficult doctrines that they can only be understood by a few theologians, or the safety of the Christian religion lay in ignorance of it.*[163]

In his 1522 A.D. edition, he wrote that he believed it would be a triumph if the Bible *is celebrated by the tongues of all men; if the farmer at the plow sings some of the mystic Psalms, and the weaver sitting at the shuttle often refreshes himself with something from the Gospel....*[164]

In 1516 A.D. Erasmus finished his translation of the New Testament into the Greek right at the time of the first rumblings of the Reformation. The 1516 A.D. edition contained the Greek text on the left side, taken from the majority of the ancient manuscripts. On the right side was Erasmus' translation of the Greek into Latin.

In translating the Bible, Erasmus used manuscripts that were part of the Majority Text family. Later critical scholars berated his translation for this reason, though these were representative of the best preserved and majority of the manuscripts. Codex Vaticanus, which later became one of the primary sources underlying the modern Greek critical text, was available to Erasmus, though he chose not to use it. He did not feel it was as accurate or pure. His reasons for this can be easily seen when we later examine that particular manuscript.

---

[163] Preserved Smith, *Erasmus*, p. 184.
[164] Preserved Smith, *Erasmus*, pp. 184-185.

In a politically savvy move, he dedicated his translation to Pope Leo X. This was meant to garner the support of the church so that the work would be able to be published without resistance. Even with this decision, the translation was almost immediately banned throughout Europe. Some claimed that if this book was tolerated, it would be the death of the papacy.

One thing that aggravated the situation even more was his choice of the word "repentance" over the Latin term "penance." Repentance was the proper translation of the Greek, but penance fit better with the Roman church's doctrine. Eventually, at the Council of Trent (1545–1563 A.D.) Erasmus was condemned as a heretic and his writings were banned by the church.

None of this resistance was able to halt its rapid spread. Many of the leaders of the Reformation obtained copies and used these to translate the Bible into their native tongues. Martin Luther translated his German Bible primarily from Erasmus' Greek New Testament. Zwingli, Calvin, and others used this translation in order to bring the Bible to Switzerland and the nations of Europe. Meanwhile, God was preparing another man to continue the work of bringing his word back to man.

WILLIAM TYNDALE

William Tyndale was born in 1494 A.D., 100 years after the death of John Wycliffe. His work in translating the Bible into English so influenced those that followed him that he was later known as the Father of the English Bible.

Tyndale studied at both Oxford and Cambridge and was considered an outstanding scholar, especially in the Greek language. It is believed that during his tenure at Cambridge he studied Greek under the tutelage of Erasmus himself. His skill with languages was attested to by Herman Buschius, a scholar and friend of Erasmus: *A man so skilled in the seven languages, Hebrew, Greek, Latin, Italian, Spanish, English, and French, that which ever he spake, you would suppose it his native tongue.*[165]

Upon his arrival at Cambridge it is believed he joined the Reformation-oriented study group at the White Horse Inn, which included Thomas Bilney and other later English martyrs. In his attacks on the established church, Tyndale became famous for his razor-sharp skills at debate. John Foxe states that Tyndale was not only a skilled secular scholar, but that he was *singularly addicted to the Scriptures.* Foxe also relates that while at Cambridge, Tyndale was involved in teaching and instructing the scriptures to his circle of friends. Foxe goes on to say that *all that knew him reputed him to be a man of most virtuous disposition, and of unspotted life* and that he was *a great student, and earnest labourer in the setting forth of the Scriptures of God.* John

---

[165] Alexander Wilson M'Clure, *Translators Revived*, pp. 27-28.

Frith stated that *For his learning and judgment in scripture, he were more worthy to be promoted than all the bishops in England.*

Tyndale's most famous statement was made during a disputation with a Catholic priest regarding the authority of the papacy versus the Bible. Tyndale's arguments were unanswerable and frustrated the priest who finally shouted out in anger, *It were better for us to be without God's laws than the Pope's.* Tyndale answered, *I defy the Pope, and all his laws; and if God spare my life, ere many years, I will cause a boy that drives a plough to know more of the Scriptures than you do!*

At about 30 years of age Tyndale decided that his life's work would be to translate the Bible into English. He requested Bishop Tunstall of London to repeal the law passed against the Lollards that had forbidden the Bible to be translated in languages other than Latin. Tunstall refused and Tyndale realized that he must leave his homeland in order to complete the work he felt called to do. Tyndale traveled to Wittenberg to sojourn with Martin Luther. It is believed that his New Testament was finished during his time with Luther. Just as Erasmus before him, he finished his translation of the New Testament in less than a year's time.

Tyndale chose to translate the Bible into English from the older Greek, rather than the Latin manuscripts. He was certainly aware of the fact that Greek translates into English more easily than Latin. This is due principally to the Greek language's flexible word order, and its preference for verbs over abstract nouns, making its sentence structure more easily comprehended by English readers.

The first copies of Tyndale's New Testament came to England in 1525. They were smuggled in sacks of flour, and thousands of copies were quickly distributed throughout England. The secular and ecclesiastical powers of England and Rome were infuriated at this influx of Bibles in the common vernacular.

The three most powerful men in England were strongly opposed to the Reformation movement and to Tyndale's English translation. Thomas Wolsey was the head of the Catholic Church in England and one of the most powerful men in the nation at that time. King Henry VIII was ruler of England and a staunch supporter of the church. The Pope had given him the title "Defender of the Church" for his literary attacks against Luther and the Reformers. The last of these three men was the Chancellor of England, Thomas More. More was a strident proponent of the Catholic faith and was considered to be one of the most intelligent and powerful debaters of his day.

More had a great hatred for Tyndale. They wrote numerous fierce polemics back and forth against one another. More made numerous accusations against Tyndale's translation, among them, the statement that *To search for errors in it was like searching for water in the sea; it was so bad it could not be mended.* More was a student of the Greek language and had enough understanding to know just how inaccurate this statement was. When Tyndale asked More to give him a specific example of an error, the only objections he presented were the translation of certain ecclesiastical terms he disagreed with.

In his translation, Tyndale had preferred the use of the Greek over that of the corrupted Latin. For example, Tyndale translated the Greek **presbyter** as elder, as this word properly means elder or senior. More was infuriated at this as he felt the word should be translated priest. The Greek word for "priest" is a different word altogether. Tyndale also translated the Greek **agape** as love, which is much clearer than the traditional word charity. The greatest issue of contention was over the word "penance." Just as Erasmus before him, he chose not to mistranslate this term. The incorrect terminology fit perfectly with the Catholic doctrines, though the correct translation is not penance but repentance, completely changing the purpose and intent.

As a result of the great resistance by the church and civil authorities, Tyndale's translation was burned wherever it was found. Bishop Tunstall, who had earlier refused Tyndale his request to allow a translation, became one of the primary persons involved in hunting down and destroying the copies. The bishop was informed that a certain printer had access to a great number of these illegal copies, and he determined to purchase them in order to burn them. The printer was a supporter of Tyndale and charged Tunstall four times the production price for the Bibles. Though they were destroyed, this allowed Tyndale to not only replace them, but to print many more! Even with these incredible events, the hatred and destruction of Tyndale's work by the church was so thorough that though there were believed to have been more than 18,000 copies made from 1525 to 1528 A.D., only one complete copy, one partial copy, and one fragment remain today.[166]

Tyndale finally relocated to Antwerp where he finished the translation of the first five books of the Old Testament. It was in Antwerp were he was eventually betrayed by a Catholic agent pretending to be his friend. He was taken north and imprisoned in the fortress at Vilvorde, where he stayed for more than 16 months. It has been said that while he was imprisoned, his great faith, like that of Paul and Silas before him, converted the prison keeper and his household. During this time he continued his translating, finishing Joshua through II Chronicles. It is believed that this manuscript was smuggled out by John Rogers, one of his disciples.

At the time of his execution on October 6, 1536 A.D., Tyndale was brought to the stake, strangled by the executioner, and burned. His last words before death were a prayer, the answer of which opened doors that had not been possible during his lifetime. It is said that he cried out with a loud voice, *Lord! Open the King of England's eyes!*

---

[166] David W. Cloud, *Rome and the Bible*, p. 147.

Within a year of his death, Henry VIII would sanction two English Bibles, both of which were based directly on Tyndale's translation. McClure records the incredible story: *What is strangest of all, and is unexplained to this day, at the very time that Tyndale by the procurement of English ecclesiastics, and by the sufferance of the English king, was burned at Vilvorde, a folio-edition of his Translation was printed at London, with his name on the title page, and by Thomas Berthelet, the king's own patent printer. This was the first copy of the Scriptures ever printed on English ground.*[167]

The King James Version was greatly influenced by Tyndale's work. Some scholars have theorized that 80–90% of its structure and wording was directly taken from Tyndale's translation. The words *Passover, scapegoat, atonement,* and *Jehovah* were all developed by Tyndale. The following phrases are a handful of the many literal adaptations of Tyndale's text found in the King James Version:

Let there be light – Genesis 1:3
my brother's keeper – Genesis 4:9
the fat of the land – Genesis 45:18
love thy neighbor as thyself – Leviticus 19:18
let my people go – Exodus 5:1
to eat, and to drink, and to be merry – Ecclesiastes 8:15
the salt of the earth – Matthew 5:13
signs of the times – Matthew 16:3
the truth shall make you free – John 8:32
a law unto themselves – Romans 2:14
the powers that be – Romans 13:1
filthy lucre – I Timothy 3:3
fight the good fight – I Timothy 6:12

---

[167] Alexander Wilson M'Clure, *Translators Revived*, p. 32.

HENRY VIII AND THE ENGLISH BIBLE

Henry VIII, who had so greatly despised the Protestant movement and had taken pleasure in the death of Tyndale, was the very instrument that would enable the Bible to be brought into the English language. He had been a hero of the Catholic Church, writing detailed theological arguments against Luther and Protestantism. It was said that Henry and Luther hated each other with a terrible hatred. It was his stand against Protestantism that had caused the Pope to give him the title "Defender of the Faith."

In 1527 A.D., during Henry's reign, Thomas Bilney was arrested while preaching publicly. Bilney had been one of the founders of the Protestant movement in England and along with Tyndale, a member of the study group that met at the White Horse Inn at Cambridge. Bilney had been a powerful voice against the Roman Church and had widely distributed the scripture.

Bilney was imprisoned, but his friends were permitted to visit him in the hopes that they would dissuade him from his beliefs. Unlike Job's friends, they succeeded. He was marched down to the public square where he was forced to listen to his heresy publicly denounced, at which point he was told to burn a stack of Tyndale's Bibles. Bilney conceded, but committing the act broke him.

He soon after returned to preaching and was arrested again in 1531 A.D. On the last night before his execution he was visited by his friends. This time they attempted to strengthen him with words of encouragement, telling him the Holy Spirit would cool the fire. Bilney opened his Bible and put one hand upon the page, stretching out his other hand over the candle on the table with his finger directly in the flame. He held his hand there till the candle had burned his finger to the bone, at no time showing any sign of pain or suffering. At last he pointed to the Bible, which was open to Isaiah 43:2: *...when thou walkest through the fire, thou shalt not be burned; neither shall the flame kindle upon thee.* He told his friends that he knew that with Christ with him in the fire he would feel no pain of burning. In the morning when he was being led to his execution he ran to the stake and embraced it, proclaiming how thankful he was to be given a second opportunity to die for his Lord.

The persecution of readers and distributors of the Bible went on through the early reign of Henry VIII. In his defense of Catholic order, he was responsible for the deaths of a number of martyrs.

- John Tewksbury was imprisoned and tortured so brutally that he was crippled. He was sentenced to death in December 1530 A.D. and burned at the stake. His crime was distributing Bibles and claiming his faith was in Christ alone.

- In November 1531 A.D., Richard Bayfield, a converted priest who had smuggled Bibles into England, was betrayed and burned at the stake.

- James Bainham was arrested in December 1531 A.D. He was accused of heresy and distributing scriptures. He was tortured until he could no longer walk. His wife was imprisoned for refusing to reveal the location of the copies of the Bible they had been distributing, and all of their property was confiscated. Bainham was burned at the stake in May 1532 A.D. After being half consumed by the flames Bainham called out that he felt no pain. His final words included the following statement: *These be the articles that I die for, which be a very truth, and grounded on God's Word, and no heresy...First, I say it is lawful for every man and woman, to have God's Book in their mother tongue. The second article is, that the Bishop of Rome is Antichrist, and that I know no other keys of heaven-gates but only the preaching of the Law and the Gospels....*[168]

- John Frythe was brought to trial in June 1533 A.D. Frythe was a disciple of William Tyndale, having come under his influence during his the meetings at Cambridge. He was offered an opportunity to escape execution but his reply was, *If I should now start aside, and run away–I should run from God, and from the testimony of his holy Word....* Frythe was burned at the stake at Smithfield in July 1534 A.D. When the fire was lit, a Catholic priest instructed the people that they were not to pray for those being executed and to consider them no more than dogs. Though the ordeal of burning was torturous, Frythe endured it without apparent pain.[169]

- Dean Forret was among five men burned at the stake at Edinburgh in March 1539 A.D. He had a great love for the Bible, having obtained a copy of Tyndale's New Testament and having memorized great portions of it. It was said that he studied the Bible from six in the morning until noon and memorized three chapters a day! The Roman Catholic authorities pronounced his crime at his execution: *Know thou not, heretic, that it is contrary to our acts and express commands, to have a New Testament or Bible in English, which is enough to burn thee for?*

The intolerant edicts and persecution continued through most of Henry's reign. Any who dared stand against Catholic doctrine, or who were courageous enough to read and spread the scriptures, were subjected to confiscation of property, torture, and death. In June 1535 A.D. the Parliament of Scotland declared that all persons possessing New Testaments or other heretical books must deliver them up within 40 days or face confiscation and imprisonment. A declaration made in

---

[168] Christopher Anderson, *Annals of the English Bible*, I, p. 334.
[169] Ibid. pp. 376-377.

May 1536 A.D. stated that the reading of the Sacred Volume in the English tongue was publicly prohibited.[170]

Henry VIII was married to Catherine of Aragon. Catherine had not been able to provide Henry with a male heir. As time passed Henry grew more and more distanced from Catherine until his roving eyes fell upon one of her ladies in waiting, Anne Boleyn. Anne would have nothing to do with Henry as long as he was married, and the Catholic Church frowned upon divorce.

Henry requested the Pope annul his marriage to Catherine on the grounds that she could not provide him with a male heir. The Pope denied his request. Henry, infuriated, removed Thomas Wolsey from his position as Archbishop of Canterbury and replaced him with Thomas Cranmer, who in 1533 A.D. annulled his marriage to Catherine and married him to Anne. Thomas More, the intensely Catholic Lord Chancellor of England, would not attend the wedding. He was later charged with treason for this action and was eventually executed in 1535 A.D.

The position of the Archbishop of Canterbury was the highest ecclesiastical office in the nation, and only the Catholic Pope could appoint a man to this seat. This caused a jagged rift between the king and the Catholic hierarchy. In order to further validate his action,

---

[170] Christopher Anderson, *Annals of the English Bible*, II, p. 487.

Henry influenced Parliament to declare that the king was the supreme head of the church in England.

Henry had previously, in his support of Catholic dogma, resisted any attempt of the Bible's translation into English. In 1530, during the beginning of the tensions between king and Church, Henry stated in a royal proclamation that he recognized the desire of the people for a Bible in their language, but that this was not yet expedient. This was the first step in opening the door for later translations.

It is very likely that Anne Boleyn exerted a great deal of influence on this process. Anne was strongly in favor of an English Bible. She also demonstrated her support numerous times for adherents of Protestant belief. Anne was presented with a copy of Tyndale's 1534 New Testament with her coat of arms on the title page and her name and title on the spine. Tyndale's work was given her "in recognition of her protection to the friends of the New Testament." It was said that she treasured this Bible more than any other. D'Aubigne writes that *Anne...often withdrew to her closet at Greenwich or at Hampton Court, to study the Gospel...she did not conceal the pleasure she found in such reading; her boldness astonished the courtiers, and exasperated the clergy.*[171] Anne was also a patron of Miles Coverdale, who would continue in Tyndale's footsteps by completing his English translation.

It is believed that Anne's presence may have alleviated much of the persecution that fell upon the Protestant Bible believers during Henry's reign. John Foxe wrote, *So great was the trouble of those times...before the coming in of Queen Anne.*

---

[171] Merle D'Aubigne, *History of the Reformation*, V, p. 324.

Anne's firstborn child was Elizabeth, who would later become one of the most powerful and influential of Protestant English rulers. Anne bore only one male child to Henry, which died soon after his birth. Like Catherine before her, this inability to provide Henry an heir would bring about her downfall.

As Henry grew more frustrated with Anne, he again sought attentions elsewhere. He quickly became infatuated with Jane Seymour. In order to replace Anne, Henry had to find some legal excuse to put her aside. False accusations of adultery were brought against her. In addition, he accused her of a conspiracy to murder him. Anne was beheaded on May 19, 1536 A.D., just months before the martyrdom of William Tyndale. She went to her death professing her innocence and begging Christ to receive her spirit. The very next day Henry married Jane Seymour.

Jane was also well disposed toward the Protestant faith. She finally gave Henry the heir he desired in 1537 A.D., but she died just 12 days after giving birth to their son, Edward VI. Henry married six times, and it is revealing that of these six wives, three (Anne Boleyn, Jane Seymour, and his sixth wife, Catherine Parr) were strong supporters of Protestantism. Though Henry resisted the Reformation, it was aided by several of his wives. Henry himself died in 1547 A.D., leaving the throne to his son.

MILES COVERDALE AND THE COVERDALE BIBLE

Miles Coverdale was a close friend of Anne Boleyn. Anne was both his patron and supporter during her short reign. Miles Coverdale would pick up the work where William Tyndale had left off.

Coverdale had been an Augustinian monk and later a priest before joining the Reformation movement. It was believed that he had been a disciple of Tyndale who had assisted him in his work on the books of Moses. Coverdale was a man of great intellect, and it was said of him that he *drank in good learning with a burning thirst.*

After converting to Protestant beliefs, Coverdale became an evangelical preacher and spoke out widely against the corruption of the Roman Catholic Church. He felt the great necessity of a Bible in the English tongue and believed that God's word was perfectly inspired: *Wherever the Scripture is known it reformeth all things. And why? Because it is given by the inspiration of God.* Due to his strong beliefs and outspoken statements he was forced to flee England in 1528 A.D. and lived in exile on the continent where he worked on his translation of the Bible until his return home in 1535 A.D.

Coverdale was skilled in Latin, but knew very little Hebrew or Greek. He recognized his limitations as a translator, writing, *Considering how excellent knowledge and learning an interpreter ought to have in the tongues, and pondering also my own insufficiency therein, and how weak I am to perform the office of a translator, I was the more loath to meddle with this work....*[172] His translation was based almost entirely on the translations done before him. This included sources as diverse as the Latin Vulgate and Luther's German translation. But it was Tyndale's translation that was the most significant influence. In order that it would be more readily accepted, he changed the terms "repentance," "elder," and "love" used by Tyndale back to the more politically acceptable terms "penance," "priest," and "charity."

Coverdale was a master wordsmith, creating many poetic passages and phrases that later became part of the King James Bible. The following literal adaptations of the Coverdale Bible made their way into the later King James Bible:

> *respect of persons* – II Chronicles 19:7 and elsewhere
> *lovingkindness* – Psalms 17:7 and elsewhere
> *the valley of the shadow of death* – Psalms 23:4
> *tender mercies* – Psalms 25:6 and elsewhere
> *Cast me not away from thy presence, and take not thy Holy Spirit from me* – Psalms 51:11
> *Forgive us our debts, as we forgive our debtors* – Matthew 6:12
> *Enter thou into the joy of thy Lord* – Matthew 25:21,23
> *the pride of life* – I John 2:16
> *the world passeth away* – I John 2:17
> *Morning star* – Revelation 2:28 and 22:16

The door was opened for Coverdale's return at the Convocation of Canterbury in 1534 A.D. The Convocation represented the southern clergy of the Church of England. In this meeting they petitioned Henry VIII that *the Holy Scriptures should be translated into the vulgar English tongue.*

---

[172] Prologue unto the Christian Reader, from the Coverdale Bible.

Coverdale's translation, known as the Coverdale Bible, was approved by Henry for limited distribution. In 1535 A.D. he ordered that the Bible was to be distributed to every church. Archbishop Parker, Anne's chaplain, recorded that even though there was great resistance to this, *through the grace and intercession of our most illustrious and virtuous mistress the Queen, permission was at length obtained from the king.* Coverdale dedicated his translation to both the king and queen. Anne Boleyn placed an open copy on a desk in the king's court so that any who wished to may read it. The 1537 A.D. edition carried the stamp of the king's license, technically making it the first authorized English Bible.

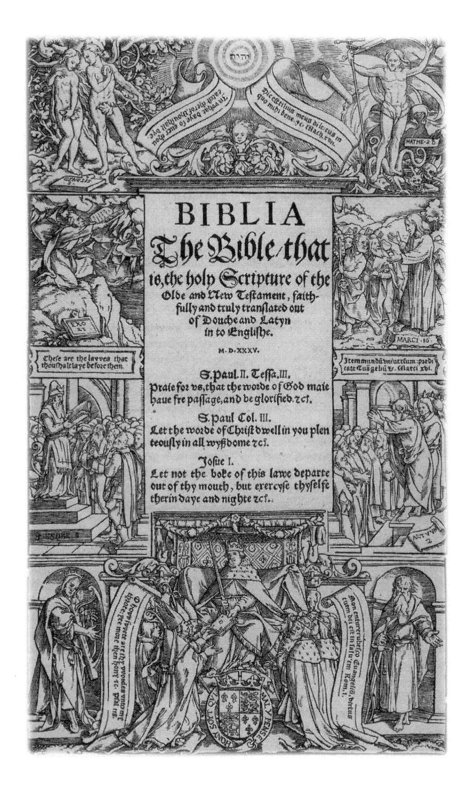

Though the translation of the Bible into English had finally begun to be officially accepted, the resistance was far from over. During a convocation of English bishops in 1537 A.D., a confrontation broke out on the subject of the Bible in the common tongue. Stephen Gardiner, the Catholic Bishop of Winchester declared, *All the heresies and extravagant opinions now in Germany and thence coming over to England, spring from the free use of the Scriptures…to offer the Bible in the English tongue to the whole nation during these distractions would prove to be the greatest snare that could be…*. Edward Fox, the Bishop of Hereford replied, *Think ye not that we can, by any sophisticated subtleties, steal out of the world again the light which every man doth see. Christ hath so enlightened the world at this time that the light of the Gospel hath put to flight all misty darkness…The lay people do now know the Holy Scripture better than many of us…*. The debate continued for some time, finally ending in agreement that the assembly would appeal to the king to permit the use of the Bible to the laity.

JOHN ROGERS AND THE MATTHEW'S BIBLE

John Rogers was the disciple of William Tyndale who carried on Tyndale's original translation. It is believed that Tyndale entrusted Rogers with his prison translation of Joshua through II Chronicles made just before his execution.

In completing his Bible translation Rogers used the pseudonym Thomas Matthew in order to hide this association with Tyndale and his work. Some historians have argued against these being the same individual, though this is clearly demonstrated by numerous witnesses. Simms records that in the Council Register of Queen Mary's reign, he is referred to as John Rogers, alias Matthew.[173]

The Matthew's Bible was completed in 1537 A.D., within a year of Tyndale's execution. Considering this translation was used in England, it is amazing to note the fact that at the end of the book of Malachi the initials W.T. (for William Tyndale) are proudly displayed in large bold letters, giving credit to the true translator of the work.

As previously stated, the Matthew's Bible was not a new translation but actually the completion of Tyndale's translation efforts. This Bible consisted of Tyndale's New Testament and his translation of Genesis through II Chronicles, the remainder of the Old Testament being taken from Coverdale's Bible.

---

[173] P. Marion Simms, *The Bible from the Beginning*, p. 176.

The Matthew's Bible was clearly Protestant. It contained numerous marginal notes of a decidedly anti-Catholic nature. Unlike the Coverdale Bible, which had Tyndale's Protestant wording and marginal notes excised, the Matthew's Bible supported these beliefs.

THE GREAT BIBLE

The Coverdale and the Matthew's Bibles had come under criticism soon after they began to be circulated. To begin with, the Coverdale Bible was associated on a number of levels with Anne Boleyn. Anne had encouraged and supported the translation. After the trial and execution of Anne by her husband, the Coverdale version bore the stigma of its association with the murdered queen. Another common criticism made against the Coverdale Bible was the fact that it had not been directly translated from the original languages.

The Matthew's Bible was so clearly Protestant that it caused the traditional and pro-Catholic bishops discomfort. This version was also very closely associated with William Tyndale. Even with the Bible's translation into English accomplished, Tyndale still was viewed as a heretic by many of the ecclesiastics.

Thomas Cranmer, Archbishop of Canterbury, and Thomas Cromwell, the Vice Regent, encouraged Miles Coverdale to make a revision of the Matthew's Bible, in order that there might be an official Bible for England that all could agree upon. It is interesting that the Matthew's Bible was the basis for this translation. The Matthew's Bible was certainly translated from the original languages, but it still bore the mark of Tyndale's hand. Though this translation was based on Tyndale's work, it was corrected in areas by the Latin Vulgate.

The Great Bible was completed during the period of 1539 to 1541 A.D. It was referred to as the Great Bible primarily due to its size. It was very thick and the pages measured about 11 inches wide by 16½ inches long. It had been designed to be chained to the church lectern. It was to be made available for the public to read, and the church was to provide a reader for those who were illiterate or incapable of reading from its pages.

All of the churches of England were required to purchase a copy of this Bible. A specified time limit was given for the purchase. At the expiration of that time, the price doubled and continued to double every month until every church had purchased a copy. This alone assured that it would become the official Bible read in the churches. Even with this fact in mind, this version was never popular with the common people, likely due to the influence of the Vulgate readings.

EDWARD VI TO MARY TUDOR

Upon the death of Henry VIII in 1547 A.D., his nine-year-old son Edward became King of England. Edward, as his mother before him, was a dedicated Protestant. He had a great love and respect for the Bible and its teaching. The story of his coronation certainly validates this fact. McClure describes the events surrounding Edward's coronation: *This intellectual and pious child was one of those "who trembled at God's Word," which he loved and venerated...At his coronation, three swords were brought, to be carried before him, in token that three realms were subject to his sway. The precocious prince said that yet another sword must be brought; and when the attending nobles asked what sword that might be, he answered, "The Bible!" That, said he, "is the sword of the Spirit, and is to be preferred before these swords."*[174]

Edward had never been a strong child, and his health slowly deteriorated over the next few years. In 1553 A.D., at just 15 years of age, Edward died of tuberculosis. There was no male heir to continue the line, so the eldest female child of Henry ascended to the throne. Mary Tudor, daughter of Catherine of Aragon, became Queen of England.

---

[174] Alexander Wilson M'Clure, *Translators Revived*, pp. 43-44.

Mary, in direct contrast to her brother, was a fanatical Roman Catholic. Her mother had sown deep seeds of hatred in her child's heart, and she was far from emotionally stable, having experienced a deeply troubled childhood. When Catherine's marriage to Henry was declared void by the church, Mary had been immediately stamped as illegitimate. There could be no divorce, so the marriage was seen as never having been legal in the church's eyes. Mary experienced great prejudice as a child, and when her mother died she was not even permitted to view the body.

Soon after rising to the throne, Mary began to reestablish the Catholic doctrines and canon laws in England. She removed the Great Bible from the churches and forbid any printing of the Bible in English. In 1554 A.D. she married the Catholic ruler Phillip II of Spain, and Catholicism was restored in all its forms, including the merciless laws against heresy. Simms states, *Reading the English Bible and offering Protestant prayers were forbidden under penalty of death. To accomplish her purpose the queen resorted freely to the rack and the fagot, and as a result came to be known as Bloody Mary.*[175]

Mary's great hatred for the English Bible is demonstrated by Robertson, as quoted in *Rome and the Bible*: *On the accession of "Bloody Mary" to the throne of England, in 1553, there existed a painting in London of King Henry VIII, in which he was represented standing holding in one hand a scepter and in the other a Bible with the words on its cover, Verbum Dei* [Word of God]. *This exhibition of the "Word of God" was so offensive to Papal eyes that it was obliterated, and a pair of gloves painted in its place. And we all know how during the reign of Mary–that same good daughter of the Church– tons of Bibles were used as* [logs] *to light the piles for martyrs, than*

---

[175] P. Marion Simms, *The Bible From the Beginning*, p. 182.

which, it was said, 'no burnt offerings could be more pleasing to Almighty God.'[176]

It has been estimated that 300 to 400 Protestant Bible believers were martyred during her short 5½-year reign. The lives of many great heroes of the English Protestant movement were taken during this time.

Nicholas Ridley and Hugh Latimer were sentenced to death in 1554 A.D. Ridley was Archbishop Cranmer's chaplain, and Latimer was a Protestant preacher who at one time had been a Catholic priest. Ridley and Latimer were brought to the stake together. Ridley, entering the place of execution, held up both of his hands to heaven. Ridley, upon seeing Latimer, ran to him and embraced him, saying, *Be of good heart brother, for God will either assuage the fury of the flames or else strengthen us to abide it.* They knelt and prayed together at the foot of the stake. After the fire was lit and the flames began to engulf them, the old man Latimer turned to the younger Ridley and told him, *Master Ridley, play the man. We shall this day light a candle by God's grace in England that shall never be put out!* That candle burns still and its torch has been carried throughout the world.

John Rogers, the faithful disciple of Tyndale and translator of the Matthew's Bible, was burned at the stake at Smithfield in February 1555 A.D. It is said that he told his executioner that he would pray for him. On the way to the place of his execution he had to pass his wife and 11 children, but was not allowed to speak to them. It is said that they gave him such words of encouragement and strength that the event seemed more a wedding than a funeral. John Foxe records Roger's last words: *...when the time had come, the prisoner was brought...to Smithfield, the place of his execution. Here Woodroofe,*

---

[176] Alexander Robertson, *The Roman Catholic Church in Italy*, p. 210 as quoted by David Cloud in *Rome and the Bible*, p. 191.

one of the sheriffs, asked him if he would change his religion to save his life; but Rogers answered, "That which I have preached, I will seal with my blood."[177] Green records that *he died bathing his hands in the fire as if it had been cold water.*[178]

Archbishop Thomas Cranmer, Henry VIII's replacement for the Catholic Thomas Wolsey, was arrested, defrocked, and ordered to stand trial for his beliefs in 1556. Cranmer, terrified at the prospect of death, wrote five recantations. Afterward, Queen Mary and Cardinal Pole burned him at the stake regardless of his recantation. They also required that he publicly testify to his return to the belief in the Catholic faith.

On March 21, 1556 A.D. he was to make his confession and be taken to the place of execution. Halfway through his public recantation, his spirit broke and he made a complete 180-degree turn. He stated, *I renounce and refuse as things written with my hand contrary to the truth in my heart, and written for fear of death; and for as much as my hand offended in writing contrary to my heart, my hand shall first be punished, for if I may come to the fire it should first be burned.* He went on to defy the Pope and the Catholic Church and was ordered to be immediately executed.

It was said that the guards had a difficult time keeping up with the old man as he rushed to the stake. When the flames were ignited he placed his hand in the fire first, and left it there until it was burned to a stump, removing it only once to wipe his face. His last recorded words were, *Lord Jesus, receive my spirit.*

---

[177] John Foxe, *Christian Martyrs*, pp. 422-423.
[178] John Richard Green, *History of the English People*, p. 372.

In May 1556 A.D. Hugh Laverick, a cripple, and John Aprice, a blind man, were burned alongside each other for their belief in the Bible alone. Foxe records their final words: *When Hugh Laverick was secured by the chain, having no further occasion for his crutch, threw it away, saying to his fellow-martyr, while consoling him, "Be of good cheer my brother; for my Lord of London is our good physician; he will heal us both shortly–thee of thy blindness, and me of my lameness.*[179]

Mary continued the persecutions and murders until her untimely end. She was eventually abandoned by her husband. Sick, depressed, and exhausted by what she believed were numerous miscarriages, she died in November 1558 A.D. She was succeeded by her half-sister Elizabeth, the daughter of Anne Boleyn. It has been said of Mary that she did all within her power to burn out Protestantism…all she did was burn it in.

---

[179] John Foxe, *Foxe's Book of Martyrs*, p. 251.

THE GENEVA BIBLE

During the reign of Queen Mary, many English Protestants fled to the continent to escape her wrath. A great number of these congregated at the Protestant city of Geneva. Geneva had become the center of the Reformation in Europe and was considered the Protestant capital of the world. In this seedbed of Protestant ideology, a new translation would be born.

This translation was believed to have been one of the first done by a committee rather than an individual, though the primary translator was most likely William Whittingham, the brother-in-law of John Calvin. Some have theorized that Coverdale was in Geneva and aided in the translation also.

The Great Bible was used as the basis of the Old Testament, though it was thoroughly revised. The intention was to translate the Old Testament more accurately from the original Hebrew, especially in the books of the Bible that Tyndale had not translated. These books had never been directly translated into English from the original tongues. The translators were so concerned with accuracy that they used the ancient rather than the modern spellings of the Hebrew names: for example, Iaakob instead of Jacob.

The New Testament was completed in 1556 A.D. It was based primarily on the Matthew's Bible, with some corrections from the Great Bible and others. The Geneva Bible was the first to completely divide the Bible into chapter and verse, and it contained words in italics to better express the flow of the language.

The entire Bible was finished by 1560 A.D. and it quickly became the most popular Bible of its day. It was widely considered the most accurate English translation made up to that time.

This was the Bible used by the great Elizabethan writers and poets; Shakespeare's quotations of scripture are taken from the Geneva Bible. This was the Bible brought over on the *Mayflower* by the Pilgrim Fathers. The translators of the King James Bible used this as their Bible of choice during that time and even quoted from it in the preface to the 1611 A.D. edition of the King James Bible.

The Geneva Bible was generally not approved by the rulers of Europe and England. This was due to its Calvinistic marginal notes of a strongly Protestant nature. These notes lashed out at the Catholic Church in a number of places. One example is the note contained at Revelation 11:7, speaking of the beast that would ascend from the bottomless pit. The Geneva Bible's marginal notes identify this beast as *the Pope which has his power out of hell and cometh thence.* These types of statements made this Bible unpopular with Queen Elizabeth and other rulers who were attempting to conciliate the differing sects. The following phrases from the Geneva Bible were literally adapted by the translators of the King James Bible:

vanity of vanities – Ecclesiastes 1:2 and 12:8
Remember now thy Creator in the days of thy youth – Ecclesiastes 12:1
My beloved Son, in whom I am well pleased – Matthew 3:17
Except a man be born again – John 3:3
A little leaven leaveneth the whole lump – I Corinthians 5:6 and Galatians 5:9
A cloud of witnesses – Hebrews 12:1

QUEEN ELIZABETH AND THE BISHOP'S BIBLE

Elizabeth was crowned Queen of England on January 15, 1559 A.D. She was a Protestant Bible believer as her mother before her. Upon hearing of her accession to the throne, she is recorded as having quoted Psalms 118:23: *This is the Lord's doing; it is marvelous in our eyes.* During her procession she was presented with a copy of the Bible, which she kissed and pledged *diligently to read therein.*

It is important to understand that though Elizabeth was Protestant herself, her intention was never to abolish Catholicism in England. She continued to believe in the efficacy of parts of the Catholic ritual and never attempted to stamp out the Catholic Church, though she made a number of strong statements against it. She called Catholicism *the darkness and filth of popery* and referred to it as the *Babylonical Beast of Rome.*

Elizabeth was completely committed to the strength and unification of England above all other things. She believed in part that religious unity could be accomplished through tolerance for both Protestant and Roman Catholic beliefs. She had no patience for anything she considered to be a fanatical religious movement and was violently opposed to the Anabaptists. Only four individuals lost their lives for their religious beliefs during her long reign, and all were Anabaptists.

Queen Elizabeth did not approve of the Geneva Bible, which had become so popular during her day. She felt that its Protestant annotations might anger the Catholics in England and bring division into its finely balanced political structure. With the counsel of Matthew Parker, the Archbishop of Canterbury, she authorized a new translation to be made that could be considered the official English Bible for the churches. Thus was born the Bishop's Bible.

The translation of the Bishop's Bible was presided over by Parker and completed in 1568 A.D. Its basic translation was taken from the Great Bible, though any offensive wording or marginal notes were avoided. This version was little more than a compromise translation. Its express intent was to avoid any type of controversy or division. It was circulated only in the churches; in all other venues the Geneva Bible continued to be the Bible of choice.

This version was considered the weakest translation made of all the Reformation Bibles. It included a number of unusual phrases, including the wording of Ecclesiastes 11:1. The King James Bible translates this verse as *cast thy bread upon the waters*, whereas the Bishop's Bible uses the phrase *lay thy bread upon wet faces*.

The Bishop's Bible did not have a great deal of influence on the later King James translation, though there were a few literal adaptations such as follow:

The voice of one crying in the wilderness – Matthew 3:3 and elsewhere
persecuted for righteousness sake – Matthew 5:10
overcome evil with good – Romans 12:2

THE KING JAMES BIBLE

14

KING JAMES I

The story of the King James Version of the Bible must, of course, begin with the man from whom it received its name, James I of England. Though he was not personally involved in the translation and distribution of the Bible that bears his name, James authorized and placed his seal upon the translation.

James became King of England in April 1603 A.D. upon the death of his cousin, Queen Elizabeth. He had ruled Scotland from 1567 to 1603 A.D. as James VI, receiving the crown upon the imprisonment of his mother, Mary, Queen of Scots.

Mary had been a devout Roman Catholic who hated the Protestant inroads that were being made in Scotland. It was said that she feared the prayers of John Knox more than all the armies of Scotland. In her political and ecclesiastical resistance to England, she made a number of attempts to overthrow her cousin Elizabeth. In 1567 she was finally imprisoned for sedition and her son James was given the crown of Scotland. Mary was eventually executed by Elizabeth in 1587.

James experienced a number of terrible tragedies in his early childhood. When he was only eight months old, his father was strangled by his enemies. His mother was deemed at least partially responsible for his father's death due to her suspected plotting with the murderers. This was the event that brought about her abdication of the throne in his favor. At five years old he had to watch his grandfather die in front of him as the results of a raid by his mother's supporters who were attempting to return her to the throne.

James later became the object of numerous assassination attempts and death threats, principally due to his commitment to Protestant beliefs. Druids cast spells upon him, and the Jesuits hatched numerous plots against him.

The most infamous attempt on his life was made in November 1605 A.D. Parliament was scheduled to hold its opening session on November 5th. A number of Jesuit agents and sympathizers, including Guy Fawkes and Robert Catesby, placed 30 barrels of gunpowder in the basement beneath the House of Parliament. Their intention was to blow up the entire assemblage, which included the king and many of the most prominent Protestant political leaders. A letter was uncovered in advance that revealed the plot, and the conspirators were captured and executed. In a statement in 1607, the Spanish ambassador inferred that the Jesuits had been behind the attempt: *He is a Protestant...The King tries to extend his Protestant religion to the whole island. The King is a bitter enemy of our religion...He is all the harsher because of this last conspiracy against his life...He understood the Jesuits had a hand in it.*[180]

Though James was weak and sickly throughout his life, he had a keen and discerning mind. He was one of the most highly educated rulers of

---

[180] Stephen A. Coston, Sr., *King James the VI of Scotland & I of England, Unjustly Accused*, 1996, p. 42.

Europe in his day. Opfell describes his mental ability: *Among those justifiably attributed refinements was his reputation as a paragon of learning, crammed with Greek and Latin and other tongues. In spite of his physical disabilities, his mind was first rate. Already at the age of seven he was able, extempore...to read a chapter of the Bible out of Latin into French and next out of French into English as well as few men could have added anything to his translation. In due time he became known as the most educated sovereign in Europe.[181]* It has been said that James had fluent mastery of Greek, Latin, and French by the age of 8.[182]

James was not only a secular scholastic; he was also a diligent student of the Bible. Coston states that James *was deeply read in the Scripture; he could quote its texts with great facility.*[183] Ralston testifies to his reputation: *King James was regarded by those of his own time as "The British Solomon." He was wise not only in politics and academics, but in Theology. He was devoutly interested in the Word of God.*[184]

Along with his authorization of the King James Bible, his accomplishments were many. Among them was the establishment of the first Christian colony in the New World. He was also the English ruler responsible for uniting the nations of England, Ireland, and Scotland and was the first to use the term "Great Britain."

Though James' moral life was later slandered by his enemies, waiting until after his death to do so, their accusations were demonstrated to be false. Many of his contemporaries testified to his morally virtuous

---

[181] Olga S. Opfell, *The King James Bible Translators*, p. 1.

[182] See *The Answer Book* by Samuel C. Gipp, Bible and Literature Missionary Foundation, 1989, p. 9. and "The Real King James," by Karen Ann Wojahn in *Moody Monthly*, July-August 1985, p. 87.

[183] Stephen A. Coston Sr., *King James the VI of Scotland & I of England, Unjustly Accused*, 1996, p. 311.

[184] David Ralston, *The Real King James, The British Solomon*, 1986, p. 8.

lifestyle. Sir Henry Wotton wrote in 1602, *There appears a certain natural goodness verging on modesty...among his good qualities none shines more brightly than the chasteness of his life, which he has preserved without stain down to the present time, contrary to the example of almost all his ancestors, who disturbed the kingdom with the great number of bastards which they left....*[185] F.A. Inderwick stated, *James had a reputation for learning, for piety, for good nature, and for liberality*[186]*and as to his personal character, it is, I think only justice to say...he was personally a man of good moral character, a quality which was probably much indebted to the strict and careful training he received from his Presbyterian tutors....*[187]

The major accusation made against him was of effeminacy and suspicion of improper relations. The evidence contained in the statements of his historical contemporaries alone makes this a ludicrous assessment. James wrote *Basilicon Doran* (The Kingly Gift) for his eldest son, Henry, who, had he not died, would have followed James in the throne. Among other things he instructed Henry not to be effeminate: *But especially eschew to be effeminate in your clothes, in perfuming, preining, or such like...and make not a fool of yourself in disguising or wearing long your hair or nails, which are but excrements of nature.*[188] Some of his other statements follow: *There are some horrible crimes that ye are bound in conscience never to forgive: such as witchcraft, willful murder, incest, and sodomy*[189] and *Keep your body clean and unpolluted while you give it to your wife whom to only it belongs.*[190] He certainly had a deep respect for marriage, writing often of his appreciation for his wife. In preparation for his marriage, he spent 15 days in prayer and meditation.

---

[185] Ibid., p. 39.
[186] Ibid., p. 43.
[187] Ibid., p. 303.
[188] Ibid., p. 4.
[189] Ibid., p. 48.
[190] Ibid., p. 44.

When it came to the church, James had firmly entrenched beliefs. He was an adamant supporter of Protestantism in the form of the Anglican Church of England. He had been brought up in Presbyterian Scotland where the church had more political power than the king. He had experienced a number of run-ins with the bishops in Scotland during his reign there, and it had affected him deeply.

The most pointed event is related by McGrath in his book *In the Beginning*: *His views on this matter were shaped to no small extent by some unpleasant experiences with Scottish presbyteries...At a heated encounter between the king and senior churchmen at Falkland Palace in October, 1596, Melville* [a Scottish Presbyterian] *had physically taken hold of James, and accused him of being "God's silly vassal." Melville pointedly declared that while they would support James as king in public, in private they knew perfectly well that Christ was the true king in Scotland, and his kingdom was the kirk-a kingdom in which James was a mere member, not a lord or head. James was shaken by this physical and verbal assault, not least because it suggested that Melville and his allies posed a significant threat to the Scottish throne. The simple fact is that James had not the slightest intention of promoting a Puritan or Presbyterian agenda in England. He thoroughly detested what he had seen in Scotland, and did not wish to encounter the same difficulties in England.*

This and other events colored James' feelings toward any but the Anglican Church. His position was that the king was divinely ordained by God and as such was the hand of God in the temporal world, including authority over the church, a position the Anglicans felt perfectly comfortable with. The Presbyterian and Puritan believers felt that no one but God alone ruled over the church. This difference of opinion set the stage for the events to come.

HAMPTON COURT

On April 5, 1603 A.D., four days after the death of Queen Elizabeth, James began his journey to London to be made King of England. As he traveled toward London he was intercepted by a delegation of Puritan ministers. The Puritans presented James with a list of grievances, which became known as the Millenary Petition, due to the fact that it contained more than 1,000 signatures of English clergymen. This was a significant number at this time, constituting about 10% of all the ministers of England.

The Millenary Petition contained grievances against the dogma of the Anglican Church of England, including the following statements: *Now we, to the number of more than a thousand of your Majesty's subjects and ministers, all groaning as under a common burden of human rites and ceremonies, do with one joint consent humble ourselves at your Majesty's feet to be eased and relieved in this behalf. Our humble suit then unto your Majesty is, that of these offences following, some may be removed, some amended, some qualified...These with such other abuses yet remaining and practised in the Church of England, we are able to shew not to be agreeable to the Scriptures....*

James had no desire to deal with the complaints of these Puritans, but he knew, considering the significant number of ministers involved, that he must at least humor them with an audience. His reply to the petition was to call *a meeting for the hearing, and for the determining, things pretended to be amiss in the church.*

The meeting between James and the churchmen was not what the Puritan ministers had expected. The assembly met at the king's residence at Hampton Court on January 14, 16, and 18, 1604 A.D. The clergymen consisted of 19 Anglicans and 4 Puritans. The Puritan representatives

were not only in the minority, but they had been hand-picked by James so he could be certain they were not extremists.

The king sat as moderator during the proceedings. For a great deal of the conference the Puritan leaders were made to sit outside the room. When they were present they were chided and harassed by both the Anglicans and the king. They made numerous requests for reform, but were brushed aside at every turn.

During the January 16 session, the Puritan Dr. John Rainolds made his famous suggestion that a new translation of the Bible be made. His specific address began with a complaint against the common prayer book. He argued that it contained numerous mistranslations due to the fact that it was based on the Great Bible and the Bishop's Bible. His original intent may have been to convince the king to sanction the Geneva Bible, which was the favored Puritan translation.

Rainold's address follows: *May your Majesty be pleased, to direct that the Bible be now translated, such versions as are extant not answering to the original....* Bishop Bancroft, the leader of the Anglicans, immediately disagreed, stating *If every man's humor might be followed, there would be no end to translating.*

To the amazement of all present, James spoke up and put an end to the debate: *I profess, I could never yet see a Bible well translated in English, but I think that of Geneva is the worst.*

Perhaps the idea of a new translation under his authorization appealed to James' pride. It is certainly true that he despised the Geneva Bible, which included numerous marginal notes that he felt undermined the office and authority of the king. Here was an opportunity to have a Bible translated on the soil of England by the greatest scholars of the nation, and one which would have no doctrinal bias.

James placed his official sanction on the translation with the following directive: *That a translation be made of the whole Bible, as consonant as can be to the original Hebrew and Greek; and this to be set out and printed, without any marginal notes, and only to be used in all churches of England, in time of Divine service.*

James was certainly excited about the prospect of this new translation. He intended that the Bible would be available to the common people in a way that it never had before. Ralston comments: *He made it clear that he wanted the Holy Word of God to be in the hands of the people and not chained to the pulpits or hoarded in cellars to be read only by Greek scholars. He had the deep conviction that the more widespread the knowledge of God's word became, the better the spiritual condition would be of his subjects.*[191]

---

[191] David Ralston, *The Real King James, The British Solomon*, 1986, p. 8.

Bishop Bancroft was ordered to begin the work. James gave him explicit instructions on his desire for the very best educated men to be involved in the translation. But even more importantly, he wanted them to be men who had *taken pains in their private study of the Scriptures.*[192] Later scholars have attempted to prove that James was not concerned with the translation, but a letter from Bishop Bancroft to one of his aides proves otherwise:

I move you in his Majesty's name that, agreeably to the charge and trust committed unto you, no time may be overstepped by you for the better furtherance of this holy work...You will scarcely conceive how earnest his Majesty is to have this work begun![193]

---

[192] Gustavus S. Paine, *The Men Behind the King James Version*, Baker, 1959, pp. 12-13.
[193] Ibid., p. 11.

THE TRANSLATION AND TRANSLATORS

Fifty-four of the greatest English scholars were selected to translate the new version. No list exists of the entire company; most range from 47 to 50 names. Part of the reason for this is that some of the older translators died during the work and were replaced by others.

Robert Louis Stevenson said *Bright is the ring of words when the right man rings them!* This was certainly the case with the translators of the King James Bible. These were not only men of the highest scholastic level of excellence; they were nearly all involved in the work of the church, being ministers in some capacity. Dr. Samuel Gipp states regarding their credentials: *The men on the translation committee of the King James Bible were, without dispute, the most learned men of their day and vastly qualified for the job which they undertook. They were both academically qualified by their cumulative knowledge and spiritually qualified by their exemplary lives. Among their company were men who, academically, took a month's vacation and used the time to learn and master an entirely foreign language; wrote a Persian dictionary; invented a specialized mathematical ruler; one was an architecht; mastered oriental languages; publicly debated in Greek; tutored Queen Elizabeth in Greek and mathematics; and of one it was said, "Hebrew he had at his fingers end."*[194]

McClure also testifies to the high educational and moral standards of these men: *It is confidently expected that...all the colleges of Great Britain and America, even in this proud day of boastings, could not bring together the same number of divines equally qualified by learning and piety for the great undertaking. Few indeed are the living names worthy to be enrolled with those mighty men.* Furthermore, *It should be noted that these men were qualified in the readings of the*

---

[194] Samuel C. Gipp, *The Answer Book*, Bible and Literature Missionary Foundation, 1989, p. 61.

church fathers which prevented them from being "locked" to the manuscripts, causing earlier readings to be overlooked. This is vastly better than the methods used by modern translators. It should be recognized that these men did not live in "ivory towers." They were men who were just as renowned for their preaching ability as they were for their esteemed education. It is a lesson in humility to see such men of great spiritual stature call themselves "poor instruments to make God's Holy Truth to be yet more and more known."

The translators were from a variety of backgrounds and doctrinal beliefs, and represented both the Puritan and Anglican camps.

The actual translation was believed to have begun in 1607 A.D. and lasted until 1611 A.D., when it went through its final editing and printing. The work was done at three locations, Westminster, Cambridge, and Oxford, and was completed by six companies of translators, with two companies at each location.

Genesis through II Kings was translated by the **First Westminster Company** led by **Lancelot Andrews**. Andrews was highly qualified for the position. At the time of the translation he was Dean of Westminster, later becoming the Bishop of Westminster. It was said of him that *he ever bore the character of "a right godly man," and "a prodigious student." One competent judge speaks of him as "that great gulf of learning!" It was also said, that "the world wanted learning*

to know how learned this man was." And a brave old chronicler remarks, that, such was his skill in all languages, especially the Oriental, that, had he been present at the confusion of tongues at Babel, he might have served as Interpreter-General! In his funeral sermon by Dr. Buckeridge, Bishop of Rochester, it is said that Dr. Andrews was conversant with fifteen languages.

The remainder of the company consisted of **Hadrian Saravia**, the oldest translator at 73; **Richard Clarke**; **John Layfield**, *Of him it is said, that being skilled in architecture, his judgment was much relied upon for the fabric of the tabernacle and temple;* **William Bedwell**, *He is spoken of in his epitaph, as being for the Eastern tongues, as learned a man as most lived in these modern times;* **Robert Thomson**; **Robert Tighe**; **Francis Burleigh**; and **Geoffrey King**.

According to Charles Butterworth in his *Literary Lineage of the English Bible*; the primary influence on the Westminster Company's rendering of the Pentateuch was (1) Tyndale, (2) the Geneva Bible, (3) Coverdale (1535 version and the Great Bible), and (4) the Bishop's Bible.

Butterworth states that in Joshua through II Kings the translators were primarily influenced by the Matthew's Bible, secondarily by the Great Bible and the Geneva Bible and in a much smaller extent from the Bishop's Bible and others.

I Chronicles through Song of Solomon was translated by the **First Cambridge Company**. The company was led by **Edward Lively**, Regius professor of Hebrew at Trinity College. Of him it was said that *he was one of the best linguists in the world.* Lively died in 1605 during the translation. The company consisted of **John Richardson** and **Lawrence Chaderton**, a Puritan and Master of Emmanuel College. Chaderton was deeply familiar with the Latin, Greek, and Hebrew and diligently investigated the writings of the rabbis so far as they might aid in the proper translation of the language. He was also considered a mighty preacher; one example of this follows: *while our aged saint was visiting some friends in his native country of Lancashire, he was invited to preach. Having addressed his audience for two full hours...he paused and said, - "I will no longer trespass on your patience." ...the whole congregation cried out with one consent, - "For God's sake, go on, go on!" He, accordingly, proceeded much longer, to their great satisfaction and delight.*[195]

Also in the company were **Francis Dillingham**; **Thomas Harrison**, a Puritan, of whom it was said, *Beloved for his meekness and charitable attitudes, he enjoyed a reputation as both Hebraist and Greek scholar, noted for his "exquisite skill in Hebrew and Greek idioms."*[196] Other members were **Roger Andrewes**, the younger brother of Lancelot Andrewes, **Andrew Bing**, and **Robert Spaulding**.

Butterworth states that the primary influence on the translation of I Chronicles through Esther was from the Geneva, Matthew's and Great Bibles.

In the poetical books it would appear that the influence was primarily from the Geneva and Bishop's Bibles, Psalms in particular shows the influence of Coverdale's versions and the Geneva Bible.

---

[195] Alexander Wilson M'Clure, *Translators Revived*, p. 115.
[196] Olga S. Opfell, *The King James Bible Translators*, p. 49.

Isaiah through Malachi was translated by the **First Oxford Company**. This company was led by **John Harding**, though **John Rainolds** likely had much more influence than Harding. Rainolds was called the "Father of the King James Version" due to his suggestion at the conference at Hampton Court. He was a Puritan and the President of Corpus Christi College. He was considered to be the most learned man in England, called a *living library, a third university....*[197] He was said to be *scholarly, gentle, incorruptible*[198] *His industry and piety are largely attested by his numerous writings, which long continued in high esteem. Old Anthony Wood, though so cynical toward all Puritans, says of him, that he was "most prodigiously seen in all kinds of learning; most excellent in all tongues." "He was a prodigy in reading," adds Anthony, "famous in doctrine, and the very treasury of erudition; and in a word, nothing can be spoken against him only that he was the pillar of Puritanism and the grand favorer of non-conformity." Dr. Cracken-thorpe, his intimate acquaintance, though a zealous churchman, gives this account of him, "He turned over all writers, profane, ecclesiastical, and divine; and all the councils, fathers, and histories of the Church. He was most excellent in all tongues useful or ornamental to a divine. He had a sharp and ready wit, a grave and mature judgment, and was indefatigably industrious. He was so well skilled in all arts and sciences, as if he had spent his whole life in each of them. And as to virtue, integrity, piety, and sanctity of life, he was so eminent and conspicuous, that to name Reynolds is to commend virtue itself." From other testimonies of a like character, let the following be given, from the celebrated Bishop flail of Norwich," He alone was a well-furnished library, full of all faculties, all studies, and all learning. The memory and reading of that man were near to a miracle."*

---

[197] Gustavus Swift Paine, *The Men Behind the King James Version*, p. 22.
[198] Olga S. Opfell, *The King James Bible Translators*, p. 56.

Also in the company were **Thomas Holland** at whose funeral sermon it was said of him *that he had a wonderful knowledge of all the learned languages, and of all arts and sciences, both human and divine.* He was also called *a prodigiously learned man, "drowned in his books,"* he was called especially *"mighty in Scripture."*[199]

Richard Kilbey was a member of the company as well as **Miles Smith**, of whom it was said *He went through the Greek and Latin fathers, making his annotations on them all. He was well acquainted with the Rabbinical glosses and comments. So expert was he in the Chaldee, Syriac, and Arabic, that were almost as familiar as his native tongue. "Hebrew he had at his fingers' ends." He was also much versed in history and general literature, and was fitly characterized by a brother bishop as "a very walking library."* Smith was said to be *covetous of nothing but books*[200] It was Smith who wrote the preface to the King James Version. As he grew older he strongly favored the Puritan views.

Richard Brett was also a member of the company. He was *famous in his time for learning as well as piety, skill'd in debate, and versed to a criticism in the Latin, Greek, Hebrew, Chaldaic, Arabic, and Ethiopic tongues,*[201] and it was said of him that *he was a most vigilant pastor, a diligent preacher of God's word....*[202] The final member of the company was **Richard Fairclough**.

Butterworth states that Isaiah through Malachi was a substantial revision of the Geneva translation with a heightening of the literary effect. After Geneva the translators appear to be influenced secondarily by Coverdale.

---

[199] Olga S. Opfell, *The King James Bible Translators*, p. 60.
[200] Alexander Wilson M'Clure, *Translators Revived*, p. 142.
[201] Olga S. Ofpell, *The King James Bible Translators*, p. 62.
[202] Alexander Wilson M'Clure , *Translators Revived*, p. 144.

The Apocrypha was translated by the **Second Cambridge Company**. These non-canonical books were inserted between the Old and New Testament and were clearly stated to have been included for historical value as they were not part of the inspired scripture. Later editions did not include the Apocrypha. This company consisted of **John Duport**; **William Brathwaite**; **Samuel Ward**; **Andrew Downes**; **Jeremiah Radcliffe**; **Robert Ward**, and **John Bois**, who was taught by his father to read Hebrew at the age of five. By six he was considered a skilled writer of Hebrew. It was said that he could read the Hebrew Bible and write its characters at this young age.

Matthew through Acts and the book of Revelation were translated by the **Second Oxford Company**. This company included **Thomas Ravis, Sir Henry Savile, George Abbot, John Harmer, John Perin**; **Giles Thomson, Richard Edes, John Aglionby, James Montague**, and **Ralph Ravens**.

In terms of the influence of prior translations on the Gospels, Butterworth states, *The simple phraseology of the Gospels represents the cumulative legacy of about twenty English versions, including various editions. Tyndale was the chief influence. Fully one third of the New Testament is worded just as Tyndale left, it, and in the remaining two-thirds, where changes have been made, the sentences still follow the general structure as Tyndale laid it down. The Beatitudes as well as the Lord's Prayer are taken almost word for word from Tyndale's translation. The secondary influence was Coverdale, then Geneva, and lastly the Bishop's Bible.*

Romans through Jude were translated by the **Second Westminster Company**. The members of this company were **William Barlow, John Spencer, Roger Fenton, Michael Rabbett, Thomas Sanderson, Ralph Hutchinson**, and **William Dakins**.

Butterworth states that Romans through Jude was most influenced by the Bishop's Bible, secondarily influenced by Coverdale's translations and the Geneva Bible, and much less by Tyndale than the other sections.

The translators in each company finished their portions at different times. As each portion was completed, it was sent to the other companies for their review, and then returned to its company with any suggestions. At the same time, advice and suggestions were received from scholars outside the translation committee, and these were weighed and analyzed.

The entire work was assembled at Stationer's Hall in London around 1610 A.D. It was here that the final review process was completed, being completed in approximately nine months.

It is believed that 6 to 12 of the translators were on the final review committee, probably one to two representatives of each company. The only names recorded as taking part in the final revision were John Bois and Andrew Downes of the Second Cambridge Company and John Harmer of the Second Oxford Company.

John Selden writes, regarding the final editorial process, *The translation in King James' time took an excellent way. That part of the Bible was given to him who was most excellent in such a tongue, and they met together, and one read the translation, the rest holding in their hands some Bible, either of the learned tongues, or French, Spanish, Italian, etc. If they found any fault, they spoke up; if not, he read on.*[203]

---

[203] John Selden, *The Table Talk of John Selden*, 1689.

The translators testified to the methodology of the translation process in its preface. The work was not to be done through the wisdom of man, but through earnest prayer and the anointing of the Spirit of God: *And in what sort did these assemble? In the trust of their own knowledge, or of their sharpness of it, or deepness of judgment, as it were in an arm of flesh? At no hand. They trusted in him that hath the key of David, opening and no man shutting; they prayed to the Lord.*

After the final editorial process was completed, Miles Smith and Thomas Bilson added the final touches, including the writing of the preface. In 1611 A.D., the King James Bible was finally completed and sent to the press by Robert Barker, the king's printer.

The final product was a masterpiece of English literature. The King James Bible is unarguably the pinnacle of the English language. The following are selected testimonies to the efficacy and enduring power of the King James Version:

Winston Churchill: *The scholars who produced this masterpiece are mostly unknown and unremembered. But they forged an enduring link, literary and religious, between the English-speaking people of the world.*

Jonathan Swift: *The translators of our Bible were masters of an English style much fitter for that work than any which we see in our present writings....*

Thomas Babington Macaulay: *A book which if everything else in our language should perish, would alone suffice to show the whole extent of its beauty and power*

Arthur Clutton-Brock: *The Authorized Version of the Bible is a piece of literature without any parallel in our modern times. Other countries, of course, have their translations of the Bible, but they are not great works of art.*

Sir Arthur Quiller-Couch: *I grant you, to be sure, that the path to the Authorized Version was made straight by previous translators, notably by William Tyndale. I grant you that Tyndale was a man of genius…But that a large committee of forty-seven should have gone steadily through the mass of Holy Writ, seldom interfering with genius, yet when interfering, seldom missing to improve; that a committee of forty-seven should have captured (or even, let us say, should have retained and improved) a rhythm so personal, so constant, that our Bible has the voice of one author speaking through its many mouths; that is a wonder before which I can only stand humble and aghast.*

Dr. Talbot W. Chambers: *The merits of the Authorized Version, in point of fidelity to the original, are universally acknowledged. No other version, ancient or modern, surpasses it, save, perhaps, the Dutch, which was made subsequently, and profited by the labors of the English translators. But a version may be faithful without being elegant. It may be accurate without adequately representing the riches of the language in which it is made. The glory of the English Bible is that while it conveys the mind of the Spirit with great exactness, it does this in such a way that the book has become the highest existing standard of our noble tongue.*

Professor Cook (Yale): *[It] is universally accepted as a literary masterpiece, as the noblest and most beautiful Book in the world, which has exercised an incalculable influence upon religion, upon manners, upon literature, and upon character….*

George Bernard Shaw: *The translation was extraordinarily well done because to the translators what they were translating was not merely a curious collection of ancient books written by different authors in different stages of culture, but the word of God divinely revealed through His chosen and expressly inspired scribes. In this conviction they carried out their work with boundless reverence and care and achieved a beautifully artistic result...they made a translation so magnificent that to this day the common human Britisher or citizen of the United States of North America accepts and worships it as a single book by a single author, the book being the Book of Books and the author being God.*

John Livingstone Lowes: *The Noblest Monument of English Prose.*

Comptons Encyclopedia (1995 Online Edition): *One of the supreme achievements of the English Renaissance came at its close, in the King James Bible...It is rightly regarded as the most influential book in the history of English civilization....*

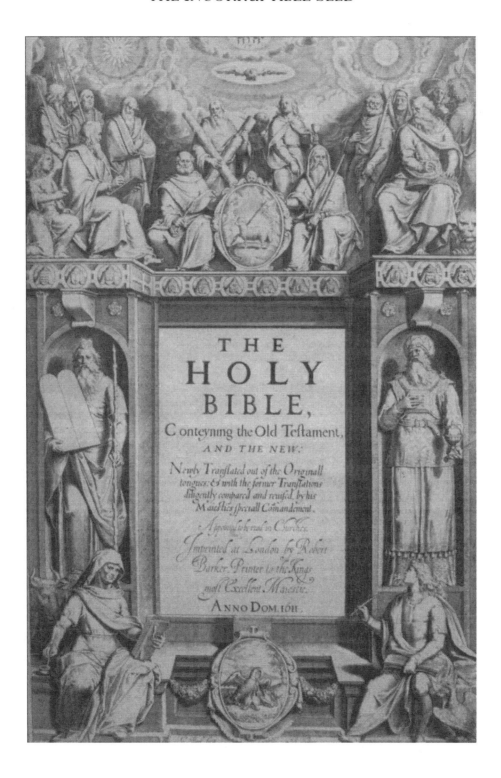

TEXTUAL CRITICISM AND THE CRITICAL TEXT

15

Psalms 118:8
It is better to trust in the Lord than to put confidence in man.

The truth and how to determine it has always been one of the intellectual pursuits that has stimulated the mind of man. There have always been those, who like Pilate, would ask, "What is truth?" When man fell, a great barrier fell between God and humankind. The brightness of God that shines out across this barrier casts a great shadow. Rather than being revealed by this light, man has chosen to live in the darkness cast by that shadow. It is in this darkness and shadowy half-light that he seeks for truth within himself.

As the years of time marched on through the centuries following the fall of the church and the rise of Romanism, man worked busily in the closing light, building empires of earth and of intellect. As darkness fell, man built on recklessly, walking in the light of his own making. The exchange of truth for a lie, of purity for harlotry is accomplished in the following stages:

Opposition to Tolerance, Tolerance to Compromise,
Compromise to Acceptance, Acceptance to Alteration,
Alteration to Assimilation, and Assimilation to Adulteration

In the beginning the thing is strongly opposed. As it works its subtle threads first of toleration and eventually of compromise into accepted thought, it quietly alters the perception of truth. Once truth is altered it is a short passage to assimilation, which finds its end in adulteration.

HIGHER (TEXTUAL) CRITICISM

Higher criticism in its modern form was born in the crucible of rationalism. Rationalistic reasoning questions all things to determine if they can be logically determined to be true. It gives no favor or precedence to a thing based on its source but treats all things with disdain.

Higher criticism focuses on the sources and historicity of the text. It makes an attempt to determine truth through humanistic reasoning. It concerns itself with the authorship, date, and place of composition of the biblical books, as well as the historical merit of the record: whether the people, events, and places were actual or fictional.

Modern higher criticism of the Bible finds it origins in the late 18th and early 19th centuries in the theological schools of Germany, especially those centered in and around Tubingen. These first critical scholars began questioning the structure and historical accounts of the Bible by using modern scientific methods and philosophical arguments.

These higher critics questioned every aspect of the Bible and its message. It was not treated as a book that was divinely inspired, but with the same indifference with which they might analyze the works of Plato or Shakespeare.

It was questioned and criticized on every level as to its accuracy and truth. The intent was not to determine whether it was true as a whole. They certainly did not believe that that was the case. According to the higher critics, the Bible was full of textual and historical errors, fables, and inventions of the imagination.

Was Moses the author of Genesis? Was Job a real person or just a poetic creation? Did David even exist? Were the prophetic books written long after the events prophesied? Did later Hebrew scribes edit and change the previous writer's words to match their own doctrinal ideas? These and many other such questions were debated and continue to be debated by the critical scholars.

The questions that higher criticism inspires are not Christian questions. Christianity is a religion established on absolute faith in the word of God. Faith, at its purest source, is without the evidences of human logic and reasoning. The questions and debates of higher critics do little more than introduce doubt to those whose faith is weak. They do not strengthen the church or the Christian faith! They are like termites gnawing away at the structure and foundation of faith.

LOWER (TEXTUAL) CRITICISM

Lower criticism or textual criticism concerns itself with attempting to establish the original version of a text. The ancient manuscripts are examined to determine which best represent the original. Once these manuscripts are agreed upon, the textual critic can piece together the best possible representative of the original.

The work of textual criticism is accomplished through a variety of methods. One of the first things is to establish a date for the manuscript. This is usually done by examining the style of writing and the materials used. Uncial writing (all uppercase) is generally considered older then minuscule writing (cursive or lowercase). The shape and style of writing are analyzed to determine the time period of its authorship

Terrance Brown stated, *Textual Criticism, the evaluation of the actual manuscripts in the ancient languages, the preparation of printed editions of the Hebrew and Greek Text, and the modern translations now being made in English and many other languages, are very largely conducted under the direction or influence of scholars who by their adoption of these erroneous theories have betrayed the unreliability of their judgment in these vital matters. We must not permit our judgment to be overawed by great names in the realm of biblical "scholarship" when it is so clearly evident that the distinguished scholars of the present century are merely reproducing the case presented by rationalists during the last two hundred years. Nor should we fail to recognise that scholarship of this kind has degenerated into a skeptical crusade against the Bible, tending to lower it to the level of an ordinary book of merely human composition.*[204]

---

[204]Terance Brown, *If the Foundations Be Destroyed*, T.B.S Article No. 14, p. 13.

BASIC TENETS OF TEXTUAL CRITICISM

Just as in any scientific method, textual criticism is made up of a number of rules and theories that attempt to categorize and confirm the manuscript evidence. What we must discern is whether these rules are based on sound facts or carnal hypotheses. The following rules and beliefs are not intended to be comprehensive, but rather to give a simplistic overview of a complex subject. Most modern scholars would agree upon these rules; each can find its roots in the critical studies developed over the last few centuries.

THE TEXTUAL FAMILIES

It is generally accepted that there are three or four textual families from which all New Testament manuscripts are descended. A textual family consists of a group of manuscripts that are in basic agreement with one another and are believed to have originated around a particular geographic area.

These textual families have changed names and shifted geographical locales as new manuscripts have been discovered and older manuscripts have been collated. Collation is the process of putting two or more texts beside one another for comparative purposes. Collation reveals where words and phrases may have been added or deleted from a manuscript through side-by-side comparison. It also reveals differences in spelling and punctuation.

The four textual families usually referred to by modern scholars are those from the areas of Byzantium (Byzantine), Alexandria (Alexandrian), Rome (Western), and Caesarea (Caesarean). These were considered to be the four main centers of Christian influence in the first few centuries A.D. The New Testament writings and epistles were copied and distributed during the expansion of the church, and eventually these centralized areas would have carried on their own copying traditions.

The Byzantine text represents by far the majority of all known manuscripts. This is why it is also called the Majority Text. Approximately 94 to 95% of all manuscripts are of the Byzantine text type. In most cases this text contains fuller readings than the other textual families. This basically means that there are more words in the Byzantine text than the minority texts.

The Byzantine text takes its name from Byzantium (Constantinople), the capital of the Eastern Roman Empire, and after the final division of Rome, the capital of the Byzantine Empire. This textual family is believed to have originated around Antioch in Syria, eventually coming to Byzantium as Antioch fell to the Muslims. The Greek New Testament continued to be faithfully copied by the scribes at Byzantium long after the split between the Eastern and Western churches. Finally in 1453 A.D. the Muslim Ottoman Turks captured Constantinople. The Greek scholars and copyists of the Eastern Church migrated to the West, bringing their precious manuscripts and knowledge of the Greek language. It was from this stream that Erasmus translated the *Textus Receptus*.

The Alexandrian textual family is believed to have originated around Alexandria, Egypt. It represents about 3 to 4% of the known manuscripts. The oldest manuscripts available are examples of the Alexandrian text. Probably the best reason for this is due to the dry desert climate of Egypt where they originated. This would allow for them to be preserved much longer than the texts of the East.

The oldest codices, or manuscripts in book form, are Alexandrian. *Codex Sinaiticus* and *Codex Vaticanus* are the two most famous. These two texts, discussed in further detail later, differ from one another in thousands of places. As we have previously seen, Alexandria was a boiling pot of philosophy and paganism. The Alexandrian texts were the seed of Origen and the disciples of the neo-Platonic schools.

The Western textual family is that which originated at Rome and to some extent Carthage. Codex D is the main example cited of the Western text. It has been said to be full of paraphrases, additions, and deletions.

The Caesarean textual family is actually a subgroup of the Alexandrian family. Some scholars believe this was the text of Origen, which originated in Alexandria and was brought to Caesarea by Eusebius and others. It contains both Alexandrian and Western influences.

CONFLATION

Conflation is the mixing of two or more passages or phrases in order to make one longer verse. It also can represent the copying of one verse into another section to add more detail. Textual critics claim that this is why the Byzantine text contains longer readings. They believe that at some point scribes combined manuscripts from various textual families together to create one uniform text.

Textual critics argue that a text that is fuller is always of lesser quality due to this effect. This theory was introduced by Westcott and Hort, whom we will discuss later. Their intention was to discredit the source of the Byzantine manuscripts. The argument they used is certainly not a logical rationale, as deletion of text is just as possible as addition. Bruce Metzger testifies to the opinion of textual critics in regard to the Byzantine copyists: *The framers of this text sought to smooth away any harshness of language, to combine two or more divergent readings into one expanded reading, and to harmonize parallel passages.*[205]

---

[205] Bruce Metzger, *A Textual Commentary on the Greek New Testament*, p. xx.

Again, it must be stressed that there is absolutely no evidence for the validity of this theory.

Truncation is just as much a danger as conflation. Truncation occurs when a scribe removes words or phrases from the text, creating a shorter or truncated reading. The minority textual families have clearly all been heavily truncated. Their readings are not shorter because they are more accurate; they are shorter because some of the Scripture has been removed or poorly copied.

AGE VERSUS WEIGHT

Textual critics believe that one older manuscript is far more valuable than the testimony of many others that are somewhat younger in age. In other words, if *Codex Sinaiticus* (Alexandrian) was written in the 4th century, it must be closer in purity to the original than 50 manuscripts from the 6th century which disagree with its reading.

This is simply not a logical conclusion. Just because a manuscript is older does not mean that it is better. The original manuscripts did not survive because they were constantly being copied and passed down. An older manuscript that was preserved could not have been heavily used. The preservation of God's word is not in the construct of man's making: ink and papyrus; it is in the life of God's word that passes down through copy after copy until it reaches down to our age from times long past.

Using the age of the manuscripts to disprove the Byzantine text will not work for the textual critics either. The very earliest papyrus fragment, known as P66, contains the Byzantine text reading of John 10:19 in contradiction to the comparable Alexandrian papyrus fragments P45 and P75.[206]

---

[206] Harry Sturz, *The Byzantine Text Type: New Testament Textual Criticism*, p. 84

FOUNDATIONS OF THE CRITICAL PHILOSOPHY

To understand the stream of thought that gave birth to the ideology of biblical criticism, we must examine some of the men who had the greatest effect on its development. As early as the 17th century, the inerrancy of the Bible was brought into question in this way. The following men and many others have worried at the Old Black Book like rabid dogs, burrowing away beneath the foundations of faith:

Richard Simon (1638–1712), according to Bruce Metzger, laid *the scientific foundations of New Testament criticism.*[207] Simon was a French Roman Catholic who *disregarded the traditional and dogmatic presuppositions of his age* and *examined critically the text of the Bible as a piece of literature.* His method was based on treating the Bible in the same manner as any other book written by carnal man. He gave its testimony no divine significance.

Richard Bentley (1662–1742), of whom Souter said *His goal, by the way, was not to attempt to publish a New Testament as it was given by the apostles but merely to "restore a Greek and Latin text to the state in which they were in the fourth century."*[208] Cloud records that *one of Bentley's principles of textual criticism was "the difficult is to be preferred to the easy reading." This was based strictly upon a humanistic perspective of the biblical text, that "a scribe is more likely to make a difficult construction easier, than make more difficult what was already easy."*[209]

Johann Bengel (1687–1752) adopted the principle of classifying manuscripts into textual families and *"recognized that the witnesses to the text must not be counted but weighed."*[210] In other words, the majority of the witnesses are of less value than one manuscript of "higher value."

---

[207] Bruce Metzger, *The Text of the New Testament*, p. 155.

[208] Alexander Souter, *The Text of the New Testament*, p. 98.

[209] David Cloud, *Textual Criticism is Drawn From the Wells of Infidelity*, Way of Life Literature.

[210] Bruce Metzger, *The Text of the New Testament*, p. 112.

Johann Griesbach (1745–1812) was highly influenced by religious rationalism. He was later to be considered one of the fathers of textual criticism. Griesbach classified the texts into three divisions: Constantinopolitan (Received Text), Alexandrian, and Western. He also created a Greek New Testament that followed the Alexandrian manuscripts.

Karl Lachmann (1793–1851) translated three Greek editions of the New Testament from 1831 to 1850 A.D. Like Griesbach before him, he was highly influenced by the skepticism introduced by religious rationalism. He introduced the method of using the same textual criticism to question the Bible as had been used in studying corrupted classical Greek works. Vincent states that to *Lachmann belongs the distinction of entirely casting aside the Textus Receptus....*[211] Lachmann did not believe it was possible to reproduce the original text of the New Testament.[212] His goal was merely to *secure the text in widest use in Jerome's time, leaving it to emendation and conjecture to get behind that.*[213] Aland tells us that Lachmann's battle cry was *Down with the late text of the Textus Receptus, and back to the text of the early fourth-century church.*[214] Scrivener said Lachmann's text seldom rested upon more than four Greek codices, primarily Codex B.[215]

Constantin von Tischendorf (1815–1874) had *a distinct respect for the conclusions of Griesbach and Lachmann.*[216] It was Tischendorf who discovered *Codex Sinaiticus*, and he obviously favored it for this reason if no other. He published his translations of the Greek New Testament between 1840 and 1872 A.D. Scrivener said that if Tischendorf could find just one or two other

[211] Marvin Richardson Vincent, *A History of Textual Criticism*, p. 110.
[212] Bruce Metzger, *The Text of the New Testament*, p. 124.
[213] Alexander Souter, *The Text and Canon of the New Testament*, 1912, p. 101.
[214] Kurt Aland, *The Text of the New Testament*, p. 11.
[215] F.H.A. Scrivener, *Introduction to the Criticism of the New Testament*, Volume II, pp. 232-233.
[216] Thompson, p. 42.

manuscripts of any type to support Sinaiticus, he would use the translation in Sinaiticus.[217] Tischendorf felt that the older texts were more accurate than the Majority Text, and he believed it was possible to find the original reading from the older texts. He himself stated that the problem was *the difficulty of finding such a text lies in that there is a great diversity among these texts.*[218] The older (minority) texts he was using were not at all in unity with one another, but he thought this must be the source of the original true text!

Samuel Tregelles (1813–1875) translated and published Greek editions of the New Testament from 1857 to 1872 A.D. As those before him, he strongly believed in the older minority of manuscripts. Metzger stated that his critical methods *paralleled to a remarkable degree those of Lachmann.*[219] David Cloud writes that *from his youth, he had a peculiar zeal to go beyond even Griesbach in rejecting the Received Text.*[220]

[217] Ibid, pp. 282-283.
[218] Constantin von Tischendorf, *Codex Sinaiticus*, p. 85.
[219] Bruce Metzger, *The Text of the New Testament*, p. 127.
[220] David Cloud, *Textual Criticism is Drawn From the Wells of Infidelity*, Way of Life Literature.

WESTCOTT AND HORT

Brooke Foss Westcott and Fenton John Anthony Hort were unarguably the most influential of all the textual critics. Their philosophy and technique were inherited directly from the critics before them, but they succeeded where none before them had. They finally overthrew the unquestioned supremacy of the King James Bible, and their ideology, no matter how skewed, colored all the textual scholars that followed them up to our present day.

Westcott and Hort were both professors at Oxford University. They not only had been brought up in the liberal environs of 19th century Oxford but were certainly influenced by the Jesuit-backed "Oxford Movement" of the early 1800's A.D. The Oxford Movement was an underground movement with the express intent of returning Catholic influence to Anglican England.

Westcott and Hort were also Anglican clergymen. Though they claimed to be Christian, it is strange to note that in all the pages of their biographies (over 1,800 pages combined), there is no testimony of their personal salvation. This is very unusual, especially considering they were both churchmen and dedicated most of their lives to translating the New Testament. Out of the massive biographical record left behind, why can we not find evidence of the event that should have been more important than any other in the life of a Christian?

About 1853 A.D., early in their careers, they came to the decision that they would jointly make their own translation of the New Testament in Greek. Their connections to the textual critics before them and to the Alexandrian manuscripts were made clear by one of Hort's letters written in 1853 A.D.: *He and I* [Westcott and Hort] *are going to edit a Greek text of the New Testament some two or three years hence, if possible. Lachmann and Tischendorf will supply rich materials* and *in 1853...the plan of a joint revision of the text of the Greek New Testament was first definitely agreed upon...Hort was to edit the text in conjunction with Mr. Westcott; the latter was to be responsible for a commentary, and Lightfoot was to contribute a New Testament Grammar and Lexicon.*[221]

Though they claimed to be Protestant, both Westcott and Hort were very pro-Catholic. There are many examples of the influence of Catholic thought on both these men; just a few of these demonstrate this clearly. Hort, in a letter to the Rev. John Ellerton, July 6, 1848 A.D., *...the pure Romish view seems to me nearer, and more likely to lead to the truth than the Evangelical.* In a letter to Westcott, September 23, 1864 A.D. he wrote, *I believe Coleridge was quite right in saying that Christianity without a substantial church is vanity and disillusion; and I remember shocking you and Lightfoot not so long ago by expressing my belief that "Protestantism" is only parenthetical and temporary.* In another letter to Westcott he wrote, *...Anglicanism, though by no means without a sound standing, seems a poor and maimed thing beside great Rome.* Again to Westcott on October 17, 1865 A.D. he wrote, *I have been persuaded for many years that Mary worship and "Jesus" worship have very much in common in their causes and in their results.*

---

[221] Arthur Hort, *Life and Letters of Fenton John Anthony Hort*, Vol. I, 1896, pp. 239-40.

Not only were they under Roman influence, but they were founding members of a spiritualistic occult group at Oxford, which they named the Ghostly Guild. The intent of the group was the study of ghostly and paranormal occurrences. Hort wrote, *Westcott, Gorham, C.B. Scott, Benson, Bradshaw, Laurd, etc. and I have started a society for the investigation of ghosts and all supernatural appearances and effects, being all disposed to believe that such things really exist....*[222] Westcott wrote, *there are many others who believe it possible that the beings of the unseen world may manifest themselves to us....*[223] This was not an isolated or adolescent fancy. They remained involved in spiritualist studies for most of their lives.

Considering that these two men would create a Greek New Testament that still remains as the most important influence underlying all modern translations, it would seem critical that they at least believe in the Bible themselves. But this was not the case. Zane Hodges noted Westcott's and Hort's apostasy: *The charge of rationalism is easily substantiated for Westcott and Hort and may be demonstrated from direct statements found in their introduction to The New Testament in the Original Greek. To begin with, Westcott and Hort are clearly unwilling to commit themselves to the inerrancy of the original Scriptures.*[224] These men, who had such a great hand in determining the interpretation of the scripture did not even believe in its inerrancy and infallibility. Westcott wrote to Hort, *For I too "must disclaim settling for infallibility." In the front of my convictions all I hold is the more I learn, the more I am convinced that fresh doubts come from my own ignorance, and that at present I find the presumption in favor of the absolute truth–I reject the word infallibility of Holy Scripture overwhelmingly.*[225]

---

[222] Ibid., p. 211.

[223] Arthur Westcott, *Life and Letters of Brooke Foss Westcott*, Vol. I, p. 117.

[224] Zane C. Hodges, *Rationalism and Contemporary New Testament Textual Criticism*, Bibliotheca Sacra, January 1971.

[225] Arthur Westcott, *Life and Letters of Brooke Foss Westcott*, Vol. I, p.207.

Not only did they distrust the Bible as being the true communication of God, but they denied many of the events in the Bible had ever happened. In regards to the creation account, both Westcott and Hort testified to their beliefs: a letter from Westcott to the Archbishop of Canterbury March 4, 1890 A.D.: *No one now, I suppose, holds that the first three chapters of Genesis, for example, give a literal history – I could never understand how any one reading them with open eyes could think they did...;* and in a letter from Hort to the Rev. John Ellerton: *I am inclined to think that no such state as "Eden" (I mean the popular notion) ever existed, and that Adam's fall in no degree differed from the fall of each of his descendants, as Coleridge justly argues.*

For those who already questioned the literal creation account, it was no small leap for them to accept Darwinian evolution. Hort especially was greatly impressed with Darwin's theories. In a letter to the Rev. John Ellerton, April 3, 1860 A.D., he wrote, *The book which has most engaged me is Darwin. Whatever may be thought of it, it is a book that one is proud to be contemporary with...My feeling is strong that the theory is unanswerable. If so, it opens up a new period.* Hort wrote to Westcott, *Such a view as Darwin's...seems to me the most probable manner of development, and the reflections suggested by his book drove me to the conclusion that some kind of development must be supposed.*[226] In a second letter to Westcott, Hort wrote, *...Have you read Darwin? How I should like to talk with you about it! In spite of difficulties, I am inclined to think it unanswerable. In any case it is a treat to read such a book.*[227]

---

[226] Arthur Hort, *Life and Letters of Fenton John Anthony Hort*, Vol. I, pp. 403-31.
[227] Ibid. p.416.

It has been said that Hort did not believe in angels. Westcott, who certainly did not believe in the traditional view of heaven, stated, *…Heaven is a state and not a place.*[228] Westcott apparently did not believe in the literal resurrection as Waite attested to: *Westcott's attack on the bodily resurrection of the Lord Jesus Christ is not by any means a direct clash of out-and-out denial, but rather an adroit, skillful, oblique undermining of the bodily resurrection of Christ by means of a re-definition of terms.*[229]

Not only did these men have these and other heretical beliefs, but they were well aware that their beliefs would be considered heretical by those of the mainstream Protestant faith. They knew that if they were to create a Greek New Testament that would be accepted, they must not allow their heresies to be made public until after their text had infiltrated itself into intellectual circles of thought and scholarship. Hort, writing to Westcott, blatantly admitted this fact: *Also–but this may be cowardice–I have a sort of craving that our text should be cast upon the world before we deal with matters likely to brand us with suspicion. I mean, a text, issued by men already known for what will undoubtedly be treated as dangerous heresy, will have great difficulties in finding its way to regions which it might otherwise hope to reach, and whence it would not be easily banished by subsequent alarms.*[230]

The subsequent translation that was created by Westcott and Hort was based entirely on Alexandrian manuscripts. The two primary manuscripts used were Sinaiticus and Vaticanus. They ignored completely the textual witnesses of the Majority Text, preferring the

---

[228] Arthur Westcott, *Life and Letters of Brooke Foss Westcott*, Vol. II, p. 49.
[229] Waite, Westcott's Denial of Bodily Resurrection, *The Bible for Today*, 1983, p. 8.
[230] Arthur Hort, *Life and Letters of Fenton John Anthony Hort*, Vol. I, p.445.

handful of manuscripts of the Alexandrian tradition over the vast majority from the Byzantine/Antiochan tradition.

Westcott and Hort felt that *Codex Sinaiticus* and *Codex Vaticanus* were superior to any and all other manuscripts. They believed if these two agreed together, then they must be the correct translation: *...with certain limited classes of exceptions, the readings of Aleph and B combined may safely be accepted as genuine in the absence of especially strong internal evidence to the contrary, and can never be safely rejected altogether.* Of these two, they gave the greatest weight of authority to Vaticanus: *even when B stands quite alone, its readings must never be rejected.*

The *Textus Receptus*, as the most important example of the Majority Text, was especially an object of their hatred. In 1851 A.D., at only 23 years of age, Hort wrote, *I had no idea till the last few weeks of the importance of the texts, having read so little Greek Testament, and dragged on with the villainous Textus Receptus...Think of that vile Textus Receptus leaning entirely on late manuscripts; it is a blessing there are such early ones.* The young Hort, who admittedly had little experience with the Greek New Testament, already had developed a hatred for the *Textus Receptus*. It is obvious that this must have been developed by the influence of some outside source as he himself had little knowledge of the Greek. Why would someone so young, without experience of a thing, despise it so much? Prejudice must be taught, and someone certainly must have taught him this hatred for the Majority Text.

The clear intention of these two men was to supplant the King James Bible and, in effect, the Majority Text and its representative, the *Textus Receptus*. The goal was to undermine the Majority Text's credibility. After it had been devalued, the time would be ripe to replace the *Textus Receptus* with their own Greek Text and in turn replace the King James Bible with a new English translation based on that text. Hort wrote,

Our object is to supply clergymen generally, schools, etc., with a portable Greek text which shall not be disfigured with Byzantine corruptions.[231]

Westcott and Hort believed in four textual families, three of which coincide with modern textual critics: the Byzantine, Alexandrian, Western, and Neutral. The Neutral textual family was believed by Westcott and Hort to represent the purest copies made from the originals, the best examples of which were Codex Vaticanus and Sinaiticus.

The understanding of the textual families has undergone numerous changes and adjustments as scholarship has developed over the last 100 years. Some scholars feel there are more than four families, some less. What most agree upon is that the Alexandrian/Neutral texts are the oldest and most accurate, whereas the Byzantine/Antiochan texts are the youngest and least accurate. An unbiased study of the facts, as has been demonstrated, will easily reveal how mistaken this view is.

In order to debase the Majority text in favor of the handful of Alexandrian/Neutral manuscripts, Westcott and Hort had to address the issue of numerical supremacy. They argued that the reason there were so many more copies of the Majority Text was due to the fact that at some point in time there had been a major recension in the textual families. By this, they meant that someone had consolidated all the available texts and made one official text from which all copies were made thereafter. According to Westcott and Hort, this would explain why the majority of the manuscripts agreed with each other. It also put the minority of Alexandrian/Neutral manuscripts on an even footing with the Majority text as they could argue that each was representative of only one original copy, thus comparing one to one rather than one Alexandrian against many Byzantine texts.

---

[231] Arthur Hort, *Life and Letters of Fenton John Anthony Hort*, Vol. I, p. 250.

They proposed the theory that Lucian of Antioch had combined all of the available texts into one authorized text around 350 A.D. This later became the Byzantine text. This Lucian Recension, as they called it, had absolutely no historical evidence to back it up. It was completely a construct of their own biased imaginations. This is especially demonstrated to be true by the many quotations of Alexandrian and Western church fathers made in the first few centuries that are found to harmonize with the Byzantine text. Dean Burgon found that of 76 Alexandrian and Western fathers quotations (4,383 total) 2,360 harmonized with the Majority (Byzantine) Text, whereas 1,753 did not. And these were the Alexandrian and Western fathers!

Though modern scholars claim to discount much of Westcott and Hort's theories, their corrupted influence has saturated the field of biblical criticism. Alfred Martin, the former Vice-President of Moody Bible Institute, wrote in 1951, *The present generation of Bible students having been reared on Westcott and Hort have for the most part accepted this theory without independent or critical examination...if believing Bible students had the evidence of both sides put before them instead of one side only, there would not be so much blind following of Westcott and Hort.* This is always how corruption, once introduced and assimilated, becomes tradition and "truth." The evidence is presented for one side only; as time passes, this erroneous belief becomes orthodox "fact" through the establishment of ongoing tradition.

Zane Hodges, professor at the Dallas Theological Seminary notes, *Modern textual criticism is psychologically addicted to Westcott and Hort.* E.C. Colwell wrote the following revealing statement: *The dead hand of Fenton John Anthony Hort lies heavy upon us...Hort did not fail to reach his major goal. He dethroned the Textus Receptus.*

THE REVISION COMMITTEE OF 1881

During the first half of the 19th century the liberal churchmen and Bible societies had been strongly petitioning the Church of England to authorize a new translation of the Bible. Small-scale revisions had been attempted in the previous two centuries but none had been approved or officially accepted by the church. Finally in February 1870 A.D., the request was brought before the Convocation of the Province of Canterbury. The American Bible Union had completed a revision in 1865 A.D., and this was used as the catalyst to authorize a British revision. The Bishop of Lincoln and others argued that this necessitated that the Church of England revise the Bible: *That it is desirable that Convocation should nominate a body of its own members to undertake the work of revision....*

The revision committee began their work in June 1870 A.D. The committee members met in the Jerusalem Chamber at Westminster four days a month, 10 months a year for 10½ years. During this time the revision committee consisted of 24 members: 17 Episcopalians, 2 of the Scottish Church, 2 dissenting Presbyterians, 1 Baptist, 1 Independent, and 1 Unitarian.

From the very beginning the committee was not only divided in doctrinal belief but was sharply divided in method and philosophy. The influential Bishop Wilberforce, whose nomination as leader of the committee had secured its authorization, quit very soon after the work began, calling the work *a miserable business.*

The dominant influences on the committee were Westcott, Hort, and Lightfoot, with Hort being the clear leader. The minority who were in opposition were led by Dr. Scrivener. Scrivener was considered to be the foremost scholar of his day in the text and history of the Greek New Testament. He was a firm supporter of the *Textus Receptus* and a critic of Hort's Alexandrian-based text.

Back and forth the battle raged between the two scholars. Scrivener would present the case for the *Textus Receptus*, and Hort would oppose him with readings from *Codex Vaticanus* or *Codex Sinaiticus*. Ellicott, the new chairman, wrote that the divisions in the committee were the results of *a kind of critical duel between Dr. Hort and Dr. Scrivener*. A large number of these divisions were based on Hort's determination to use *Codex Vaticanus* over all other manuscripts. The majority of the committee, under Hort's dominance, continuously and systematically outvoted Scrivener's suggestions.

Westcott and Hort's Greek New Testament had just been completed, and it was certainly a great influence on the committee. John Burgon recorded that members of the committee had been secretly given copies of this as yet unpublished translation and that they were bound to a pledge of silence in regard to its use. Burgon wrote, *A "confidential" copy of their work having been already entrusted to every member of the New Testament Company of Revisionists to guide them in their labours, under pledge that they should neither show nor communicate its contents to any one else.* The inclusion of this text in determining the manner of translation for the revision committee is not surprising. Phillip Schaff, a strong supporter of the critical text, stated,

The Greek New Testament of Westcott and Hort...harmonizes essentially with the text adopted by the Revisers.

The Revised Version was completed in 1881 A.D. At the same time as its publication, Westcott and Hort's Greek New Testament was released. This was surely not coincidental. As could be expected, the Revised Version was vastly different from the King James Version. One reviser stated that in comparison with the King James Version, it contained *between eight and nine changes in every five verses, and in about every ten verses, three of these were made for critical purposes.* This Revised Version was the predecessor for all of the many 20th century versions and revisions to come.

Dean John Burgon was the greatest defender of the King James Version during this time of revision. He was an active opponent of Westcott and Hort and of their revision in particular. Through his studies he gave strong testimony against the Greek text of the revisers and the revisers themselves. Many of his arguments were avoided rather than answered.

Regarding the issue of the replacement of the Authorized Version with the new revision, Burgon stated, *Destroy my confidence in the bible as an historical record, and you destroy my confidence in it altogether; for by far the largest part of the bible is an historical record. If the Creation of Man, the longevity of the Patriarchs, the account of the Deluge; if these be not true histories, what is to be said of the lives of Abraham, of Jacob, of Joseph, of Moses, of Joshua, of David, of our Saviour Christ Himself?...Will you then reject one miracle and retain another? Impossible! You can make no reservation, even in favour of the Incarnation of our Lord, the most adorable of all miracles, as it is the very keystone of our Christian hope. Either, with the best and wisest of all ages, you must believe the whole of holy scripture; or, with the narrow-minded infidel, you must disbelieve the whole. There is no middle course open to you.*[232]

Comparing the King James Bible to the Revised Version, he testified of the former as having *the living freshness, and elastic freedom, and habitual fidelity of the Grand Old Version which we inherited from our Fathers, and which has sustained the spiritual life of the Church of England, and of all English-speaking Christians, for 350 years.*[233] He encouraged his readers to *cling the closer to the priceless treasure which was bequeathed to them by the piety and wisdom of their fathers.*[234]

---

[232] Dean Burgon, *Sermon II*, p. 46.
[233] Dean Burgon, *Revision Revised*, p. 225.
[234] Ibid. p. 232.

THE NESTLE/ALAND
AND
THE UBS CRITICAL TEXT

A number of other Greek New Testaments were published near the end of the 18th century, but the most influential was Nestle's Greek New Testament. Eberhard Nestle published his version in 1898. The Nestle's critical text is the father of the Nestle/Aland critical text and the grandfather of the United Bible Societies text.

Nestle used the texts of Westcott and Hort, Tischendorf, and Weymouth to create his critical Greek text. Weymouth's text was replaced with the Weiss text in the third edition. Nestle's method was simply to compare the three texts and accept the reading that the majority agreed upon. This is the reading he would use as his text.

Eberhard's son Erwin took over the text in 1927. Erwin updated his father's edition and added a critical apparatus. Essentially the underlying Greek text remained unchanged.

Around 1950 Kurt Aland assumed ownership of the Nestle's text, thus making it the Nestle/Aland text. He had been co-editor of the text since the 1940's. Under Aland, the Nestle/Aland text went through further editions until its final 26th and 27th edition. The 26th edition of 1979 was concurrent with the United Bible Societies (UBS) Greek text, which was also overseen by Aland. The 27th edition of 1993 was precisely the same as the 26th with the exception of the critical apparatus and appendixes. The UBS and Nestle/Aland texts are virtually identical in all respects other than punctuation and format. With the last editions of the Nestle/Aland text, the UBS text became the major Greek text.

The committee of editors overseeing the UBS text consisted of Kurt Aland, Matthew Black, Roman Catholic Cardinal Carlo Martini (2nd and 3rd editions), Bruce Metzger, and Alan Wilkgren. Eugene Nida became the administrator of the work. The 4th edition of 1993 was prepared by Aland, his wife, Barbara, Cardinal Martini, Metzger, and Johannes Karavidopolous. Kurt Aland died in 1994.

Cardinal Carlo Martini, who died in 2002, was archbishop over the largest Catholic diocese in Europe with authority over 2,000 priests and 5 million laity. In the December 26, 1994 edition, of *Time* magazine, he was named as one of the most likely persons to become the next Pope. He was famous for, among other things, bringing together a convocation of over 100 religious leaders to promote a one-world religious platform. Is this a person that we would choose to translate and interpret the word of God for us?

Bruce Metzger has written numerous books on the biblical text. His comments in regard to its infallibility and truth are interesting. Consider his introduction to the Old Testament in the New Oxford Annotated Bible RSV: *Out of a matrix of myth, legend, and history, there had appeared the earliest written form of the story of the saving acts of God from creation to the conquest of the Promised Land, an account which later in modified form became a part of Scripture.* He certainly did not believe in a worldwide flood: *Traditions of a prehistoric flood covering the whole earth are heightened versions of local inundations....* In his introduction to the following respective books, he called Job *an ancient folktale* and Jonah a *popular legend.* Metzger also consistently gave the books of the Bible much later dates, claiming the prophetic writings were written after the prophesied events happened. Considering his disbelief in the historicity and verity of the Bible, is this a person that we would choose to translate and interpret the word of God for us?

Eugene Nida, who oversaw the production of the UBS, was noted as having been the developer of dynamic equivalency. He himself did not believe that the Bible was literally true; perhaps this is why he chose to translate it in a dynamic style. He wrote, *God did not give eternal truths, but granted communication...Biblical revelation is not absolute....* Here is a man, who by his own testimony, does not believe God's truths are eternal, or that His revelation is absolute. Is this a person that we would choose to translate and interpret the word of God for us?

The modern Greek critical texts beginning with Westcott and Hort and continuing through Nestle, Aland, and the UBS versions underlie nearly all the translations from the time of the 1881 Revision Committee forward. These are little more than repackaged versions of the same old tainted manuscripts and textual prejudices.

It is important for anyone trying to grasp the differences between modern translations of the Bible to understand the origin of their source material. To begin with, the Greek critical texts use only a handful of manuscripts to determine their translation. These minority text manuscripts are primarily Alexandrian.

There are three major manuscripts in codex form that overshadow all modern translations. Modern textual critics fallaciously consider these codices to be far superior to any other manuscript evidence, including the 90 to 95% of all manuscripts that make up the Byzantine textual family. These, in order of importance to the critics, are the *Codex Sinaiticus*, *Codex Vaticanus* and *Codex Alexandrinus*.

SINAITICUS
Aleph

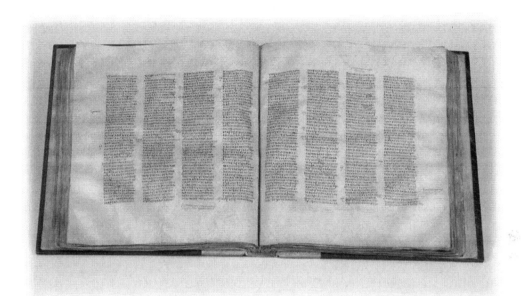

Codex Sinaiticus or **Aleph**, along with *Codex Vaticanus* and *Codex Alexandrinus*, is one of the primary manuscripts underlying the modern Greek New Testaments, and thus the modern translations of the Bible. It has been dated from the 4th century.

Codex Sinaiticus contains part of the Old Testament, as well as the Gospels, Acts, the Epistles, and Revelation. It also contains the non-canonical books: the Epistle of Barnabas and the Shepherd of Hermas. It is primarily of the Alexandrian textual family. The New Testament is made up of 148 leaves measuring 15 by 14 inches. The text is written in 4 columns with 48 lines per column and about 12 to 16 letters per line.

Kenyon states that *its origin has been assigned to Rome, Southern Italy, Egypt, and Caesarea, but cannot be determined.*[235] A number of modern scholars have theorized that *Codex Sinaiticus* and *Codex Vaticanus*, were two of the Bibles that Constantine commissioned Eusebius to prepare in the 4th century. Thus its physical origin may have been in Caesarea, whereas its philosophical origin was with Origen in Egypt. This seems even more likely when considering that one of its correctors added this note: *This codex was compared with a very ancient exemplar which had been corrected by the hand of the holy martyr Pamphilus; which exemplar contained at the end of the subscription in his own hand: "Taken and corrected according to the Hexapla of Origen: Antonius compared it: I, Pamphilus, corrected it."*

Sinaiticus is full of corrections, additions, and omissions. A look at the actual manuscript reveals numerous changes that were introduced by a number of different editors. Scrivener wrote, *From the number of errors, one cannot affirm that it is very carefully written. The whole manuscript is disfigured by corrections, a few by the original scribe, very many by an ancient and elegant hand of the 6th century...some again by a hand a little later, for the greatest number by a scholar of the 7th century who often cancels the changes by the 6th century amender, others by as many as (8) different later writers.*[236]

The story of the discovery of *Codex Sinaiticus* is somewhat unusual. In May 1844 A.D., Constantin von Tischendorf was at the monastery of St. Catherine at Mt. Sinai. Tischendorf was a textual scholar and explorer who was always on the lookout for manuscripts and antiquities. As Tischendorf was preparing to leave the monastery he noticed a refuse bin full of discarded parchments. The monks were

---

[235] Frederic G. Kenyon, *Handbook to the Textual Criticism of the New Testament*, London, 1901, p. 56.

[236] F.H.A. Scrivener, *A Plain Introduction to the Criticism of the New Testament*, Volume I, p. 93.

burning these parchments for heat. Tischendorf examined the parchments, discovering that they consisted of 129 leaves of the Old Testament in Greek. He asked permission to keep them and was allowed to leave with 43 of the pages.

Tischendorf returned, but was denied his request for more of the pages. The monks clearly recognized that the pages were considered valuable. Tischendorf again returned a few years later under the patronage of Alexander II, the Russian Czar. He convinced the monks to give the codex as a gift to the Czar. It remained in the Imperial Library of St. Petersburg until 1933 A.D. when it was purchased by the British government.

Dr. R.L. Hymers visited St. Catherine's monastery at Mount Sinai in 1987 A.D., and recorded these observations: *I was struck by the queer and even satanic characteristics of this monastery. The skulls of the monks from across the centuries are heaped in a large room. This heap of skulls is seven or eight feet high. The skeleton of one of the monks is chained to a door adjacent to this mound of skulls, left there as an ageless guard. Within the sanctuary at the monastery itself, ostrich eggs hang from the ceiling, lamps dimly illuminate the gloomy atmosphere, and strange drawings and unscriptural paintings decorate the entire edifice...As I stood in front of the case where the Sinaiticus scroll had been kept prior to its being (taken) by Tischendorf, I had the distinct impression that nothing in the way of spiritual light could come from this place.*[237]

---

[237] Dr. R.L. Hymers, *The Ruckman Conspiracy*, p. 1.

Dean John Burgon collated *Codex Sinaiticus* with the edition of the *Textus Receptus* that underlies the King James Version and found the following:

- 3,455 words omitted
- 839 words added
- 1,114 words substituted
- 2,229 words transposed
- 1,265 words modified
- 8,972 total changes

ALEXANDRINUS
A

Codex Alexandrinus, known as "A," has been dated from about the 5th century. It contains most of the Gospels, Acts, the Epistles, and Revelation with the exception of portions of Matthew, John, and II Corinthians. It also contains the non-canonical book the Epistle of Clement.

The Gospels are primarily Byzantine, whereas the remainder of the manuscript is of the Alexandrian textual family. It consists of 773 parchment leaves measuring about 12½ by 10½ inches. The text was written in two columns per page with 46 to 52 lines and 20 to 25 letters in each line.

In 1627 A.D., Cyril Lucar, the Patriarch of the Greek Orthodox Church, was the first recorded owner of *Codex Alexandrinus*. Before being made Patriarch over all the Greek Church, Cyril had been the Patriarch of Alexandria, and it is believed he brought the manuscript with him from Egypt. Cyril sent the codex to King James I of England as a gift, but James died before the manuscript reached him and King Charles I received it. It may have been the providence of God that James did not have this polluted manuscript during the time of the translation of the King James Bible.

It is not considered nearly as important to the critics as a textual witness as is *Codex Sinaiticus* and *Codex Vaticanus*. Like its harlot sisters though, it bears the marks of its descent. *It is found, however, to bear a great affinity to the text embodied in Origen's Hexapla and to have been corrected in numberless passages according to the Hebrew.*[238]

---

[238] *The Catholic Encyclopedia*, "Alexandrinus" entry.

VATICANUS
B

Codex Vaticanus, known as "B," is the second of the two "false witnesses" of Alexandria. It is believed to have been written during the 4th century, and some scholars believe that it, like *Codex Sinaiticus*, may have been one of the copies Eusebius was commissioned to compile by Constantine. It is of a mixed textual family, though the greatest influence is Alexandrian.

In the New Testament it contains the Gospels, Acts, and the Epistles. It is missing portions of I Timothy through Philemon, Hebrews, and the entire book of Revelation. It also contains the non-canonical books of the Epistle of Barnabas and the Old Testament apocrypha. The fact that all of Revelation is missing is not surprising as it is Revelation that most clearly testifies to the fallen Roman church and its expected end.

The Old Testament is mostly complete and contains 617 leaves. The New Testament consists of 142 leaves. The leaves measure about 10.8 inches on each side. The text is written in three columns with 40 to 44 lines of per column and about 16 to 18 letters per line. It appears that soon after it was written a corrector went through the manuscript. A second corrector worked on the manuscript around the 10th or 11th century, tracing over the faded letters with fresh ink and adding accent and breathing marks. During this process he omitted numerous letters and words he thought to be incorrect.

It is not certain when *Codex Vaticanus* was discovered, though it was reported to be catalogued in the Vatican Library as early as 1481 A.D. The most common opinion is that it originated in Egypt. The Catholic Church testifies to its origin: *It may be said that the Vatican Codex, written in the first half of the fourth century, represents the text of one of those recensions of the Bible which were current in the third century, and that it belongs to the family of manuscripts made use of by Origen in the composition of his Hexapla.*[239]

Frederic Kenyon made these revealing statements regarding *Codex Vaticanus*: *As its name shows* [Vaticanus] *is in the Great Vatican Library at Rome, which has been its home since some date before 1481...For some reason which does not clearly appear, the authorities of the Vatican Library put continual obstacles in the way of all who wished to study it in detail. A correspondent of Erasmus in 1533 sent that scholar a number of selected readings from it, as proof of its superiority to the received Greek text* [Erasmus certainly did not see it as superior, as he rejected the use of the Vaticanus readings]. *In 1843 Tischendorf, after waiting for several months, was allowed to see it for six hours.....In 1845...Tregelles was allowed indeed to see it but not to copy a word. His pockets were searched before he might open it, and all writing materials were taken away. Two clerics stood beside him*

---

[239] *The Catholic Encyclopedia,* "Vaticanus" entry.

and snatched away the volume if he looked too long at any passage!...In 1866 Tischendorf once more applied for permission to edit the MS., but with difficulty obtained leave to examine it for the purpose of collating difficult passages...Renewed entreaty procured him six days longer study, making in all fourteen days of three hours each; and by making the very most of his time Tischendorf was able in 1867 to publish the most perfect edition of the manuscript which had yet appeared. An improved Roman edition appeared in 1861-1881.[240]

The veil of secrecy covering this manuscript was not removed until 1890 A.D. when the Vatican had a facsimile copy made. The poor condition and numerous corrections and mutilations were not made apparent in this way. *The Catholic Encyclopedia* itself testifies to the corrupted condition of the manuscript: *Unfortunately, the codex is mutilated....*[241]

In his collation of *Codex Vaticanus* compared to the *Textus Receptus*, Dean Burgon found the following in the Gospels alone:
- 2,877 words changed
- 536 words added
- 935 words substituted
- 2,098 words transposed
- 1,132 words modified
- Total of 7,578 changes in relation to the *Textus Receptus*

These codices and the Alexandrian papyri that support their readings have been the evidence used by textual critics to make changes and adjustments from the traditional Majority Text that underlies the King James Bible. The apparent hatred of the critics and the itching ears of the laity have led to the proliferation of many new translations in the 100 years following the 1881 Revision. More versions of the Bible

---

[240] Frederic Kenyon, *Our Bible and the Ancient Manuscripts*, 4th edition, 1939, pp. 138-39.
[241] *The Catholic Encyclopedia*, "Vaticanus" entry.

have been presented in this hundred-year period than in all of its history! Thus the author of confusion sells his imitations to the hungry masses.

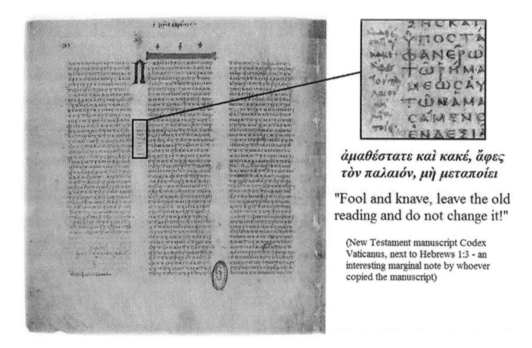

ἀμαθέστατε καὶ κακέ, ἄφες τὸν παλαιόν, μὴ μεταποίει

"Fool and knave, leave the old reading and do not change it!"

(New Testament manuscript Codex Vaticanus, next to Hebrews 1:3 - an interesting marginal note by whoever copied the manuscript)

THE BIBLE AND THE MODERN AGE

16

Psalms 11:3
If the foundations be destroyed, what can the righteous do?

MODERN TRANSLATIONS AND TRANSLATORS

An enormous profusion of translations and versions was released during the 20th century. Many of these were little more than revisions of older versions. The two earliest versions that propagated many other translations were the American Standard Version of 1901 and the Revised Standard Version of 1946.

THE AMERICAN STANDARD VERSION

The American Standard Version (ASV) of 1901 was the immediate successor of Westcott and Hort's 1881 Revision of the King James Bible. The American Committee had agreed with the Revision Committee of England not to publish their version for 14 years.

The ASV differs from the King James Version in over 36,000 places.

The ASV never gained public support or popularity. The common people apparently did not consider replacing the King James Version with this truncated and poorly translated imitator.

THE REVISED STANDARD VERSION

The Revised Standard Version (RSV) was published in 1946. It was a revision of the American Standard, changes being made to update that version and to make it more palatable to the masses.

The RSV was copyrighted by the ecumenical National Council of Churches and was at one time the preferred version used by much of the Catholic Church. Its preface states, *The Revised Standard Version Bible committee...has become both ecumenical and international, with Protestant and Catholic active members....*

Members of the translation committee were both ecumenical and strong proponents of higher criticism. The testimony of the translators themselves is very revealing.

- Edgar Goodspeed described the book of Ruth as belonging to *Israel's fiction, rather than to its history, and should be read among its tales and stories.* He called the book of Job *religious fiction* and the book of Jonah *fiction.*
- Julius Brewer wrote, *The dates and figures found in the first five books of the Bible turn out to be altogether unreliable.*
- Henry Cadbury stated concerning Jesus, *He was given to overstatements....*
- Walter Bowie believed that *the story of Abraham comes down from ancient times; and how much of it is fact and how much of it is legend, no one can possibly tell.*
- James Moffatt undermined the inerrancy of the Bible in commenting that *the writers of the New Testament made mistakes in interpreting some of the Old Testament prophecies....*
- Millar Burrows wrote, *We cannot take the Bible as a whole and in every part as stating with divine authority what we must believe and do....* He believed that the cloud by day and fire by night that led the children of Israel was *a volcano far off on the eastern horizon,*

to which they were guided by the smoke it emitted in the daytime and by its red glow at night.

- Clarence Craig did not even believe in the resurrection: *It is to be remembered there were no eyewitnesses of the resurrection of Jesus. No canonical gospel presumed to describe Jesus emerging from the tomb. The mere fact that a tomb was found empty was capable of many explanations. The very last one that would be credible to a modern man would be the explanation of a physical resurrection of the body.*

- William Irwin believed that the idea of God's sovereignty was developed over time by the Hebrews: *The prophets were forced by the disasters that befell them to do some hard, painful thinking. They were forced by the history of their own times to revise their own messages again and again in order to keep up with the progress of the age. The Assyrians and the Babylonians forced them to revise their conception of Yahweh from time to time until they finally made Him God of the universe.*

This version is infamous for removing the word virgin in Isaiah 7:14. This verse, as translated in the King James Version is, …*Behold, a virgin shall conceive, and bear a son, and shall call his name Emmanuel.* The Revised Standard Version replaces the word "virgin" with "young woman," completing changing the prophetic meaning of the verse.

THE NEW INTERNATIONAL VERSION

The New International Version is perhaps arguably the worst of all modern translations. It was translated with the principles of dynamic equivalency rather than literal interpretation. This makes for a simplistic and modern flavor that strips away the poetic grandeur and linguistic power of the King James Version readings. Dynamic equivalency also allows for a very wide range of meaning in translation and thus passages can come across with a very different phraseology than that intended by the original authors.

The chairman of the Old Testament translation committee was Martin Woudstra. Woudstra was a supporter of alternative lifestyles. He maintained a close relationship with Evangelicals Concerned, an organization dedicated to Christian persons involved in alternative lifestyles and their friends. In the face of solid scriptural evidence, he stated that he believed these lifestyles were acceptable to God. It is interesting to note that the terms "sodomy" and "sodomite" are not contained in the New International Version's Old Testament, over which Woudstra held sway.

Another adherent to these beliefs involved with the project was Virginia Mollenkott. Mollenkott was a literary consultant to the translation committee. Mollenkott was a supporter of a feminist form of Christianity in which God was represented as female. She was strongly pro-abortionist and argued for the alternative lifestyle she practiced, demanding that her sexual preference *is simply a good gift, as all sexuality is a good gift.*[242]

---

[242] Virginia Mollenkott, *Sensuous Spirituality*, p. 158.

Many of the modern Bibles are descended directly from the work of the Revision Committee of 1881, as well as the underlying Greek critical texts of Westcott and Hort, Nestle/Aland, and the UBS. This fact alone should cause us to reject their readings, but there are a number of other factors to consider when evaluating these modern versions. Following are a few selected examples:

- **The New American Standard Bible** of 1963 – The Lockman Foundation that publishes this translation would not even release the names of the translators until 30 years after it had been released.

- **The New Scofield Bible** of 1967 – The original Scofield Bible was a King James Version with Scofield's study notes. This revision is merely called an update, though the translation is altered in numerous places and Scofield's notes have been updated by modern scholars.

- **The New English Bible** of 1970 – Produced by a mixed committee of Protestants and Roman Catholics. C.H. Dodd, who oversaw much of the work, was also the VP of the British and Foreign Bible Society and a founding member of the United Bible Society. In describing the Old Testament, he said that it *contains incongruities and contradictions, not merely in matters of fact, but in spiritual outlook and moral evaluation.*[243] He also stated, *Creation, the Fall of Man, the Deluge and the Building of Babel are symbolic myths*[244] and *it has long ago become clear that in claiming for the Bible accuracy in matters of science and history its apologists had chosen a hopeless position to defend.*[245]

- **The Living Bible** of 1971 – This is little more than a poorly written paraphrase taken primarily from the American Standard Version of 1901. Many critical concepts, such as grace and repentance, are left out of passages. In modernizing the language, strong and vulgar

---

[243] C.H. Dodd, *The Bible Today*, p. 1.0
[244] Ibid., p. 112.
[245] C.H. Dodd, *The Authority of the Bible*, p. 13.

expressions are used in a number of passages, many of which were later softened. Compare the original wording in I Samuel 20:30, II Kings 18:27, and John 9:34 and 11:39.

- **Today's English Version** of 1976 – Robert Bratcher, chief translator stated, *Only willful ignorance or intellectual dishonesty can account for the claim that the Bible is inerrant and infallible* and *words spoken by Jesus…do not necessarily wield compelling authority over us today.*[246] *If we build our faith wholly on the Bible, then we are building our faith on shifting sand….*[247]

- **The New Revised Standard Version** of 1990 – This was a revision of the original Revised Standard Version. Just as with its predecessor, the copyright is held by the ecumenical National Council of Churches. This version was translated by Catholic, Protestant, and Jewish scholars.

---

[246] Southern Baptist Life Commission Seminar, Dallas, TX 1981.
[247] Lecture at Furman University, November 5, 1970.

THE KING JAMES BIBLE
VERSUS MODERN TRANSLATIONS

The question that must be asked is not which Bible best conveys the human writer's words, but which best conveys the intention of the eternal author. The Bible must be taken as a construct of divine communication first, and then it can be interpreted into the words of mortal men. The argument is not only over manuscripts and interpretation; every interpretation of man will have errors and mistakes. Anything that man takes in his hand will be tainted with his mortality. Our question must be, Which translation of the Bible best expresses the communication of the living God?

Another critical question to be asked regards the character of those who handle God's word. Are these men who are seeking after God's will? Are they obedient to His word? Are they examples of commitment and dedication to Christian principles? Do they treasure the revealed word of God above all other things? If these questions cannot be answered in the affirmative for the translators, then it is certain they should not take up the precious word. Filthy hands and corrupted minds must never handle this message that is so critical to mankind.

In distinct contrast to the aforementioned beliefs of many of the translators of the last two centuries, consider some of the following statements of the King James Bible translators, in reference to the inspiration and inerrancy of the manuscripts they were translating, taken from the preface to their 1611 translation: *The original thereof being from Heaven, not from earth; the author being God, not man; the editor, the Holy Spirit, not the wit of the apostles or prophets....*

There is a great gulf between the King James Bible and modern translations. There are several key separation points that become more distinct as they are further investigated.

THE KING JAMES VERSION IS NOT COPYRIGHTED

MODERN VERSIONS ARE COPYRIGHTED

One of the first things that separates the King James Version from the modern versions is the lack of copyright. The modern committees and organizations are careful to copyright their versions. Why is this an important difference? To answer this question we must ask another. Why would it be necessary to copyright the Bible at all?

Copyright ensures that the author of a work retains control over his work. It also makes certain that all money generated from its sales or use finds its way back to the publisher and originator of the work. The subsidizers of the modern Bibles have every intention of making a profit off of their sales. The Bible, the Holy word of God, is treated like a product in the marketplace! There is a vast difference between scripture that has been translated and subsidized by God's people for the purpose of disseminating the Gospel of Christ and a book that has been translated and published with the intention of turning a profit. The work of translating a Bible should be a sacrifice of joy, not a profitable enterprise.

THE KING JAMES VERSION IS BASED ON
THE MAJORITY OF GREEK AND LATIN TEXTS

MODERN VERSIONS ARE BASED ON
A SMALL MINORITY OF DISCORDANT MANUSCRIPTS

The KJV, having been translated from the *Textus Receptus* and the majority of the texts, finds it origin in the vast majority of Greek and Latin manuscripts. These manuscripts of the Greek text underlying the KJV make up 90 to 95% of all the Greek and Latin manuscripts! The modern versions are based on a small handful of slightly older manuscripts that not only are the minority, but do not even agree among themselves!

Modern critics argue that the translators of the King James Bible did not have the oldest and best manuscripts available to them when they were completing their work. These critics present the manuscript discoveries of the 19th and 20th centuries as being older and more accurate renditions of the scripture. As can be seen by comparing and collating these manuscripts, this is certainly not the case. The translators authorized by King James had a wide selection of texts available to them. These consisted primarily of the Majority Text family of Greek manuscripts as well as Hebrew texts, rabbinical commentary and Targums, the Peshitta, Old Latin texts, and all of the English and foreign translations available. F.F. Bruce states, *all of the existing English versions lay before the translators, and every available foreign version, Latin translations, ancient and recent, the Targums and the Peshitta–all as aids to the elucidation of the Hebrew and Greek originals*[248]

The age of the manuscripts is certainly not a valid argument for their value. Most of the oldest manuscripts were discovered in Egypt where

---

[248] F.F. Bruce, *The Books and the Parchments*, 3rd Revised Edition, Revell Co., 1950, p. 229.

the climate allows for these materials to be preserved much longer. Many of these "older" manuscripts were found in refuse pits and graveyards! In addition, the older manuscripts were often preserved by lack of use. They were buried or placed on a shelf and seldom used. The Majority Text manuscripts preserved the oldest readings through use. They were copied and recopied until the oldest manuscripts were worn out, so it is not likely that the best manuscripts will be found to be the oldest.

THE KING JAMES VERSION FINDS ITS TEXTUAL ORIGIN IN ANTIOCH

THE MODERN VERSIONS HAVE THEIR ORIGIN IN ALEXANDRIA

As has been previously demonstrated, the Majority Text manuscripts originated around Antioch and Constantinople. The minority selection of manuscripts used by the modern versions are principally descendants of the Alexandrian tradition. Why is this critical? Antioch was one of the seats of the Early Church. Paul and the apostles were recorded as having visited Antioch during their ministries, and it was there that they were first called Christians.

Alexandria, on the other hand, has a completely different claim to fame. It is best known as a seat of philosophical and intellectual study, primarily rooted in the pagan mystery religions and teachings of the Greek philosophers. There is no biblical record of any work in Alexandria during the Early Church period. As has been demonstrated, the leaders of the "Christian" schools in Alexandria left much to be desired both in doctrine and philosophy.

THE KING JAMES VERSION WAS TRANSLATED BY THE GREATEST SCHOLARS OF ITS DAY, IN A DAY OF HIGH EDUCATIONAL STANDARDS

THE MODERN VERSIONS ARE TRANSLATED BY THE INTELLECTUAL ELITE, IN A DAY OF COMPROMISED EDUCATIONAL STANDARDS

The scholars who translated the KJV were some of the greatest minds of their day. This was a period of intense scholasticism and sacrifice, and these men were not only incredibly intelligent and skilled, they were committed to the cause of Christ.

It is often claimed that we have access to more knowledge and understanding than those who came before us. Though our modern technology and level of knowledge may be greater than ever before in history, individual educational standards are at a low. Bell curves and lower standards allow modern men to achieve positions and influence without the level of commitment and sacrifice of earlier days. It must also be understood that technical mastery of a subject is not the same thing as practical mastery.

THE KING JAMES BIBLE WAS TRANSLATED IN A PERIOD OF MORAL ASCENDANCY, SPIRITUAL DEDICATION, AND REFORMATION, BY MEN OF HIGH CHARACTER

THE MODERN VERSIONS HAVE BEEN TRANSLATED IN A PERIOD OF MORAL DECLINE, CRITICISM, AND COMPROMISE, BY MEN OF QUESTIONABLE CHARACTER

The 16th and 17th centuries marked the beginning of the Reformation of the church. Standards of holiness and dedication were rising. The work of these early centuries set the tone for the great revivals of the 19th century, the Holiness movement, and the Pentecostal rebirth of the 20th century. The translators were not only intellectual scholars, but demonstrated their character through their involvement and commitment to the church.

The modern age is one of spiritual decline. It was born in the critical thoughts and theories of the 19th century ideas of evolution, communism, and higher criticism. Salvation, rather than being a thing of value, is little more than a sugar-coated children's story. No great stress is placed on personal holiness or depth of doctrine. Modern lifestyles and ease have colored the religious messages of our day. Many of the most well-known "Christian" scholars are entrenched in the beliefs of higher criticism, philosophy, and carnal psychology. Ecumenicism has crept into many of the churches, compromising truth for peace and a false sense of harmony. The modern translators, beginning with Westcott and Hort, have been found to be men of questionable character and beliefs.

THE KING JAMES VERSION DESCENDED FROM TRANSLATIONS BOUGHT WITH THE BLOOD OF MARTYRS

MODERN VERSIONS DESCENDED FROM TRANSLATIONS CREATED BY THE INTELLECTUAL ELITE

The men who translated the versions that influenced and allowed for the creation of the KJV endured severe persecution for their beliefs. Many gave their lives so that the Bible could be made available to men in their own language. Many martyrs shed their blood to sow the seed that would eventually become the King James Bible.

Modern translators, as a whole, have been sheltered from the struggles of the past. There has been no terrible price paid or sacrifice of blood made to inaugurate the modern versions, and it can be clearly seen in their lack of depth and intensity.

THE USE OF ONE AUTHORIZED BIBLE ENCOURAGES MEMORIZATION AND UNITY

THE USE OF MANY DIFFERENT VERSIONS DISCOURAGES MEMORIZATION AND BRINGS CONFUSION

As we know God is not the author of confusion; it is easy to narrow down who is. Imagine a church where every member used a different translation of the Bible. Any public reading of the Bible would be confusing at best. Whose version is best? Which verse is the one that should be quoted? How can you memorize verses when your version may not only contain different wording, but may be missing essential components that are contained in another version?

THE KING JAMES BIBLE RETAINS
THE HEBREW CULTURAL IDIOMS

THE MODERN VERSIONS USE UPDATED LANGUAGE
AND REPLACE THE HEBREW IDIOMS WITH MODERN IDEAS

God communicated the Old Testament to His people in the Hebrew language. The idioms and picturesque words of that language were designed by Him to convey His thoughts in His preferred way. This was a language created by God for religious use. Replacing Hebrew cultural design and idiomatic language with modern slang and dynamic misinterpretation is an atrocity. God had a specific intention in influencing the words and expressions used in the Bible. Modern versions attempt to reinterpret God's communication in their own words.

CHARTS
AND
TABLES

TABLE OF THE BIBLICAL WRITERS

BOOK	AUTHORSHIP	TRIBE	DATE (Approximate)[249]
GENESIS	MOSES Hebrew, Christian, and Talmudic tradition,[250] Joshua 1:7-8, I Kings 2:3, II Chronicles 34:14, Nehemiah 8:1,14, 13:1, Luke 24:27, John 1:45, 5:45-47, Acts 28:23	LEVI	Events took place about 4000 B.C. Moses edited records around 1462–1423 B.C. while Israel was in the wilderness
EXODUS	------- (see Genesis) Exodus 24:4	-------	(see Deuteronomy)
LEVITICUS	------- (see Genesis)	-------	1461 B.C. Possibly 2nd year after leaving Egypt, probably 1st month of the 2nd year[251]
NUMBERS	------- (see Genesis)	-------	1423 B.C. (directly before Moses' death)
DEUTERONOMY	------- (see Genesis) Deuteronomy 31:9	-------	By 1423 B.C.[252] (events took place 1462–1423)

---

[249] Dates based on those used by Dr. R.C. Wetzel in *A Chronology of Biblical Christianity*. Many differing dates have been presented for the occurrence of biblical events, as Wetzel's dates are fairly traditional and in order to maintain consistency, these dates are used throughout.

[250] The five books of the Torah have long been believed to have been authored and/or edited by Moses.

[251] Exodus 40:17. The tabernacle was set up on the 1st day of the 1st month of the second year after Israel left Egypt.

[252] 40 years after the exodus from Egypt, believed to have been about 1463–1462 B.C.

JOSHUA	JOSHUA Joshua 24:26, Hebrew tradition	EPHRAIM	By 1372 B.C.[253] (events took place 1422–1372)
JUDGES	SAMUEL	EPHRAIM	1073–1025 B.C.[254]
RUTH	------- Talmudic tradition	-------	1073–1025 B.C.
I and II SAMUEL	SAMUEL / GAD or NATHAN?	-------	1073–1025 B.C. and 1025–985 B.C.[255]
I and II KINGS	JEREMIAH Talmudic tradition	LEVI	By 572 B.C. (647–572)
I and II CHRONICLES	EZRA Talmudic tradition[256]	LEVI	By 424 B.C.
EZRA	-------	-------	(see above)
NEHEMIAH	NEHEMIAH Jewish tradition	UNKNOWN	By 425 B.C.
ESTHER	MORDECAI or EZRA[257] Jewish tradition	BENJAMIN	About 473 B.C.[258] If compiled by Ezra, then by 424 B.C.
JOB	JOB or MOSES Talmudic tradition (Moses)[259]	N/A[260]	If Job, possibly 1900 B.C. If Moses, 1462–1423 B.C.
PSALMS (75 or more)	DAVID Authorship attested to in the Psalm titles	JUDAH	1055–985 B.C.

---

[253] Joshua would have died around 1372 B.C. at age 110.

[254] Judges had to have been written during the first few years after David became king as it record s events after the fall of Shiloh (Judges 18:31) and before the capture of Jerusalem as Jebusites are mentioned as living there (Judges 1:21).

[255] King David died around 985 B.C. at age 70 (I Kings 2:10).

[256] II Esdras 14 (Jewish apocrypha) states that Ezra was inspired of God to rewrite the law, which had been destroyed during the exile.

[257] Ezra is considered the author by traditional sources. Mordecai may have recorded the events with Ezra compiling them at a later date.

[258] Esther became queen about 479 B.C.

[259] *Baba Bathra* 14b.

[260] Job is believed to have lived before the time of Jacob (Israel) and thus would have been of the Sethly line prior to the Abrahamic line.

PSALMS 50, 73-83	ASAPH Authorship attested to in the Psalm titles	LEVI	1018–945 B.C.[261]
PSALMS 42, 44-49, 84, 85, 87	SONS OF KORAH Authorship attested to in the Psalm titles	LEVI	(see above)
PSALM 88	HEMAN[262] Authorship attested to in the Psalm title	LEVI	(see above)
PSALM 89	ETHAN Authorship attested to in the Psalm title	LEVI	(see above)
PSALM 90	MOSES Authorship attested to in the Psalm title	-------	1400's B.C.
PSALMS 127	DAVID or SOLOMON[263] Title of the Psalm "for Solomon"	JUDAH	1003–945 B.C.
PROVERBS	SOLOMON (AGUR and LEMUEL)[264] Proverbs 1:1, 10:1, 25:1, 30:1, 31:1	JUDAH	985–945 B.C. (727–697 B.C.)[265]

---

[261] It is most likely these Psalms would have been written during the reigns of David and Solomon as the authors are believed to have lived during this time.

[262] Some traditions consider Heman and Ethan to have been Gentiles who were given a place in the Levitical genealogies because of their work of the music staff in the temple.

[263] There are two conflicting traditions regarding authorship of this Psalm. A number of sources attribute it to Solomon himself, whereas others say the title and nature of the Psalm argue for authorship by his father David.

[264] Little is known of Agur and some have argued that this may have been a pen name of Solomon. Lemuel has been traditionally believed by the Jewish rabbis to have been a title or phrase (meaning "toward God" or "spoken by God"), and they believe this refers to Solomon's authorship rather than an individual (See Cohen, Proverbs SonB, p. 209).

[265] Proverbs 25–29 were compiled from Solomon's writings by scribes of Hezekiah.

ECCLESIASTES	SOLOMON Ecclesiastes 1:1 and internal evidence[266]	JUDAH	985–945 B.C.
SONG OF SOLOMON	SOLOMON Song of Solomon 1:1, Jewish tradition and internal evidences	JUDAH	(see Proverbs)
ISAIAH	ISAIAH[267] Isaiah 1:1, 2:1, 13:1, 37:21, 38:1, 39:3	UNKNOWN (JUDAH)[268]	784–697 B.C.
JEREMIAH	JEREMIAH Jeremiah 1:1, 36:1-2, et al.	LEVI	647–522 B.C.
LAMENTATIONS	------- Originally part of the book of Jeremiah	-------	586 B.C. or after [269]

---

[266] The writer is called the son of David in 1:1; in 1:16 he claims that he has gotten more wisdom than all they who have been before him in Jerusalem. Knowing the legendary wisdom of Solomon and the lives of those who followed him on the throne of David, this gives us a solid argument for Solomon's authorship. See also 2:3-8 as descriptive of his wealth and 12:9 testifying to his proverbs and teachings.

[267] Modern critics believe that Isaiah did not write the entire book given his name but the latter parts that contain specific fulfilled prophecy had to have been written by someone who was witness to the events. Up until the 18th century the book of Isaiah was universally believed to have been written by Isaiah himself. In 1775 J.C. Doderlein began the critical attack against the sole authorship of Isaiah, which has continued to our day. Modern critics believe chapters 40–54 and 55–66 were written by two later authors after the events prophesied had already happened. This is nothing more than false and blasphemous belief, only held by those who cannot accept that Isaiah prophesied these events so accurately more than 100 years before they came about.

[268] Some Jewish traditions hold that Isaiah was the son of a prince of Judah; his bearing before rulers and his depth of vocabulary would suggest this is a possibility.

[269] The destruction of Jerusalem and the Babylon captivity would have begun about 586 B.C. (II Kings 25:1-11).

EZEKIEL	EZEKIEL Ezekiel 1:1-3	LEVI[270]	593–571 B.C.[271]
DANIEL	DANIEL Daniel 12:4, also attested to by Jesus in Matthew 24:15 and Mark 13:14	UNKNOWN	605–536 B.C.
HOSEA	HOSEA Hosea 1:1-2	UNKNOWN	784–697 B.C.
JOEL	JOEL Joel 1:1	UNKNOWN	889–885 B.C.
AMOS	AMOS Amos 1:1	UNKNOWN	798–747 B.C.
OBADIAH	OBADIAH Obadiah 1:1	UNKNOWN	About 886 B.C.
JONAH	JONAH Jonah 1:1	UNKNOWN	About 772 B.C.
MICAH	MICAH Micah 1:1	UNKNOWN	747–697 B.C.
NAHUM	NAHUM Nahum 1:1	UNKNOWN	697–642 B.C.
HABAKKUK	HABAKKUK Habakkuk 1:1	UNKNOWN	About 605 B.C.
ZEPHANIAH	ZEPHANIAH Zephaniah 1:1	UNKNOWN	640–609 B.C.
HAGGAI	HAGGAI Haggai 1:1	UNKNOWN	About 520 B.C.
ZECHARIAH	ZECHARIAH Zechariah 1:1	LEVI	About 520 B.C.
MALACHI	MALACHI Malachi 1:1	UNKNOWN	431–425 B.C.

---

[270] Ezekiel 1:3 clearly defines his vocation as that of a priest, though some have argued that this may not be the case. Ezekiel uses a great deal of priestly symbolism and had a thorough working knowledge of the temple activities. Based on these facts it would seem very likely that he was of a priestly line.

[271] Ezekiel would have died in Babylon around 571 B.C.

BOOK	AUTHORSHIP	TRIBE	DATE (approximate)[272]
MATTHEW	MATTHEW Authorship assumed in title and tradition	UNKNOWN	37–68 A.D.[273]
MARK	MARK Authorship assumed in title and tradition	UNKNOWN	50–68 A.D.
LUKE	LUKE Authorship assumed in title and tradition	N/A GENTILE	58–60 A.D.[274]
JOHN	JOHN Authorship assumed in title and tradition	UNKNOWN	85–90 A.D.
ACTS	LUKE[275] Christian tradition and internal evidences[276]	-------	60–63 A.D.[277]
ROMANS	PAUL Romans 1:1	BENJAMIN	58 A.D. (probably from Corinth)

---

[272] Dates based on those used by Dr. R.C. Wetzel in *A Chronology of Biblical Christianity*. Many differing dates have been presented for the occurrence of biblical events, as Wetzel's dates are fairly traditional and in order to maintain consistency, these dates are used throughout.

[273] All the gospels except John's are believed to have been written before 68 A.D., which is the traditional date of Paul's death.

[274] Luke is believed to have used Mark's gospel as one source, and at least one other gospel had been written at the time of Luke's record (Luke 1:1-2). This would infer that Luke would have been written after the time of Mark.

[275] Luke and Acts are considered to be one history in two parts, both written by Luke. See Luke 1:3 and Acts 1:1.

[276] The author of Luke and Acts was traditionally held to be Luke the Physician who was a fellow traveler with Paul (Colossians 4:14, II Timothy 4:11, etc.). The author was clearly a fellow labourer with Paul as he uses the term "we" in relating their experiences (Acts 16:9-12, 20:5-21:18, 27:1-28:16).

[277] Clearly written before the death of Paul around 68 A.D.

I CORINTHIANS	PAUL (with Sosthenes) I Corinthians 1:1	-------	55–57 A.D. (probably from Ephesus, I Cor. 16:8)
II CORINTHIANS	PAUL (with Timothy) II Corinthians 1:1	-------	55–57 A.D. (probably from Macedonia)
GALATIANS	PAUL Galatians 1:1	-------	55–57 A.D.
EPHESIANS	------- Ephesians 1:1	-------	61–62 A.D. (during his 1st imprisonment in Rome)
PHILIPPIANS	PAUL (with Timothy)[278] Philippians 1:1	-------	During the same period as Ephesians (see above)
COLOSSIANS	PAUL (with Timothy) Colossians 1:1	-------	During the same period as Ephesians (see above)
I and II THESSALONIANS	PAUL (with Silas and Timothy) I Thessalonians 1:1 II Thessalonians 1:1	-------	51–52 A.D.
I TIMOTHY	PAUL I Timothy 1:1	-------	63–66 A.D. (after his release from his 1st imprisonment in Rome)
II TIMOTHY	PAUL II Timothy 1:1	-------	67–68 A.D. (during his 2nd imprisonment in Rome and close to his execution)
TITUS	PAUL Titus 1:1	-------	During the same period as I Timothy (see above)
PHILEMON	PAUL (with Timothy) Philemon 1:1	-------	61–62 A.D. (during his 1st imprisonment in Rome)
HEBREWS	PAUL[279] Christian tradition	-------	64–68 A.D.

---

[278] Though Timothy is mentioned with Paul in the introduction of both Philippians and Colossians, Paul was probably the sole writer, as these epistles are written in the first person throughout.

[279] It is uncertain who wrote Hebrews, though tradition holds it was Paul. Other authors suggested: Barnabas, Apollos, Silas, Clement of Rome, and even Aquila and Priscilla.

JAMES	JAMES[280] James 1:1	JUDAH[281]	45–49 A.D.[282]
I PETER	PETER I Peter 1:1	UNKNOWN	63–64 A.D. (from Rome, I Pet. 5:13)
II PETER	------- II Peter 1:1	-------	66–67 A.D. (just prior to his execution in Rome)
I, II AND III JOHN	JOHN Christian tradition and internal evidences[283]	UNKNOWN	90 A.D.
JUDE	JUDE Jude 1:1	JUDAH[284]	70–80 A.D.[285]
REVELATION	JOHN Revelation 1:1, Christian tradition and internal evidences[286]	UNKNOWN	90's A.D.

---

[280] It has been debated which James is author. James, the brother of John, was martyred around 44 A.D. James, the brother of Jesus, would be the likely author as the epistle is believed to have been written at a later date. The author speaks with authority and this would also coincide with the latter James as he was one of the leaders in the Jerusalem church (Acts 12:17, 15:13, and 21:18). This conclusion has also been given support by the style of Greek used.

[281] If Jesus' brother James, he would be of the tribe of Judah through Joseph or Mary.

[282] James is considered by many scholars to have been the earliest epistle.

[283] Writers in the first centuries are generally unanimous in crediting John with authorship of these epistles. There are also many terms used in them that are found only in the Gospel of John: *Word, paraclete, to do the truth, the true light, little children, begotten of God, no man hath beheld God at any time, to overcome the world*, etc.

[284] Also a brother of Jesus and thus of the tribe of Judah.

[285] Written after II Peter as Jude quotes from Peter's epistle in verses 17-18.

[286] The writers of the church in the first few centuries generally agreed that the Apostle John was the author. The Apostle was also the only well-known John at this period in the church's history. Just as in the Epistles of John, there are many internal phrases that give evidence that this was the same author. Phrases such as *the Word, the Lamb of God,* and *overcome* found in Revelation are used in the Gospel of John or the Epistles of John.

CHRONOLOGICAL TABLE OF THE BIBLICAL BOOKS

BOOK	DATE WRITTEN	TIME PERIOD COVERED
GENESIS	1462–1423 B.C.	Approx. 4000–1606 B.C. (Creation to Joseph's death)
JOB	1462–1423 B.C. (about 1900 B.C. if written by Job)	About 1900 B.C.
EXODUS	1462–1423 B.C.	1542–1461 B.C. (Moses' birth to the building of the Tabernacle)
LEVITICUS	1462–1423 B.C.	1461 B.C. (Giving of the Levitical law)
NUMBERS	1462–1423 B.C.	1461[287]–1423 B.C. (40 years in the wilderness)
DEUTERONOMY	1423 B.C.	1461–1423 B.C. (Review of 40 years in the wilderness to Moses' death)
JOSHUA	By 1372 B.C.	1423–1372 B.C. (Moses' death to Joshua's death)
JUDGES	1073–1027 B.C.	1372–1076 B.C. (Joshua's death to Samson's death)
RUTH	1030–1027 B.C.	1251–1055 B.C. (Elimelech's migration to Moab to David's birth)
I and II SAMUEL	1073–985 B.C.	1103–988 B.C. (Samuel's birth to David's census
PSALMS	1055–945 B.C.	1055–945 B.C. (David's birth to Solomon's death)[288]
I and II CHRONICLES	By 424 B.C.	1025–536 B.C. (Saul's death to the decree of Cyrus to rebuild the temple)
PROVERBS/ECCLESIASTES/ SONG OF SOLOMON	985–945 B.C.	985–945 B.C. (During the reign of Solomon)

---

[287] Begun on the 1st day of the 2nd month of the 2nd year after leaving Egypt.
[288] With the exception of Psalm 90, which would have been written about 1462 B.C.

I and II KINGS	By 572 B.C.	985–561 B.C. (David's death/Solomon made king to the release of Jehoiachin in Babylon)
JOEL	889–885 B.C.[289]	889–885 B.C. (dating is uncertain)
OBADIAH	886 B.C.[290]	886 B.C. (dating is uncertain)
AMOS	798–747 B.C.	798–747 B.C. (Jeroboam II made king over Israel to the leprosy of Uzziah, king of Judah)
HOSEA	784–697 B.C	784–697 B.C. (Jeroboam's reign to the death of Hezekiah)
ISAIAH	784–697 B.C. (764–677 B.C.)[291]	784–697 B.C. (The end of Uzziah's reign to the reign of Manasseh)
JONAH	About 772 B.C.	About 772 B.C. (During the reign of Jeroboam II)
MICAH	747–697 B.C.	747–697 B.C. (From the time of Uzziah being stricken with leprosy to the death of Hezekiah)
NAHUM	697–642 B.C.	697–642 B.C. (The death of Hezekiah to the death of Manasseh)
ZEPHANIAH	640–621 B.C.[292]	640–621 B.C. (During the reign of Josiah)
JEREMIAH/LAMENTATIONS	627–586 B.C.	627–586 B.C. (The 13th year of Josiah's reign to after the destruction of Jerusalem)

[289] Joel has been alternately dated at about 835 B.C. by some scholars.

[290] Obadiah has been alternately dated at about 840 B.C. by some scholars.

[291] Possible alternate dating. Sennacherib was slain by his sons in 681 B.C. and this is recorded in Isaiah 37:38. Thus the traditional dating for Isaiah's ministry may not be accurate.

[292] Zephaniah probably prophesied up until the time of the great reforms of Josiah in 621 B.C. as he alludes to the moral state of the nation.

HABAKKUK	606 B.C.	606 B.C. (During the reign of Nebuchadnezzar probably before the battle of Carchemish)
DANIEL	605–536 B.C.	605–536 B.C. (From the first deportation to Babylon to the 3rd year of the reign of Cyrus)
EZEKIEL	593–571 B.C.	593–571 B.C. (From the 5th year of Jehoiachin's through part of the Babylonian captivity under Nebuchadnezzar)
HAGGAI	520	520 B.C. (During the reign of Darius I of Persia and the repopulation of Jerusalem after the exile)
ZECHARIAH	520–518 B.C.	520–518 B.C. (During the reign of Darius I of Persia and the repopulation of Jerusalem after the exile)
EZRA	457–433 B.C.	538–433 B.C. (From the decree of Cyrus to the rebuilding of the walls of Jerusalem)
ESTHER	486–465 B.C. (464–424 B.C.)[293]	486–465 B.C. (During the reign of Ahaseurus, king of Persia)
NEHEMIAH	445–433 B.C.	445–433 B.C. (From the decree of Artaxerxes to rebuild Jerusalem to the completion of the work)
MALACHI	425 B.C.	431–425 B.C.

[293] Ahaseurus has traditionally been held to have been Xerxes I, though the Septuagint names him as Artaxerxes I who sent Ezra to Jerusalem. Josephus also testifies to Artaxerxes as the husband of Esther, which would have made her queen in Nehemiah's day)

BOOK	DATE WRITTEN	TIME PERIOD COVERED
MATTHEW	37–68 A.D.[294]	5 B.C.–29 A.D.
LUKE	58–60 A.D.[295]	5 B.C.–29 A.D.
JOHN	85–90 A.D.	5 B.C.–29 A.D.
MARK	50–68 A.D.	25 A.D.–29 A.D.
ACTS	60–63 A.D.[296]	29–61 A.D. (From the ascension of Jesus to Paul's arrival in Rome)
JAMES	45–49 A.D.[297]	45–49 A.D.
I AND II THESSALONIANS	51–52 A.D.	51–52 A.D.
I AND II CORINTHIANS and GALATIANS	55–57 A.D.	55–57 A.D.
ROMANS	58 A.D.	58 A.D.
EPHESIANS, PHILIPPIANS, COLOSSIANS, PHILEMON	61–62 A.D.	61–62 A.D. (probably during Paul's 1st imprisonment in Rome)
I TIMOTHY and TITUS	63–66 A.D.	63–66 A.D. (after Paul's release from his 1st imprisonment in Rome)
I PETER	63–64 A.D.	63–64 A.D.
II PETER	66–67 A.D.	66–67 A.D. (just prior to Peter's execution in Rome)
II TIMOTHY and HEBREWS	67–68 A.D.	67–68 A.D. (during Paul's 2nd imprisonment in Rome, and close to his execution)
JUDE	70–80 A.D.[298]	70–80 A.D.
I, II and III JOHN	90 A.D.	90 A.D.
REVELATION	90's A.D.	90's A.D.

---

[294] All the gospels except John's are believed to have been written before 68 A.D., which is the traditional date of Paul's death.

[295] Luke is believed to have used Mark's gospel as one source, and at least one other gospel had been written at the time of Luke's record (Luke 1:1-2). This would infer that Luke would have been written after the time of Mark.

[296] Clearly written before the death of Paul around 68 A.D.

[297] James is considered by many scholars to have been the earliest epistle.

[298] Written after II Peter as Jude quotes from Peter's epistle in verses 17-18.

TABLES OF PROPHETIC EVIDENCE
FOR THE BIBLE[299]

PROPHECIES ABOUT THE NATION OF ISRAEL

PROPHECY	DATE PROPHESIED	FULFILLMENT	DATE FULFILLED
If Judah and Israel failed to serve the Lord they would be cast out and scattered among the nations *Moses*[300] Leviticus 26:27-33, Deuteronomy 4:23-28, 28:63-66 *Hosea* Hosea 9:17 *Jeremiah* Jeremiah 16:10-13 *Ezekiel* Ezekiel 22:14-16	Moses 1460–1423 B.C. Hosea 784–697 B.C. Jeremiah 647–522 B.C. Ezekiel 593–571 B.C.	Assyrian Captivity of Israel and Judah (II Kings 15:29, 18:13, I Chronicles 5:26) Babylonian Captivity of Judah (II Kings 24:14, 25:11, II Chronicles 36:20, Jeremiah 52:28-30) Roman Destruction of Jerusalem Final Roman Dispersion of the Jews	721 B.C. 586–516 B.C. 70 A.D. 135 A.D.
The Division of the Kingdom of Israel into the separate nations of Israel and Judah (Division into 10 and 2 tribes) *Ahijah* I Kings 11:29-40	962 B.C.	I Kings 12	945 B.C.
70 years of Babylonian captivity *Jeremiah* Jeremiah 25:11-14	626 B.C.	II Kings 24 and 25 II Chronicles 36:20-21	586–516 B.C.

---

[299] These tables are intended to give an overview of major Biblical prophecies and are not intended to represent every prophecy on these subjects. Dates are approximate and based on Wetzel's chronology (*A Chronology of Biblical Christianity*).
[300] The captivity witnessed to be part of Moses' prophecy in Nehemiah 1:8.

End of the 70-year captivity (Dedication of the 2nd Temple) *Jeremiah* Jeremiah 25:11-14,[301] 29:10	626 B.C.	II Chronicles 36:22-23 Ezra 1	516 B.C.[302]
The Jews will return to repossess Israel *Moses* Deuteronomy 30:1-5 *Amos* Amos 9:14-15 *Isaiah* 27:12-13, 43:5-7, 66:7-8[303] *Jeremiah* Jeremiah 23:3, 29:10-14, 31:10, 32:37[304] *Ezekiel* Ezekiel 11:17, 20:34, 34:11-16, 36:24, 37:21-22 *Zechariah* Zechariah 8:7-8	Moses 1460–1423 B.C. Amos 798–747 B.C. Isaiah 784–697 B.C. Jeremiah 647–522 B.C. Ezekiel 593–571 B.C. Zechariah 520 B.C.	These prophecies began to come to fruition in the late 1800's when Jews began returning to Palestine (Israel) to make their home there. The nation of Israel was established in 1948 and millions of Jews began immigrating to their homeland from all parts of the world. The prophecies are still in the process of coming to full completion. It is believed that approximately 1 in 3 Jews in the world now live in Israel.	Late 1800's A.D. 1948 A.D. to Present
The Jews would buy back land *Jeremiah* Jeremiah 32:15	647–522 B.C.	During the late 1800's and early 1900's A.D., large numbers of Jews returned to Palestine, began buying parcels of land, and repopulating the ancient places.	Late 1800 to early 1900's A.D.

---

[301] Isaiah also speaks of the return under Cyrus' decree in Isaiah 44:28; see note below.
[302] Cyrus decreed in 536 B.C. that the first group of Jews could return to their homeland, but the actual captivity did not end until the temple was rebuilt and dedicated in 516 B.C. Haggai prophesied around 520 B.C. that the Jews should finish the work on the Lord's house even though the 70 years had not been finished (Haggai 1:1-4).
[303] This has been considered typologically to both the births of the Church (Acts 2) in one day and the modern nation of Israel on May 14, 1948.
[304] The first dispensation of this prophecy was begun in the return from Babylonian captivity, the second dispensation in these latter days which began with the return of Jews to Palestine in the late 1800s and the restoration of Israel in 1948.

The nation of Israel would be militarily more powerful than their enemies, even though disproportionately much smaller in number *Moses* Leviticus 26:7-8	1460–1423 B.C.	Fulfilled throughout Israel's history under Moses, Joshua, David, and others. In 1948 Israel defeated the invading armies of Egypt, Syria, Lebanon, Jordan, and Iraq that outnumbered them 20 to 1. In 1967 and 1973 Israel won victories against staggering odds once again, and in each of these wars Israel not only drove back the enemy but took land.	Early nation of Israel 1948 A.D. 1967 A.D. 1973 A.D.
The Jews would have a great influence on the entire world through the gifts of God bestowed upon them *God to Abraham and his descendants* Genesis 12:2-3, 18:18, 22:18, 26:4, and mentioned in Psalms 72:17, Acts 3:25, and Galatians 3:8	To Abraham 1967–1792 B.C.	**The Jews have been blessed in intellect and ability in many fields in a way very disproportionate to their small numbers.**	Throughout history

PROPHECIES ABOUT JESUS THE MESSIAH

PROPHECY	DATE PROPHESIED	FULFILLMENT	DATE FULFILLED
The Messiah would be born of a woman (he did not just appear but went through the natural birth process) *God to Adam* Genesis 3:15 and inferred in Micah 5:3	About 4000 B.C.	Matthew 1:21, Luke 1:31, 2:7, and mentioned in Galatians 4:4	5 B.C.
The Messiah would be born of a virgin *Isaiah* Isaiah 7:14	784–697 B.C.	Matthew 1:18-23, Luke 1:26-35	5 B.C.
The Messiah would be of the tribe of Judah *Jacob to his sons* Genesis 49:10 *Isaiah* Isaiah 11:1	Jacob 1660 B.C. or before Isaiah 784–697 B.C.	Matthew 1:1-17, Luke 3:23, mentioned in Romans 1:3, Hebrews 7:14, and Revelation 5:5	5 B.C.
The Messiah would be of the house of David *God to David* II Samuel 7:12, Psalm 132:11 *Isaiah* Isaiah 11:1 *Jeremiah* Jeremiah 23:5	David 1018–985 B.C. Isaiah 784–697 B.C. Jeremiah 647–522 B.C.	Matthew 1:1, 22:42, Luke 3:31, John 7:42, mentioned in Acts 2:29-30, 13:22-23, and Romans 1:3	5 B.C.
The Messiah would be born in Bethlehem *Micah* Micah 5:2	747–697 B.C.	Matthew 2:5-6, Luke 2:4-7	5 B.C.
The Messiah would be anointed by the Holy Spirit *Isaiah* Isaiah 11:2, 42:1	784–697 B.C.	Matthew 3:16-17, Mark 1:10, Luke 3:22, John 1:32	25 A.D.

The messenger of the Lord would go before the Messiah to prepare for his arrival *Isaiah* Isaiah 40:3 *Malachi* Malachi 3:1	Isaiah 784–697 B.C. Malachi 431–425 B.C.	Matthew 3:1-3, 11:10, Mark 1:1-4, Luke 7:26-27	25 A.D.
The Messiah would be rejected *David (in the Spirit)* Psalm 22:6 *Isaiah* Isaiah 49:7, 53:3	David 1055–985 B.C. Isaiah 784–697 B.C.	John 1:10-11, 7:5,48 and demonstrated in his non-acceptance by the Jews throughout his ministry and crucifixion. Jesus speaks of this in a parable in Luke 19:14.	25–29 A.D.
He would enter Jerusalem on a donkey *Zechariah* Zechariah 9:9	520 B.C.	Matthew 21:1-10, Mark 11:1-10, Luke 19:29-44, John 12:12-16	29 A.D.
The Messiah would be betrayed by a friend who broke bread with him *David* (in the Spirit) Psalm 41:9	1055–985 B.C.	Matthew 26:21-24, Mark 14:18-21, Luke 22:21-22, John 13:18	29 A.D.
He would be betrayed and sold to his enemies for 30 pieces of silver *Zechariah* Zechariah 11:12	520 B.C.	Matthew 26:15, 27:9	29 A.D.
The 30 pieces of silver would be cast down in the temple and eventually given to the potter *Zechariah* Zechariah 11:13	520 B.C.	Matthew 27:5-8	29 A.D.
The Messiah would suffer a humiliating death *David* Psalm 22 *Isaiah* Isaiah 53	David 1055–985 B.C. Isaiah 784–697 B.C.	Matthew 26:57-27:66, Mark 14:53-15:41, Luke 22:54-23:49, John 18:12-19:37	29 A.D.

The Messiah would be silent before his accusers *Isaiah* Isaiah 53:7	784–697 B.C.	Matthew 26:63, 27:12-14, Mark 14:61, 15:5, and mentioned in I Peter 2:23	29 A.D.
He would be beaten and spit upon *Isaiah* Isaiah 50:6, 53:5	784–697 B.C.	Matthew 27:26-30, Mark 15:15-20, John 19:1-3	29 A.D.
The Messiah would die for the sins of the people *Isaiah* Isaiah 53:4-6,10-12	784–697 B.C.	See above (Messiah to suffer death) II Corinthians 5:21, Galatians 3:13, I Peter 2:24, I John 3:5, and many others	29 A.D.
He would be the Lamb of God offered for our sins (typified by the Passover lamb of Exodus 12) *Isaiah* Isaiah 53:7 *John the Baptist* John 1:29, 36	Isaiah 784–697 B.C. John the Baptist 25 A.D.	See above, Acts 8:32-35, I Peter 1:19, Revelation 5:6,12-13, 6:1, and others	29 A.D. to present
His hands and feet would be pierced *David* (in the Spirit) Psalm 22:16 *Zechariah* Zechariah 12:10	David 1055–985 B.C. Zechariah 520 B.C.	Matthew 27:35, Mark 15:24, Luke 23:33, John 19:23, 37	29 A.D.
He would be given vinegar and gall to drink *David* (in the Spirit) Psalm 69:21	1055–985 B.C.	Matthew 27:34,48, Mark 15:36, Luke 23:36, John 19:29	29 A.D.
The Messiah would die with criminals *Isaiah* Isaiah 53:9,12	784–697 B.C.	Matthew 27:38, Mark 15:27-28, Luke 22:37	29 A.D.

He made intercession for his persecutors *Isaiah* Isaiah 53:12	784–697 B.C.	Luke 23:34 (Matthew 5:44)	29 A.D.
Lots would be cast for his clothes *David* Psalms 22:18	1055–985 B.C.	Matthew 27:35, Mark 15:24, Luke 23:34, John 19:23-24	29 A.D.
He would be buried in a rich man's tomb *Isaiah* Isaiah 53:9	784–697 B.C.	Matthew 27:57-60, Mark 15:42-47, Luke 23:50-55, John 19:38-42	29 A.D.
The Messiah would rise from the dead *David* (in the Spirit) Psalm 16:10, 49:15	1055–985 B.C.	Matthew 28:5-6, Mark 16:6, Luke 24:5-6, John 20:1-18	29 A.D.
The Messiah would ascend to heaven *David* (in the Spirit) Psalm 68:18	1055–985 B.C.	Mark 16:19, Luke 24:51, John 20:17 (inferred), Acts 1:9	29 A.D.
The Messiah would be seated at the right hand of God *David* (in the Spirit) Psalm 110:1 alluded to by Jesus in Matthew 22:44-45, Mark 12:35-37, and Luke 20:41-44	1055–985 B.C.	Acts 7:56, Romans 8:34, Colossians 3:1, Ephesians 1:20, Hebrews 1:3, 8:1, 10:12, 12:2, I Peter 3:22	29 A.D. to present

COMPARISON OF PRESERVATION
OF ANCIENT MANUSCRIPTS
WITH BIBLICAL MANUSCRIPTS

MANUSCRIPT	DATE WRITTEN	DATE OF OLDEST COPY	TIME BETWEEN WRITING AND OLDEST COPY	TOTAL COPIES IN EXISTENCE
THE BIBLE: NEW TESTAMENT	40–96 A.D.	125 A.D.	29+ YEARS	24,000
HOMER	900 B.C.	400 B.C.	500 YEARS	653
DEMOSTHENES	383–322 B.C.	1100 A.D.	1,422+ YEARS	200
SOPHOCLES	496–404 B.C.	1000 A.D.	1,404+ YEARS	193
ARISTOTLE	384–322 B.C.	1100 A.D.	1,422+ YEARS	49
ANNALS OF TACITUS	100 A.D.	1100 A.D.	1,000 YEARS	20
CAESAR	100–44 B.C.	900 A.D.	944+ YEARS	10
ARISTOPHANES	450–385 B.C.	900 A.D.	1,285+ YEARS	10
EURIPIDES	480–406 B.C.	1100 A.D.	1,506+ YEARS	9
HERODOTUS' HISTORY	480–425 B.C.	900 A.D.	1,325+ YEARS	8
THUCYDIDES' HISTORY	460–400 B.C.	900 A.D.	1,300+ YEARS	8
TETRALOGIES OF PLATO	427–347 B.C.	900 A.D.	1,247+ YEARS	7
PLINY THE YOUNGER'S HISTORY	61–113 A.D.	850 A.D.	737+ YEARS	7

THE KING JAMES BIBLE
COMPARED TO
THE MODERN VERSIONS

THE KING JAMES BIBLE (RECEIVED TEXT)	MODERN BIBLES (CRITICAL TEXT)
NOT COPYRIGHTED	COPYRIGHTED
BASED ON THE MAJORITY OF GREEK AND LATIN TEXTS (90–95%)	BASED ON THE MINORITY OF GREEK AND LATIN TEXTS (5–10%)
TRANSLATED FROM THE MAJORITY OF AVAILABLE MANUSCRIPTS	TRANSLATED PRIMARILY FROM 2 MANUSCRIPTS: SINAITICUS AND VATICANUS
TRADITIONAL ORIGIN IS ANTIOCH	TRADITIONAL ORIGIN IS ALEXANDRIA
BYZANTINE STREAM OF TRANSMISSION	ALEXANDRIAN AND WESTERN (ROMAN) STREAM OF TRANSMISSION
PRESERVED PRIMARILY IN THE BYZANTINE CHURCHES	PRESERVED PRIMARILY IN THE ROMAN CHURCHES
TRANSLATED BY THE GREATEST SCHOLARS OF THEIR DAY, IN A DAY OF HIGH EDUCATIONAL STANDARDS	TRANSLATED BY GREAT SCHOLARS OF THEIR DAY, IN A DAY OF MUCH LOWER EDUCATIONAL STANDARDS
TRANSLATED IN A PERIOD OF MORAL ASCENDANCY, SPIRITUAL DEDICATION, AND REFORMATION	TRANSLATED IN A PERIOD OF MORAL DECLINE, CRITICISM, AND COMPROMISE
TRANSLATED IN AN AGE OF FAITH	TRANSLATED IN AN AGE OF DOUBT
DESCENDED FROM TRANSLATIONS BOUGHT WITH THE BLOOD OF MARTYRS	DESCENDED FROM TRANSLATIONS CREATED BY THE INTELLECTUAL ELITE
PRESERVED BY USE: BY COPYING AND PASSING DOWN	PRESERVED BY AGE: UNUSED AND ABUSED COPIES
TRANSLATED BY MEN OF HIGH CHARACTER AND PROTESTANT BELIEFS	TRANSLATED BY MEN OF QUESTIONABLE CHARACTER AND ECUMENICAL BELIEFS
CONTEMPORARY WITH THE PURITANS AND THE ROOTS OF THE HOLINESS MOVEMENT	CONTEMPORARY WITH DARWIN AND MARX, AMID THE ROOTS OF EVOLUTION AND COMMUNISM
YOUNGER MANUSCRIPTS (OLDER WORN OUT THROUGH USE)	OLDER MANUSCRIPTS (PRESERVED THROUGH LACK OF USE)
ONE SINGLE TRANSLATION FOR NEARLY 300 YEARS	MANY TRANSLATIONS OVER ONLY 100 YEARS

THE USE OF ONE AUTHORIZED BIBLE ENCOURAGES MEMORIZATION AND THEOLOGICAL UNITY	THE USE OF VARIOUS VERSIONS DISCOURAGES MEMORIZATION AND BRINGS CONFUSION
HEBREW IDIOMS AND CULTURE MAINTAINED	HEBREW REPLACED WITH MODERN IDIOMS AND CULTURE
THE PINNACLE OF THE ENGLISH LANGUAGE	THE DECLINE OF THE ENGLISH LANGUAGE
THE ENGLISH OF THE BIBLE IS UNIQUE IN ITS FORM: IT IS BIBLICAL ENGLISH, UNKNOWN ANYWHERE ELSE[305]	THE ENGLISH OF THE MODERN VERSIONS IS BASED ON THE CULTURAL LANGUAGE OF THE DAY: MAN'S DIALECT, NOT GOD'S
FULLER TEXT	ABBREVIATED TEXT
TRANSLATED IN A TIME WHEN THE LIGHT HAD BEGUN TO SHINE OUT OF DARKNESS	TRANSLATED IN A TIME OF FALLING DARKNESS

---

[305] The language of the King James Version was not the language of England in that day. It was structured specifically to demonstrate and communicate the glory of God's word. This can easily be seen in the difference between the language of the preface to the KJV written by the translators and the translation itself. As far as words like "thee" and "thou," they were not in common usage during this period. This terminology was brought together to best express the most faithful rendering of the Hebrew and Greek languages.

THE KING JAMES AND MODERN BIBLES[306]
TRANSLATION COMPARISON

TRANSLATION IN THE KING JAMES VERSION	TRANSLATION IN THE MODERN VERSIONS[307]	SIGNIFICANCE AND COMMENTS
Riches and honour are with me; yea, durable riches and righteousness. Proverbs 8:18	*With me are riches and honor, enduring wealth and prosperity.* (NIV) *Riches and honor are with me, enduring wealth and prosperity.* (RSV)	The Hebrew word ***tsedaqah*** means righteousness
Therefore the Lord himself shall give you a sign; Behold, a virgin shall conceive, and bear a son, and shall call his name Immanuel. Isaiah 7:14	*Therefore the Lord himself will give you a sign. Behold, a young woman shall conceive and bear a son, and shall call his name Immanu-el.* (RSV and the NRSV)	Most versions translate this properly
How art thou fallen from heaven, O Lucifer, son of the morning! Isaiah 14:12	*How you have fallen from heaven, O morning star, son of the dawn!* (NIV) *How you have fallen from heaven, O star of the morning, son of the dawn!* (NASB) *How you are fallen from heaven, O Day Star, son of Dawn!* (RSV)	Not only is the name Lucifer rendered as a title, it is imitative of the titles given to Jesus, who is the bright and morning star,[308] and of the revelation of God through Jesus referred to as the day star that arises in our hearts[309]

---

[306] Verses are selected for comparative purposes and are by no means a comprehensive list.
[307] Most examples are taken from three of the most influential and best-selling versions. These only are used for the sake of brevity though there are many others.
[308] Revelation 22:16.
[309] II Peter 1:19.

And one shall say unto him, What are these wounds in thine hands? Then he shall answer, Those with which I was wounded in the house of my friends. Zechariah 13:6	If someone asks him, 'What are these wounds on your body? he will answer, The wounds I was given at the house of my friends. (NIV) And one will say to him, What are these wounds between your arms? Then he will say, Those with which I was wounded in the house of my friends. (NASB) And if one asks him, What are these wounds on your back? he will say, The wounds I received in the house of my friends. (RSV)	This is a prophecy of the nail prints in the hands of Jesus. The modern versions describe the wounds as being anywhere but specifically in his hands! The NEB even translates this as "scars on your chest." The Hebrew word here is **yad**, which means "hands," not body, back, chest, etc.
And [Joseph] knew her not till she had brought forth her firstborn son:.... Matthew 1:25	But he had no union with her until she gave birth to a son. (NIV) but kept her a virgin until she gave birth to a Son. (NASB) but knew her not until she had borne a son. (RSV)	The Catholic belief that Mary was a perpetual virgin is given support by the modern versions Jesus was Mary's firstborn son, as he had later siblings
This kind can come out by nothing, but by prayer and fasting. Mark 9:29	This kind come out only by prayer. (NIV) This kind cannot come out by anything but prayer. (NASB) This kind cannot be driven out by anything but prayer. (RSV)	Removes the power of fasting coupled with prayer in order to overcome the adversary Change made in the UBS Greek text due to Alexandrian manuscripts
...Children, how hard is it for them that trust in riches to enter into the kingdom of God! Mark 10:24	...Children, how hard it is to enter the kingdom of God. (NIV, NASB, and RSV)	This truncation completely changes the intention of the writer
And Jesus answered and said unto him, Get thee behind me, Satan: for it is written... Luke 4:8	Jesus answered, It is written.... (NIV) Jesus answered him, It is written.... (NASB and RSV)	Get thee behind me, Satan is cut from the text, obliterating one of Jesus' most powerful statements of resistance to the adversary

But he turned, and rebuked them, and said, Ye know not what manner of spirit ye are of. For the Son of man is not come to destroy men's lives, but to save them. And they went to another village. Luke 9:55-56	*But Jesus turned and rebuked them, and they went to another village.* (NIV) *But he turned and rebuked them. And they went on to another village.* (RSV) The NASB has the correct wording here.	Another example of translational truncation removing an important statement by the Savior
...we beheld his glory, the glory as of the only begotten of the Father,.... John 1:14	*We have seen his glory, the glory of the One and Only.* (NIV)	Nearly all other versions translate this verse properly
In these lay a great multitude of impotent folk, of blind, halt, withered, waiting for the moving of the water. For an angel went down at a certain season into the pool, and troubled the water: whosoever then first after the troubling of the water stepped in was made whole of whatsoever disease he had. And a certain man was there, which had an infirmity thirty and eight years. John 5:3-5	*Here a great number of disabled people used to lie—the blind, the lame, the paralyzed. One who was there had been an invalid for thirty-eight years.* (NIV) *In these lay a multitude of invalids, blind, lame, paralyzed. One man was there, who had been ill for thirty-eight years.* (RSV) The NASB contains the passage, but with a marginal note that verses 3 and 4 were not contained in the early manuscripts.	The entire background regarding the troubling of the water and the angelic visitation are removed
A little while, and ye shall not see me: and again, a little while, and ye shall see me, because I go to the Father. John 16:16	*In a little while you will see me no more, and then after a little while you will see me.* (NIV) *A little while, and you will no longer see Me; and again a little while, and you will see Me.* (NASB) *A little while, and you will see me no more; again a little while, and you will see me.* (RSV)	Jesus qualified this statement by saying that he was going to the Father, a fact not mentioned by the modern versions

...Ye men of Athens, I perceive that in all things ye are too superstitious. Acts 17:22	*Men of Athens! I see that in every way you are very religious.* (NIV) *Men of Athens, I observe that you are very religious in all respects.* (NASB) *Men of Athens, I perceive that in every way you are very religious.* (RSV)	There is a very different intention behind these translations Being religious is generally considered a good thing The activity of the Athenians was superstition, not true religion, and the modern versions give a slanted perspective of this in their choice of words
For the invisible things of him from the creation of the world are clearly seen, being understood by the things that are made, even his eternal power and Godhead; so that they are without excuse: Romans 1:20	*For since the creation of the world God's invisible qualities—his eternal power and divine nature...* (NIV) *For since the creation of the world His invisible attributes His eternal power and divine nature...* (NASB) *Ever since the creation of the world his invisible nature, namely, his eternal power and deity...* (RSV)	The term "godhead" defines the structure of the divine order The modern versions make it a term describing the characteristics of God. Acts 17:29 is also translated in this manner
But I keep under my body, and bring it into subjection.... I Corinthians 9:27	*I beat my body and make it my slave...* (NIV) *I pommel my body and subdue it.* (RSV)	The heretical sects and mystery religions believed in physical punishment of the body to bring it closer to the divine presence
But we have this treasure in earthen vessels,.... II Corinthians 4:7	*But we have this treasure in jars of clay...* (NIV) *We carry this precious message around in the unadorned clay pots of our ordinary lives.* (The Message)	These and others are examples of the dumbing down of passages by the use of dynamic equivalency This passage in the KJV demonstrates that the treasure is in an earthen vessel, just as man is made of earth

And this I say, that the covenant, that was confirmed before of God in Christ, the law, which was four hundred and thirty years after, cannot disannul, that it should make the promise of none effect. Galatians 3:17	*What I mean is this: The law, introduced 430 years later, does not set aside the covenant previously established by God and thus do away with the promise.* (NIV) *What I am saying is this: the Law, which came four hundred and thirty years later, does not invalidate a covenant previously ratified by God, so as to nullify the promise.* (NASB) *This is what I mean: the law, which came four hundred and thirty years afterward, does not annul a covenant previously ratified by God, so as to make the promise void.* (RSV)	None of these versions contain the words *in Christ*! The entire purpose of this statement is that the covenant was confirmed by God <u>in Christ</u>, yet the modern versions infer that this was just a covenant of God alone
I would they were even cut off which trouble you. Galatians 5:12	*As for those agitators, I wish they would go the whole way and emasculate themselves!* (NIV) *I wish that those who are troubling you would even mutilate themselves.* (NASB) *I wish those who unsettle you would mutilate themselves!* (RSV)	This phrase is meant to refer to them being cut off, the spiritual separated from the carnal as in the act of circumcision referred to in the prior verses The modern versions skew this understanding completely
...God, who created all things by Jesus Christ: Ephesians 3:9	*God who created all things.* (NIV, NASB, RSV)	The modern versions state that God created all things, not by Jesus as the majority of manuscripts states
For this cause I bow my knees unto the Father of our Lord Jesus Christ, Ephesians 3:14	*For this reason I kneel before the Father.* (NIV) *For this reason I bow my knees before the Father.* (NASB and RSV)	Just the Father, not the Father of Jesus

For the perfecting of the saints, for the work of the ministry, for the edifying of the body of Christ: Till we all come in the unity of the faith, and of the knowledge of the Son of God, unto a perfect man, unto the measure of the stature of the fulness of Christ: Ephesians 4:12-13	...to prepare God's people for works of service, so that the body of Christ may be built up until we all reach unity in the faith and in the knowledge of the Son of God and become mature, attaining to the whole measure of the fullness of Christ... (NIV) ...to equip the saints for the work of ministry, for building up the body of Christ, until we all attain to the unity of the faith and of the knowledge of the Son of God, to mature manhood, to the measure of the stature of the fulness of Christ. (RSV)	To attain to the measure of the fullness of Christ is to be a perfect man, not just mature The modern versions consistently translate "perfect" as "mature" or "complete"
For we are members of his body, of his flesh, and of his bones. Ephesians 5:30	...for we are members of his body. (NIV) ...because we are members of his body. (NASB and RSV)	That we are of his flesh and bones is left out of the passage
In whom we have redemption through his blood, ...: Colossians 1:14	...in whom we have redemption... (NIV, NASB, and RSV)	Where is the precious blood of Christ in this passage?
Let no man beguile you of your reward in a voluntary humility and worshipping of angels, intruding into those things which he hath not seen, ..., Colossians 2:18	Do not let anyone who delights in false humility and the worship of angels disqualify you for the prize. Such a person goes into great detail about what he has seen... (NIV) Let no one keep defrauding you of your prize by delighting in self-abasement and the worship of the angels, taking his stand on visions he has seen... (NASB) Let no one disqualify you, insisting on self-abasement and worship of angels, taking his stand on visions... (RSV)	The mistranslation of the word "not" here, though seemingly minor, completely reverses the meaning of the phrase

For which things' sake the wrath of God cometh on the children of disobedience: Colossians 3:6	*Because of these, the wrath of God is coming.* (NIV) *On account of these the wrath of God is coming.* (RSV)	The NASB includes the phrase regarding the children of disobedience with a marginal note stating that two of the early manuscripts do not contain it
Perverse disputings of men of corrupt minds, and destitute of the truth, supposing that gain is godliness: from such withdraw thyself. I Timothy 6:5	*And constant friction between men of corrupt mind, who have been robbed of the truth and who think that godliness is a means to financial gain.* (NIV) *And constant friction between men of depraved mind and deprived of the truth, who suppose that godliness is a means of gain.* (NASB) *And wrangling among men who are depraved in mind and bereft of the truth, imagining that godliness is a means of gain.* (RSV)	This removes the critical statement that from such you should withdraw yourself Changes were made based on Sinaiticus and Vaticanus
That the man of God may be perfect, thoroughly furnished unto all good works. II Timothy 3:17	*...so that the man of God may be thoroughly equipped for every good work.* (NIV) *so that the man of God may be adequate, equipped for every good work.* (NASB) *that the man of God may be complete, equipped for every good work.* (RSV)	There is a great difference between being adequate or complete and being perfect

For verily he took not on him the nature of angels, but he took on him the seed of Abraham. Hebrews 2:16	*For surely it is not angels he helps, but Abraham's descendants.* (NIV) *For assuredly he does not give help to angels, but he gives help to the descendant of Abraham.* (NASB) *For surely it is not with angels that he is concerned, but with the descendants of Abraham.* (RSV)	This type of translation completely changes the meaning of the verse The key thought here is that Jesus took on the physical and spiritual nature of man
Through faith also Sarah herself received strength to conceive seed, and was delivered of a child when she was past age, because she judged him faithful who had promised. Hebrews 11:11	*By faith Abraham, even though he was past age—and Sarah herself was barren—was enabled to become a father because he considered him faithful who had made the promise.* (NIV)	The NIV inserts this statement regarding Abraham with no textual evidence whatsoever, as it is not found in any Greek manuscript!
And I beheld, and heard an angel flying through the midst of heaven, saying with a loud voice,...! Revelation 8:13	*As I watched, I heard an eagle that was flying in midair call out in a loud voice...* (NIV) *Then I looked, and I heard an eagle flying in midheaven, saying with a loud voice...* (NASB) *Then I looked, and I heard an eagle crying with a loud voice, as it flew in midheaven...* (RSV)	This translation is ridiculous for multiple reasons. To begin with the angel's declaration in the latter part of the verse is...*Woe, woe, woe to the inhabiters of the earth by reason of the other voices of the trumpet of the three angels which are yet to sound!* **Aggelos**, the Greek word translated angels in the latter part of the verse is the exact same word as that translated angel at the first, and this first angel refers to the **other** voices, i.e., the other angels

And the nations of them which are saved shall walk in the light of it... Revelation 21:24	*The nations will walk by its light...* (NIV and NASB) *By its light shall the nations walk...* (RSV)	The omission of *them which are saved* shows the ecumenical bias of the translators This gives the impression that all the nations will walk in its light, where the KJV makes it clear that this will the those who are saved

OMISSIONS AND TRUNCATION IN THE MODERN VERSIONS[310]

SCRIPTURE IN THE KING JAMES VERSION	PRIMARY MANUSCRIPT TESTIMONY	SCRIPTURE IN THE MODERN VERSIONS	PRIMARY MANUSCRIPT TESTIMONY
...bless them that curse you, do good to them that hate you, and pray for them which despitefully use you, and persecute you; Matthew 5:44 (also in NKJV)	D, L, W, and the Majority Text manuscripts	*...pray for those who persecute you...* (RSV, NRSV, NASB, NIV, NEB, NLT)	Aleph, B, Coptic
And lead us not into temptation, but deliver us from evil: For thine is the kingdom, and the power, and the glory, for ever. Amen Matthew 6:13 (also in NKJV and NASB)	L, W, and the Majority Text manuscripts	*...but rescue us from evil.* (RSV, NRSV, NIV, NEB, NLT)	Aleph, B, D, Z
Howbeit this kind goeth not out but by prayer and fasting. Matthew 17:21 (also in NKJV and NASB)	One of the correctors of Aleph as well as C, D, L, W, and the Majority Text manuscripts	VERSE OMITTED (RSV, NRSV, NIV, NEB, NLT)	First scribe of Aleph as well as B
For the Son of man is come to save that which was lost. Matthew 18:11 (also in NKJV and NASB)	D, a corrector of L, W, and the Majority Text manuscripts	VERSE OMITTED (RSV, NRSV, NIV, NEB, NLT)	Aleph, B, L and Origen's writings
...for many be called, but few chosen. Matthew 20:16 (also in NKJV)	C, D, W, the Syriac versions, Old Latin versions, and Majority Text manuscripts	OMITTED (RSV, NRSV, NASB, NIV, NEB, NLT)	Aleph, B, L, Z

---

[310] These are selected examples and by no means constitute an exhaustive list.

And he saith unto them, Ye shall drink indeed of my cup, and be baptized with the baptism that I am baptized with:.... Matthew 20:23 (also in NKJV)	C, W, and the Majority Text manuscripts	*He says to them, Indeed you will drink my cup.* (RSV, NRSV, NASB, NIV, NEB, NLT)	Aleph, B, D, L, Z
Woe unto you, scribes and Pharisees, hypocrites! for ye devour widows' houses, and for a pretence make long prayer: therefore shall ye receive the greater damnation. Matthew 23:14 (also in NKJV and NASB)	In the Old Latin and in the Majority Text manuscripts before verse 13	OMITTED (RSV, NRSV, NIV, NEB, NLT)	Aleph, B, D, L, Z, Omega
If any man have ears to hear, let him hear. Mark 7:16 (also in NKJV and NASB)	A, D, W, and the Majority Text manuscripts	OMITTED (RSV, NRSV, NIV, NEB, NLT)	Aleph, A, B, C, D
But if ye do not forgive, neither will your Father which is in heaven forgive your trespasses. Mark 11:26 (also in NKJV and NASB)	A, C, D, and the Majority Text manuscripts	OMITTED (RSV, NRSV, NIV, NEB, NLT)	Aleph, B, L, W
And the scripture was fulfilled, which saith, And he was numbered with the transgressors. Mark 15:28 (also in the NKJV and NASB)	L and the Majority Text manuscripts	OMITTED (RSV, NRSV, NIV, NEB, NLT)	Aleph, B, C, D

Mark 16:9-20 (in no version but the KJV)	A, C, D, K, X, and the Majority Text manuscripts	*So they went out and fled from the tomb, for terror and amazement had seized them; and they said nothing to anyone, for they were afraid.* (NRSV, NEB, NLT end with verse 8 above) A number of other modern versions that contain this verse have it either bracketed or separated with an explanation that it should not be included. Some of the modern versions have both the shorter and longer sections with explanation as above.	Aleph, B, and the writings of Origen
....It is written, That man shall not live by bread alone, but by every word of God. Luke 4:4 (also in the NKJV)	A, D, and the Majority Text manuscripts	*...It is written, man shall not live by bread alone.* (RSV, NRSV, NASB, NIV, NEB, NLT)	Aleph, B, L, W

And when his disciples James and John saw this, they said, Lord, wilt thou that we command fire to come down from heaven, and consume them, even as Elias did? But he turned, and rebuked them, and said, Ye know not what manner of spirit ye are of. For the Son of man is not come to destroy men's lives, but to save them. And they went to another village. Luke 9:54-56 (also in the NKJV and NASB)	C, D, W, and the Majority Text manuscripts	*And when his disciples James and John saw it, they said, "Lord, do you want us to bid fire come down from heaven and consume them?" But he turned and rebuked them. And they went on to another village.* (RSV, NRSV, NIV, NEB, NLT)	Aleph, B, L
...Thy will be done, as in heaven, so in earth. Luke 11:2 (also in the NKJV[311])	Aleph, A, C, D, W, and the Majority Text manuscripts	OMITTED (RSV, NRSV, NASB, NIV, NEB, NLT)	B, L and the writings of Origen
Two men shall be in the field; the one shall be taken, and the other left. Luke 17:36 (also in the NKJV[312] and NASB)	D, the Old Latin and Syriac versions, and the Textus Receptus	OMITTED (ASV, RSV, NRSV, NIV, NEB, NLT)	Aleph, A, B, L and W
(For of necessity he must release one unto them at the feast.) Luke 23:17 (also in the NKJV and NASB)	Aleph, W, and the Majority Text manuscripts	OMITTED (RSV, NRSV, NIV, NEB, NLT)	A, B, L and T

---

[311] The margin states that it should be excluded.
[312] The margin states that it should be excluded.

Then said Jesus, Father, forgive them; for they know not what they do.... Luke 23:34 (in all English translations)	Aleph, A, C, one of the correctors of D, L, and the Majority Text manuscripts	Note in the margin excluding this verse. (ASV, NKJV, RSV, NRSV, NASB, NIV, NEB, NLT)	One of the correctors of Aleph, B, D, W and Omega
In these lay a great multitude of impotent folk, of blind, halt, withered, waiting for the moving of the water. For an angel went down at a certain season into the pool, and troubled the water: whosoever then first after the troubling of the water stepped in was made whole of whatsoever disease he had. John 5:3-4 (also in the NKJV and NASB)	Aleph, one of the correctors of C, the Old Latin, and the Majority Text manuscripts	*In these lay a multitude of invalids, blind, lame, paralyzed.* (ESV, NIV)	Aleph, B, and C
John 7:53–8:11 (also in the NKJV, NASB, RSV (2nd printing), NRSV, NIV, NLT)	D, G, H, K, M, U, and the Majority Text manuscripts	OMITTED	Aleph, B, C, L, N, T, W, and the writings of Tertullian and Origen
And Phillip said, If thou believest with all thine heart, thou mayest. And he answered and said, I believe that Jesus Christ is the Son of God. Acts 8:37 (also in the NKJV and NASB)	E, the Old Latin, and the Textus Receptus	OMITTED (RSV, NRSV, NIV, NEB, NLT)	Aleph, A, B, and C
And when he had said these words, the Jews departed, and had great reasoning among themselves. Acts 28:29 (also in the NKJV and NASB)	The Old Latin and Majority Text manuscripts	OMITTED (ASV, RSV, NRSV, NIV, NEB, NLT)	Aleph, A, B, E, and the Coptic versions

The grace of our Lord Jesus Christ be with you all. Amen Romans 16:24 (also in the NKJV and NASB)	D, F, G, and the Majority Text manuscripts	OMITTED (RSV, NRSV, NIV, NEB, NLT)	Aleph, A, B, C, and the Coptic versions
This is he that came by water and blood, even Jesus Christ; not by water only, but by water and blood. And it is the Spirit that beareth witness, because the Spirit is truth. For there are three that bear record in heaven, the Father, the Word, and the Holy Ghost: and these three are one. And there are three that bear witness in earth, the Spirit, and the water, and the blood: and these three agree in one. I John 5:6-8 (also in the NKJV)	The Latin Vulgate and the Textus Receptus (3rd edition)[313]	*This is the One who came by water and blood, Jesus Christ; not with the water only, but with the water and with the blood. It is the Spirit who testifies, because the Spirit is the truth. For there are three that testify: the Spirit and the water and the blood; and the three are in agreement.* (The phrase *…For there are three that bear record in heaven, the Father, the Word, and the Holy Ghost: and these three are one…* was the later addition.) (RSV, NRSV, NASB, NIV, NEB, NLT)	Aleph, B, the Syriac, Coptic, Aramaic and Ethiopian versions, as well as the Majority Text manuscripts

[313] Erasmus did not put this insertion into his first two editions of the Greek text. He was criticized for this by supporters of the Latin Vulgate. He told them if they could find one Greek manuscript with this insertion, he would include it in his next edition. One was quickly produced, though it was likely a forgery.

TABLE OF MAJOR ANCIENT MANUSCRIPTS

OLD TESTAMENT

NAME	LETTER DESIG. [314]	DATE	SOURCE	COMMENTS
NASH PAPYRUS	-------	200 B.C.– 100 A.D.	-------	Deuteronomy 6:4-9 Exodus 20:2ff Deuteronomy 5:6ff
DEAD SEA SCROLLS (COMPLETE COLLECTION)	-------	150 B.C.– 70 A.D.	Essene community at Qumran	Over 40,000 fragments from more than 500 books, 100 of which are of the Hebrew Old Testament

All the books of the Old Testament are represented except Esther |
| DEAD SEA SCROLLS (ISAIAH SCROLL) | ------- | 125–100 B.C. | Essene community at Qumran | The entire book of Isaiah,

This manuscript was found to be 95% identical[315] with the later Masoretic texts of the 10th and 11th centuries A.D. |
ORIENTALES 4445	-------	820– 1000 A.D.[316]	Masoretic scribes	Genesis 39:20–Deuteronomy 1:33 (less Numbers 7:47-73 and 9:12-10:18)
CAIRO CODEX[317]	C	895 A.D.	Masoretic scribes	Joshua, Judges, I and II Samuel, I and II Kings, Isaiah, Jeremiah, Ezekiel, and the 12 Minor Prophets

---

[314] As designated in the *Biblia Hebraica Stuttgartensia.*

[315] The 5% deviation was found to be in minor issues of spelling and incidental errors.

[316] Ginsburg dates it between 820 and 850 A.D., but Kahle argues that it should be from the ben Asher period (10th century) due to the vowel pointing, etc.

[317] Also called the Codex Cairensis.

ST PETERSBURG CODEX OF THE PROPHETS[318]	V(ar)^p	916 A.D.	Masoretic scribes at Babylon	Isaiah, Jeremiah, Ezekiel, and the 12 Minor Prophets
ALEPPO CODEX	-------	925 A.D.	Masoretic scribes (ben Asher)	Portions of the Old Testament
BRITISH MUSEUM CODEX	-------	950 A.D.	Masoretic scribes	Part of Genesis through Deuteronomy
LENINGRAD CODEX[319]	L	1000 – 1008 A.D.	Masoretic scribes[320] (ben Asher)	Entire Old Testament
REUCHLIN CODEX OF THE PROPHETS	--------	1105 A.D.	ben Naphtali Masoretic scribes	Most of the Prophetic books

---

[318] Also called the Leningrad Codex of the Prophets or the Babylonian Codex of the Latter Prophets.

[319] Also called the Codex Leningradensis.

[320] According to a note at the end, it was copied by Samuel ben Jacob (1008 A.D.) from a manuscript written by Aaron ben Moses ben Asher (1000 A.D.).

NEW TESTAMENT

PAPYRI

NAME	LETTER[321]	DATE[322] and LOCATION	TEXT TYPE	TEXT CONTAINED
OXYRHYNCHUS PAPYRI	P[1]	200–250 A.D. Oxyrhynchus (El Bahnasa), Egypt[323]		Matthew 1:1-9,12,14-20
(UNNAMED)	P[4]	150 A.D. Coptos (Qift), Egypt	Primarily Alexandrian[324]	Luke 1:58-59, 1:62–2:1,6-7, 3:8–4:2, 29-32, 34-35, 5:3-8, 5:30–6:16
OXYRHYNCHUS PAPYRI	P[5]	200–300 A.D. Oxyrhynchus (El Bahnasa), Egypt		John 1:23-31,33-40, 20:11-17
OXYRHYNCHUS PAPYRI	P[13]	200–300 A.D.	Somewhat Alexandrian	Hebrews 2:14-5:5, 10:8-22, 10:29-11:13, 11:28–12:7
OXYRHYNCHUS PAPYRI	P[20]	200–250 A.D.	Somewhat Alexandrian[325]	James 2:19–3:9
OXYRHYNCHUS PAPYRI	P[23]	200 A.D.	Somewhat Alexandrian[326]	James 1:10-12,15-18
OXYRHYNCHUS PAPYRI	P[24]	250–300 A.D.	Somewhat Alexandrian[327]	Revelation 5:5-8, 6:5-8
OXYRHYNCHUS PAPYRI	P[30]	200–250 A.D.		I Thessalonians 4:12-13, 16-17, 5:3,8-10, 12-18,25-28, II Thessalonians 1:1-2

[321] Letter designations of papyri are numbered by their order of discovery.
[322] Dates are approximate calculations.
[323] All the Oxyrhynchus Papyri were found in an ancient rubbish heap.
[324] Affinities with Codex Vaticanus.
[325] Generally concurs with Codex Vaticanus.
[326] Generally concurs with Codices Vaticanus, Sinaiticus, and Ephraemi Rescriptus.
[327] Generally agrees with Codex Alexandrinus.

JOHN RYLANDS PAPYRI 5	p^{32}	150–175 A.D.	Alexandrian[328]	Titus 1:11-15, 2:3-8
OXYRHYNCHUS PAPYRI	p^{39}	200–300 A.D.	Alexandrian[329]	John 8:14-22
PAPYRUS HEIDELBERG 645	p^{40}	200–300 A.D.	Somewhat Alexandrian	Romans 1:24-27, 1:31 – 2:3, 3:21 – 4:8, 6:2-5,15-16, 9:16-17,27
CHESTER BEATTY PAPYRI	p^{45}	200–250 A.D. Egypt[330]	Mixed Text	Portions of the Gospels and Acts
CHESTER BEATTY PAPYRI	p^{46}	150–250 A.D.	Somewhat Alexandrian[331]	Portions of Paul's Epistles
CHESTER BEATTY PAPYRI	p^{47}	250 A.D.	Somewhat Alexandrian[332]	Revelation 9:10-17:2
OXYRHYNCHUS PAPYRI	p^{48}	250 A.D. Oxyrhynchus (El Bahnasa), Egypt	Independent (D) Text	Acts 23:11-17,23-29
OXYRHYNCHUS PAPYRI	p^{49}	200–300 A.D.		Ephesians 4:16-29, 4:31 – 5:13
JOHN RYLANDS PAPYRI 457	p^{52}	110–125 A.D.		John 18:31-33, 37-38
(UNNAMED)	p^{64}	150 A.D. Coptos (Qift), Egypt	Primarily Alexandrian	Small portions of Matthew
OXYRHYNCHUS PAPYRI	p^{65}	200–300 A.D. Oxyrhynchus (El Bahnasa), Egypt		I Thessalonians 1:3-10, 2:1, 6-13
BODMER PAPYRI	p^{66}	200 A.D. or earlier Jabal Abu Manna, Egypt	Alexandrian and Western	John 1:1-6:11, 6:35b–14:26, 29-30, 15:2-26, 16:2-4, 6-7, 16:10–20:20, 22-23, 20:25–21:9

[328] Generally agrees with Codex Sinaiticus.

[329] Exact word for word with Codex Vaticanus.

[330] All the Chester Beatty Papyri were found in a Coptic graveyard.

[331] Shares affinities with Codex Vaticanus and Sinaiticus.

[332] Often agrees with Codex Sinaiticus.

(UNNAMED)	P[67]	150 A.D. Coptos (Qift), Egypt	Primarily Alexandrian	Small portions of Matthew
BODMER PAPYRI	P[72]	300 A.D. Jabal Abu Manna, Egypt	Somewhat Alexandrian with other influences[333]	Jude, I and II Peter, as well as a collection of Apocryphal books
BODMER PAPYRI	P[74]	600–700 A.D.	Primarily Alexandrian	Acts and the General Epistles
BODMER PAPYRI	P[75]	175–200 A.D.	Primarily Alexandrian[334]	Luke 3:18–4:2, 4:34–5:10, 5:37–18:18, 22:4–24:53, John 1:1–11:45, 48-57, 12:3–13:1, 8-9, 14:8-30, 15:7-8
OXYRHYNCHUS PAPYRI	P[77]	150–200 A.D. Oxyrhynchus (El Bahnasa), Egypt	Somewhat Alexandrian[335]	Small portion of Matthew 23
(UNNAMED)	P[87]	150–250 A.D.		Philemon 13-15, 24-25
-------	P[90]	150–200 A.D.		John 18:36–19:7
(UNNAMED)	P[98]	100–200 A.D.		Revelations 1:13–2:1
-------	P[104]	323 B.C.–200 A.D.[336]		Matthew 21:34-37, 43
-------	P[115]	300 A.D.	Somewhat Alexandrian[337]	Various portions of Revelation 2–15[338]

[333] I Peter has affinities with Codex Vaticanus and Alexandrinus; II Peter and Jude are mixed with possible Western influence.

[334] Calvin Porter collated this manuscript with Codex Vaticanus, demonstrating that they were approximately 87% in harmony.

[335] Some similarities with Codex Sinaiticus.

[336] Possibly the earliest of all the New Testament manuscripts; the style this papyrus was written in was begun during the Ptolemaic period (323 –30 B.C. and lasted until the end of the 2nd century).

[337] Generally agrees with Codex Alexandrinus and Ephraemi Rescriptus.

[338] In Revelation 13:18 the number of the beast is written "616" rather than "666."

CODICES
UNCIAL MANUSCRIPTS

NAME	LETTER[339]	DATE[340] and LOCATION	TEXT TYPE	TEXT CONTAINED
CODEX SINAITICUS	ALEPH	340 A.D. St. Catherine's Monastery at Mt. Sinai	Primarily Alexandrian with Western influence	Over half of the Old Testament and all of the New Testament with the exception of Mark 16:9-20 and John 7:53–8:11 Also includes all the Old Testament Apocrypha and the New Testament Apocryphal books of the Epistle of Barnabas, and most of the Shepherd of Hermas

---

[339] Letter designations of codices.
[340] Dates are approximate calculations.

| CODEX ALEXANDRINUS | A | 450 A.D. (Alexandria, Egypt) | The Gospels are primarily Byzantine, whereas the rest is primarily Alexandrian | All of the Old Testament with the exception of numerous small sections Most of the New Testament with the exception of Matthew 1:1-25:6, John 6:50-8:52 and II Corinthians 4:13-12:6

Also included are most of the Apocryphal books of I and II Clement and the Psalms of Solomon |

CODEX VATICANUS	B	325–350 A.D. Vatican Library, Vatican City, Rome	Primarily Alexandrian	Most of the Old Testament except Genesis 1:1-46:28, II Kings 2:5-7 and 10–13, Psalms 106:27–138:6 Most of the New Testament except I Timothy through Philemon, and Hebrews 9:14 through Revelation Mark 16:9-20 and John 7:53–8:11 were omitted[341] Also includes the majority of the Apocrypha.

---

[341] Norman Geisler and William Nix, *A General Introduction to the Bible*, p. 392.

CODEX EPHRAEMI RESCRIPTUS	C	345 A.D.	Mixture of text types	Parts of Job, Proverbs, Ecclesiastes, and Song of Solomon in the Old Testament Most of the New Testament with the exceptions of II Thessalonians, II John, and portions of various books Also includes the apocryphal Wisdom of Solomon, and Ecclesiasticus.
CODEX BEZAE	D	450–550 A.D.	The Gospels are somewhat Western but overall it is a mixture of text types	Most of the 4 Gospels, Acts, and III John, with various omissions in each
CODEX CLAROMONTANUS	D^2	550 A.D.	Primarily Western	All of Paul's Epistles and Hebrews, with various omissions in each
CODEX BASILENSIS	E	700–800 A.D.	Primarily Byzantine	Most of the 4 Gospels
CODEX LAUDIANUS	E^2	550–650 A.D.	Primarily Byzantine with Western influences	Most of Acts
CODEX SANGERMANENSIS	E^3	800–900 A.D.	Primarily Western	Copy of Codex Claromontanus
CODEX BOREELIANUS	F	800–900 A.D.	Primarily Byzantine	The 4 Gospels

CODEX AUGIENSIS	F²	800–900 A.D.	Primarily Western	Paul's Epistles in Greek and Latin, with Hebrews in Latin only
CODEX WOLFII A	G	900–1000 A.D.		Most of the 4 Gospels
CODEX BOERNERIANUS	G³	800–900 A.D.	Primarily Western	Paul's Epistles in Greek with a literal Latin interlinear translation
CODEX WOLFII B	H	800–1000 A.D.	Primarily Byzantine	Most of the 4 Gospels
CODEX MUTINENSIS	H²	800–900 A.D.	Primarily Byzantine	Part of Acts (7 chapters missing)
CODES COISLINIANUS	H³	500–600 A.D.	Primarily Alexandrian	Paul's Epistles
CODEX WASHINGTONIANUS II	I	400–600 A.D.	Primarily Alexandrian	Pauline Epistles and Hebrews with Romans missing
CODEX CYPRIUS	K	800–1000 A.D.	Primarily Byzantine	The 4 Gospels
CODEX MOSQUENSIS	K²	800–1000 A.D.	Mixture of text types	Acts, the General Epistles, and Paul's Epistles with Hebrews
CODEX REGIUS	L	700–800 A.D.	Somewhat Alexandrian[342]	The 4 Gospels with two endings in Mark[343]
CODEX ANGELICUS	L²	800–900 A.D.	Primarily Byzantine	Acts, the General Epistles, and Paul's Epistles
CODEX PAMPIANUS	M	800–900 A.D.	Primarily Byzantine with Caesarean influences	The 4 Gospels

---

[342] Shares affinities with Codex Vaticanus.
[343] First ending does not include verses 9-20, whereas the second ending does.

CODEX PURPUREUS PETROPOLITANUS	N	500–600 A.D.	Primarily Byzantine	The 4 Gospels
CODEX SINOPENSIS	O	500–600 A.D.	Primarily Byzantine with Caesarean influences	Most of the 4 Gospels
CODEX PORPHYRIANUS	P[2]	?	Primarily Byzantine with a mixture of text types	Most of Acts, the General and Pauline Epistles and Revelation
CODEX NITRIENSIS	R	500–600 A.D.	Primarily Western	Luke with Homer's Iliad and a treatise by Severus of Antioch overwritten
CODEX VATICANUS 354	S	949 A.D.	Primarily Byzantine	The 4 Gospels
CODEX BORGIANUS	T	400–500 A.D.	Somewhat Alexandrian[344]	Luke 22–23 and John 6–8
CODEX MOSQUENSIS	V	700–900 A.D.	Primarily Byzantine	Most of the 4 Gospels
CODEX WASHINGTONIANUS I	W	300–450 A.D.	Mixture of text types	Most of the 4 Gospels, portions of Paul's Epistles except Romans and portions of Hebrews, as well as Deuteronomy, Joshua, and Psalms
CODEX DUBLIENSIS	ZETA	400–600 A.D.	Primarily Alexandrian[345]	Most of Matthew
CODEX SANGALLENSIS	DELTA	800–900 A.D.	Primarily Byzantine with Alexandrian influence in Mark	The 4 Gospels in a Greek and Latin interlinear translation

---

[344] Generally agrees with Codex Vaticanus.
[345] Generally agrees with Codex Sinaiticus.

CODEX KORIDETHI	THETA	800–900 A.D	Primarily Byzantine with Alexandrian influence in Mark	The 4 Gospels
CODEX TISCHENDORFIANUS III	LAMBDA	800–900 A.D.	Primarily Byzantine	Luke and John
CODEX ZACYNTHIUS	XI	1100–1300 A.D.	Primarily Alexandrian[346]	Luke 1:1–11:33
CODEX PETROPOLITANUS	PI	800–900 A.D.	Primarily Byzantine	Most of the 4 Gospels
CODEX ROSSANENSIS	SIGMA	500–600 A.D.	Primarily Byzantine with Caesarean influences	Matthew and Mark
CODEX BERATINUS	PHI	500–600 A.D.	Mixture of text types	Most of Matthew and Mark
CODEX ATHOUS LAURAE	PSI	700–900 A.D.	Primarily Byzantine with some Alexandrian influences	Mark 9–16, Luke, John, Acts, the General Epistles, Paul's Epistles and Hebrews
CODEX ATHOUS DIONYSIOU	OMEGA	700–900 A.D.	Primarily Byzantine	Most of the 4 Gospels

MINUSCULE MANUSCRIPTS
AMOUNTING TO 2,795 MANUSCRIPTS AND 1,964 LECTIONARIES
(Approximately 90% Byzantine)

---

[346] Affinities with Codex Vaticanus.

TABLES OF SCRIPTURE TRANSLATIONS

OLD TESTAMENT TRANSLATIONS AND VERSIONS

NAME	DATE	TRANSLATOR(S)	OLD TESTAMENT BASE TEXT	COMMENTS
SAMARITAN PENTATUECH	432 B.C or later	Traditionally Manasseh under the direction of Sanballat	Hebrew Torah	The oldest known copy is from the mid 11th century A.D. Translated from the Torah with Samaritan biases
THE ARAMAIC TARGUMS	450 B.C.– 200 A.D.	Traditionally Ezra began the work, which was carried on by the scribal guilds	Hebrew scriptures	Paraphrases of the Hebrew Scriptures in the common tongue of Aramaic
THE SEPTUAGINT (LXX)	250– 150 B.C.	According to legend, 72 Hebrew scribes sent from Israel and Judah	Hebrew scriptures	Many variant renderings from the Masoretic text. This is the text most likely to have been used by the later Alexandrian church fathers and translators
AQUILA'S VERSION	130 A.D.	Aquila, a Jewish proselyte	Hebrew scriptures	Translated into Greek for Greek speaking Jews Extremely literal translation

THEODOTIAN'S REVISION	180–190 A.D.	Theodotian of Ephesus, a Jewish proselyte or Ebionite Christian	Hebrew scriptures and/or earlier translations	A revision either of Aquila's earlier work or of the Septuagint
SYMMACHUS'S REVISION	170 A.D.	Symmachus, a Samaritan convert to Judaism or an Ebionite Christian	Hebrew scriptures and/or earlier translations	A revision of earlier works Idiomatic Greek
ORIGEN'S HEXAPLA	240–250 A.D.	Origen of Alexandria	Hebrew scriptures, the Septuagint, Aquila's version, Theodotian's revision, and Symmachus's revision	Origen put all of the aforesaid versions in parallel columns with a Greek transliteration of the Hebrew scriptures
MASORETIC TEXT (BEN CHAYYIM)	1524–1525 A.D.	Abraham (Jacob) ben Chayyim, Hebrew scholar and rabbi who converted to Christianity	Hebrew scriptures copied through the scribal tradition	Published in the Second Great Rabbinic Bible by Daniel Bomberg Based on the accepted Masoretic texts.
MASORETIC TEXT (MODERN "BEN ASHER")	1008 A.D.	Aaron ben Moses ben Asher, Hebrew scholar and rabbi	Hebrew scriptures copied through the scribal tradition	Based primarily upon the Leningrad and Aleppo Codices.

BIBLIA HEBRAICA[347]	1906–1937 A.D.	Rudolf Kittel with Paul Kahle (1937 Edition)	Masoretic ben Chayyim text and later the ben Asher text of the Leningrad Codex (Codex Leningradensis)	Kittel used the ben Chayyim Masoretic Text in his 1906 and 1912 editions In his 1937 edition he changed to the ben Asher Masoretic Text
BIBLIA HEBRAICA STUTTGARTENSIA	1967–1977 A.D.		Masoretic ben Asher text of the Leningrad Codex	Stuttgart version of the Biblia Hebraica
BIBLIA HEBRAICA LENINGRADENSIA		Aron Dotan, Jewish scholar	Masoretic Text of the Leningrad Codex	Dotan's modern translation of the ben Asher Masoretic Text

---

[347] The Biblia Hebraica editions are based on the ben Asher text, taken from a smaller number of manuscripts and differing in the Biblia Hebraica footnotes in 15 to 20 places per page.

EARLY COMPLETE BIBLE TRANSLATIONS AND VERSIONS

NAME	DATE	TRANSLATOR(S)	HEBREW AND GREEK BASE TEXTS	COMMENTS
THE OLD LATIN VERSION	Before 200 A.D.	Unknown	O.T. believed to have been translated from the Septuagint N.T. was likely translated from the early Greek and Aramaic manuscripts	The Bible of the Western church before Jerome's Vulgate became the official Bible Used and copied up to the 13th century
COPTIC VERSIONS (SAHIDIC, BOHAIRIC, AND MIDDLE EGYPTIAN DIALECTS)	250–350 A.D.	Unknown	O.T. from the Septuagint. N.T. from Alexandrian-type Greek text	The Bibles of the Egyptian churches translated into the various dialects of Egypt
ETHIOPIC VERSION	300–700 A.D.	Unknown	O.T. probably from the Septuagint or another Greek O.T. N.T. appears to be based on Byzantine Greek text	The Bible for the churches in Ethiopia This went through several recensions, and was later influenced by Coptic and Arabic versions
GOTHIC VERSION	350 A.D.	Ulfilas, "apostle to the Goths"	O.T. is primarily from Byzantine Greek text N.T. is almost literal translation of the Byzantine text	Ulfilas was said to have created an alphabet and written language from the oral language of the Goths to make this translation Copies of this version date back to the 5th and 6th centuries

THE LATIN VULGATE	382–405 A.D.	Jerome, commissioned by Damasus, bishop of Rome	O.T. from the Septuagint and Hebrew scriptures N.T. from the Old Latin and Alexandrian texts	A revision of the Old Latin Version intended as an official Bible of the Western church
THE ARMENIAN VERSION	390–439 A.D.	Sahak	O.T. and N.T. most likely from the Syriac versions, and Byzantine Greek texts	Revised before the 8th century The oldest manuscripts date to the 9th century
THE SYRIAC PESHITTA	411–435 A.D.	Traditionally Rabullah, bishop of Edessa	O.T. from the Hebrew scriptures, Septuagint, and others Byzantine manuscripts and earlier Syriac versions for the N.T.	Possibly a recension of earlier Syriac versions Unlike the Alexandrian Codices, it omits any apocryphal books
THE SYRO-HEXAPLARIC VERSION	616 A.D.	Under the direction of Bishop Paul of Tella	O.T. from Origen's Hexapla translation from the Septuagint The N.T. is Byzantine with Western influences	Literal rendering

LATER AND MODERN GREEK TRANSLATIONS
OF THE NEW TESTAMENT

NAME	DATE	TRANSLATOR(S)	BASE TEXTS USED	COMMENTS
ERASMUS' GREEK NEW TESTAMENT (TEXTUS RECEPTUS)	1516 A.D.	Desiderius Erasmus	The Majority Text (Byzantine and Caesarean)	5 Editions released in 1516, 1519, 1522, 1527, and 1535 A.D.
ESTIENNE'S (STEPHANUS) GREEK NEW TESTAMENT	1546 A.D.	Robert Estienne[348]	The Complutensian Polyglot and the Textus Receptus	4 Editions released in 1546, 1549, 1550, and 1551 A.D.
BEZA'S GREEK NEW TESTAMENT	1565–1604 A.D.	Theodore Beza[349]	The Majority Text (Byzantine and Caesarean)	10 Editions
ELZEVIR'S GREEK NEW TESTAMENT	1624–1678 A.D.	Bonaventure and Abraham Elzevir	The Majority Text (Byzantine and Caesarean) Primarily taken from the versions of Estienne and Beza.	7 Editions Their second edition in 1633 had the phrase in Latin "the text new received by all" from which the term Textus Receptus was coined
BENGEL'S GREEK NEW TESTAMENT	About 1734 A.D.	Johann Albrecht Bengel	Mixed textual families with a prejudice toward the Alexandrian text	Bengel was a strong proponent of the Alexandrian (what he called the African texts) over the Byzantine Majority texts

---

[348] Also known as Robert Stephanus.
[349] John Calvin's successor.

GRIESBACH'S GREEK NEW TESTAMENT	1777–1806 A.D.	Johann Jakob Griesbach	Mixed textual families with a prejudice towards the Alexandrian text.	2 Editions Griesbach believed the Textus Receptus was inferior to the Alexandrian texts Origen's citations had influence on his textual selections
LACHMAN'S GREEK NEW TESTAMENT	1831–1850 A.D.	Karl Lachman	Primarily Alexandrian	2 Editions Lachman went farther in debasing the Byzantine Majority text than those before him The citations of Origen and Irenaeus had influence on his textual selections
TISCHENDORF'S GREEK NEW TESTAMENT	1841–1872 A.D.	Constantin von Tischendorf	Primarily Alexandrian	8 Editions Tischendorf primarily used Codex Vaticanus and Sinaiticus
TREGELLES' GREEK NEW TESTAMENT	1857–1872 A.D.	Samuel Tregelles	Primarily Alexandrian	Tregelles editions were not considered as accurate as Tischendorf's, as his translation of the Gospels was completed before the release of Codex Sinaiticus in 1868
ALFORD'S GREEK NEW TESTAMENT	1849–1861 A.D.	Henry Alford	Primarily Alexandrian	6 Editions, each of which progressively drifted further from the Majority Text readings

THE NEW TESTAMENT IN THE ORIGINAL GREEK (WESTCOTT AND HORT)	1870–1881 A.D.	Brooke F. Westcott and Fenton J.A. Hort	Primarily Codex Sinaiticus and Vaticanus as well as the Greek critical texts of the 18th and 19th centuries	Released concurrently with the publication of the Revised Version

This Greek New Testament is the strongest influence on the modern Bibles |
| SCRIVENER'S TEXTUS RECEPTUS | 1881 A.D. | F.H.A. Scrivener | Primarily Majority Text | Scrivener was a defender of the Majority Text and the Textus Receptus |
| WEYMOUTH'S GREEK NEW TESTAMENT | 1886 A.D. | Richard Weymouth | Primarily Alexandrian texts and the Greek critical text of the 19th century | 1 Edition |
| WEISS GREEK NEW TESTAMENT | 1894–1905 A.D. | Bernhard Weiss | Primarily Alexandrian texts | 2 Editions

The largest textual influence was Westcott and Hort's Greek New Testament |

NESTLE'S GREEK NEW TESTAMENT	1898–1913 A.D.	Eberhard Nestle	Primarily Westcott and Hort's Greek New Testament as well as Alexandrian manuscripts, especially Codex D	26 Editions Upon Eberhard's death it was taken over by his son Erwin in 1913, who edited the 10th edition (1914) through the 25th editions Nestle used 3 Greek New Testaments to develop his edition: Weymouth's 1892, Westcott and Hort's 1881, and Tischendorf's 1869 He later replaced Weymouth's with Weiss's 1894 edition
NESTLE–ALAND GREEK NEW TESTAMENT (NOVUM TESTAMENTUM GRAECE)	1952–1979 A.D.	Kurt Aland	Westcott and Hort's Greek New Testament, as well as Alexandrian manuscripts, primarily Aleph and B	Aland was executive editor of the Nestle's Greek New Testament from the 21st edition till he took over the Nestle's with the 26th edition, replacing the older text with the text of the UBS
NOVI TESTAMENTI BIBLIA GRAECA ET LATINA	1943 A.D.	Jose Maria Bover	Latin text is from the Vulgate Greek text is eclectic, but primarily Alexandrian	

UNITED BIBLE SOCIETY (UBS) GREEK NEW TESTAMENT	1966–1993 A.D.	Kurt Aland, Matthew Black, Bruce Metzger, Allen Wikren, Cardinal Carlo Martini (1968) 1993 edition editors were Kurt Aland, Barbara Aland, Johannes Karavidopoulos, Cardinal Carlo Martini, And Bruce Metzger	Primarily Alexandrian texts	4 Editions

1966 edition was intended as a revision of the 1927 Nestle's Greek New Testament

Numerous Catholic leaders are involved in this ecumenical work, including Cardinal Onitsha, Cardinal Martini, and Bishop Alilona |

MAJOR BIBLE VERSIONS

VERSION	DATE	TRANSLATORS (THEOLOGY)	TEXT[350]	STYLE
KING JAMES	1611 A.D.	47–54 Scholars (Anglican/Puritan)	OT: Masoretic text NT: Textus Receptus and Majority Text	Literal
REVISED VERSION	1881–1885 A.D.	24 scholars led by Westcott and Hort (varied denominational)	OT: Masoretic text NT: Westcott and Hort's Greek text, Tregelle's 1857 Greek text, and others	Literal
AMERICAN STANDARD VERSION	1901 A.D.	Led by Phillip Schaff (ecumenical, varied denominational)	OT: Masoretic text NT: Westcott and Hort, and other critical texts	Literal
REVISED STANDARD VERSION	1946 A.D.	20–32 scholars led by Luther Weigle (ecumenical, National Council of Churches)	OT: Masoretic text NT: Nestle 17th edition, and others	Somewhat dynamic (revision of the American Standard Version)
NEW WORLD TRANSLATION OF THE HOLY SCRIPTURES	1961 A.D.	Jehovah's Witness scholars led by Frederick Franz[351] (Jehovah's Witness)	OT: Masoretic text NT: Primarily Westcott and Hort's Greek text	Literal

---

[350] The "eclectic" text is primarily that influenced by Westcott and Hort's Greek New Testament.
[351] Franz was likely to have been the primary translator.

NEW AMERICAN STANDARD BIBLE	1963 A.D. (NT) 1971 A.D.	39 scholars (NT) and 58 scholars (OT/NT) (Lockman Foundation, non-denominational)	OT: Primarily Masoretic text NT: Nestle 23rd edition	Literal Updated in 1995
AMPLIFIED BIBLE	1964 A.D.	Primarily Mary Francis Siewert (Lockman Foundation, non-denominational)	OT: Masoretic text (Biblia Hebraica) NT: Westcott and Hort's Greek text, Nestle's 23rd edition, and others	Paraphrase
JERUSALEM BIBLE (ENGLISH EDITION)	1966 A.D.	27 Roman Catholic scholars led by A. Jones (Catholic)	OT: Masoretic text NT: Eclectic	Literal
NEW ENGLISH BIBLE	1970 A.D.	28 scholars led by C.H. Dodd (Churches of England and Scotland)	OT: Masoretic text (Biblia Hebraica), Samaritan Pentateuch, and others NT: Eclectic	Dynamic equivalency
NEW AMERICAN BIBLE	1970 A.D.	59 Roman Catholic and several Protestant scholars (Catholic)[352]	OT: Masoretic text, Septuagint and others NT: Nestle-Aland 25th edition	Literal
LIVING BIBLE	1971 A.D.	Kenneth Taylor	See American Standard Version	Freely paraphrased from the American Standard Version

---

[352] The most widely used Bible by American Roman Catholics.

TODAY'S ENGLISH VERSION (GOOD NEWS FOR MODERN MAN)	1976 A.D.	Small committee of scholars led by Robert Bratcher	OT: Masoretic text (Biblia Hebraica) NT: UBS 1966 1st and 3rd editions	Dynamic equivalency
NEW INTERNATIONAL VERSION	1978 A.D.	About 110 scholars	OT: Masoretic text (Biblia Hebraica Stuttgartensia), Samaritan Pentateuch, and others NT: Eclectic, but primarily UBS 1966 1st edition, and Nestle-Aland	Dynamic equivalency
NEW KING JAMES	1982 A.D.	130 evangelical scholars (evangelical)	OT: Masoretic text NT: Primarily Textus Receptus with influences and marginal notes from the UBS 1975 3rd edition, and Hodges and Farstad's 1982 edition	Literal
NEW JERUSALEM BIBLE	1986 A.D.	Committee of editors led by Henry Wansbrough (Catholic)[353]	OT: Masoretic text, Syriac Peshitta, Septuagint, and others NT: Eclectic (Western textual influences)	Mixed (dynamic equivalency)

---

[353] This is the most widely used Bible by Roman Catholics outside the United States.

REVISED ENGLISH BIBLE	1989 A.D.	About 26 British scholars	OT: Masoretic text (Biblia Hebraica Stuttgartensia), Septuagint, and others NT: Nestle–Aland 26th edition	Mixed (dynamic equivalency)
NEW REVISED STANDARD VERSION	1990 A.D.	30 scholars led by Bruce Metzger (ecumenical, National Council of Churches)	OT: Masoretic text and others NT: UBS 3rd edition	Literal (revision of the Revised Standard)
NEW CENTURY VERSION (THE EVERYDAY BIBLE)	1991 A.D.	Primarily Ervin Bishop, vice president of the World Bible Translation Center	OT: Masoretic text (Biblia Hebraica Stuttgartensia) NT: UBS 3rd edition	Limited vocabulary (3rd grade) Heavy dynamic equivalency
NEW LIFE VERSION[354]	1993 A.D.	Gleason Ledyard	?	Limited vocabulary Dynamic equivalency
THE MESSAGE	1993–1997 A.D.	Eugene Peterson	OT: N/A NT: UBS 4th edition	Paraphrase
CONTEMPORARY ENGLISH VERSION	1994 A.D.	Barclay Newman and members of the American Bible Society	OT: ? NT: UBS 3rd corrected edition	Paraphrase

---

[354] Precious Moments Bible, etc.

NEW LIVING TRANSLATION	1996 A.D.	Kenneth Taylor with more than 90 translators	OT: Masoretic text (Biblia Hebraica Stuttgartensia), Septuagint, and others NT: Nestle-Aland 27th edition, UBS 4th edition	Dynamic equivalence (revision of the Living Bible)
ENGLISH STANDARD VERSION	2001 A.D.	14-member translation committee with 100 advisory and review scholars (evangelical)	OT: Masoretic text (Biblia Hebraica Stuttgartensia) NT: Nestle-Aland 27th edition, UBS 4th edition	Mixed revision of the Revised Standard Version
TODAY'S NEW INTERNATIONAL VERSION	2002 A.D. (NT) 2005 A.D. (OT)	12-member translation committee led by John Stek (various denominations)	See New International Version	Update of the New International Version

MATERIALS FOR FURTHER STUDY

THE TABERNACLE

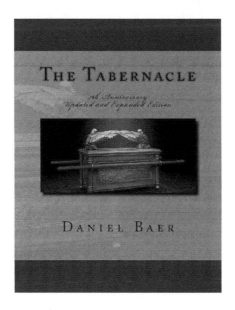

THE FEASTS OF ISRAEL

GENESIS

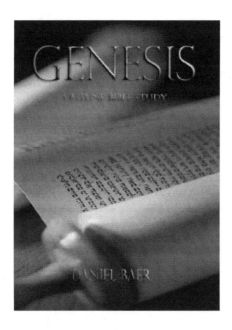

FOUNDATIONS OF BIBLICAL HEBREW

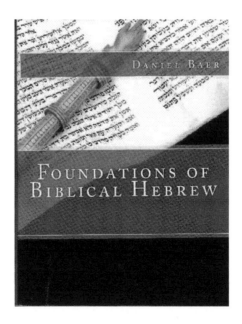

THE SONG OF SONGS Part 1

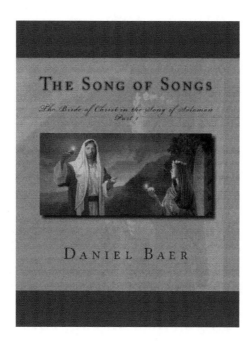

THE BOOK OF RUTH

THE FEASTS OF ISRAEL
CD Set
14 Audio CDs

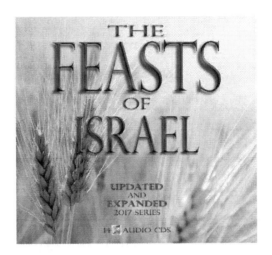

THE DOCTRINE OF GOD
CD Set
12 Audio CDs and 1 Data CD

THE DOCTRINE OF CHRIST
CD Set
9 Audio CDs and 1 Data CD

THE DOCTRINE OF THE DEVIL CD Set
(available to regional ministry or by ministerial approval only)
15 Audio CDs and 1 Data CD

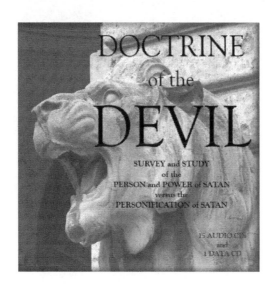

THE DOCTRINE OF THE RESURRECTION Part 1
CD Set
19 Audio CDs and 1 Data CD

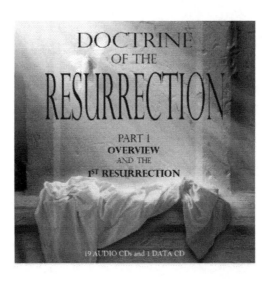

THE DOCTRINE OF BAPTISMS CD Set
10 Audio CDs

BAPTISM AND WORK OF THE HOLY SPIRIT
CD Set
9 Audio CDs and 1 Data CD

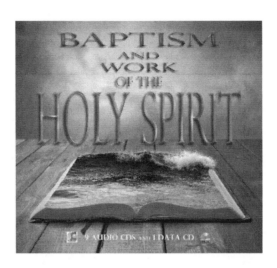

THE BRIDE MESSAGE Part 1
CD Set
12 Audio CDs

THE DOCTRINE OF HELL
CD Set
14 Audio CDs and 1 Data CD

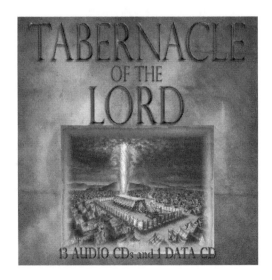

THE TABERNACLE
CD Set
13 Audio CDs and 1 Data CD

THE SABBATH
CD Set
7 Audio CDs

HISTORY OF THE CHURCH Part 1
CD Set
8 Audio CDs and 1 Data CD

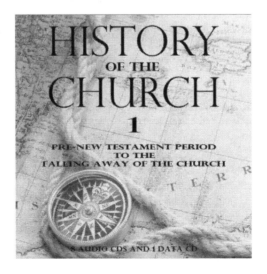

REVELATION Part 2
CD Set
12 Audio CDs and 1 Data CD

THE 7 SPIRITS OF GOD
CD Set
15 Audio CDs and 1 Data CD

THE SONG OF SOLOMON Part 1 CD Set
24 Audio CDs

RUTH
CD Set
22 Audio CDs

ELIJAH Part 1
CD Set
8 Audio CDs

10 YEAR ANNIVERSARY MULTIMEDIA COLLECTION
MP3 audio files, books and charts on a 32 GB FLASH DRIVE

HUNDREDS OF HOURS OF SERMONS, BIBLE STUDIES,
AND TOPICAL STUDIES INCLUDING:
100+ Sermons from 2005 to 2015

ALL topical Bible Study subjects taught from 2005 to 2015:
The Doctrine of God, The Doctrine of Christ, The Bride Message part 1,
The Doctrine of the Devil, The Doctrine of Baptisms,
The Doctrine of the Resurrection part 1, The Doctrine of Hell, The Book
of Revelation, The Book of Exodus part 1, The Song of Solomon part 1,
The History of the Church part 1
The Sabbath: Spiritual and Physical, and The Tabernacle

More than 30 Ministerial Bible study sessions with visiting ministers

**All books published prior to 2016 in PDF format able to be printed
out or read on computers or with PDF reader apps on smartphones or
tablets**

Charts and handouts from Bible study classes

2016 ANNUAL MULTIMEDIA COLLECTION
MP3 audio files of Sermons, Bible Studies, and Ministerial Sessions,
as well as PDF files of books and charts
on an 8 GB FLASH DRIVE

2017 ANNUAL MULTIMEDIA COLLECTION
MP3 audio files of Sermons, Bible Studies, and Ministerial Sessions,
as well as numerous PDF files of books and Bible study outlines
on a 16 GB FLASH DRIVE

For information, or to attend a local service or Bible study,
you may contact us at:

GOSPEL ASSEMBLY CHURCH

1100 S. Trimble Rd.
Mansfield, Ohio 44906
mansfieldgac@yahoo.com

Information, multimedia files, and other materials
may also be found on the church website at:
www.mansfieldgac.com
or at
www.facebook.com/MansfieldGAC/

Made in the USA
Monee, IL
11 June 2021